Essential Papers on Obsessive-Compulsive Disorder

ESSENTIAL PAPERS IN PSYCHOANALYSIS
General Editor: Leo Goldberger

Essential Papers on Borderline Disorders
Edited by Michael H. Stone, M.D.

Essential Papers on Object Relations
Edited by Peter Buckley, M.D.

Essential Papers on Narcissism
Edited by Andrew P. Morrison, M.D.

Essential Papers on Depression
Edited by James C. Coyne

Essential Papers on Psychosis
Edited by Peter Buckley, M.D.

Essential Papers on Countertransference
Edited by Benjamin Wolstein

Essential Papers on Character Neurosis and Treatment
Edited by Ruth F. Lax

Essential Papers on the Psychology of Women
Edited by Claudia Zanardi

Essential Papers on Transference
Edited by Aaron H. Esman, M.D.

Essential Papers on Dreams
Edited by Melvin R. Lansky, M.D.

Essential Papers on Literature and Psychoanalysis
Edited by Emanuel Berman

Essential Papers on Object Loss
Edited by Rita V. Frankiel

Essential Papers on Masochism
Edited by Margaret Ann Fitzpatrick Hanly

Essential Papers on Short-Term Dynamic Therapy
Edited by James E. Groves, M.D.

Essential Papers on Suicide
Edited by John T. Maltsberger and Mark J. Goldblatt

Essential Papers on Obsessive-Compulsive Disorder
Edited by Dan J. Stein, M.B., and Michael Stone, M.D.

Essential Papers on Obsessive-Compulsive Disorder

Edited by
Dan J. Stein, M.B., and
Michael Stone, M.D.

NEW YORK UNIVERSITY PRESS
New York and London

Copyright © 1997 by New York University

Library of Congress Cataloging-in-Publication Data
Essential papers on obsessive-compulsive disorder / edited by Dan J.
Stein and Michael Stone.
p. cm.
Includes bibliographical references and index.
ISBN 0-8147-8057-1. — ISBN 0-8147-8056-3
1. Obsessive-compulsive disorder.   I. Stein, Dan J.   II. Stone,
Michael H., 1933–   .
RC533.E87   1997
616.85′227—dc20   96-46090
                                CIP

New York University Press books are printed on acid-free paper,
and their binding materials are chosen for strength and durability.

Manufactured in the United States of America

10 9 8 7 6 5 4 3 2 1

For Heather, Gabriella, and Joshua
For Beth

Contents

Preface

Dan J. Stein

SIGMUND FREUD (1926) wrote that obsessional neurosis was "unquestionably the most interesting and repaying subject of analytic research." Although the entity currently known as obsessive-compulsive disorder (OCD) had been described previously by others (Adams 1973; Pitman 1994), Freud coined the term *obsessional neurosis* and provided some of the most detailed descriptions of the syndrome to date. He also emphasized that patients are able to conceal their illness, so that "many more people suffer from these forms of obsessional neurosis than doctors hear of" (Freud 1907). This important contribution to psychiatric nosology and phenomenology was complemented by theoretical innovation—early psychoanalytic writing provided a comprehensive description of the underlying psychic structures and mechanisms thought to be responsible for obsessive-compulsive symptoms.

Indeed, psychoanalytic understanding of obsessional neurosis on the one hand, and of hysteria on the other, can be seen as comprising the clinical keystones on which Freud constructed his understanding of the unconscious and its role in psychopathology. Whereas the hysteric—often a woman—repressed ideas, the obsessive—often a man—repressed affect. Again and again Freud returned to these two disorders, contrasting and comparing their manifestations and psychodynamics.

And yet, OCD has taken a back seat in modern psychoanalysis. Recent years have seen very few theoretical contributions to this subject. Furthermore, it is not clear that psychoanalysis is a useful treatment for OCD. Indeed, a thorough review of the psychoanalytic literature concludes that there is little evidence that psychoanalysis constitutes an effective intervention for patients with this condition (Esman 1989).

At the same time, we have seen a vast increase in knowledge about OCD. Epidemiologists have noted that OCD is far more common than some have thought, with a lifetime prevalence of 2 to 3 percent in the United States and a range of other countries. Biologically oriented psychiatrists have documented that OCD has a specific mediating neurochemistry and neuroanatomy, and they have found that specific medications are useful in its treatment. Cognitive-behavioral psychotherapists have similarly documented the efficacy of certain nonpsychodynamic techniques in the treatment of OCD.

1

Given the recency of this knowledge, what is the justification for a volume that attempts to look back over the past hundred years or so of writing on obsessive-compulsive disorder? Surely papers more than a few years old are merely historical curiosities?

Despite the advances in our modern understanding of the neurobiology and cognitive-behavioral therapy of OCD, there are important reasons to return to the classics. First, despite the dramatic advances made in biological psychiatry, there are still many aspects of this disorder that require further investigation; the older literature may provide an important source of constructs and hypotheses. Second, despite the tremendous success of pharmacotherapy and cognitive-behavioral psychotherapy, there are still many cases where psychodynamic psychotherapy plays an important role, either in encouraging patients to employ these modalities or as a supplement to them.

Thus the question is perhaps not so much whether to return to Freud and other early authors, but rather how best to incorporate their findings. We based our selection of papers not only on the grounds of whether particular papers are widely quoted, but also whether together they represent adequately the different strands of thinking about OCD. In this way we hope to provide the most comprehensive framework for theoretical and clinical integration possible. For the sake of convenience, we have divided the selections into three sections: classical psychoanalysis, psychological research, and neuro-psychiatric approaches.

CLASSICAL PSYCHOANALYSIS

The tremendous influence of Freud is reflected in his strong impact upon all subsequent psychoanalytic writing on obsessive-compulsive psychopathology. The papers in the "Classical Psychoanalysis" section of the book in turn exemplify the development of psychoanalytic thought from Freud's earliest models of the mind to his later structural approach, as well as the shift within psychoanalysis from drive theories to object relations approaches. OCD has been crucial to psychoanalytic thought, and as psychoanalytic theory has developed there have been important revisions and alterations in psychodynamic models of this disorder.

The first paper of this volume is Freud's "The Defence Neuro-Psychoses," published in 1894. At this point, Freud's model of the mind is based on the laws of nineteenth-century physics. He states that "in mental functions something is to be distinguished—a quota of affect or sum of excitation—which possesses all the characteristics of a quantity (though we have no means of measuring it), which is capable of increase, diminution, displacement, and discharge, and which is spread over the memory-traces of ideas somewhat as an electric charge is spread over the surface of a body." Similarly, he explains psychopathology in terms of particular configurations of psychic energy.

Central to the pathogenesis of obsessive-compulsive psychopathology in patients is the moment "at which an occurrence of incompatability took place in their ideational lives—that is to say, until their ego was faced with an experience, an idea or feeling which aroused such a distressed affect that the subject decided to forget about it." Freud postulates that in both obsessive-compulsive neurosis and hysteria, "Incompatible ideas of this sort arise chiefly on the soil of sexual experience and sensation," resulting in a defensive effort to suppress the thought.

In hysteria, "The incompatible idea is rendered innocuous by its sum of excitation being transformed into something somatic," a process that Freud terms *conversion*. In obsessive-compulsive neurosis, the patient defends against the idea by "separating it from its affect," which then "attaches itself to other ideas which are not in themselves incompatible; and, thanks to this 'false connection', those ideas turn into obsessional ideas." Importantly, these "are processes which occur without consciousness." Logically, treatment involves "leading back the attention of patients . . . to the repressed sexual ideas in spite of all their protestations."

In a subsequent paper, Freud (1896) went so far as to state that "obsessional ideas are invariably transformed self-reproaches which have re-emerged from repression and which always relate to some sexual act that was performed with pleasure in childhood," with obsessional actions resulting from a successful secondary defense against the "return of the repressed." Whereas hysteria is characterized by "passive" childhood sexual experiences, in obsessive-compulsive neurosis these sexual experiences are carried out actively and with pleasure.

Freud later came to doubt this theory of the etiology of hysteria and obsessional neurosis, arguing that patients' apparent recollections were often fantasies. Nevertheless, in a footnote added in 1924 Freud argues that his 1896 paper should not be rejected in total: "Seduction retains a certain aetiological importance, and even to-day I think some of these psychological comments are to the point."

Freud's hydraulic model of the mind finds little support in the writings of modern authors (Mitchell 1988). Nevertheless, "The Defence Neuro-Psychoses" makes several fundamental contributions. It provides a vivid and detailed depiction of the symptoms of OCD. In particular, it empathically details the "craziness" of the symptoms for the patient. There is a disjunction, Freud asserts, between ideas and affects. Whether or not one agrees with this concept, there is undoubtedly a rupture in OCD between the patient's drive to perform compulsions and his or her acknowledgment that these are excessive or senseless.

Freud's assertion that obsessions and compulsions are the sequelae of sexual trauma is currently being reassessed. In the last decade there has been an explosion of theoretical and empirical research on child abuse, and Freud's abandonment of his seduction theory has been viewed by many authors as a fundamental error (Masson 1984). Empirical research has confirmed that sexual and physical trauma plays a significant role in adult psychopathology. Nevertheless, there is little literature so far indicating that sexual trauma is important in the etiology of OCD. On the other hand, a history of sexual abuse can be found in some patients with OCD (Stone et al., unpublished data), and in these cases psychotherapeutic interventions must, as Freud pointed out, address the trauma.

The next paper in the volume is an extract from Freud's case study of the "Rat Man," "Notes upon a Case of Obsessional Neurosis" (1909), a classic in the field. Freud emphasizes the value of case studies in his observation that "it would be a most desirable thing if the philosophers and psychologists who develop brilliant theoretical views on the unconscious . . . would first submit to the convincing impressions which may be gained from a first-hand study of the phenomena of obsessional thinking." Certainly, the material in the "Rat Man" provides a detailed description of the clinical phenomenology of OCD and gives subsequent generations of theorists much food for thought.

In his theoretical formulation of the case, Freud further develops his early libidinal theory of the specific instincts (e.g., sadistic impulses) and defenses (e.g., withdrawal of affect) involved in obsessional neurosis. He also extends his account of the need to translate the meaning of symptoms, arguing that while "patients themselves do not know the wording of their own obsessional ideas," the obsessional idea "exhibits . . . in its distortion from its original wording, traces of the primary defensive struggle." At the heart of this kind of linguistic approach is the insistence that obsessive-compulsive symptoms are only apparently senseless. Thus, "in obsessive actions everything has its meaning and can be interpreted" (Freud 1907). Obsessive actions are "consequently to be interpreted either historically or symbolically" (Freud 1907).

This too is an argument that many modern readers may be unwilling to accept. A dominant argument in the current literature is that obsessions and compulsions may be meaningful from an ethological perspective—for example, as dysfunctional grooming behaviors (Rapoport, Ryland, and Kriete 1992; Stein et al. 1992)—but that these symptoms are essentially meaningless from the perspective of the patient. Nevertheless, a return to Freud raises this issue for debate (Gabbard 1992).

Freud goes on to describe the importance of unconscious hatred and sadistic impulses in obsessional neurosis. Thus, "in the cases of unconscious hatred with which we are concerned the sadistic components of love have, from constitutional causes, been exceptionally strongly developed, and have consequently undergone a premature and all too thorough suppression, and . . . the neurotic phenomena . . . arise on the one hand from conscious feelings of affection . . . , and on the other hand from sadism persisting in the unconscious in the form of hatred." He uses this formula to explain symptoms of compulsion and doubt. While the notion of unconscious hatred is rarely considered in current research on OCD, researchers are increasingly looking at the relationship between OCD and impulsive-aggression, and indeed between compulsivity and impulsivity (Stein and Hollander 1993a, 1993b).

In his 1913 paper "Hate and Anal Erotism in the Obsessional Neurosis," Ernest Jones elaborates on the importance of hate and anal erotism in the pathogenesis of obsessional neurosis. This work complements Freud's (1913) assertion that obsessional neurosis results from a regressive return to the anal phase, which is characterized by sadistic libidinal drives. Like Freud, Jones argues that paralysis of love and hate underlies the alternation between compulsion and doubt in obsessional neurosis. He also attempts to draw a connection between anal erotism and the "omnipotence of thought," which Freud (1909) described as characteristic of obsessional neurosis.

While the construct of anal erotism in the work of Jones (1913) and Freud (1913) is perhaps increasingly discordant with modern psychological constructs, the notion that brain-based cognitive-affective structures are intimately concerned with dirt (at a basic level) and contamination (at a more abstract level) remains intriguing (Rapoport, Ryland, and Kriete 1992; Stein et al. 1992). Current thinking also posits that such structures may have some relationship to the expression of anger and aggression (Stein and Hollander 1993a, 1993b).

Karl Abraham's 1921 paper "Contributions to the Theory of the Anal Character" also draws closely on Freud's concepts of anality, returning to the anal character triad of orderliness, parsimony, and obstinancy (Freud 1908). Like Freud, Abraham views the anal libidinal organization as underlying both symptom formation (obsessional neurosis) and character type (anal triad)—with the difference lying only in the fact that in the anal character there is no failure of repression and no return of the repressed (Freud 1913). Abraham hypothesizes that when cleanliness or other tasks are demanded too soon by parents, a conflict may result between a conscious attitude of submissiveness and an unconscious desire for vengeance. These patients develop traits such as having to do everything themselves because no one else can do it as well, indexing and registering everything, giving gratification in small and insufficient amounts, and overemphasizing possession.

While Abraham's argument that all these so-called anal traits have analogues in the patient's attitude to feces and defecation may be questioned, his depiction of these patients is another important contribution to the clinical phenomenology of the entity currently known as obsessive-compulsive personality disorder (OCPD). Although a distinction has increasingly been drawn between OCD and OCPD, their relationship has been a subject of considerable debate and has not yet been fully resolved (Stein, Hollander, and DeCaria 1994; Stein et al, 1995).

By the time of his 1926 paper "Inhibitions, Symptoms, and Anxiety," Freud had moved from his early topographic model to a structural model, in which the id, ego, and super-ego are depicted. He notes that "the ego and the super-ego have a specially large share in the formation of symptoms" of obsessional neurosis. When the ego defends against the libidinal demands of the Oedipus complex, it regresses to the earlier sadistic-anal level. As a result, "The superego becomes exceptionally severe and unkind, and the ego, in obedience to the super-ego, produces strong reaction-formations in the shape of conscientiousness, pity and cleanliness." In hysteria, on the other hand, the defensive process is limited to repression. The development of obsessional neurosis may be a result of "constitutional factors," or it may be because "opposition of the ego begins too early, while the sadistic phase is at its height."

On many occasions, Freud's focus on sexuality seems absurd. For example, he writes that the "chief task during the latency period seems to be the fending-off of the temptation to masturbate." The idea that the threatened punishment of the super-ego is an extension of the punishment of castration is also difficult to accept. It may be argued, however, that this view that in obsessional neurosis the "very process of thinking becomes hypercathected and erotized" provides a detailed, empathic window on the illness. For example, Freud uses his libidinal theory to explain the defenses of undoing and isolating—and in so doing again makes an important contribution to the phenomenological description of OCD. Similarly, his focus on touching and physical contact as immediate aims of id drives again foreshadows current views of OCD as a disorder of innate grooming mechanisms (Rapoport, Ryland, and Kriete 1992; Stein et al. 1992).

Anna Freud's 1966 paper "Obsessional Neurosis" provides a summary of views of obsessional neurosis presented at the Twenty-Fourth International Psycho-Analytical Congress. She begins with her own view of obsessional neurosis, which succintly summarizes much of her father's work on the spectrum of obsessional disorders and their id content, defense mechanisms, and etiology. She argues that the defenses associated with the disorder—reaction formations and intellectualization—differentiate obsessions from repetitive behaviors (e.g., in mental defectives) and id-driven behavior (e.g., in addicts and psychopaths).

Anna Freud points out a number of newer foci, such as developments in ego psychology. She notes, for example, that the extension of defensive devices to include the ego's "everyday functioning such as perceiving, thinking, abstracting, conceptualizing ... represents an attempt to embrace the area of conflict as well as the conflict-free area of secondary process functioning." She also suggests a number of interesting hypotheses (e.g., positing a link between failed object relations and heightened anality) and formulas (e.g., noting that "in hysteria the body behaves as if on its own, the mind does the same in obsessional neurosis").

All in all, Anna Freud provides a cogent analysis of past theory and unresolved issues in the psychoanalytic approach to obsessional neurosis. She remains optimistic that the general framework of psychoanalysis is correct, and that psychoanalytic understanding of obsessional neurosis will progress. However, in her criticisms there are also hints of the limits of psychoanalytic understanding—leaving the modern reader with the sense that other constructs and models will be necessary for progress in this area.

Peter E. Sifneos (1966) has argued that many patients respond to brief, psychoanalytically oriented, dynamic therapy. In his paper in this volume, he applies this view to obsessional neurosis, arguing that there are patients who suffer from mild obsessional-compulsive neuroses of sudden onset who respond well to short-term dynamic psychotherapy. Often environmental factors, such as criticism from an authority, act as a precipitant, resulting in the use of defense mechanisms that prove to be unsuccessful.

Sifneos outlines several criteria for selecting patients for such therapy. These include acute onset of obsessive-compulsive symptoms in a well-adjusted person facing an emotional crisis and a general fluidity of the defenses used. His techniques for treatment include early utilization of the positive transference, concentration on unresolved conflicts, avoidance of characterological complication, and avoidance of the development of a trans- ference neurosis. This paper is useful in that it points to the possibility of transient psychogenic OCD—a phenomenon that has not received much attention lately.

Leonard Salzman's 1968 book *Treatment of the Obsessional Personality* was one of the first full-length volumes on this condition. Like so many other psychoanalysts, Salzman begins with the classical model of Freud. However, he extends the classical model in new directions, focusing, as Sullivan (1956) did earlier, on understanding the interpersonal relationships of patients with obsessional neurosis, and paying particular attention to the issue of control.

"The essential task in the therapy of the obsessive-compulsive disorders," Salzman writes, "is that of conveying insight and initiating learning and change without getting caught in the 'obsessional tug-of-war.' " He argues that "most of the obsessional patterns of behavior arise from feelings of powerlessness and uncertainty" rather than from hostility per se. He describes how psychotherapy can therefore be transformed by the obsessional patient from "a collaborative adventure" to "a struggle for control and position."

Salzman provides specific and practical advice about psychotherapy with the obsessional patient. In particular, he encourages therapists to actively participate, combine firmness with flexibility, be aware of countertransference feelings, and emphasize the here and now. In these respects his remarks are typical of much other post-Freudian theory and practice, which veers away from the classical insistence on, say, analytic neutrality and genetic recon- struction.

How important is Salzman's work for contemporary clinicians, given the current focus on pharmacotherapy and behavior therapy for OCD? We would argue that even these therapies take place within an interpersonal context, and that control issues are very often present, perhaps particularly in patients with OCPD. At times, these issues may defeat the best intentions of the psychopharmacologist or behavior therapist. Thus, Salzman's contribution continues to be relevant to current practice.

PSYCHOLOGICAL RESEARCH

Although psychoanalytic theory is based on clinical material, detailed re- search on the psychopathology and psychotherapy of OCD required research- ers to adopt a more rigorous empirical investigative approach. The second section of this volume focuses on early work in this direction. To the credit of psychoanalysis, some of these empirical studies were initially conducted by psychoanalysts. Increasingly, however, psychological research on OCD has fallen in the arena of researchers with a behaviorist or cognitivist orientation.

Joseph Sandler and Anandi Hazari (1960) made an important contribution to empirical investigation of OCD by studying the relationship between obsessive-compulsive symptoms and traits. They provide a clear definition of obsessions and compulsions that is remarkably similar to the one currently used in the *Diagnostic and Statistical Manual of Mental Disorders* (DSM-IV). They note that while some authors see the difference between obsessional symptoms and traits as merely a matter of degree, others hold that patients with an obsessional character often experience depression and other pathological reactions rather than obsessional neurosis.

Sandler and Hazari gave a battery of forty items for assessing obsessive and compulsive symptoms and traits to one hundred patients and subjected the data to factor analysis. Two relatively independent constellations were derived, termed the *A-type* and *B-type*. The A-type is similar to the current concept of OCPD, while the B-type is more redolent of the symptoms of OCD. Subsequent research has confirmed the psychometric independence of OCD and OCPD (Slade 1974; Stein, Hollander, and DeCaria 1994).

Nevertheless, Sandler and Hazari make the point that even in the B-type constellation there may be a spectrum of symptoms, with some patients having a milder picture. They use the term "obsessional personality" to describe this milder entity. Perhaps a less confusing term would be subclinical OCD. This entity arguably remains relevant to understanding the phenomenology and psychobiology of OCD.

Lewis L. Judd (1965) provides one of the earliest comprehensive descriptive studies of OCD in children. Although the study is limited by its retrospective nature, the findings that OCD is not an uncommon condition in this population and that, although difficult to treat, it can respond to psychotherapy remain relevant. The observation that there were no reported difficulties or adverse conditions associated with toilet training marks a turn against psychodynamic hypotheses. Similarly, Judd was able to establish rigorous criteria for differentiating normal compulsions and ritualization from pathological symptoms. His paper sets an exemplary tone for modern criteria-based nosological and phenomenological psychopathological research on both children and adults with OCD.

Heinz Hartmann's (1933) experimental research on OCD goes beyond factor analysis to tests of psychological functioning. In particular he is interested in B. Zeigarnik's (1927) work showing that recall of uncompleted tasks is higher than recall of completed tasks. Hartmann noted that incompleteness or inability of closure is characteristic of the thinking of obsessive-compulsive neurotics and decided to assess the Zeigarnik effect in these patients. This kind of research was of particular interest to Hartmann and other psychoanalysts interested in ego functioning.

Although his sample size was small, Hartmann found that obsessive-compulsive neurotics did not recall uncompleted tasks significantly better than completed ones. In contrast, Zeigarnik had found that impulsive subjects recalled uncompleted tasks more readily than other subjects. These findings are consistent with the report that OCD patients are dissatisfied with their performance even on subjectively completed tasks. As Hartmann notes, "Subjective incompletion of a task and the tendency for repetition must be recognized as influences upon recall."

Hartmann concludes with the assertion that psychological models such as Kurt Lewin's theory of needs (which encompassed Zeigarnik's work) could usefully be based on psychoanalytic drive theory. Whether or not we accept this argument, Hartmann's paper opens the way to empirical research on the neuropsychology of OCD, an area of investigation that remains important (Stein, Hollander, and Cohen 1994).

Rigorous experimental methodologies were first applied to the treatment of OCD by behaviorists. In their 1971 paper "The Treatment of Chronic Obsessive-Compulsive Neurosis," Stanley Rachman, Ray Hodgson, and Isaac M. Marks report on a controlled study of modeling and flooding. Both treatments were found to produce significantly more improvement than did relaxation control treatment.

Behavior therapy continues to remain the psychotherapeutic treatment of choice for patients with OCD. Particular success has been achieved with exposure and response prevention techniques. There is also increasing evidence that therapeutic success obtained with behavioral therapy can be long-lasting (Baer and Minichiello 1990).

In his 1985 paper "Obsessional-Compulsive Problems: A Cognitive-Behavioural Analysis," Paul M. Salkovskis argues that a behavioral model of OCD must be supplemented by a cognitive one. He notes that obsessional thinking can be considered the archetypal example of a cognitive disorder in the neuroses. Furthermore, behavioral therapy often appears to require supplementation by cognitive techniques.

Salkovskis suggests that intrusive thoughts are best regarded as cognitive stimuli. Cognitive responses to these intrusive thoughts are typically linked to beliefs concerning responsibility or blame for harm. This formula allows Salkovskis to explain a number of clinical phenomena (e.g., heightened depression results in increased accessibility to concerns about responsibility and so to increased obsessive-compulsive symptoms) and to suggest a number of clinical interventions (e.g., contradicting the beliefs concerning responsibility and blame).

Salkovskis's paper is of particular interest given the increasing amount of work on cognitive models of the mind and its disorders (Stein and Young 1992). It seems clear that an integrative model of OCD must incorporate a description and explanation of cognitive structures and processes. Hopefully, the work of Salkovskis and others will encourage such integration to proceed.

NEUROPSYCHIATRIC APPROACHES

Freud noted that obsessional neurosis involved constitutional factors (1909, 1926) and "similar heredity" (1895) and wrote that "before the question as to what factors can bring about such disturbances of development the work of psycho-analysis comes to a stop: it leaves that problem to biological research" (1913). Although the study of the biology of OCD is relatively young, a number of investigators have already made significant contributions that are likely to have lasting value. Work demonstrating the mediation of OCD symptoms by specific brain regions and neurotransmitters has been particularly exciting.

In an early paper, Paul Schilder (1938) reviewed some of the earliest evidence for a neurobiological basis for OCD—the association between OCD and encephalitis lethargica, a neurological sequela of the influenza epidemic that occurred early in the twentieth century. Patients with these symptoms often demonstrated involuntary movements, presumably on the basis of basal ganglia pathology. Conversely, Schilder found that a subgroup of OCD patients had increased neurological soft signs suggesting brain dysfunction. Schilder remains strongly supportive of psychodynamic thinking, arguing that at bottom, OCD is an impulse disturbance that is either organic or psychogenic in nature.

Subsequent investigation has confirmed that OCD is associated with a number of basal ganglia neurological disorders (e.g., Sydenham's chorea, Tourette's syndrome) and that OCD patients may have specific neuropsychiatric abnormalities (Stein, Hollander, and Cohen 1994). Such work provides important clues to tracing the ultimate genetic and molecular mechanisms responsible for the pathogenesis of OCD (Pauls et al. 1986; Swedo, Leonard, and Kiessling 1994).

Steven P. Wise and Judith L. Rapoport (1989) synthesize additional evidence for the link between basal ganglia dysfunction and OCD. In particular, they review brain imaging studies, psychosurgery data, and neuropharmacology data that support a role for basal ganglia dysfunction in OCD. Parallel loops between the basal ganglia and cortex mediate motor, cognitive, and perceptual functions and are good candidates for involvement in OCD. Thus, impairment in the basal ganglia gating mechanism for sensory input may underly OCD. Similarly, a repository of innate motor programs in the basal ganglia may be responsible for the kinds of symptom seen in this disorder. Indeed, this hypothesis provides the basis for the current exciting work on animal analogues of OCD (Rapoport, Ryland, and Kriete 1992; Stein et al. 1992).

In addition to advances in understanding the neuroanatomy of OCD, there is now increased understanding of the neurochemistry of the disorder. Involvement of serotonin in OCD was surmised when early investigators found that a serotonergic tricyclic, clomipramine, was particularly helpful in alleviating obsessive and compulsive symptoms. Joseph Zohar and Thomas R. Insel's 1987 paper summarizes their pioneering work on the serotonin system in OCD.

These authors reach a number of significant conclusions. First, the serotonergic antidepressant clomipramine is more effective than the noradrenergic antidepressant desipramine in the treatment of OCD. Second, the serotonin agonist m-chlorophenylpiperazine (m-CPP) results in a significant increase in obsessive-compulsive symptoms. In contrast, administration of the serotonin antagonist metergoline results in a decrease in obsessive-compulsive symptoms. These results points to the specific role of the serotonin neurotransmitter system in mediating OCD.

Given the role of serotonin in OCD, the introduction of medications that act specifically on serotonin receptors comprised an important step forward in the treatment of OCD. There are now several serotonin specific reuptake inhibitors on the market, all of which appear useful in OCD. Michael A. Jenike (1992) summarizes current knowledge of the use of these and other medications in the management of OCD and discusses current pharmacological approaches to the treatment-resistant patient.

An immediate question is how to integrate work on the neuroanatomy and neurochemistry of OCD. The work of Lewis R. Baxter and colleagues (1992) not only addresses this question, but also provides an approach to the integration of behavioral and pharmacotherapeutic data about OCD. Functional brain imaging has become increasingly sophisticated in recent years, with techniques such as single photon emission computed tomography (SPECT) and positron emission tomography (PET) allowing researchers to investigate activity in specific brain regions in fine detail. Baxter and colleagues report on the use of PET scans before and after both behavior therapy and pharmacotherapy with a serotonin reuptake inhibitor (SRI) for OCD. The results indicate that similar changes are seen in the basal ganglia after both forms of intervention.

Thus, even if brain dysfunction is an important factor in the etiology of some OCD patients, psychotherapy—which also has effects at a brain level—may be an important intervention. This work makes an important contribution to dissolving the mind–brain gap. This kind of research moves OCD from its central role in psychodynamic theory, where it was said to shed light on the unconscious, to an important role in neuropsychiatric science, where it may well be able to illuminate some general principles of psychopathology.

Susan E. Swedo, Henrietta L. Leonard, and Judith L. Rapoport (1992) follow through on the early work of Judd (1965) and other authors (Despert 1955; Adams 1973) in their thorough prospective investigation of a large sample of children and adolescents with OCD. They detail clinical presentation, co-morbidity, treatment, and course. OCD is unusual among psychiatric disorders in having so similar a clinical phenomenology and treatment response in children and adults. This work is crucial in alerting clinicians to the importance of diagnosing OCD in children, and in reminding researchers of the necessity for investigating the psychobiology of OCD in both younger and older populations.

Psychoanalytic theory postulated a spectrum from obsessive-compulsive character through to obsessive-compulsive symptoms. The neuropsychiatric perspective has highlighted observations that several neurological disorders (e.g., Tourette's syndrome) and psychiatric disorders (e.g., body dysmorphic disorder, hypochondriasis, and perhaps trichotillomania) are characterized by intrusive thoughts or ritualistic behaviors and may also respond selectively to SRIs. Indeed, the notion of an obsessive-compulsive spectrum of disorders has received increasing attention.

Dan J. Stein and Eric Hollander (1993b) discuss the advantages and disadvantages of various OCD spectrum concepts. On the one hand, the idea of a neuropsychiatric spectrum of OCD disorders runs the risk of being overinclusive and of overgeneralizing. On the other hand, the notion of a spectrum provides a heuristic for research on the phenomenology and psychobiology of a range of possibly related disorders and also provides the clinician with guidelines for assessment and treatment of these disorders. Taken together, it would seem that advances in our understanding of the neurobiology and pharmacotherapy of OCD provide a useful way for the researcher and clinician to approach a series of other possibly related conditions.

CONCLUSION

Freud writes that "obsessional neurosis presents such a vast multiplicity of phenomena that no efforts have yet succeeded in making a coherent synthesis of all its variations" (1926). While much remains to be understood about OCD, many important advances have been made over the past century. Psychodynamic theorists, psychological researchers, and neuropsychiatrically oriented investigators have all contributed to these advances.

The psychodynamic approach pioneered by Freud has made a significant contribution to the nosology and phenomenology of obsessive-compulsive disorder. Each of the major models of psychoanalysis—classical drive theory, ego psychology, interpersonal and object relations theory—has been applied to this condition (Nagera 1976). Early psychodynamic writing provides a rich source of data and hypotheses about these conditions, challenging researchers to incorporate a wealth of clinical observations into their models. Later psychodynamic writing emphasizes the interpersonal context of OCD symptoms and their management and continues to be a helpful clinical resource.

The emphasis of ego psychology on cognitive functioning gave an important impetus to a neuropsychological perspective on OCD (Hartmann 1933; Shapiro 1965; Sandler and Joffe 1965; Barnett 1966). Subsequent research from the perspective of academic psychology further investigated the underlying neuropsychology of OCD and documented the efficacy of specific psychotherapeutic techniques in its management. Given that OCD is manifested by abnormalities of behavior and cognition, this level of investigation cannot be ignored. Researchers need to address cognitive-behavioral structures and processes in their models of OCD. Clinicians can successfully incorporate a range of cognitive-behavioral assessment and intervention techniques in their management of OCD.

The neuropsychiatric approach has led to an increasingly detailed understanding of the neuroanatomy and neurochemistry of OCD. Current brain imaging techniques are particularly exciting insofar as they allow detailed investigation of the neurobiology of both psychotherapeutic and pharmacotherapeutic interventions. Indeed, current research on OCD is beginning to illuminate some important principles of general psychopathology. Such work has already led to significant advances in the management of OCD, and progress in this area should lead to further improvements in treatment.

We have undoubtedly omitted some papers on OCD that researchers or clinicians consider to be their favorites. Clearly, space limitations have made it impossible for us to include even a small portion of the many important contributions that have been made over the past century to the study of this intriguing disorder. We particularly regret having to omit early papers on OCD spectrum disorders such as Tourette's disorder and trichotillomania; important papers on the epidemiology (Karno et al. 1988) and assessment (Goodman et al. 1989a, 1989b) of OCD; psychoanalytically oriented writing that has focused on cognitive (Shapiro 1965; Barnett 1966), linguistic (Schneiderman 1986), and sociocultural (Adams 1973) aspects of OCD; psychological research that has investigated normal obsessions and habits (Rachman and De Silva 1978; Martin and Tesser 1989); and recent studies at the forefront of cognitive-behavioral and neuropsychiatric investigation of OCD (Baer and Minichiello 1990; Goodman et al. 1990; Swedo et al. 1994).

The contributions included here, however, provide the reader with an inclusive and useful framework for beginning to formulate an integrated theoretical and clinical approach to obsessive-compulsive disorder. We hope this collection of papers will encourage such integrative work to proceed.

ACKNOWLEDGMENT

Dan J. Stein is supported by a grant from the Medical Research Council of South Africa and the Lundbeck Fellowship Award.

REFERENCES

Abraham K. [1921] 1953. Contributions to the theory of the anal character. Pp. 370–92 in Selected Papers, vol. 1. London: Hogarth Press.

Adams P. L. 1973. Obsessive Children: A Sociopsychiatric Study. New York: Brunner/Mazel.

Baer L., Minichiello W. E. 1990. Behavior therapy for obsessive-compulsive disorder. In M. A. Jenike, L. Baer, W. E. Minichiello, eds., Obsessive-Compulsive Disorders: Theory and Management, 2nd ed. Chicago: Year Book Medical Publishers.

Barnett J. 1996. On cognitive disorders in the obsessional. Contemporary Psychoanalysis, 2: 122–34.

Baxter L. R., Schwartz J. M., Bergman K. S. et al. 1992. Caudate glucose metabolic rate changes with both drug and behavior therapy for OCD. Arch Gen Psychiatry 49: 681–89.

Despert L. 1955. Differential diagnosis between obsessive-compulsive neurosis and schizophrenia in children. P. H. Hock, J. Zubin, eds., Psychopathology of Childhood. New York: Grune and Stratton.

Esman A. H. 1989. Psychoanalysis and general psychiatry: obsessive-compulsive disorder as paradigm. J Am Psychoanal Assoc 37: 319–36.

Freud A. 1966. Obsessional neurosis: a summary of psycho-analytic views as presented at the congress. Int J Psychoanal 47: 116–23.

Freud S. 1894. The defence neuro-psychoses. Standard Edition 3: 45–61.

———. 1895. Obsessions and phobias: their physical mechanisms and their etiology. Standard Edition 1: 70–84.

———. 1896. Further remarks on the neuro-psychoses of defence. Standard Edition 3: 162–89.

———. 1907. Obsessive actions and religious practices. Standard Edition 9: 115–28.

———. 1908. Character and anal erotism. Standard Edition 9: 167–76.

———. 1909. Notes upon on a case of obsessional neurosis. Standard Edition 10: 221–49.

———. 1913. The disposition towards obsessional neurosis. Standard Edition 12: 311–26.

———. 1926. Inhibitions, symptoms, and anxiety. Standard Edition 20: 111–31.

Gabbard G. O. 1992. Psychodynamic psychiatry in the "decade of the brain." Am J Psychiatry 149: 991–98.

Goodman W. K., McDougle C. J., Price L. H. et al. 1990. Beyond the serotonin hypothesis: a role for dopamine in some forms of obsessive compulsive disorder? J Clin Psychiatry 51: S36–S43.

Goodman W. K., Price L. H., Rasmussen S. A. et al. 1989a. The Yale-Brown Obsessive Compulsive Scale. I. Development, use and reliability. Arch Gen Psychiatry 46: 1006–11.

———. 1898b. The Yale-Brown Obsessive Compulsive Scale. II. Validity. Arch Gen Psychiatry 46: 1012–16.

Hartmann H. 1933. An experimental contribution to the psychology of obsessive-compulsive neurosis—on remembering completed and uncompleted tasks. In Essays on Ego Psychology. Reprint, London: Hogarth Press and London Institute of Psychoanalysis, 1964.

Jenike M. A. 1992. Pharmacologic treatment of obsessive compulsive disorders. Psych Clin N Am 15: 895–19.

Jones E. 1913. Hate and anal erotism in the obsessional neurosis. Pp. 553–61 in Papers on Psychoanalysis. Baltimore: Williams and Wilkins.

Judd L. L. 1965. Obsessive compulsive neurosis in children. Arch Gen Psychiatry 12: 136–43.

Karno M., Golding J. M., Sorenson S. B. et al. 1988. The epidemiology of obsessive-compulsive disorder in five US communities. Arch Gen Psychiatry 45: 1094–99.

Martin L. L., Tesser A. 1989. Toward a motivational and structural theory of rumina-

tive thought. Pp. 306–26 in J. S. Uleman, J. A. Bargh, eds., Unintended Thought. *New York: Guilford Press.*

Masson J. M. 1984. The Assault on Truth: Freud's Suppression of the Seduction Theory. *New York: Farrar, Straus and Giroux.*

Mitchell S. A. 1988. Relational Concepts in Psychoanalysis: An Integration. *Cambridge: Harvard University Press.*

Nagera H. 1976. Obsessional Neurosis: Developmental Psychopathology. *Northvale, N.J.: Jason Aronson.*

Pauls D. L., Towbin K. E., Leckman J. F. et al. 1986. Gilles de la Tourette's syndrome and obsessive compulsive disorder: evidence supporting genetic relationship. Arch Gen Psychiatry *43: 1180–82.*

Pitman R. K. 1994. Obsessive compulsive disorder in Western history. In E. Hollander, J. Zohar, D. Marazzati, B. Olivier, eds., Current Insights in Obsessive-Compulsive Disorder. *Chichester, Eng.: Wiley.*

Rachman S., De Silva P. 1978. Abnormal and normal obsessions. Behav Res Therapy *16: 233–48.*

Rachman S., Hodgson R., Marks I. M. 1971. The treatment of chronic obsessive-compulsive neurosis. Behav Res Therapy *9: 237–47.*

Rapoport J. L., Ryland D. H., Kriete M. 1992. Drug treatment of canine acral lick: an animal model of obsessive-compulsive disorder. Arch Gen Psychiatry *48: 517–21.*

Salkovskis P. M. 1985. Obsessional-compulsive problems: a cognitive-behavioral analysis. Behav Res Therapy *23: 571–83.*

Salzman L. 1968. Therapy of the obsessive personality. In Treatment of the Obsessive Personality. *New York: Jason Aronson, 1968.*

Sandler J., Hazari A. 1960. The 'obsessional': on the psychological classification of obsessional character traits and symptoms. Br J Med Psychol *33: 113–22.*

Sandler J., Joffe W. G. 1965. Notes on obsessional manifestations in children. Psychoanalytic Study of the Child *20: 425–41.*

Schilder P. 1938. The organic background of obsessions and compulsions. Am J Psychiatry *94: 1397–1413.*

Schneiderman S. 1986. Theory of obsessional neurosis. In Rat Man. *New York: New York University Press.*

Shapiro D. 1965. Neurotic Styles. *New York: Basic Books.*

Sifneos P. E. 1966. Psychoanalytically oriented short-term dynamic or anxiety-producing psychotherapy for mild obsessional neuroses. Psych Quarterly *40: 277–82.*

Slade P. D. 1974. Psychometric studies of obsessional illness and obsessional personality. Pp. 95–109 in H. R. Beech, ed., Obsessional States. *London: Methuen.*

Stein D. J., Hollander E. 1993a. Impulsive aggression and obsessive-compulsive disorder. Psychiatric Annals *23: 389–95.*

———. *1993b. The spectrum of obsessive-compulsive related disorders. In E. Hollander, ed.,* Obsessive-Compulsive Related Disorders. *Washington D.C.: American Psychiatric Press.*

Stein D. J., Hollander E., Cohen L. 1994. Neuropsychiatry of Obsessive-Compulsive Disorder. In E. Hollander, J. Zohar, D. Marazzati, B. Olivier, eds., Current Insights in Obsessive-Compulsive Disorder. *Chichester, Eng.: Wiley.*

Stein D. J., Hollander E., DeCaria C. M. 1994. Personality disorders and obsessive-compulsive disorder. In E. Hollander, Z. Zohar, D. Marazzati, B. Olivier, eds., Current Insights in Obsessive-Compulsive Disorder. *Chichester, Eng.: Wiley.*

Stein D. J., Shoulberg N., Helton K., Hollander E. 1992. The neuroethological model of obsessive-compulsive disorder. Comprehensive Psychiatry *33: 274–81.*

Stein D. J., Trestman R., Coccaro E. et al. 1995. Serotonergic responsivity in compulsive personality disorder. Biol Psychiatry *37: 645.*

Stein D. J., Young J. E., eds. 1992. Cognitive Science and Clinical Disorders. *San Diego: Academic Press.*

Sullivan H. S. 1956. Obsessionalism. Pp. 229–83 in S. Perry et al., eds., Clinical Studies in Psychiatry. *New York: Norton.*

Swedo S. E., Leonard H. L., Kiessling L. S. 1994. Speculations on antineuronal antibody-mediated neuropsychiatric disorders of childhood. Pediatrics *93: 323–26.*

Swedo S. E., Leonard H. L., Rapoport J. L. 1992. Childhood-onset obsessive compulsive disorder. Psychiatric Clin N Am *15: 767–75.*

Wise S., Rapoport J. L. 1989. Obsessive-compulsive disorder: is it basal ganglia dysfunction. Pp. 327–47 in J. L. Rapoport, ed., Obsessive-Compulsive Disorder in Children and Adolescents. *Washington, D.C.: American Psychiatric Press.*

Zeigarnick B. 1927. Das Behalten von erledigten und unerledigten Handlungen. Psychologie Forschung *9: 1–85.*

Zohar J., Insel T. R. 1987. Obsessive-compulsive disorder: psychobiological approaches to diagnosis, treatment, and pathophysiology. Biol Psychiatry *22: 667–87.*

Introduction: The History of Obsessive-Compulsive Disorder from the Early Period to the Turn of the Twentieth Century

Michael H. Stone, M.D.

THE MISTS OF HISTORY still lay thick over the first persons who suffered from obsessive-compulsive disorder (OCD) and the first physicians who described the condition. If, as some writers have claimed, intense religiosity can at times predispose to obsessive scrupulosity and compulsive, overly ritualized behavior, then the first instances of what we now call OCD must go back very far indeed. Actually, it is not always easy to determine whether fanatic religiosity literally predisposes to OCD or is merely the form OCD (stemming from other, including hereditary, factors) may assume in persons who coincidentally are deeply religious. Religions that encourage the suppression of sexual urges (such as the early Christian church, Puritanism, and certain Buddhist and Orthodox Jewish groups) may foster a program of self-control, along with feelings of guilt. Condemnation of all feelings of anger (as stressed by these same religions) can likewise promote exaggerated feelings of unworthiness and lead to a redoubling of efforts to rise above one's natural impulses. These efforts often take the form of obsessional self-criticism and of compulsive, ritualized acts of cleansing or self-mortification.

In the Tenth Century, the Persian Muslim medical writer Najab ud din Unhammad—a contemporary of the great Islamic physician Rhazes (c. 865–925)—described ruminative states of doubt. Unhammad called the condition *Murrae Souda* and felt it stemmed from excessive love of philosophy and law (Zilboorg 1941, 123).

Paul Adams (1973) has chronicled the medieval and Renaissance writers who dealt with the topic, especially with "obsessions." Paracelsus, the maverick sixteenth-century Swiss physician, spoke of *obsessio* as an imperious craving that derived from one's "animal nature." H. F. Ellenberger (1970) reminds us that in the Catholic theology of Paracelsus's day, alien, disturbing thoughts and tendencies were understood as coming literally from the outside: if this occurred while one was asleep, this so-called somnambulic phenomenon was called *possessio;* if it happened while one was awake or "lucid," the term *obsessio* was used. Since this possession or obsession was thought to result from infiltration into one's body by daemons—the agents who presumably forced one to think unclean or irreligious thoughts, or to have unnatural fears or inhibitions (especially sexual ones)—the notion of "daemonic possession" took hold and became widespread in the Catholic world.

Under the influence of the Protestant Reformation, writers in the formerly Catholic, mostly Northern European countries no longer adhered to the belief in daemonic influences. In the 1650s, English writer Richard Flecknoe spoke of the obsessional person simply as one who, "when he begins to deliberate, never makes an end" (Adams 1973, 251).

Around this time, an English doctor of divinity, Jeremy Taylor (1613–1667), wrote the treatise *Ductor dubitantium, or the rules of conscience* (1660), describing the obsessive person as one in whom irrational fears, but most especially *religious scruples,* became excessive and morbid, sometimes progressing to mental breakdown.

In the eighteenth century, the great English man of letters Samuel Johnson suffered various obsessive, melancholic, and hypochondriacal symptoms, which he described with the authenticity of one who has experienced such ailments. He declared, "No disease of the imagination is so difficult of cure, as that which is complicated with the dread of guilt" (Hunter and Macalpine 1963, 417).

In the 1770s, the Austrian miracle-healer Johann Gassner—apparently still believing in the daemonic, externally imposed nature of obsessions—practiced exorcism in cases of *obsessio.*

Among the earliest of the modern-sounding comments on the condition is that of the English alienist John Haslam (1764–1844), apothecary to the Bethelehem Hospital in London and later a physician and medical writer on psychiatric themes. Concerning obsessional patients, he commented (in 1798): "Certain notions are forced into their minds, of which they see the folly and incongruity, and complain that they cannot prevent their intrusion" (Hunter and Macalpine 1963, 632). Haslam was aware that many obsessive patients harbored extreme religious scruples, but he hastened to add that religion itself was not to blame (1809)—indeed, it was sinful to suppose so. Rather, certain persons of meager education or mental adjustment were prone to misuse and misconstrue their religious teachings, exaggerating various moral precepts into a state of religious preoccupation and pathological guilt.

The French alienists of the nineteenth century paid considerable attention to obsessive disorders. Esquirol, arguably the most prominent figure in nineteenth-century French psychiatry, wrote of them in his 1838 textbook under the heading of *monomanie raisonnante,* implying a state in which one's rational mind, without veering off into delusion (or what we would call *psychosis*), nevertheless was abnormally fixated on certain worries and concerns, to the exclusion of other symptoms (hence, only a *mono*manie). The worries were not only irrational but seemingly discordant with the previous character of the person in question. Because excessive doubting was a common feature of the condition, Jean-Pierre Falret, writing in 1850, preferred the term *folie du doute.*

In the 1860s, Benedict Morel, to whom we owe the term *démence précoce,* was one of the first to use obsession in the contemporary sense of "unwelcome recurring thoughts" (Adams 1973, 253). A little later, in 1875, Henri Le Grand du Saulle wrote a monograph on the subject, the details of which have a modern ring. At the end of this chapter, I have translated some portions of that work by way of acquainting the reader with the similarities and differences between OCD as we depict it today and as it was understood a century ago. Le Grand du Saulle, who called the condition *folie du doute avec délire de toucher,* thought that OCD evolved along a certain path, from lesser to greater severity as time went on, passing through "three stages." This three-stage concept was typical of French nosologists of the nineteenth century. Felix Voisin, for example, had earlier (in 1826) described even nymphomania as showing a three-stage course, the final one being a life-threatening, all-consuming sexual hunger. The idea that a psychological disorder could remain mild throughout life was not widely accepted at the time. (In more recent times, prominent analysts have spoken of various "borderline" conditions, including the As-If personality, as "incipient" forms of schizophrenia, destined later to harden into the full-blown illness.) As for Le Grand du Saulle's clinical description, many symptoms were included that we would categorize as belonging to the depressive axis, as will be noted in the passages and vignettes below. This is not surprising; although we can delineate OCD in a way that discriminates it from depressive illness, in actual experience it often shows comorbidity for depression: both relate to harm-avoidant (Cloninger 1986), inhibited reaction-patterns that are largely innate. Many depressed patients also brood and worry and ruminate like OCD patients do, though not necessarily to the extreme degree characteristic of the latter. One might say there is a larger-scale condition, involving guilt and harm-avoidance, whose cognitive component resembles OCD and whose affective component is depression (of greater or lesser severity). Distinctions and accompaniments of this sort formed the basis of controversy among the nosologists of nineteenth-century France—a controversy that has not been put altogether to rest in our own day. Henry Maudsley expressed the view in 1879 that OCD was related to the affective disorders, such as manic-depressive illness (Adams 1973, 253). In our own day, Joseph Zohar and Thomas Insel (1987) concluded that depression and OCD are best considered separable and separate entities, despite the tendency for many OCD patients to experience depression and at least some depressive patients to manifest OCD.

Toward the end of the nineteenth century, Sigmund Freud (1895) was to describe a clinical condition showing a mixture of phobia and anxiety-neurosis as *Zwangsneurose* (literally, compulsion-neurosis) and noted in the following year (1896) that obsessions were a type of self-reproach with which one castigated oneself out of guilt over having enjoyed childhood sexual acts. From the side of traditional (as opposed to the new psychoanalytic) psychology, Richard von Krafft-Ebing (1965) introduced the term *obsessive idea* in 1897.

Concerning the life-course of the OCD patient, whereas Le Grand du Saulle situated the onset at puberty, Pierre Janet, who saw obsessions, tics, phobias, and neurasthenia as related phenomena, described obsessional illness as manifesting itself sometimes even in children of five or six (Janet and Raymond 1903). Janet, like Le Grand du Saulle, also pictured OCD as proceeding in stages. As Pitman (1987) has summarized, Janet characterized the first stage as a *psychasthenic* state in which the patient is tormented by the conviction of being imperfect, despite reassurances from other people that his tasks have been performed well. The patient may succumb to morbid doubts, including doubts as to his very existence. One may see other symptoms, such as derealization, depersonalization, and déjà-vu. Typically, the patient will be indecisive to the point of severe procrastination, and blunted emotionally to the point of being numb to joy or sorrow. Pleasurable activities may become interdicted because of the patient's scrupulosity, especially in the area of sex. Janet envisioned a second stage, which he labeled *forced agitation*. Here, repetitive, excessive behaviors are the order of the day, along with ruminations and compulsive acts ("tics"). There is an exaggerated need for precision and perfection. This may be accompanied by phobia and anxiety when the patient (inevitably) falls short of these goals. As an example, a dread of knives may derive from the fear of harming or killing a family member. Constant checking-behavior may occur in this stage, and the patient may show a "mania" (i.e., a grossly exaggerated need) for symmetry and order. It was the third and final stage to which Janet gave the name *obsessions and compulsions*. Here, the patient is tormented by forbidden thoughts, usually in the domain of violence, sacrilege, or lust—that is, *anything* that is proscribed by the patient's culture. One may carry certain obsessive ideas close to, or beyond, the boundary with delusion—as when certain anorexics feel "fat" while being dangerously thin. As R. K. Pitman (1987) points out, the idea that OCD could develop *de novo* in full-blown form during adult life was uncongenial to Janet, who felt, as did his French predecessors, that there had to have been premonitory signs and symptoms. Patients with OCD are prone to exhibit personality disorders as well, but Janet seemed aware, as we are today (Insel 1982), that the personality disorder need not be "obsessive-compulsive" but can be of a different type, such as depressive or paranoid. Whereas we tend, at the close of the twentieth century, to view patients with complex clinical pictures as harboring several "separate" categories of illness at once, Janet, at the close of the nineteenth century, was more of a "lumper" than a "splitter." He preferred to describe OCD as a core condition with which many other anxious and depressive symptom-disorders could become merged. The resolution to the debate implied by these two contrasting positions depends mostly on the task at hand. The clinician may prefer the "lumper" position, while the researcher may find the "splitter" position the more useful (Pitman 1987, 227).

Regarding theories about the etiology of OCD, the ideas that were current, and competing, in the nineteenth century included autonomic nervous system dysfunction, psychological abnormalities concerning the will (Esquirol), the emotions (Morel), or the intellect (Westphal). It was Westphal, a German psychiatrist, who introduced the term *Zwang* (compulsion) in referring to the behavioral manifestations (when present) of OCD (Tallis 1995). Although the theory of OCD as an emotional disturbance gained supremacy at the turn of the century, the condition had been classified in many different ways in France over the preceding seventy years. As G. E. Berrios (1989) points out, OCD was viewed initially as a variety of insanity or psychosis (viz. by Esquirol in the 1830s, using the term *monomania*), and later as a neurosis (implying the preservation of reality-testing). Berrios also makes the point that considering OCD as an emotional disturbance allowed it to be retained as a "functional" disorder, while "at the same time maintaining its relationship to the autonomic nervous system" (1989, 292). This in turn influenced Freud, who was to comprehend the bulk of mental illnesses as emotional in origin.

No matter how tightly and rigorously we define OCD in contemporary psychiatry, there is still conceptual overlap with various "diagnostic near-neighbors." Obsessions can at the extreme take on the coloration of delusion—schizophrenics, after all, often have obsessional preoccupations, as do many other "psychotic" patients. And there is no fine line demarcating *compulsion* from *impulsion* such as to rid these concepts satisfactorily of all overlap. Those who feel *com*pelled to pull out their hair will, every so often, feel *im*pelled actually to do so. The *DSMIV* classifies this condition, trichotillomania, with the impulsive disorders—but for reasons having more to do with the toss of the coin than with scientific accuracy. In nineteenth-century France, the problem of semantic disentanglement was even more acute, probably because the popular nosologic terms in 1800 were so vague and all-inclusive. Terms like *délire* and *manie* and *folie* are maddeningly imprecise (and remain so to this day)—sometimes signifying delusion *(folie à deux)* or psychosis; sometimes, a milder condition *(folie du doute*—our OCD). By Le Grand du Saulle's day, in the 1870s, *obsession* (i.e., *folie du doute*) had finally been separated conceptually from the psychotic-level *délire* (Berrios 1989, 292). But the common "fellow-travelers" of OCD (phobia, panic, depression) and the fairly wide range of severity among bona fide cases of OCD will ensure a level of semantic confusion well beyond our day, even as the neuroanatomic substrates of the condition become better and better elucidated. Precisely because of progress in the latter area, and because of the development of effective serotonergic medications over the past fifteen years, our view of OCD is now more complex; and, correspondingly, we rely less on purely psychodynamic explanations and treatments than did the generation of the psychoanalytic pioneers.

APPENDIX

Excerpts from *La Folie du Doute avec Délire de Toucher* by Le Docteur Henri Le Grand du Saulle of the Bicêtre Hospital (Paris: Adrien Delahaye, 1875).

Doubting mania (with touching mania) is one of the four nosologic varieties of mania with conscience. This form is characterized by a sort of active frenzy that becomes more and more widespread. It is unrelated to persecutory delusions or to melancholia, and is incorrectly regarded as a part of the clinical picture of either hypochondriasis or of hysteria. Little recognized or scarcely suspected by most authors, not described or even classified (though glimpsed hazily by Esquirol, Falret Sr., Baillarger, Griesinger, E. Blanche, Marcé and Jules Falret—who reported several examples under various names and in a quite provisional or sketchy manner), the condition easily conceals itself from careful study. It is elusive as to its onset, in its essentially spasmodic course, in its various manifestations, and in its three distinguishable phases. For these reasons the condition often leads to mistaken clinical assessments and at times to rather embarrassing prognostic miscalculations.

I will try to show how this particular mental condition deserves separate classification—a condition that constitutes an all too real chapter in the pathology of the intellectual faculties, yet that lends itself all the same to an easily recognizable account of its typical symptomatology. Every clinician can probably recall one or two cases that are similar, if not altogether parallel, to those I am about to describe.

The phrase *folie du doute (avec délire de toucher)* speaks of my clear desire to name this condition according to its salient clinical features; namely, a mental questioning prompted by doubt and by fear of contact with certain external objects. *Doubt* begins the morbid drama. Long afterward, eccentricities about *touching* bring the drama to a close. In giving a name to the illness, *doubt* and *touching* should be juxtaposed. This would probably be the only way of lastingly fixing one's attention on these two fundamental peculiarities of the neurosis in question.

To begin with we should briefly point out that the condition scarcely pursues a smooth course; it progresses by spurts and thrusts, punctuated by quiescent phases that may on occasion be rather lengthy. The condition passes nevertheless, in its slow evolution, through these stages, subtle in their expression, though ultimately quite different one from the other.

The *first* period, compatible with otherwise excellent physical and intellectual well-being, consists in the spontaneous production, involuntary and irresistible, of a certain chain of thoughts on one or another abstract or absurd subject, although without either illusions or hallucinations. This sequence of thoughts manifests itself through minute questioning on the part of the patient, by a feeling—at once profound and vague—of doubt, and by a kind of internal and essentially monotonous deliberation that is stubborn, persistent, and oppressive, and focused on the same subject. In some cases this deliberation takes the form of mental representations of certain images, as well as of fixed *ruminations* that are related to and defined by these images. So far, the struggle is silent: the besieged person does not as yet complain of his oppression.

The *second* period can be recognized by the following signs: unexpected revelations to one's family, friends, and acquaintances; exaggerated scruples; fanciful fears; overwhelming worries; ideas of suicide and at times suicidal acts; crises of excitability preceded by an aura of abdominal discomfort; dread and avoidance of an animal; an appreciable lessening of doubt and of one's personal interpretations; a morbid re-hashing of the same concerns to the same family member or friend—couched in the very same wording. In additions there will be fear of touching certain objects along with a grossly abnormal preoccupation with cleanliness and repeated washing. There will be eccentricities of every sort, and spontaneous confessions of foolish acts. Longish quiescent phases are still a possibility, and the preservation of one's intellectual faculties remains always intact.

The *third* period is characterized by a morbid state at once grave and permanent. The situation grows more intolerable day by day. The capacity for socialization is lost. Many of the normal acts of everyday life now become impossible. Going out of doors, for instance, may no longer be acceptable or be done only with the greatest of reluctance and later on refused altogether. All the patient's movements are slowed down such that one's morning ablutions take up hours, as do the meals of the day. The gamut of irrational ideas narrows, and anxiety heightens in proportion. The fears of walking, sitting, brushing against somebody, of shaking hands, of opening a window or a door, and the unconquerable revulsion for various objects—all become more pronounced. One's terrors are no longer openly expressed, and the movements of the lips betray only the persistence of one's inner thoughts. Even so, the conscience remains intact, madness does not develop, and it is in a state of near immobility that one lives out one's days.

Such is the history in brief of a neurosis whose first signs appear usually at puberty, and whose manifestations, however long they may remit, eventually reappear to make a torture of one's earthly existence as long as life goes on. . . .

Clinical Vignette (Illustrating the First Period)

Miss Hortense G., twenty-four years old, a musician of high reputation, gave music lessons in a large city. She is intelligent, active, punctual, conscientious, and enjoys the good opinion of all who know her. When she is by herself in the street, she has preoccupations of the following sort: "What if somebody falls from a window up above and lands right at my feet? Would it be a man or a woman? Would the person be injured or actually die? If injured: would it be in the head or the feet? Would there be blood on the sidewalk? If the person were to die from the impact, would I be able to tell this? Should I call for help, flee the scene, or recite right then and there a *pater noster* or an *ave?* Might others accuse *me* of having been responsible for the occurrence? And then would my pupils all quit me? Or perhaps people might realize I was innocent." All these thoughts would crowd her mind and affect her emotions. She would begin to tremble. Her one regret was that no one was there to give her a reassuring word once she arrived at the home of one of her pupils.

The Second Period

After no end of anxiety, efforts, struggle and suffering, the patients, after having sought stubbornly the origins of their fixed ideas, their strange disturbances and bizarre actions, finally consult a doctor—hoping to be enlightened about their anomalous condition and about their inability to conquer it; also, about the likelihood of improvement, worsening, or recurrence. They become the most implacable of interrogators. The doctor himself, searching for the answers to all these questions, takes heed of the difficulties of the situation, and replies in the least upsetting way he can, though inwardly reminding himself of what the philosopher [Pierre] *Maine de Biran* said: "Whence comes it about that our usual ways are suddenly without effect? What does it mean—that our inclinations and stubborn ideas suddenly take possession of our imagination against our better judgment, and then persist despite our Will, invading and replacing habits of long standing?"

What I maintain as the *discriminating* feature of this second period or "phase" from the first—is the quite unanticipated revelations on the part of the patient, in the form of extremely detailed recitations of his hitherto unsuspected suffering, in the inception of an endless chain of questions, in the repeated imploring of reassuring words, and in the extraordinary ease with which an acquaintance can—for the moment at least—dispel the patient's seemingly deepest fears. . . .

Feelings of revulsion toward an animal is generally noted in these patients. Dogs, cats, mice, frogs or toads are the most common objects of this pathological dread. But fear of rabid dogs, of bites and of the spittle of such dogs—is the primary cause of these intense apprehensions and unwarranted frights and even nervous attacks. Once the fear of rabid dogs is in place in the patient's mind, every mental effort henceforth centers around this predominant anxiety, and of the possible consequences of an encounter. This invariably leads to peculiar and bizarre behavior—totally discordant with the patient's previous way of life.

Clinical Vignette

A woman of fifty-two imagined that her husband's dog had been beaten only because of its having been "rabid." Though mistaken, from that moment on the idea of having touched a rabid dog took over her mind day and night. In the garden near the animal, there had been some laundry hung out to dry. Could that laundry, she wondered, have been in contact with the dog's drool? Once folded in the closet, next to various other household effects, might not that laundry have infected her, her husband, and the whole family? The woman no longer dared put her arms around her husband, nor could she bring herself to touch anything in the whole house. She couldn't touch her clothes, and indeed, wore the same outfit for two months. "Am I crazy or not?" she asked Professor Morel [whom she saw in consultation]. "Will they have to lock me up in an asylum because I shudder at the sight of a dog or because I can't touch anything in my home? So what good are my reasoning powers anyway?" She was willing to undergo hydrotherapy, provided that one gave her only brand-new clothes and blankets that had never been used by anyone else.

Vignette #2

A young woman who around age twelve had already been tormented with religious scruples, happened to see a person with a cancerous facial ulceration come to her father's home. At first she registered neither disgust, repulsion, nor fear—though people observed that she became mournful and preoccupied afterward, responding evasively when one put any questions to her. Eventually it became clear to everybody that she was obsessed with the thought that all the clothes and objects around the house were more or less tainted and covered with cancerous matter. Weighed down by this apprehension, she was no longer able to sleep, no longer knew what attitude to take, and spent all her time brushing, rubbing, and washing. She understood perfectly well that her fears were without foundation, but she was powerless to dispel them. Her life became a continual torture. Slowly and gradually her fears did lessen and then disappear and her life returned to normal.

A few years later this young woman, whose health had been excellent both physically and mentally, married and became a mother. There had been no mental problems during either her pregnancy or delivery. She was without anxieties and felt very happy. One day it chanced that someone mentioned to her that a "mad dog" had wandered briefly into her house. She herself had not noticed this, nor had she been in any contact with the dog—yet she was very shaken. She became more and more worried, grew depressed, spoke to no one, dozed a bit now and then, or, when speaking to her husband—allowed as how she really had no reason to be upset. Even so, she could not bring herself to touch the "rabid dust" on her furniture, on the chimney, the floors, her pockets, other people's clothes, kitchen utensils . . . in a word, anywhere. She wiped, scoured, brushed or washed everything she touched, even when at other people's homes, nor did she dare touch the door-knocker at her own home. She bewailed her current state (she was now thirty-six), understood that her anxieties were groundless, and beseeched the doctors to cure her. . . .

The Third Period

In the grip of unceasing anxieties and of suffering without end, having lost with each succeeding day a little of that normal activity by which they were once known, disillusioned with everyone—especially with doctors and the medical profession—and, with their intelligence well preserved, aware at every moment of the bizarreness of their behavior, the patients in this "phase" create a kind of a cure of their own. They venture out less and less, they give up sitting in the waiting rooms of consultants, seek treatment no longer, and take to staying voluntarily in their own quarters. Incapable of reestablishing normalcy in public settings, or of carrying out the customary activities of everyday life, they *remove* themselves *from* life, becoming asocial in the process. They *avoid* the world. . . .

[Citing Jules Falret's *La Folie Raisonnante* of 1866, page 43, the author continues:] "These patients manage to withstand, often for months or even years, their ceaseless preoccupations—without any major shock to their bodily health and without significant weakening of their intellectual powers. It is in fact noteworthy that this mental state, which often stretches out over their whole life-span, with remissions and relapses (the latter sometimes very severe), never culminates in a true psychosis *[démence]*." . . .

Clinical Vignette

In 1869 I saw in consultation a man from Nogent-sur-Marne, seventy years old, a former merchant, widowed and without children, cared for by an old relative and a maidservant—who had not left his house in nine years. He spoke scarcely a word, though in cordial language; he made himself read the *Voyage Around the World;* he no longer touched anything, no longer ate alone or dressed himself. He spent his days in a large wheelchair in the middle of his bedroom, during winter—or, if during the summer, in the middle of his garden. With his eyes turned always toward the entrance door, he would become restless every time he heard someone ring the bell. His housemaid would then open the door ever so slightly and with infinite carefulness—a shutter having been placed in the door—with instructions that no one was to be allowed entry unless he swore that he had no dog with him and had not encountered any dog in the vicinity. Even then she would not open the door, until these reassurances had been given repeatedly. The old man, whose intellectual faculties had in no way declined, would become wretched and tremulous with fear if he so much as heard a dog barking somewhere off in the neighborhood. He spoke to himself in a scarcely audible voice, and with the air of someone preoccupied. He was almost immobile. "You see," he told me, "that I am neither crazy nor agitated; I may be an old coward, but I know perfectly well what I have to do." His physician, his relative, and his maidservant are far from considering him a "mental case" *[aliéné]* . . . well, perhaps a mental case, but certainly not a person with delusions.

REFERENCES

Adams, P. L. 1973. Obsessive Children: A Sociopsychiatric Study. *New York: Brunner/ Mazel.*

Berrios, G. E. 1989. *Obsessive-compulsive disorder: Its conceptual history in France during the nineteenth century.* Comprehen. Psychiat. *30:283–95.*

Cloninger, C. R. 1986. *A unified biosocial theory of personality and its role in the development of anxiety states.* Psychiatric Developments *3:167–226.*

Ellenberger, H. F. 1970. The Discovery of the Unconscious: The History and Evolution of Dynamic Psychiatry. *New York: Basic Books.*

Esquirol, J. 1838. Des Maladies Mentales. *Paris: J.-B. Baillière.*

Freud, S. 1895. *On the grounds for detaching a particular syndrome from neurasthenia under the description of "anxiety neurosis."* Standard Edition, *3:87–115.*

——. 1896. *Further remarks on the neuro-psychoses of defense.* Standard Edition *3:150–85.*

Haslam, J. 1809. Observations on Madness. *London: J. Callow.*

Hunter, R., and Macalpine, I. 1963. Three Hundred Years of Psychiatry. *London: Oxford University Press.*

Insel, T. R. 1982. *Obsessive-compulsive disorder: Five clinical questions and a suggested approach.* Comprehen. Psychiat. *23:241–51.*

Janet, P., and Raymond, F. 1903. Obsessions et la Psychasthenie. *Paris: F. Alcan.*

Krafft-Ebing, Richard von. 1965. Psychopathia Sexualis. *New York: Stein and Day.*

Le Grand du Saulle, H. 1875. La Folie du Doute avec Délire du Toucher. *Paris: Delahaye.*

Pitman, R. K. 1987. *Pierre Janet on obsessive-compulsive disorder (1903).* Arch. Gen. Psychiat. *44:226–32.*

Tallis, F. 1995. Obsessive Compulsive Disorder: A Cognitive and Neuropsychological Perspective. *New York: John Wiley.*

Voisin, F. 1826. Des Causes Morales et Physiques des Maladies Mentales. *Paris: J.-B. Baillière.*

Zilboorg, G. 1941. A History of Medical Psychology. *New York: W. W. Norton.*

Zohar, J., and Insel, T. R. 1987. *Obsessive-compulsive disorder: Psychobiological approaches to diagnosis, treatment and pathophysiology.* Biol. Psychiat. *22:667–87.*

PART I

Classical Psychoanalysis

1. The Defence Neuro-Psychoses

An endeavour to provide a psychological theory of acquired hysteria, many phobias and obsessions, and certain hallucinatory psychoses.

Sigmund Freud

AFTER A CLOSE STUDY of several patients suffering from phobias and obsessions a tentative explanation of these symptoms forced itself upon me; and as it later enabled me successfully to divine the origin of similar pathological ideas in other cases, I consider it worthy of publication and of further tests.[1] Along with this 'psychological theory of phobias and obsessions', observation of these patients has resulted in a contribution to the theory of hysteria, or rather an alteration in it, which appears to account for an important characteristic common both to hysteria and to the neuroses mentioned above. Further, I had opportunities of gaining some insight into the psychological mechanism of a form of disease that is undoubtedly of mental origin, and then found that the tentative point of view I had adopted established an intelligible connection between these psychoses and the two neuroses mentioned. At the end of this essay I shall bring forward an hypothesis which I have employed in all three cases.

I

Let me begin with the alteration that in my view we are called upon to make in the theory of the hysterical neurosis.

Since the publication of the fine work carried out by P. Janet, J. Breuer and others, it may be taken as generally acknowledged that the syndrome of hysteria, in so far as it permits of understanding up to the present, justifies the concept of a splitting of consciousness, with the formation of separate psychical groups; opinions are less definite, however, concerning the origin

Authorized translation of *The Collected Papers*, vol. 1 by Sigmund Freud under the supervision of Joan Riviere published by Basic Books, Inc., by arrangement of Random House UK, Ltd., and The Institute of Psycho-Analysis, London. Reprinted by permission of Basic Books, Inc., a division of HarperCollins Publishers, Inc., and Random House UK, Ltd.

of this splitting of consciousness and the part which this character plays in the structure of the hysterical neurosis.

According to Janet's theory[2] the splitting of consciousness is a primary feature of the hysterical change. It is dependent on an inborn weakness in the capacity for psychical synthesis, on the narrowness of the 'field of consciousness' *(champ du conscience)* which in the form of a psychic stigma is evidence of the degeneration of hysterical persons.

In contradistinction to Janet's view, which seems to me to admit of many and various objections, we have that advocated by J. Breuer in our joint publication.[3] According to Breuer, the 'foundation and condition' of hysteria is the occurrence of peculiar dream-like states of consciousness with diminished capacity for association, for which he suggests the name 'hypnoid states'. The splitting of consciousness is then secondary and acquired; it occurs because the ideas which emerge in hypnoid states are cut off from associative connection with the remaining contents of consciousness.

I can now bring forward evidence of two other more extreme forms of hysteria in which it is impossible to regard the splitting of consciousness as primary in Janet's sense. In the first of these forms I repeatedly succeeded in demonstrating that the splitting of the contents of consciousness is the consequence of a voluntary act on the part of the patient; that is to say, it is instituted by an effort of will, the motive of which is discoverable. By this I do not of course mean that the patient intends to produce a splitting of his consciousness; the patient's aim is a different one, but instead of attaining its end it produces a splitting of consciousness.

In the third form of hysteria, as shown by the mental analysis of intelligent patients, the splitting of consciousness plays an insignificant part, or perhaps none at all. These are the cases in which all that had happened was that the reaction to traumatic stimuli had failed to occur, so that they are accordingly dissolved and cured by 'abreaction'[4]—they are the pure 'retention' hysterias.

In connection with what I have to say about phobias and obsessions I shall here deal only with the second form of hysteria, which for reasons that will soon be evident I shall designate as *defence hysteria,* and distinguish by this name from *hypnoid* and *retention hysteria.* I may also provisionally represent my cases of defence hysteria as cases of 'acquired hysteria', because there was in them no question either of grave hereditary taint or of individual atrophic degeneration.

These patients whom I analysed had enjoyed good mental health up to the time at which an intolerable idea presented itself within the content of their ideational life; that is to say, until their ego was confronted by an experience, an idea, a feeling, arousing an affect so painful that the person resolved to forget it, since he had no confidence in his power to resolve the incompatibility between the unbearable idea and his ego by the processes of thought.

Such unbearable ideas develop in women chiefly in connection with sexual experiences and sensations, and the patients can recollect with the most satisfactory minuteness their efforts at defence—their resolution to 'push the thing out', not to think of it, to suppress it. I will give from my experience some examples which I could easily multiply: A young girl who disapproved of herself because while nursing her sick father she had let her mind dwell on the thought of a young man who had made a slight erotic impression on her; a governess who had fallen in love with her employer and had resolved to thrust this affection from her mind because it appeared to her incompatible with her pride; and so on.[5]

I do not of course assert that an effort of will to thrust such things out of the mind is a pathological act, nor am I able to say whether and in what manner intentional forgetting is successful in people who remain healthy, although subject to similar mental impressions. I only know that this kind of 'forgetting' did not succeed with the patients whom I analysed, but led to various pathological reactions, giving rise either to hysteria, or to an obsession, or to an hallucinatory psychosis. The ability to bring about by an effort of will one of these states, which are all of them associated with splitting of consciousness, is to be regarded as the manifestation of a pathological disposition—which, however, is not necessarily identical with personal or hereditary 'degeneration'.

In regard to the intermediate processes between the patient's effort of will and the onset of the neurotic symptom, I have formed an opinion which may be expressed in the customary psychological abstractions somewhat as follows: The task which the ego undertakes in defence—of treating the unbearable idea as 'non arrivée'—is absolutely insoluble; both the memory-trace and the affect attached to the idea are there once and for all, and it is no longer possible to extirpate them. But it amounts to an approximate fulfillment of this task if the ego succeeds in transforming a strong idea into a weak one, in depriving it of its affect—the quantity of excitation with which the idea is charged. The weak idea will then make practically no demands on the work of association; the quantity of excitation, however, which is then detached from the idea, must be utilized in another direction.

Up to this point the processes are the same in hysteria and in phobias and obsessions; from now onwards their ways diverge. In hysteria the unbearable idea is rendered innocuous by the quantity of excitation attached to it being transmuted into some bodily form of expression, a process for which I should like to propose the name of conversion.

The conversion may be either total or partial, and it proceeds along the line of the motor or sensory innervation that is more or less intimately related to the traumatic experience. Thus the ego succeeds in resolving the incompatibility within itself; but instead it has burdened itself with a memory-symbol, which dwells in consciousness, like a sort of parasite, either in the form of a persistent motor innervation or else as a constantly recurring hallucinatory sensation, and remains until a reversion takes place in the opposite direction. The memory-trace of the repressed idea is not, however, annihilated by this process; on the contrary, from now onwards it forms the nucleus of a secondary psychical group.

I will only add a few more words to this conception of the psycho-physical processes in hysteria. When once such a nucleus of an hysterical splitting has been formed owing to a 'traumatic' factor it will be developed by the influence of other factors (which might be called 'auxiliary traumatic' factors) as soon as an impression of a similar kind, subsequently experienced, succeeds in breaking through the barriers erected by the will, in furnishing the weakened idea with fresh affect and in re-establishing for a time an associative connection between the two psychical groups—until a further conversion creates a defence against it. The distribution of excitation thus brought about in hysteria proves as a rule an unstable one; the excitation which is directed into a wrong channel (into somatic innervation) now and then finds its way back to the idea from which it was detached, and then compels the subject either to undertake the work of associative absorption or else to discharge it by the way of hysterical attacks—a conclusion which is supported by the familiar opposition between the hysterical attack and chronic symptoms. Breuer's cathartic method achieves its results by deliberately effecting such a re-transmutation of the excitation from the somatic into the mental field, in order then to enforce a resolution of the opposed elements by a process of thought and a discharge of the excitation in speech.

The conclusion that the splitting of consciousness in acquired hysteria is based on an act of will also explains with surprising simplicity the remarkable fact that hypnosis regularly widens the narrowed consciousness of the hysteric and makes the psychical group which has been split off accessible. Indeed, we know it to be a peculiarity of all sleep-like conditions that they abrogate that distribution of excitation upon which the 'will' of the conscious personality depends.

Thus we can see that the characteristic factor in hysteria is not to be found in the splitting of consciousness but in the *capacity for conversion,* and we may assume that the psycho-physical capacity to transmute such large quantities of excitation into somatic innervation is an important element of the disposition to hysteria, which in other respects is still unknown.

This capacity does not in itself preclude mental health and leads to hysteria only where there is some mental incompatibility or an accumulation of excitation. With this new turn in the theory Breuer and I approach Oppenheim's[6] and Strümpell's[7] well-known definition of hysteria, and recede from Janet[8] who assigns too great importance to the splitting of consciousness as a characteristic of hysteria. The presentation here given may claim to have rendered the relation between conversion and the hysterical splitting of consciousness intelligible.

II

If the capacity for conversion does not exist in a person predisposed to hysteria and yet the separation of its affect from an unbearable idea is nevertheless undertaken as a defence against the latter, then this affect must persist in the psychical sphere. Thus weakened, the idea remains present in consciousness, detached from all associations; but its affect, now freed from it, attaches itself to other ideas which are not in themselves unbearable, but which through this 'false connection' grow to be obsessions. This is shortly the psychological theory of obsessions and phobias which I mentioned to start with.

I will now enumerate the various elements necessary to the structure of this theory that admit of direct proof, and then describe those that I have myself supplied. Apart from the final result of the process, that is, the obsession, it is possible in the first place to demonstrate the ultimate source of the affect which is now falsely attached to some other idea. In all the cases I have analysed it was in the sexual life that a painful affect—of precisely the same quality as that attaching to the obsession—had originated. On theoretical grounds it is not impossible that this affect may at times arise in other spheres; I have merely to state that hitherto I have not discovered any other origin of it. Incidentally, it is easy to see that it is precisely in regard to the sexual life that unbearable ideas most frequently arise.

Further, we have the most unequivocal utterances on the part of patients in proof of the effort of will, the attempt at defence, upon which the theory lays emphasis; and in at least a number of cases the patients themselves will inform us of the fact that the phobia or obsession first made its appearance after this effort of will had apparently succeeded in its aim. 'Once something very disagreeable happened to me, and I did my utmost to thrust it out of my mind, to think no more about it. Finally I succeeded, but then I got this, which since then I have never been rid of.' With these words a patient confirmed the chief points of the theory I have developed here.

Not all those who suffer from obsessions are themselves so clear about the origin of them. As a rule, when one draws these patients' attention to the original idea of a sexual nature, the answer is, 'It can't come from that; indeed, I thought very little about that. For a moment I was scared, but I turned my mind to something else and since then it hasn't troubled me.' In this frequent objection we have a proof that the obsession represents a substitute or surrogate for the unbearable sexual idea, and has taken its place in consciousness.

Between the patient's effort of will which successfully represses the intolerable sexual idea, and the appearance of the obsessional idea, which though having little intensity in itself is now endowed with incomprehensibly strong affect, there lies a gap which the theory here developed aims at filling in. The detachment of the sexual idea from its affect and the connection of the latter with another idea, suited to it but not intolerable, are processes which occur outside consciousness—they may be presumed but they cannot be proved by any clinical-psychological analysis. Perhaps it would be more correct to say: These processes are not of a psychical nature at all, but are physical processes the psychical consequences of which are so represented as if what is expressed by the words 'detachment of the idea from its affect and false connection of the latter' had really happened.

Alongside the cases which show the unbearable sexual idea followed subsequently by the obsession, there is another series in which obsessions and painful sexual ideas are present simultaneously. We cannot very well call the latter 'sexual obsessions', for *one* essential feature of obsessions is missing from them; they are fully justified, whereas the painfulness of the ordinary obsession constitutes a problem for both physician and patient. So far as I have been able to see in cases of this kind, it appears that in them a perpetual defence is going on against sexual ideas continually arising anew; that is, we are here concerned with an operation that has not yet been completed.

As long as they are conscious of the sexual origin of their obsessions, the patients often keep them concealed. When they complain about them, they as a rule express their astonishment that they are subject to the affect in question—that they feel anxious, or that they have such and such an impulse, and so on. To the experienced physician this affect appears, on the contrary, to be justified and comprehensible; he only finds it surprising that an affect of that kind should be associated with an inappropriate idea. The affect of the obsession appears to him, in other words, to be *dislocated* or *transposed,* and if he is proceeding on the assumptions here laid down he can in a great number of cases attempt its re-translation into the sexual.

Any idea which is either suited by nature to be associated with an affect of this quality or else bears a certain relation to the unbearable idea—in consequence of which it appears practicable to employ it as a surrogate for the latter—may be made use of in secondary connection with the detached affect. Thus for example, an unattached anxiety, the sexual origin of which the patient is unable to recall, will seize upon the common primary phobias of mankind in regard to animals, thunderstorms, darkness and the like, or upon things which are manifestly associated with the sexual in some way or other, such as urination, defæcation, defilement and contagion generally.

The ego gains considerably less advantage by choosing the method of *transposition* of affect as a measure of defence than it does by the hysterical conversion of psychical excitation into somatic innervation. The affect which the ego had to endure remains unchanged and undiminished, just as before—the only difference being that the unbearable idea is suppressed and cut off from recollection. The repressed ideas then form again the nucleus of a second psychical group, which, as it seems to me, is accessible even without the aid of hypnosis. If in phobias and obsessions the striking symptoms which in hysteria accompany the formation of an independent psychical group fail to appear, this is probably because in the former the whole transformation takes place within the psychical sphere—the relation between psychical excitation and somatic innervation has undergone no change.

To illustrate what has been said concerning obsessions I will give a few examples, which are probably typical:

1. A young girl suffered from obsessive reproaches. If she read in the papers about counterfeiting coinage the thought occurred to her that she also had forged coins; if an unknown criminal had committed a murder she asked herself anxiously whether she had not done the deed. At the same time she was quite conscious of the absurdity of these obsessive reproaches. This sense of guilt gained for a time such an influence over her that her critical faculty was stifled, so that she accused herself to her relations and her physician of having really committed all these crimes (psychosis through simple intensification—overwhelming-psychosis—*Überwältigungspsychose*). A close examination then revealed the source in which her sense

of guilt arose: Accidentally stimulated by a voluptuous sensation, she had allowed herself to be led astray by a friend into masturbation and had practised it for years, with full knowledge of her wrong-doing and accompanied by most intense self-reproaches, which as usual were of no avail. An excessive indulgence after attending a ball had evoked the intensification leading to the psychosis. After a few months of treatment and close watching the patient was cured.

2. Another young girl had suffered from the dread of being forced to pass water and wet herself ever since the time when an impulse of this kind had really obliged her to leave a concert during a performance. This phobia had gradually made her completely unable to enjoy herself or to go into society. She only felt well if there was a closet near at hand to which she could have access without arousing attention. Any organic complaint justifying this lack of confidence in her control of the bladder was excluded; at home under quiet conditions and at night the urgency did not arise. A penetrating enquiry showed that the urgency had appeared for the first time in the following circumstances: A gentleman to whom she was not indifferent had been sitting not far from her at the concert; she began to think about him and to imagine how she would sit beside him as his wife. During this erotic reverie she had that bodily sensation which is to be compared with erection in men and which in her case—I do not know if it is always so—ended with a slight desire to micturate. She became greatly frightened by the sexual sensation, to which she was otherwise quite accustomed, because she had resolved within herself to overcome her affection for this man as well as for all others, and the next moment the affect transferred itself to the accompanying desire to micturate and compelled her to leave the hall after a very painful struggle. In her life she was so prudish that she positively shuddered at anything sexual and could not even contemplate the thought of marrying; on the other hand, she was sexually so hyperæsthetic that during every erotic reverie, which she willingly indulged in, that pleasurable sensation appeared. The erection was always accompanied by the desire to micturate which, up to the time of the scene at the concert, had made no impression on her. Treatment led to a nearly complete mastery of the phobia.

3. A young woman who in five years of married life had had only one child complained to me of an obsessive impulse to throw herself from the window or balcony, and also of the fear of stabbing her child which seized her at the sight of a sharp knife. She confessed that marital relations seldom occurred, and only with precautions against conception; but she added that this was no

privation to her as she was not of a sensual nature. I ventured to tell her that at the sight of a man she had erotic ideas and that she had therefore lost confidence in herself and regarded herself as a depraved person, capable of anything. The re-translation of the obsession into the sexual was successful; in tears she confessed at once to her long-concealed misery in her marriage and later on related in addition some painful thoughts of an unchanged sexual nature, such as the often-recurring sensation of something forcing itself under her skirts.

I have turned experiences of this kind to therapeutic advantage by re-directing the attention of patients with phobias and obsessions, in spite of all their protestations, back to the repressed sexual ideas and, where feasible, in blocking the source whence they arose. I naturally cannot assert that *all* phobias and obsessions arise in the manner here described; for, first, my experience of them embraces only a limited number as compared with the relative frequency of these neuroses, and secondly, I myself know that these 'psychasthenic' symptoms, as Janet terms them, are not all to be estimated alike.[9] There are, for example, pure hysterical phobias. I believe, however, that the mechanism of transposition of affect will be found to exist in the great majority of phobias and obsessions; and I would therefore urge that these neuroses, which are as often found in an isolated form as combined with hysteria or neurasthenia, should not be loosely classified together with ordinary neurasthenia, in which there is absolutely no ground for assuming a psychical mechanism of the principal symptoms.

III

In both the cases described above defence against an unbearable idea was effected by detachment of its affect from it; the idea itself remained in consciousness, although weakened and isolated. Now there exists a very much more energetic and successful kind of defence, which takes the following form: the ego rejects the unbearable idea together with its associated affect and behaves as if the idea had never occurred to the person at all. But, as soon as this process has been successfully carried through, the person in question will have developed a psychosis, and his state can only be described as one of 'hallucinatory confusion'. A single example will serve to illustrate this.

A young girl gave her first impulsive affection to a man and firmly believed in the return of her love. As a matter of fact she was mistaken; the young man had another motive for visiting the house. Disappointments were not spared her; first of all she defended herself against her experiences by means of hysterical conversion, thus preserving her belief that he would one day come and seek her hand; but at the same time she felt unhappy and ill on account of incomplete conversion and of the perpetual experience of fresh painful impressions. Finally on a certain day, the day of a family festival, she waited for him in a state of intense excitement. The day wore on without his coming; after all the trains by which he could arrive had gone by, her condition passed into one of hallucinatory confusion. He *is come,* she hears his voice in the garden, hastens downstairs in her night-dress to receive him. From that time she lived for two months in a happy dream, of which the content was that he is there, ever by her side, everything is as it was a little while ago (before the time of the disappointment against which she had so strenuously defended herself). The hysteria and the depression of spirits were both overcome; nothing of the latter period of doubt and suffering was alluded to during her illness; she was happy as long as she was left undisturbed, and only raved when some circumstance of her surroundings prevented her from carrying out the logical promptings of her blissful dream. This psychosis, which at the time of its occurrence had been unintelligible, was explained ten years later with the aid of an hypnotic analysis.

The fact to which I now wish to call attention is that the content of such an hallucinatory psychosis consists precisely in the accentuation of the very idea which was first threatened by the experience occasioning the outbreak of the illness. One is therefore justified in saying that the ego has averted the unbearable idea by a flight into psychosis; and the process by which this result is obtained again withdraws itself out of range of self-perception as well as of psychological-clinical analysis. It is to be regarded as the expression of a high degree of pathological predisposition and may perhaps be described somewhat as follows: The ego has broken away from the unbearable idea; but, the latter being inseparably bound up with a part of reality, in so far as the ego achieves this result it has also cut itself loose from reality, totally or in part. In my opinion, this is the condition under which certain ideas acquire hallucinatory vividness, and consequently when this form of defence is successfully carried through the person finds himself in a state of hallucinatory confusion.

I have very few analyses of psychoses of this kind at my disposal; but I think we must here be concerned with a type of psychical illness that is very frequently developed, for in no insane asylum are analogous examples wanting—for instance, the mother who, falling ill after the loss of her baby, is to be seen incessantly rocking a log of wood in her arms, or the jilted bride arrayed in all her finery who has for years been awaiting her betrothed.

It is perhaps not superfluous to point out that the three modes of defence here described, together with the three forms of illness to which they lead, may all be combined in the same person. The simultaneous appearance of phobias and hysterical symptoms, observed so often in practice, is one of those factors which render it difficult to distinguish hysteria in a clear-cut manner from other neuroses, and make it necessary to set up the category of 'mixed neuroses'. To be sure, hallucinatory confusion is not often compatible with a continuance of hysteria, nor of clear-cut manner from other neuroses, and make it necessary to set up the category of 'mixed neuroses'. To be sure, hallucinatory confusion is not often compatible with a continuance of hysteria, nor of obsessions, as a rule. On the other hand, it is not rare for a defence psychosis to break out episodically in the course of an hysterical or mixed neurosis.

I should like finally to dwell for a moment on the hypothesis which I have made use of in the exposition of the defence neuroses. I mean the conception that among the psychic functions there is something which should be differentiated (an amount of affect, a sum of excitation), something having all the attributes of a quantity—although we possess no means of measuring it—a something which is capable of increase, decrease, displacement and discharge, and which extends itself over the memory-traces of an idea like an electric charge over the surface of the body. We can apply this hypothesis, which by the way already underlies our theory of 'abreaction',[10] in the same sense as the physicist employs the conception of a fluid electric current. For the present it is justified by its utility in correlating and explaining diverse psychical conditions.

NOTES

1. First published in the *Neurologisches Zentralblatt,* 1894, Nos. 10 and 11. [Translated by John Rickman.]

2. *Etat mental des hystériques,* Paris, 1893 and 1894. Quelques définitions récentes de l'hystérie, *Archives de Neurologie,* 1893, xxxv–xxxvi.

3. [*Ed. note:* See Joseph Breuer and Sigmund Freud, "Studies on Hysteria," in Sigmund Freud, *The Collected Papers,* vol. 2 (London: Hogarth, 1893–95)]

4. [*Ed. note:* See ibid.]

5. These examples are more fully described in *Studien über Hysterie,* Breuer and Freud. 1895.

6. Oppenheim: Hysteria is an intensified expression of emotion. The 'expression of emotion', however, represents that quantity of the psychical excitation which normally undergoes conversion.

7. Strümpell: In hysteria the disturbance lies in the psycho-physical sphere, where body and mind have their connection with each other.

8. In the second edition of his ingenious paper, '*Quelques definitions, etc.*', Janet has himself dealt with the objection that splitting of consciousness occurs also in the psychoses and in psychasthenia, so-called, but in my judgement he has not solved the difficulty satisfactorily. It is essentially this objection that has forced him to regard hysteria as a form of degeneration. He cannot, however, adequately distinguish the hysterical splitting of consciousness from the psychotic and other such forms by any characterization.

9. The group of typical phobias, of which agoraphobia is a model, cannot be traced back to the psychical mechanism mentioned above; on the contrary, the mechanism of agoraphobia differs from that of true obsessions, and of the phobias derived from them, in *one* decisive particular—there is here no repressed idea from which the affect of anxiety would be detached. The anxiety of these phobias has another origin.

10. [*Ed. note:* See Breuer and Freud, "Studies on Hysteria," 24.

2. Theoretical (from "Notes upon a Case of Obsessional Neurosis")

Sigmund Freud

SOME GENERAL CHARACTERISTICS OF OBSESSIONAL FORMATIONS[1]

In the year 1896 I defined obsessional or compulsive ideas as 'reproaches re-emerging in a transmuted form from under repression—reproaches which invariably relate to a sexual deed performed with pleasure in childhood'.[2] This definition now seems to me to be open to criticism upon formal grounds, though its component elements are unobjectionable. It was aiming too much at unification, and took as its model the practice of obsessional neurotics themselves, when, with their characteristic liking for indeterminateness, they heap together under the name of 'obsessional ideas' the most heterogeneous psychological formations.[3] In point of fact, it would be more correct to speak of 'obsessive thinking', and to make it clear that obsessional structures can correspond to every sort of mental act. They can be distinctively classed as wishes, temptations, impulses, reflections, doubts, commands, or prohibitions. Patients endeavour in general to tone down such distinctions and to regard what remains of these mental acts after they have been deprived of their affective index simply as 'obsessional ideas'. Our present patient gave an example of this type of behaviour in one of his first sittings, when he attempted to reduce a wish to the level of a mere 'connection of thought' (see p. 316).

It must be confessed, moreover, that even the phenomenology of obsessional thinking has not yet had sufficient attention paid to it. During the secondary defensive struggle, which the patient carries on against the 'obsessional ideas' that have forced their way into his consciousness, psychological formations make their appearance which deserve to be given a special name.

Authorized translation of *The Collected Papers,* vol. 3 by Sigmund Freud under the supervision of Alix and James Strachey published by Basic Books, Inc., by arrangement of Random House UK, Ltd., and The Institute of Psycho-Analysis, London. Reprinted by permission of Basic Books, Inc., a division of HarperCollins Publishers, Inc., and Random House UK, Ltd.

(Such, for example, were the sequences of thoughts that occupied our patient's mind on his journey back from the manœuvres.) They are not purely reasonable considerations which arise in opposition to the obsessional thoughts, but, as it were, hybrids between the two species of thinking; they accept certain of the premises of the obsession they are combating, and thus, while using the weapons of reason, are established upon a basis of pathological thought. I think such formations as these deserve to be given the name of 'deliria'. To make the distinction clear, I will give an instance, which should be inserted into its proper context in the patient's case history. I have already described the crazy conduct to which he gave way at one time when he was preparing for an examination—how, after working till far into the night, he used to go and open the front door to his father's ghost, and then look at his genitals in the looking-glass (see p. 342). He tried to bring himself to his senses by asking himself what his father would say to it all if he were really still alive. But the argument had no effect so long as it was put forward in this rational shape. The spectre was not laid until he had transformed the same idea into a 'delirious' threat to the effect that if he ever went through this nonsense again some evil would befall his father in the next world.

The distinction between a primary and a secondary defensive struggle is no doubt well founded, but we find its value unexpectedly diminished when we discover that *the patients themselves do not know the wording of their own obsessional ideas.* This may sound paradoxical, but it is perfectly good sense. During the progress of a psycho-analysis it is not only the patient who plucks up courage, but his disease as well; it grows bold enough to speak more plainly than before. To drop the metaphor, what happens is that the patient, who has hitherto turned his eyes away in terror from his own pathological productions, begins to attend to them and obtains a clearer and more detailed view of them.[4]

There are, besides, two particular ways in which a more precise knowledge of obsessional formations can be gained. In the first place, experience shows that an obsessional command (or whatever it may be), which in waking life is known only in a truncated and distorted form, like a mutilated telegraph message, may have its actual text brought to light in a dream. Such texts appear in dreams in the shape of speeches, and are thus an exception to the rule that speeches in dreams are derived from speeches in real life.[5] Secondly, in the course of the analytic examination of a case history, one becomes convinced that if a number of obsessions succeed one another they are often—even though their wording is not identical—ultimately one and the same. The obsession may have been successfully shaken off on its first appearance, but it comes back a second time in a distorted form and without being recognized, and may then perhaps be able to hold its own in the defensive struggle more effectively, precisely because of its distortion. But the original form is the correct one, and it often displays its meaning quite openly. When we have at great pains elucidated an unintelligible obsessional idea, it often happens that the patient informs us that just such a notion, wish, or temptation as the one we have constructed did in fact make its appearance on one occasion before the obsessional idea had arisen, but that it did not persist. It would unfortunately involve us in too lengthy a digression if we were to give instances of this from the history of our present patient.

What is officially described as an 'obsessional idea' exhibits, therefore, in its distortion from its original wording, traces of the primary defensive struggle. Its distortion enables it to persist, since conscious thought is thus compelled to misapprehend it, just as though it were a dream; for dreams also are a product of compromise and distortion, and are also misapprehended by waking thought.

This misapprehension on the part of consciousness can be seen at work not only in reference to the obsessional ideas themselves, but also in reference to the products of the secondary defensive struggle, such, for instance, as the protective formulas. I can produce two good examples of this. Our patient used to employ as a defensive formula a rapidly pronounced *'aber'* ['but'] accompanied by a gesture of repudiation. He told me on one occasion that this formula had become altered recently; he now no longer said *'áber'* but *'abér'*. When he was asked to give the reason for this new departure, he declared that the mute *'e'* of the second syllable gave him no sense of security against the intrusion, which he so much dreaded, of some foreign and contradictory element, and that he had therefore decided to accent the *'e'*. This explanation (an excellent sample of the obsessional neurotic style) was, however, clearly inadequate; the most that it could claim to be was a rationalization. The truth was that *'abér'* was an approximation towards the similar-sounding *'Abwéhr'* ['defence'], a term which he had learnt in the course of our theoretical discussions of psycho-analysis. He had thus put the treatment to an illegitimate and 'delirious' use in order to strengthen a defensive formula. Another time he told me about his principal magic word, which was an apotropaic against every evil; he had put it together out of the initial letters of the most powerfully beneficent of his prayers and had clapped on an 'amen' at the end of it. I cannot reproduce the word itself, for reasons which will become apparent immediately. For, when he told it me, I could not help noticing that the word was in fact an anagram upon the name of his lady. Her name contained an 's', and this he had put last, that is, immediately before the 'amen' at the end. We may say, therefore, that by this process he had brought his *'Samen'* ['semen'] into contact with the woman he loved; in imagination, that is to say, he had masturbated with her. He himself, however, had never noticed this very obvious connection; his defensive forces had allowed themselves to be fooled by the repressed ones. This is also a good example of the rule that in time the thing which is meant to be warded off invariably finds its way into the very means which is being used for warding it off.

I have already asserted that obsessional thoughts have undergone a distortion similar to that undergone by dream thoughts before they become the manifest content of a dream. The technique of this distortion may therefore be of interest to us, and there should be nothing to prevent our exhibiting its various modes by means of a series of obsessions which have been translated and made clear. But here again the conditions governing the publication of this case make it impossible for me to give more than a few specimens. Not all of the patient's obsessions were so complicated in their structure and so difficult to solve as the great rat idea. In some of the others a very simple technique was employed—namely, that of distortion by omission or ellipsis. This technique is pre-eminently applicable to jokes, but in our present case it also did useful work as a means of protecting things from being understood.

For instance, one of the patient's oldest and favourite obsessions (which corresponded to an admonition or warning) ran as follows: *'If I marry the lady, some misfortune will befall my father'* (in the next world). If we insert the intermediate steps, which had been skipped but were known to us from the analysis, we get the following train of thought: 'If my father were alive, he would be as furious over my design of marrying the lady as he was in the scene in my childhood; so that I should fly into a rage with him once more and wish him every possible evil; and thanks to the omnipotence of my wishes[6] these evils would be bound to come upon him.'

Here is another instance in which a solution can be reached by filling out an ellipsis. It is once more in the nature of a warning or an ascetic prohibition. The patient had a charming little niece of whom he was very fond. One day this idea came into his head: *'If you indulge in a coitus, something will happen to Ella'* (*i.e.* she will die). When the omissions have been made good, we have: 'Every time you copulate, even with a stranger, you will not be able to avoid the reflection that in your married life sexual intercourse can never bring you a child (on account of the lady's sterility). This will grieve you so much that you will become envious of your sister on account of little Ella, and you will grudge her the child. These envious impulses will inevitably lead to the child's death.' [7]

The technique of distortion by ellipsis seems to be typical of obsessional neuroses; I have come across it in the obsessional thoughts of other patients as well. One example, a particularly transparent one, is of especial interest on account of a certain structural similarity with the rat idea. It was a case of doubting, and occurred in a lady who suffered principally from obsessional acts. This lady was going for a walk with her husband in Nuremberg, and made him take her into a shop, where she purchased various objects for her child and amongst them a comb. Her husband, finding that the shopping was too long a business for his taste, said that he had noticed some coins in an old curiosity shop on the way which he was anxious to secure, adding that after he had made his purchase he would come and fetch her in the shop in which they at present were. But he stayed away, as she thought, far too long. When he came back she accordingly asked him where he had been. 'Why,' he replied, 'at the old curiosity shop I told you about.' At the same instant she was seized by a tormenting doubt whether she had not as a matter of fact always possessed the comb which she had just bought for her child. She was naturally quite unable to discover the simple mental link that was involved. There is nothing for it but to regard the doubt as having become displaced, and to reconstruct the complete chain of unconscious thoughts as follows: 'If it is true that you were only at the old curiosity shop, if I am really to believe that, then I may just as well believe that this comb that I bought a moment ago has been in my possession for years.' Here, therefore, the lady was drawing a derisive and ironical parallel, just as when our patient thought: 'Oh yes, as sure as those two' (his father and the lady) 'will have children, I shall pay back the money to A.' In the lady's case the doubt was dependent upon her unconscious jealousy, which led her to suppose that her husband had spent the interval of his absence in paying a visit of gallantry.

I shall not in the present paper attempt any discussion of the psychological significance of obsessional thinking. Such a discussion would be of extraordinary value in its results, and would do more to clarify our ideas upon the nature of the conscious and the unconscious than any study of hysteria or the phenomena of hypnosis. It would be a most desirable thing if the philosophers and psychologists who develop brilliant theoretical views on the unconscious upon a basis of hearsay knowledge or from their own conventional definitions would first submit to the convincing impressions which may be gained from a first-hand study of the phenomena of obsessional thinking. We might almost go to the length of requiring it of them, if the task were not so far more laborious than the methods of work to which they are accustomed. I will only add here that in obsessional neuroses the unconscious mental processes occasionally break through into consciousness in their pure and undistorted form, that such incursions may take place at every possible stage of the unconscious process of thought, and that at the moment of the incursion the obsessional ideas can, for the most part, be recognized as formations of very long standing. This accounts for the striking circumstance that, when the analyst tries, with the patient's help, to discover the date of the first occurrence of an obsessional idea, the patient is obliged to place it further and further back as the analysis proceeds, and is constantly finding fresh 'first' occasions for the appearance of the obsession.

SOME PSYCHOLOGICAL PECULIARITIES OF OBSESSIONAL NEUROTICS: THEIR ATTITUDE TOWARDS REALITY, SUPERSTITION AND DEATH

In this section I intend to deal with a few mental characteristics of obsessional neurotics which, though they do not seem important in themselves, nevertheless lie upon the road to a comprehension of more important things. They were strongly marked in our present patient; but I know that they are not attributable to his individual character, but to his disorder, and that they are to be met with quite typically in other obsessional patients.

Our patient was to a high degree superstitious, and this although he was a highly educated and enlightened man of considerable acumen, and although he was able at times to assure me that he did not believe a word of all this rubbish. Thus he was at once superstitious and not superstitious; and there was a clear distinction between his attitude and the superstition of uneducated people who feel themselves at one with their belief. He seemed to understand that his superstition was dependent upon his obsessional thinking, although at times he gave way to it completely. The meaning of this inconsistent and vacillating behaviour can be most easily grasped if it is regarded in the light of a hypothesis which I shall now proceed to mention. I did not hesitate to assume that the truth was not that the patient still had an open mind upon this subject, but that he had two separate and contradictory convictions upon it. His oscillation between these two views quite obviously depended upon his momentary attitude towards his obsessional disorder. As soon as he had got the better of one of these obsessions, he used to smile in a superior way at his own credulity, and no events occurred that were calculated to shake his firmness; but the moment he came under the sway of another obsession which had not been cleared up—or, what amounts to the same thing, of a resistance—the strangest coincidences would happen to support him in his credulous belief.

His superstition was nevertheless that of an educated man, and he avoided such vulgar prejudices as being afraid of Friday or of the number thirteen, and so on. But he believed in premonitions and in prophetic dreams; he would constantly meet the very person of whom, for some inexplicable reason, he had just been thinking; or he would receive a letter from some one who had suddenly come into his mind after being forgotten for many years. At the same time he was honest enough—or rather, he was loyal enough to his official conviction—not to have forgotten instances in which the strangest forebodings had come to nothing. On one occasion, for instance, when he went away for his summer holidays, he had felt morally certain that he would never return to Vienna alive. He also admitted that the great majority of his premonitions related to things which had no special personal importance to him, and that, when he met an acquaintance of whom, until a few moments previously, he had not thought for a very long time, nothing further took place between himself and the miraculous apparition. And he naturally could not deny that all the important events of his life had occurred without his having had any premonition of them, and that, for instance, his father's death had taken him entirely by surprise. But arguments such as these had no effect upon the discrepancy in his convictions. They merely served to prove the obsessional nature of his superstitions, and that could already be inferred from the way in which they came and went with the increase and decrease of his resistance.

I was not in a position, of course, to give a rational explanation of all the miraculous stories of his remoter past. But as regards the similar things that happened during the time of his treatment, I was able to prove to him that he himself invariably had a hand in the manufacture of these miracles, and I was able to point out to him the methods that he employed. He worked by means of indirect vision and reading, forgetting, and, above all, errors of memory. In the end he used himself to help me in discovering the little sleight-of-hand tricks by which these wonders were performed. I may mention one interesting infantile root of his belief that forebodings and premonitions came true. It was brought to light by his recollection that very often, when a date was being fixed for something, his mother used to say: 'I sha'n't be able to on such-and-such a day. I shall have to stop in bed then.' And in fact when the day in question arrived she had invariably stayed in bed!

There can be no doubt that the patient felt a need for finding experiences of this kind to act as props for his superstition, and that it was for that reason that he occupied himself so much with the inexplicable coincidences of everyday life with which we are all familiar, and helped out their shortcomings with unconscious activity of his own. I have come across a similar need in many other obsessional patients and have suspected its presence in many more besides. It seems to me easily explicable in view of the psychological characteristics of the obsessional neurosis. In this disorder, as I have already explained (see p. 333), repression is effected not by means of amnesia but by a severance of causal connections brought about by a withdrawal of affect. These repressed connections appear to persist in some kind of shadowy form (which I have elsewhere compared to an entoptic perception),[8] and they are thus transferred, by a process of projection, into the external world, where they bear witness to what has been effaced from consciousness.

Another mental need, which is also shared by obsessional neurotics and which is in some respects related to the one just mentioned, is the need for *uncertainty* in their life, or for *doubt.* An inquiry into this characteristic leads deep into the investigation of instinct. The creation of uncertainty is one of the methods employed by the neurosis for drawing the patient away from *reality* and isolating him from the world—which is among the objects of every psycho-neurotic disorder. Again, it is only too obvious what efforts are made by the patients themselves in order to be able to avoid certainty and remain in doubt. Some of them, indeed, give a vivid expression to this tendency in a dislike of—clocks and watches (for they at least make the time of day certain), and in the unconscious artifices which they employ in order to render these doubt-removing instruments innocuous. Our present patient had developed a peculiar talent for avoiding a knowledge of any facts which would have helped him in deciding his conflict. Thus he was in ignorance upon those matters relating to his lady which were the most relevant to the question of his marriage: he was ostensibly unable to say who had operated upon her and whether the operation had been unilateral or bilateral. He had to be forced into remembering what he had forgotten and into finding out what he had overlooked.

The predilection felt by obsessional neurotics for uncertainty and doubt leads them to turn their thoughts by preference to those subjects upon which all mankind are uncertain and upon which our knowledge and judgements must necessarily remain open to doubt. The chief subjects of this kind are paternity, length of life, life after death, and memory—in the last of which we are all in the habit of believing, without having the slightest guarantee of its trustworthiness.[9]

In obsessional neuroses the uncertainty of memory is used to the fullest extent as a help in the formation of symptoms; and we shall learn directly the part played in the actual content of the patients' thoughts by the questions of length of life and life after death. But as an appropriate transition I will first consider one particular superstitious trait in our patient to which I have already alluded and which will no doubt have puzzled more than one of my readers.

I refer to the *omnipotence* which he ascribed to his thoughts and feelings, and to his wishes, whether good or evil. It is, I must admit, decidedly tempting to declare that this idea was a delusion and that it oversteps the limits of obsessional neurosis. I have, however, come across the same conviction in another obsessional patient; and he was long ago restored to health and is leading a normal life. Indeed, all obsessional neurotics behave as though they shared this conviction. It will be our business to throw some light upon these patients' over-estimation of their powers. Assuming, without more ado, that this belief is a frank acknowledgement of a relic of the old megalomania of infancy, we will proceed to ask the patient for the grounds of his conviction. In reply, he adduces two experiences. When he returned for a second visit to the hydropathic establishment at which his disorder had been relieved for the first and only time, he asked to be given his old room, for its position had facilitated his relations with one of the nurses. He was told that the room was already taken and that it was occupied by an old professor. This piece of news considerably diminished his prospects of successful treatment, and he reacted to it with the unamiable thought: 'I wish he may be struck dead for it!' A fortnight later he was woken up from his sleep by the disturbing idea of a corpse; and in the morning he heard that the professor had really had a stroke, and that he had been carried up into his room at about the time he himself had woken up. The second experience related to an unmarried woman, no longer young, though with a great desire to be loved, who had paid him a great deal of attention and had once asked him point-blank whether he could not love her. He had given her an evasive answer. A few days afterwards he heard that she had thrown herself out of window. He then began to reproach himself, and said to himself that it would have been in his power to save her life by giving her his love. In this way he became convinced of the omnipotence of his love and of his hatred. Without denying the omnipotence of love we may point out that both of these instances were concerned with death, and we may adopt the obvious explanation that, like other obsessional neurotics, our patient was compelled to overestimate the effects of his hostile feelings upon the external world, because a large part of their internal, mental effects escaped his conscious knowledge. His love—or rather his hatred—was in truth overpowering; it was precisely they that created the obsessional thoughts, of which he could not understand the origin and against which he strove in vain to defend himself.[10]

Our patient had a quite peculiar attitude towards the question of death. He showed the deepest sympathy whenever any one died, and religiously attended the funeral; so that among his brothers and sisters he earned the nickname of 'bird of ill omen'.[11] In his imagination, too, he was constantly making away with people so as to show his heartfelt sympathy for their bereaved relatives. The death of an elder sister, which took place when he was between three and four years old, played a great part in his phantasies, and was brought into intimate connection with his childish misdemeanours during the same period. We know, moreover, at what an early age thoughts about his father's death had occupied his mind, and we may regard his illness itself as a reaction to that event, for which he had felt an obsessional wish fifteen years earlier. The strange extension of his obsessional fears to the 'next world' was nothing else than a compensation for these death-wishes which he had felt against his father. It was introduced eighteen months after his father had died, at a time when there had been a revival of his sorrow at the loss, and it was designed—in defiance of reality, and in deference to the wish which had previously been showing itself in phantasies of every kind—to undo the fact of his father's death. We have had occasion in several places to translate the phrase 'in the next world' by the words 'if my father were still alive'.

But the behaviour of other obsessional neurotics does not differ greatly from that of our present patient, even though it has not been their fate to come face to face with the phenomenon of death at such an early age. Their thoughts are unceasingly occupied with other people's length of life and possibility of death; their superstitious propensities have, to begin with, had no other content and have perhaps no other source whatever. But these neurotics need the help of the possibility of death chiefly in order that it may act as a solution of conflicts they have left unsolved. Their essential characteristic is that they are incapable of coming to a decision, especially in matters of love; they endeavour to postpone every decision, and, in their doubt which person they shall decide for or what measures they shall take against a person, they are obliged to choose as their model the old German courts of justice, in which the suits were usually brought to an end, before judgement had been given, by the death of the parties to the dispute. Thus in every conflict which enters their lives they are on the look out for the death of some one who is of importance to them, usually of some one they love—such as one of their parents, or a rival, or one of the objects of their love between which their inclinations are wavering. But at this point our discussion of the death-complex in obsessional neuroses touches upon the problem of the instinctual life of obsessional neurotics. And to this problem we must now turn.

THE INSTINCTUAL LIFE OF OBSESSIONAL NEUROTICS, AND THE ORIGINS OF COMPULSION AND DOUBT

If we wish to obtain a grasp of the psychical forces whose interplay built up this neurosis, we must turn back to what we have learnt from the patient on the subject of the exciting causes of his falling ill as a grown-up man and as a child. He fell ill when he was in his twenties on being faced with a temptation to marry another woman instead of the one whom he had loved so long; and he avoided a decision of this conflict by postponing all the necessary preliminary actions. The means for doing this was given him by his neurosis. His hesitation between the lady he loved and the other girl can be reduced to a conflict between his father's influence and his love for his lady, or, in other words, to a conflicting choice between his father and his sexual object, such as had already subsisted (judging from his recollections and obsessional ideas) in his remote childhood. All through his life, moreover, he was unmistakably victim to a conflict between love and hatred, in regard both to his lady and to his father. His phantasies of revenge and such obsessional phenomena as his obsession for understanding and his exploit with the stone in the road bore witness to his discordant feelings; and they were to a certain degree comprehensible and normal, for the lady by her original refusal and subsequently by her coolness had given him some excuse for hostility. But his relations with his father were dominated by a similar discordance of feeling, as we have seen from our translation of his obsessional thoughts; and his father too must have given him an excuse for hostility in his childhood, as indeed we have been able to establish almost beyond question. His attitude towards the lady—a compound of tenderness and hostility—came to a great extent within the scope of his conscious knowledge; at most he deceived himself over the degree and strength of his negative feelings. But his hostility towards his father, on the contrary, though he had once been acutely conscious of it, had long since vanished from his ken, and it was only in the teeth of the most violent resistance that it could be brought back into his consciousness. We may regard the repression of his infantile hatred of his father as the event which brought his whole subsequent career under the dominion of the neurosis.

The conflicts of feeling in our patient which we have here enumerated separately were not independent of each other, but were bound together in pairs. His hatred of his lady was inevitably coupled with his attachment to his father, and inversely his hatred of his father with his attachment to his lady. But the two conflicts of feeling which result from this simplification— namely, the opposition between his relation to his father and to his lady, and the contradiction between his love and his hatred within each of these relations—had no connection whatever with each other, either in their content or in their origin. The first of these two conflicts corresponds to the normal vacillation between male and female which characterizes every one's choice of a love-object. It is first brought to the child's notice by the time-honoured question: 'Which do you love most, Papa or Mamma?' and it accompanies him through his whole life, whatever may be the relative intensity of his feelings to the two sexes or whatever may be the sexual aim upon which he finally becomes fixed. But normally this opposition soon loses the character of a hard-and-fast-contradiction, of an inexorable 'either'–'or'. Room is found for satisfying the unequal demands of both sides, although even in a normal person the higher estimation of one sex is always thrown into relief by a depreciation of the other.

The other conflict, that between love and hatred, strikes us more strangely. We know that incipient love is often perceived as hatred, and that love, if it is denied satisfaction, may easily be partly converted into hatred, and poets tell us that in the more tempestuous stages of love the two opposed feelings may subsist side by side for a while as though in rivalry with each other. But the chronic coexistence of love and hatred, both directed towards the same person and both of the highest degree of intensity, cannot fail to astonish us. We should have expected that the passionate love would long ago have conquered the hatred or been devoured by it. And in fact such a protracted survival of two opposites is only possible under quite peculiar psychological conditions and with the co-operation of the state of affairs in the unconscious. The love has not succeeded in extinguishing the hatred but only in driving it down into the unconscious; and in the unconscious the hatred, safe from the danger of being destroyed by the operations of consciousness, is able to persist and even to grow. In such circumstances the conscious love attains as a rule, by way of reaction, an especially high degree of intensity, so as to be strong enough for the perpetual task of keeping its opponent under repression. The necessary condition for the occurrence of such a strange state of affairs in a person's erotic life appears to be that at a very early age, somewhere in the prehistoric period of his infancy, the two opposites should have been split apart and one of them, usually the hatred, have been repressed.[12]

If we consider a number of analyses of obsessional neurotics we shall find it impossible to escape the impression that a relation between love and hatred such as we have found in our present patient is among the most frequent, the most marked, and probably, therefore, the most important characteristics of the obsessional neurosis. But however tempting it may be to bring the problem of the 'choice of neurosis' into relation with the instinctual life, there are reasons enough for avoiding such a course. For we must remember that in every neurosis we come upon the same suppressed instincts behind the symptoms. After all, hatred, kept suppressed in the unconscious by love, plays a great part in the pathogenesis of hysteria and paranoia. We know too little of the nature of love to be able to arrive at any definite conclusion here; and, in particular, the relation between the *negative* factor[13] in love and the sadistic components of the libido remains completely obscure. What follows is therefore to be regarded as no more than a provisional explanation. We may suppose, then, that in the cases of unconscious hatred with which we are concerned the sadistic components of love have, from constitutional causes, been exceptionally strongly developed, and have consequently undergone a premature and all too thorough suppression, and that the neurotic phenomena we have observed arise on the one hand from conscious feelings of affection which have become exaggerated as a reaction, and on the other hand from sadism persisting in the unconscious in the form of hatred.

But in whatever way this remarkable relation of love and hatred is to be explained, its occurrence is established beyond any possibility of doubt by the observations made in the present case; and it is gratifying to find how easily we can now follow the puzzling processes of an obsessional neurosis by bringing them into relation with this one factor. If an intense love is opposed by an almost equally powerful hatred, and is at the same time inseparably bound up with it, the immediate consequence is certain to be a partial paralysis of the will and an incapacity for coming to a decision upon any of those actions for which love ought to provide the motive power. But this indecision will not confine itself for long to a single group of actions. For, in the first place, what actions of a lover are not brought into relation with his one principal motive? And secondly, a man's attitude in sexual things has the force of a model to which the rest of his reactions tend to conform. And thirdly, it is an inherent characteristic in the psychology of an obsessional neurotic to make the fullest possible use of the mechanism of *displacement*. So the paralysis of his powers of decision gradually extends itself over the entire field of the patient's behaviour.

And here we have the domination of *compulsion* and *doubt* such as we meet with in the mental life of obsessional neurotics. The doubt corresponds to the patient's internal perception of his own indecision, which, in consequence of the inhibition of his love by his hatred, takes possession of him in the face of every intended action. The doubt is in reality a doubt of his own love—which ought to be the most certain thing in his whole mind; and it becomes diffused over everything else, and is especially apt to become displaced on to what is most insignificant and trivial.[14] A man who doubts his own love may, or rather *must,* doubt every lesser thing.[15]

It is this same doubt that leads the patient to uncertainty about his protective measures, and to his continual repetition of them in order to banish that uncertainty; and it is this doubt, too, that eventually brings it about that the patient's protective acts themselves become as impossible to carry out as his original inhibited decision in connection with his love. At the beginning of my investigations I was led to assume another and more general origin for the uncertainty of obsessional neurotics and one which seemed to be nearer the normal. If, for instance, while I am writing a letter some one interrupts me with questions, I afterwards feel a quite justifiable uncertainty as to what I may not have written under the influence of the disturbance, and, to make sure, I am obliged to read the letter over after I have finished it. In the same way I might suppose that the uncertainty of obsessional neurotics, when they are praying, for instance, is due to unconscious phantasies constantly mingling with their prayers and disturbing them. This hypothesis is correct, but it may be easily reconciled with our earlier statement. It is true that the patient's uncertainty whether he has carried through a protective measure is due to the disturbing effect of unconscious phantasies; but the content of these phantasies is precisely the contrary impulse—which it was the very aim of the prayer to ward off. This became clearly evident in our patient on one occasion, for the disturbing element did not remain unconscious but made its appearance openly. The words he wanted to use in his prayer were, *'May*

God protect her', but a hostile *'not'* suddenly darted out of his unconscious and inserted itself into the sentence; and he understood that this was an attempt at a curse. If the 'not' had remained mute, he would have found himself in a state of uncertainty, and would have kept on prolonging his prayers indefinitely. But since it became articulate he eventually gave up praying. Before doing so, however, he, like other obsessional patients, tried every kind of method for preventing the opposite feeling from insinuating itself. He shortened his prayers, for instance, or said them more rapidly. And similarly other patients will endeavour to *'isolate'* all such protective acts from other things. But none of these technical procedures are of any avail in the long run. If the impulse of love achieves any success by displacing itself on to some trivial act, the impulse of hostility will very soon follow it on to its new ground and once more proceed to undo all that it has done.

And when the obsessional patient lays his finger on the weak spot in the security of our mental life—on the untrustworthiness of our memory—the discovery enables him to extend his doubt over everything, even over actions which have already been performed and which have so far had no connection with the love-hatred complex, and over the entire past. I may recall the instance of the woman who had just bought a comb for her little daughter in a shop, and, becoming suspicious of her husband, began to doubt whether she had not as a matter of fact been in possession of the comb for a long time. Was not this woman saying point-blank: 'If I can doubt your love' (and this was only a projection of her doubt of her own love for him), 'then I can doubt this too, then I can doubt everything'—thus revealing to us the hidden meaning of neurotic doubt?

The *compulsion* on the other hand is an attempt at a compensation for the doubt and at a correction of the intolerable conditions of inhibition to which the doubt bears witness. If the patient, by the help of displacement, succeeds at last in bringing one of his inhibited intentions to a decision, then the intention *must* be carried out. It is true that this intention is not his original one, but the energy dammed up in the latter cannot let slip the opportunity of finding an outlet for its discharge in the substitutive act. Thus this energy makes itself felt now in commands and now in prohibitions, according as the affectionate impulse or the hostile one snatches control of the pathway leading to discharge. If it happens that a compulsive command cannot be obeyed, the tension becomes intolerable and is perceived by the patient in the form of extreme anxiety. But the pathway leading to a substitutive act, even where the displacement has been on to a triviality, is so hotly contested, that such an act can as a rule be carried out only in the shape of a protective measure intimately associated with the very impulse which it is designed to ward off.

Furthermore, by a sort of *regression,* preparatory acts become substituted for the final decision, thinking replaces acting, and, instead of the substitutive act, some thought preliminary to it asserts itself with all the force of compulsion. According as this regression from acting to thinking is more or less marked, a case of obsessional neurosis will exhibit the characteristics of obsessive thinking (that is, of obsessional ideas) or of obsessive acting in the narrower sense of the word. True obsessional acts such as these, however, are only made possible because they constitute a kind of reconciliation, in the shape of a compromise formation, between the two antagonistic impulses. For obsessional acts tend to approximate more and more—and the longer the disorder lasts the more evident does this become—to infantile sexual acts of an onanistic character. Thus in this form of the neurosis acts of love are carried out in spite of everything, but only by the aid of a new kind of regression; for such acts no longer relate to another person, the object of love and hatred, but are auto-erotic acts such as occur in infancy.

The first kind of regression, that from acting to thinking, is facilitated by another factor concerned in the production of the neurosis. The histories of obsessional patients almost invariably reveal an early development and premature repression of the sexual instinct of looking and knowing (the scoptophilic and epistemophilic instinct); and, as we know, a part of the infantile sexual activity of our present patient was governed by that instinct.[16]

We have already mentioned the important part played by the sadistic instinctual components in the genesis of obsessional neuroses. Where the epistemophilic instinct is a preponderating feature in the constitution of an obsessional patient, brooding becomes the principal symptom of the neurosis. The thought process itself becomes sexualized, for the sexual pleasure which is normally attached to the content of thought becomes shifted on to the act of thinking itself, and the gratification derived from reaching the conclusion of a line of thought is experienced as a *sexual* gratification. In the various forms of obsessional neurosis in which the epistemophilic instinct plays a part, its relation to thought processes makes it particularly well adapted to attract the energy which is vainly endeavouring to make its way forward into action, and divert it into the sphere of thought, where there is a possibility of its obtaining pleasurable gratification of another sort. In this way, with the help of the epistemophilic instinct, the substitutive act may in its turn be replaced by preparatory acts of thought. But procrastination in action is soon replaced by dilatoriness in thought, and eventually the whole process, together with all its peculiarities, is transferred into the new sphere, just as in America an entire house will sometimes be moved from one site to another.

I may now venture, upon the basis of the preceding discussion, to determine the psychological characteristic, so long sought after, which lends to the products of an obsessional neurosis their 'obsessive' or compulsive quality. A thought process is obsessive or compulsive when, in consequence of an inhibition (due to a conflict of opposing impulses) at the motor end of the psychical system, it is undertaken with an expenditure of energy which (as regards both quality and quantity) is normally reserved for actions alone; or, in other words, *an obsessive or compulsive thought is one whose function it is to represent an act regressively.* No one, I think, will question my assumption that processes of thought are ordinarily conducted (on grounds of economy) with smaller displacements of energy, probably at a higher level, than are acts intended to discharge an affect or to modify the external world.

The obsessive thought which has forced its way into consciousness with such excessive violence has next to be secured against the efforts made by conscious thought to resolve it. As we already know, this protection is afforded by the *distortion* which the obsessive thought has undergone before becoming conscious. But this is not the only means employed. In addition, each separate obsessional idea is almost invariably removed from the situation in which it originated and in which, in spite of its distortion, it would be most easily comprehensible. With this end in view, in the first place *an interval of time is inserted* between the pathogenic situation and the obsession that arises from it, so as to lead astray any conscious investigation of its causal connections; and in the second place the content of the obsession is taken out of its particular setting by being *generalized*. Our patient's 'obsession for understanding' is an example of this. But perhaps a better one is afforded by another patient. This was a woman who prohibited herself from wearing any sort of personal adornment, though the exciting cause of the prohibition related only to one particular piece of jewellery: she had envied her mother the possession of it and had had hopes that one day she would inherit it. Finally, if we care to distinguish verbal distortion from distortion of content, there is yet another means by which the obsession is protected against conscious attempts at solution. And that is the choice of an indefinite or ambiguous wording. After being misunderstood, the wording may find its way into the patient's 'deliria', and whatever further processes of development or substitution his obsession undergoes will then be based upon the misunderstanding and not upon the proper sense of the text. Observation will show, however, that the deliria constantly tend to form new connections with that part of the matter and wording of the obsession which is not present in consciousness.

I should like to go back once more to the instinctual life of obsessional neurotics and add one more remark upon it. It turned out that our patient, besides all his other characteristics, was a *renifleur* (or osphresiolagniac). By his own account, when he was a child he had recognized every one by their smell, like a dog; and even when he was grown up he was more susceptible to sensations of smell than most people.[17] I have met with the same characteristic in other neurotics, both in hysterical and in obsessional patients, and I have come to recognize that a tendency to osphresiolagnia, which has become extinct since childhood, may play a part in the genesis of neurosis.[18] And here I should like to raise the general question whether the atrophy of the sense of smell (which was an inevitable result of man's assumption of an erect posture) and the consequent organic repression of his osphresiolagnia may not have had a considerable share in the origin of his susceptibility to nervous disease. This would afford us some explanation of why, with the advance of civilization, it is precisely the sexual life that must fall a victim to repression. For we have long known the intimate connection in the animal organization between the sexual instinct and the function of the olfactory organ.

In bringing this paper to a close I may express a hope that, though my communication is incomplete in every sense, it may at least stimulate other workers to throw more light upon the obsessional neurosis by a deeper investigation of the subject. What is characteristic of this neurosis—what differentiates it from hysteria—is not, in my opinion, to be found in instinctual life but in psychological relations. I cannot take leave of my patient without putting on paper my impression that he had, as it were, disintegrated into three personalities: into one unconscious personality, that is to say, and into two preconscious ones between which his consciousness could oscillate. His unconscious comprised those of his impulses which had been suppressed at an early age and which might be described as passionate and evil impulses. In his normal state he was kind, cheerful, and sensible—an enlightened and superior kind of person, while in his third psychological organization he paid homage to superstition and asceticism. Thus he was able to have two different creeds and two different outlooks upon life. This second preconscious personality comprised chiefly the reaction-formations against his repressed wishes, and it was easy to foresee that it would have swallowed up the normal personality if the illness had lasted much longer. I have at present an opportunity of studying a lady suffering severely from obsessional acts. She has become similarly disintegrated into an easy-going and lively personality and into an exceedingly gloomy and ascetic one. She puts forward the first of them as her official ego, while in fact she is dominated by the second. Both of these psychical organizations have access to her consciousness, but behind her ascetic personality may be discerned the unconscious part of her being— quite unknown to her and composed of ancient and long-repressed conative impulses.[19]

NOTES

1. Several of the points dealt with in this and the following section have already been mentioned in the literature of obsessional neuroses, as may be gathered from Löwenfeld's exhaustive study, *Die psychischen Zwangserscheinungen,* 1904, which is the standard work upon this form of disease.

2. 'Further Remarks on the Defence Neuro-Psychoses' (1896), *Collected Papers,* vol. 1., p. 162.

3. This fault in my definition is to some extent corrected in the paper itself. The following passage will be found on p. 163: 'The reanimated memories and the self-reproach which is built up on them, however, never appear in consciousness unchanged. The obsessional idea and the obsessive affects which appear in consciousness and take the place of the pathogenic memory in conscious life are *compromise-formations* between the repressed and the repressing ideas.' In the definition, that is to say, especial stress is to be laid upon the words 'in a transmuted form'.

4. Many patients carry the diversion of their attention to such lengths that they are totally unable to give the content of an obsessional idea or to describe an obsessional act though they have performed it over and over again.

5. Cf. Freud, *Die Traumdeutung* (1900), First Edition, p. 283.

6. This omnipotence is discussed further on.

7. An example from another of my works, *Der Witz* (1905), Fourth Edition, p. 63, will recall to the reader the manner in which this elliptical technique is employed in making jokes: 'There is a witty and pugnacious journalist in Vienna, whose biting invective has repeatedly led to his being physically maltreated by the subjects of his attacks. On one occasion, when a fresh misdeed on the part of one of his habitual opponents was being discussed, somebody exclaimed: "If X. hears of this, he'll get his ears boxed again." . . . The apparent absurdity of this remark disappears if between the two clauses we insert the words: "he'll write such a scathing article upon the man, that, etc." '—This elliptical joke, we may note, is similar in its content, as well as in its form, to the first example quoted in the text.

8. *Zur Psychopathologie des Alltagslebens* (1905), Tenth Edition, p. 287.

9. As Lichtenberg says, 'An astronomer knows whether the moon is inhabited or not with about as much certainty as he knows who was his father, but not with so much certainty as he knows who was his mother'. A great advance was made in

civilization when men decided to put their inferences upon a level with the testimony of their senses and to make the step from matriarchy to patriarchy.—The prehistoric figures which show a smaller person sitting upon the head of a larger one are representations of patrilineal descent; Athena had no mother, but sprang from the head of Zeus. A witness who testifies to something before a court of law is still called 'Zeuge' [literally, 'begetter'] in German, after the part played by the male in the act of procreation; so too in hieroglyphics a 'witness' is represented pictorially by the male genitals.

10. (*Additional Note*, 1923.)—The omnipotence of thoughts, or, more accurately speaking, of wishes, has since been recognized as an essential element in the mental life of primitive people. (See *Totem und Tabu*.)

11. [In the original '*Leichenvogel*', literally 'corpse-bird'.—*Trans.*]

12. Compare the discussion on this point during one of the first sittings.—(*Additional Note*, 1923). Bleuler subsequently introduced the appropriate term 'ambivalence' to describe this emotional constellation. See also a further development of this line of thought in my paper 'The Predisposition to Obsessional Neurosis' (1913), *Collected Papers*, vol. 2.

13. Alcibiades says of Socrates in the *Symposium:* 'Many a time have I wished that he were dead, and yet I know that I should be much more sorry than glad if he were to die: so that I am at my wits' end' [Jowett's Translation].

14. Compare the use of 'representation by a triviality' as a technique in making jokes. Freud, *Der Witz* (1905), Fourth Edition, p. 65.

15. So in the love-verses addressed by Hamlet to Ophelia:

> 'Doubt thou the stars are fire;
>   Doubt that the sun doth move;
> Doubt truth to be a liar;
>   But never doubt I love.'

16. The very high average of intellectual capacity among obsessional patients is probably also connected with this fact.

17. I may add that in his childhood he had been subject to strong coprophilic propensities. In this connection his anal erotism has already been noticed.

18. For instance, in certain forms of fetishism.

19. (*Additional Note*, 1923.)—The patient's mental health was restored to him by the analysis which I have reported upon in these pages. Like so many other young men of value and promise, he perished in the Great War.

3. Hate and Anal Erotism in the Obsessional Neurosis

Ernest Jones

I N A RECENT contribution on the subject of the obsessional neurosis,[1] one to which this paper is really an addendum, I laid stress on the remarkable prominence of the part played in the disease by anal erotism,[2] and the experience of other psycho-analysts of whom I have since inquired coincides in this respect with my own. As is well known, Freud in his chief contribution to the subject[3] directed especial attention to the predominating influence of hate in the genesis of the disease, the alternation of the affects of love and hate and the mutual interaction between these being mainly responsible for the characteristic features of compulsion and doubt (obsessions and *folie du doute*), with which they are strictly to be correlated; I may add that my own experience, as illustrated in the cases reported in the contribution just referred to, confirms Freud's conclusions on these points in every respect. If, therefore, my finding, mentioned above, is correct, it is to be expected that there must be some inherent connection between hate and anal erotism, certainly in the obsessional neurosis, and perhaps altogether.

Of the psychogenesis of hate there is not a great deal known. That it often bears a close relation to sadism is a familiar fact of experience, though there is much reason for doubting whether this is necessarily a primary one. As it appears to me, the genesis of hate is probably preceded by an earlier undifferentiated state in which pain *(Unlust)*, annoyance, and perhaps anger, is experienced when the infant finds that any of his wishes are not being immediately gratified, and particularly when the gratification of these wishes is being actively prevented. We can speak of anger only when feelings of this kind become attached to certain definite persons, but this in itself does not constitute hate. For hate to arise, it is necessary that a durable affective bond be established between the two persons concerned, or at least that the one hated be a replacement-figure for some one who is the bearer of this bond.

Reprinted by permission of Williams and Wilkins, a Waverly Co., from *Papers on Psychoanalysis* by Ernest Jones, Baltimore, 1918, pp. 553–61.

Like all affective bonds, this one, too, is primarily a positive one, and it remains such in the unconscious. It may have at one time manifested itself consciously as love, in which case we have the familiar event of love being turned to hate, or there may have been only an unconscious attempt to establish a love relationship, which has failed. In any case the hate is to be regarded as an expression of disappointed or baulked love, which doubtless is the reason why the most intense and furious hatreds are to be met with in regard to members of the same family or other persons where love might have been expected—*e.g.,* between lovers or married partners.

There also seems to be regularly concerned in the genesis of hate some admixture of fear, though this is by no means always conscious, and the suggestion of such an idea is often repudiated with indignation. We never hate a person who is not in some way or other, often not at all obviously, superior to or stronger than ourselves, or who at all events has some power over us. Thus, we may be angry with an inferior, a stranger, or someone who is quite indifferent to us, but in order to hate properly we must be concerned with a person who is in some way superior to ourselves, with whom we have or have had much to do, and whom we had hoped to love. These conditions are most often fulfilled in the case of someone standing in a near relationship to us, especially a member of our own family, and it is likely that all hate, like charity, begins at home, later and outside manifestations of it being merely displacements of this primary form.

Leaving now the subject of the nature of hate, and passing to that of its origin, we have to consider the occasions in the child's early life where the conditions just mentioned are in operation. To the infant, and, indeed, to a large extent to older children, love on the part of a parent or other member of the environment is synonymous with the giving of pleasure to it. The child feels that he is loved when the person obeys his commands and gratifies his wishes, or at least refrains from interfering with their gratification. Any behaviour of the opposite kind on the part of anyone on whom the child makes demands is at once interpreted by the latter as a sign of insufficient love, or even hostility, and becomes the basis in later years of such reactions as the chronic feeling of being slighted or, in insanity, delusions of persecution. In paranoia, for instance, it is now known that such delusions always arise to begin with in connection with persons whom the patient has tried to love, but for internal reasons (repression of homosexuality) has been unable to.[4]

Perhaps the most familiar example of this situation in the infant's life is the common Œdipus one, where the parent of the same sex acts as either a passive or an active obstacle in the way of the child's desire for contact with the other parent. The child's annoyance and anger, which cannot, of course, be gratified, are apt to pass over into chronic hatred, either conscious or—more often—repressed, and the far-reaching consequences of this in later life are too well known to this audience for me to have to discuss them here. In this situation we have a typical illustration of the conditions necessary for the development of hate, a would-be loved being, stronger than the person, acting as an obstacle to the obtaining of pleasure and hence becoming both feared and hated.

It is sometimes forgotten, however, that there is a still earlier situation in infancy which may lead to the same result, and the consequences of which may in certain circumstances be no less significant. This is the situation where the infant for the first time finds itself in serious conflict with the outer world, probably one of the chief ways in which it comes to appreciate the very existence of an outer world as something distinct from itself—namely, during the education of the sphincters. There is no doubt that, especially in cases where the anal erotism is unusually pronounced and where the child is exceedingly loath to relinquish its supreme control over the functions in question, this conflict can become one of the greatest importance, the interference of the nurse or mother being resented in a high degree.[5] The lasting effect of this early experience was strikingly illustrated in a paraphrenic patient of mine, a man aged twenty-five, whose chief delusion was that his mother was interfering with him in every possible way. He was a most pronounced anal-erotist, and whenever he went to the water-closet he had the visual hallucination of his mother being there disturbing him; he usually took about an hour to accomplish the act of defæcation, most of the time being occupied in performing various ceremonies to exorcise this hallucination. As might be expected, his attitude towards his mother was one of open hatred. The conflict involved in the interference with anal erotism on the part of the mother, therefore, must be regarded as one of the important sources of chronic hatred, and in this connection it is interesting to note that Federn, in his detailed essay on the subject of pain lust,[6] lays great stress on the part played by anal-erotic sensations themselves (apart from the conflict here mentioned) in the genesis of sadism, which is so often associated with hate; I might, further, recall the case related by Brill[7] at our last meeting, one in which the ideas of defæcation and cruelty were so closely connected in the patient's mind that he was able to carry out the act only by having recourse to the aid of sadistic phantasies and symptomatic actions.

In the obsessional neurosis the association just described between hate and anal erotism is certainly very frequent, being in my experience a constant occurrence, and the recognition of it seems to me to throw some light on the structure of the disease itself. As is now known, the chief characteristic in the psychology of the neurosis is the mutual paralysis of the tendencies of love and hate, with the resulting alternation of compulsion and doubt. This curious phenomenon becomes more intelligible when we remember that the hate, according to my view, is first developed towards the *Imago* of all later love-objects, the mother herself; thus the capacity to love is impeded or paralysed at its very inception. It is only to be expected that anyone whose love towards the mother has from the beginning alternated with hate should shew the same alternation towards all secondary love-objects. This seems to me to be the real explanation of the profound ambivalency that runs through the whole of such patients' love-life.

This consideration perhaps also explains—it certainly accords with the fact—why the obsessional neurosis occurs with so much greater frequency in men than in women, or at least it indicates the presence of one more factor in addition to those already pointed out. For the effect of the anal-erotic conflict in women is in harmony with that of the normal incestuous one, whereas in men it stands in contradiction to this. It leads a girl to hate her mother, either consciously or unconsciously, merely a little earlier and a little more cordially than she otherwise would, but her maximum capacity for love—towards her father—is left unimpaired. With a boy, on the other hand, it leads to a much more involved state of affairs; he is hostile to his father for other reasons (Œdipus-complex), and now he is made to hate the person whom by nature he is most intended to love—namely, his mother. The paralysis of the capacity to love is therefore necessarily greater in the case of the male, and one cannot help correlating this with the much higher incidence of the obsessional neurosis in the male sex.

Another matter that the preceding association throws more light on is the attitude of defiance towards a stronger person, which is an essential constituent of hate. Since anal erotism is the chief source of the character trait of defiance in general, this being one of the triad of character attributes originally described by Freud,[8] it is probable that from it arises the defiance always found in the obsessional neurosis, just as Federn[9] has suggested it is in the case of that accompanying sadism. In the neurosis it is most often transferred on to the person of the father, who for Œdipus reasons is the most suitable object to receive it, the transference being also favoured by the homosexual tendencies that are always abnormally pronounced in this disease.

Before concluding, I may add some further considerations as to the part played by anal erotism in the genesis of the obsessional neurosis, and particularly in regard to the sense of power. It is known that one of the most remarkable psychological characteristics of the obsessional neurosis is the patient's inordinate belief in the 'omnipotence of his thoughts' *(Allmathi der Gedanken)*, the conviction that his mere wishes are followed by immediate results in the external world. It is further known that ideas of power, just as the allied ones of contempt and of money, are intimately connected with the anal-erotic impulse, a circumstance which Federn[10] relates—rightly or wrongly—to the use that infants make of it to display their power over the persons of their environment. This may explain the bringing of the idea of power into relation with certain definite persons, but there are deeper connections between this idea and anal erotism itself. In his recent work on animism[11] Freud correlated the feeling of omnipotence, of supreme power, with the narcissistic phase of development, which arises through the fusion and directing of the various discrete auto-erotic impulses of infancy, and among these the anal-erotic is certainly one of the two most important. Ferenczi writes:[12] 'Psycho-analytical experience has made it clear to me that this symptom, the feeling of omnipotence, is a projection of the observation that one has slavishly to obey certain irresistible instincts.' This statement applies to anal erotism more strikingly than to any other part of the infantile 'sexual hunger' *(Libido)*, and I would relate the sense of compulsion in the obsessional neurosis, one which in its genesis is closely connected with the feeling of omnipotence, in part to the overpowering force with which an anal-erotic desire may present itself.

As is well known, the feeling of omnipotence is in the obsessional neurosis most typically shewn in the belief that has been well called the omnipotence of thoughts, a fact which becomes quite intelligible when we remember that sexualisation of the thought processes is highly characteristic of this neurosis as distinct from any other.[13] Now, I have pointed out elsewhere[14] that both the ideas of speech and of thinking are equivalent in the unconscious with that of passing flatus, which they frequently symbolise in consciousness, and in the light of the preceding considerations I am inclined to think that this bears some relation to the genesis of the patient's faith in the omnipotence of his thoughts. In a recent illuminating essay[15] Ferenczi has divided the development of the sense of reality into four stages, and these stages also represent the progressive series of efforts that the infant has to make in order to retain, so far as is possible, his primary inborn feeling of omnipotence. The third of these stages Ferenczi terms the 'period of omnipotence by the help of magic gestures.' In it the child has to give certain 'signals' to the persons of his environment in order to bring about the alteration it desires in the outer world. Provided only that it gives these signals it can retain its ancient belief in the omnipotence of its wishes, in their power to secure fulfilment. The signals have to be either visible movements—chiefly of the hands—or else sounds, and the latter are evidently the more important, if only for the reason that they are the only ones that can be perceived both by day and by night, both when the nurse is in the same room and when she is in an adjoining one. Amongst these signals, sounds accompanying anal activities play a part second only in significance to the voice itself, so that they constitute one of the chief means through which the infant retains its belief in its omnipotence, a consideration that throws some light on the above-mentioned association between the belief and anal erotism in the obsessional neurosis. The fourth stage of development is called by Ferenczi the 'period of magic thoughts and magic words,' the signalling gestures being here largely replaced by the beginnings of speech, and it is interesting in the present connection that he should at this point refer to a previous article of his in which he shewed that the superstitious belief in the omnipotence of thoughts and words is retained in adult life in connection with obscene words and phrases to a more striking extent than with any others.

If followed, however, these considerations would lead us far away from the purpose of the present paper, which was merely to call attention to the prominent part played by anal erotism in the obsessional neurosis, and, if possible, to throw some light on the connection between it and hate.

In a subsequent paper [16] Freud has confirmed my conclusions that the general association between hate and anal erotism is important, and that a high development of this combination is the most specific characteristic of the obsessional neurosis. He then proceeds to explain the meaning of this empirically discovered state of affairs. It will be remembered that he conceives of the course of development of the infantile sexuality as consisting first in a grouping together of the originally discrete auto-erotic 'component impulses' into a whole, secondly in these being directed towards an object, which to begin with is the self (stage of infantile narcissism) and only later is an external object. After the last of these stages is accomplished (the choice of an external object) there emerges from the fused and co-ordinated impulses one which achieves a permanent primacy—namely, the genital erotogenic zone. He now gives a number of grounds for holding that there is normally an intermediate stage between the two last mentioned—that is, after the choice of external object, but before the primacy of the genital zone is achieved—and this he terms the 'pregenital' stage of development.[17] There are perhaps several varieties or sub-stages of this. Two at least are known. The most important is the sadistic-analerotic one discussed above, and the characteristic of the obsessional neurosis is that the regression on which it is based reaches back to its 'fixation-point' in this sadistic-analerotic phase of normal development; such patients have, no doubt for congenital, constitutional reasons, never properly traversed this phase in the course of development.[18]

The other pregenital stage is the 'oral' or 'cannibalistic' phase of development, one to the study of which Abraham[19] has recently made an interesting contribution.

NOTES

1. *Jahrbuch der Psychoanalyse,* Bde. iv. and v.

2. I wish particularly to thank Drs. Ferenczi and Seif for the information they have given me regarding their experience.

3. Freud, 'Bemerkungen über einen Fall von Zwangsneurose,' *Jahrbuch der Psychoanalyse,* Bd. i., S. 357.

4. Freud, 'Psychoanalytische Bemerkungen über einen autobiographisch beschriebenen Fall von Paranoia.' *Jahrbuch der Psychoanalyse,* Bd. iii.; and Ferenczi, 'Contributions to Psycho-Analysis,' 1916, ch. v.

5. In an interesting essay on the subject, Lou Andreas-Salomé (*Imago,* 1916, Jahrg. iv., S. 249) has confirmed and developed my suggestion as to the importance of the conflict with the outer world that arises in this situation.

6. Federn, *Internationale Zeitschrift für drztliche Psychoanalyse,* Jahrg. i., S. 42–44.

7. Brill, *Journal of Abnormal Psychology,* August, 1912, Case III.

8. Freud, 'Charakter und Analerotik,' reprinted in his 'Sammlung kleiner Schriften,' 2ᵉ Folge, Kap. iv.

9. Federn, *op. cit.,* S. 42.

10. Federn, *op. cit.,* S. 41.

11. Freud, 'Animismus, Magie und Allmacht der Gedanken,' *Imago,* Jahrg. ii., Heft i.; reprinted in his 'Totem und Tabu,' 1913.

12. Ferenczi, *op. cit.,* p. 183.

13. See on this matter Freud, *op. cit., Jahrbuch,* Bd. i.

14. 'Essays in Applied Psycho-Analysis,' 1923, ch. viii.

15. Ferenczi, *op. cit.,* ch. viii.: 'Stages in the Development of the Sense of Reality.'

16. Freud, 'Die Disposition zur Zwangsneurose,' *Internat. Zeitschr. f. drstl. Psychoanalyse,* Jahrg. i., Heft 6.

17. The social consequences of this gain in knowledge will prove to be more far-

reaching than might appear. Some years ago, on hearing M. Anatole France make the remark that the two great forces which socialism had to overcome were militarism and capitalism (force and possession), I realised that these corresponded in society with the sadistic and anal-erotic components of the pregenital stage of individual development, so that the world movement to transcend the present pregenital civilisation by developing a higher social level has a profound psycho-biological meaning.

18. See also Freud, 'Allgemeine Neurosenlehre,' 1917, S. 375 *et seq.*

19. Abraham, 'Untersuchungen über die früheste prägenitale Entwicklungsstufe der Libido,' *Internat. Zeitschr. f. drstl. Psychoanalyse,* Jahrg. iv., S. 71.

4. Contributions to the Theory of the Anal Character

Karl Abraham

THE WIDE FIELD which is open to the science of psycho-analysis at the present time offers an abundance of instances of the rapid increase of psychological knowledge along the lines of purely inductive investigation. Perhaps the most remarkable and instructive of these is the development of the theory of the anal character. In 1908, about fifteen years after the appearance of his first contributions to the psychology of the neuroses, Freud published a short paper entitled 'Character and Anal Erotism'. It occupied only three pages of a journal, and was a model of condensed statement and of cautious and clear summing up. The gradually increasing number of his co-workers, among whom may be mentioned Sadger, Ferenczi, and Jones, has helped to extend the range of ascertained knowledge. The theory concerning the products of the transformation of anal erotism gained unsuspected significance when in 1913, following on Jones' important investigation on 'Hate and Anal Erotism in the Obsessional Neurosis', Freud formulated an early 'pregenital' organization of the libido. He considered that the symptoms of the obsessional neurosis were the result of a regression of libido to this stage of development, which is characterized by a preponderance of the anal and sadistic component instincts. This threw a new light both on the symptomatology of the obsessional neurosis and on the characterological peculiarities of the person suffering from it—on the so-called 'obsessional character'. I might add, anticipating a future publication, that very similar anomalies of character are found in those people who tend to melancholic or manic states of mind. And the strictest possible study of the sadistic-anal character-traits is necessary before we can proceed to investigate those last mentioned diseases which are still so enigmatical to us. The present study is mainly concerned with the anal contributions to the formation of character. Jones'[1] last great work on this subject presents an abundance of valuable

Reprinted by permission of Random House UK, Ltd., and Brunner/Mazel from *Selected Papers*, vol. 1 by Karl Abraham, New York, 1953, pp. 370–92.

material, but it does not exhaust it. For the work of a single person cannot do justice to the multiplicity and complexity of the phenomena; each analyst who possesses data of his own should publish them, and so help to contribute to the body of psycho-analytical knowledge. In the same way the purpose of the following remarks is to extend the theory of the anal character-traits in certain directions. Another problem of great theoretical importance will be very frequently alluded to in this study. Up to the present we understand only very incompletely the particular psychological connections that exist between the two impulses of sadism and anal erotism which we always mention in close association with each other, almost as a matter of habit. And I shall attempt the solution of this question in a later paper.

In his first description of the anal character Freud has said that certain neurotics present three particularly pronounced character-traits, namely, a love of orderliness which often develops into pedantry, a parsimony which easily turns to miserliness, and an obstinacy which may become an angry defiance. He established the fact that the primary pleasure in emptying the bowels and in its products was particularly emphasized in these persons; and also that after successful repression their coprophilia either becomes sublimated into pleasure in painting, modelling, and similar activities, or proceeds along the path of reaction-formation to a special love of cleanliness. Finally he pointed out the unconscious equivalence of fæces and money or other valuables. Among other observations Sadger [2] has remarked that persons with a pronounced anal character are usually convinced that they can do everything better than other people. He also speaks of a contradiction in their character, namely, great perseverance side by side with the tendency to put off doing everything till the last moment.

I will pass over isolated remarks in psycho-analytic literature by other authors and turn to Jones' very thorough and comprehensive study on this subject. I might remark in advance that I do not differ from this author on any points, but that nevertheless I feel that his statements need amplification and completion in certain respects.

Jones quite rightly distinguishes two different acts in the process we usually designate as the education of the child in cleanly habits. The child has not only to be taught not to soil its body and surroundings with excreta, but it has also to be educated to perform its excretory functions at regular times. In other words, it has to give up both its coprophilia and its pleasure in the process of excretion. This double process of limitation of infantile impulses together with its consequences in the psychical sphere requires further investigation.

The child's primitive method of evacuation brings the entire surface of its buttocks and lower extremities in contact with urine and fæces. This contact seems unpleasant, even repulsive, to adults, whose repressions have removed them from the infantile reaction to these processes. They cannot appreciate the sources of pleasure on which the libido of the infant can draw, in whom the stream of warm urine on the skin and contact with the warm mass of fæces produce pleasurable feelings. The child only begins to give signs of discomfort when the excreted products grow cold against its body. It is the same pleasure which the child seeks when it handles its fæces at a somewhat later period. Ferenczi[3] has traced the further development of this infantile tendency. It must not be forgotten, moreover, that pleasure in the sight and smell of fæces is associated with these feelings.

The special pleasure in the *act* of excretion, which we must differentiate from pleasure in the *products* of the excretory process, comprises besides physical sensations a psychical gratification which is based on the *achievement* of that act. Now in that the child's training demands strict regularity in its excretions as well as cleanliness it exposes the child's narcissism to a first severe test. The majority of children adapt themselves sooner or later to these demands. In favourable cases the child succeeds in making a virtue out of necessity, as it were; in other words, in identifying itself with the requirements of its educators and being proud of its attainment. The primary injury to its narcissism is thus compensated, and its original feeling of self-satisfaction is replaced by gratification in its achievement, in 'being good', in its parents' praise.

All children are not equally successful in this respect. Particular attention should be drawn here to the fact that there are certain over-compensations behind which is hidden that obstinate holding fast to the primitive right of self-determination which occasionally breaks out violently later. I have in mind those children (and of course adults also) who are remarkable for their 'goodness', polite manners, and obedience, but who base their underlying rebellious impulses on the grounds that they have been forced into submission since infancy. These cases have their own developmental history. In one of my patients I could trace back the course of events to her earliest infancy, in regard to which, it is true, previous statements of her mother were of assistance.

The patient was the middle one of three sisters. She showed unusually clearly and completely the traits characteristic of a 'middle' child, which Hug-Hellmuth[4] has recently described in such an illuminating way. But her refractoriness, which was associated in the clearest manner with her assertion of the infantile right of self-determination in the sense mentioned above, went back, in the last instance, to a particular circumstance of her childhood.

When she was born her elder sister had been still under a year old. Her mother had not quite succeeded in educating the elder child to habits of cleanliness when the newcomer had imposed on her a double amount of washing, both of clothes and body. When the patient was a few months old her mother had become pregnant for the third time, and had determined to hasten the education of her second child in cleanly habits, so that she should not still be too much taken up with her when the third child was born. She had demanded obedience on its part regarding the carrying out of its needs earlier than is usual, and had reinforced the effect of her words by smacking it. These measures had produced a very welcome result for the harassed mother. The child had become a model of cleanliness abnormally early, and had grown surprisingly submissive. When she was grown up, the patient was in a constant conflict between a conscious attitude of submissiveness, resignation and willingness to sacrifice herself on the one hand, and an unconscious desire for vengeance on the other.

This brief account illustrates in an instructive manner the effect of early injuries to infantile narcissism, especially if these injuries are of a persistent and systematic nature, and force a habit prematurely upon the child before it is psychically ready for it. This psychical preparedness only appears when the child begins to transfer on to objects (its mother, etc.) the feelings which are originally bound narcissistically. Once the child has acquired this capacity it will become cleanly 'for the sake of' this person. If cleanliness is demanded too soon, it will acquire the habit through fear. Its inner resistance will remain and its libido will continue in a tenacious narcissistic fixation, and a permanent disturbance of the capacity to love will result.

The full significance of such an experience for the psychosexual development of the child only becomes apparent if we examine in detail the course of narcissistic pleasure. Jones lays stress on the connection between the child's high self-esteem and its excretory acts. In a short paper[5] I have brought forward some examples to show that the child's idea of the omnipotence of its wishes and thoughts can proceed from a stage in which it ascribed an omnipotence of this kind to its excretions. Further experience has since convinced me that this is a regular and typical process. The patient about whose childhood I have spoken had doubtless been disturbed in the enjoyment of a narcissistic pleasure of this sort. The severe and painful feelings of insufficiency with which she was later afflicted very probably went back in the last instance to this premature destruction of her infantile 'megalomania'.

This view of the excretions as a sign of enormous power is foreign to the consciousness of normal adults. That it persists in the unconscious, however, is shown in many everyday expressions, mostly of a jocular nature; for example, the seat of the closet is often denoted as the 'throne'. It is not to be wondered at that children who grow up in a strong anal-erotic environment incorporate these kinds of comparisons which they so frequently hear, in the fixed body of their recollections and make use of them in their later neurotic phantasies. One of my patients had a compulsion to read a meaning of this kind into the German national anthem. By transposing himself in his phantasies of greatness into the Kaiser's place he pictured to himself 'the high delight' of 'bathing in the glory of the throne', *i.e.* of touching his own excreta.

Once again language gives us characteristic instances of this over-estimation of defæcation. In Spanish, the common expression for it, *'regir el vientre'* ('to rule the belly'), which is used quite seriously, clearly indicates the pride taken by the person in the functioning of his bowels.

If we recognize in the child's pride in evacuation a primitive feeling of power we can understand the peculiar feeling of helplessness we so often find in neurotically constipated patients. Their libido has been displaced from the genital to the anal zone, and they deplore the inhibition of the bowel function just as though it were a genital impotence. In thinking of the person who is hypochondriacal about his motions one is tempted to speak of an *intestinal* impotence.

Closely connected with this pride is the idea of many neurotics, which was first described by Sadger, that they must do everything themselves because no one else can do it as well. According to my experience this conviction is often exaggerated until the patient believes that he is a unique person. He will become pretentious and arrogant and will tend to under-estimate everyone else. One patient expressed this as follows: 'Everything that is not me is dirt'. These neurotics only take pleasure in possessing a thing that no one else has, and will despise any activity which they have to share with other people.

The sensitiveness of the person with an anal character to external encroachments of every kind on the actual or supposed field of his power is well known. It is quite evident that psycho-analysis must evoke the most violent resistance in such persons, who regard it as an unheard-of interference with their way of life. 'Psycho-analysis pokes about in my affairs', one patient said, thereby indicating unconsciously his passive-homosexual and anal attitude towards his analyst.

Jones emphasizes the fact that many neurotics of this class hold fast obstinately to their own system of doing things. They refuse altogether to accommodate themselves to any arrangement imposed from without, but expect compliance from other people as soon as they have worked out a definite arrangement of their own. As an example, I might mention the introduction of strict regulations for use in the office, or possibly the writing of a book which contains binding rules or recommendations for the organization of all offices of a certain kind.

The following is a glaring example of this kind. A mother drew up a written programme in which she arranged her daughter's day in the most minute manner. The orders for the early morning were set out as follows: (1) Get up. (2) Use the chamber. (3) Wash, etc. In the morning she would knock from time to time at her daughter's door, and ask, 'How far have you got now?' The girl would then have to reply, '9' or '15', as the case might be. In this way the mother kept a strict watch over the execution of her plan.

It might be mentioned here that all such systems not only testify to an obsession for order in its inventor, but also to his love of power which is of sadistic origin. I intend later to deal with the combination of anal and sadistic impulses in detail.

Allusion may be made here to the pleasure these neurotics take in indexing and registering everything, in making up tabular summaries, and in dealing with statistics of every kind.

They furthermore show the same self-will in regard to any demand or request made to them by some other person. We are reminded of the conduct of those children who become constipated when defæcation is demanded of them, but afterwards yield to the need at a time that is agreeable to themselves. Such children rebel equally against the "shall" (being told to empty their bowels) as against the 'must' (a child's expression for the need to defæcate); their desire to postpone evacuation is a protection against both imperatives.

The surrender of excrement is the earliest form in which the child 'gives' or 'presents' a thing; and the neurotic often shows the self-will we have described in the matter of giving. Accordingly in many cases he will refuse a demand or request made to him, but will of his own *free choice* make a person a handsome present. The important thing to him is to preserve his right of decision. We frequently find in our psycho-analyses that a husband opposes any expenditure proposed by his wife, while he afterwards hands her of his 'own free will' more than what she first asked for. These men delight in keeping their wives permanently dependent on them financially. Assigning money in portions which they themselves determine is a source of pleasure to them. We come across similar behaviour in some neurotics regarding defæcation, which they only allow to take place *in refracta dosi*. One special tendency these men and women have is to distribute food in portions according as they think best, and this habit occasionally assumes grotesque forms. For instance, there was a case of a stingy old man who fed his goat by giving it each blade of grass separately. Such people like to arouse desire and expectation in others and then to give them gratification in small and insufficient amounts.

In those instances where they have to yield to the demand of another person some of these neurotics endeavour to maintain a semblance of making a personal decision. An example of this is the tendency to pay even the smallest amounts by cheque; in this way the person avoids using current notes and coin, but creates his 'own money' in each case. The displeasure of paying out is thereby diminished by just as much as it would be increased if payment were made in coin. I should like to make it quite clear, however, that other motives are also operative here.

Neurotics who wish to introduce their own system into everything are inclined to be exaggerated in their criticism of others, and this easily degenerates into mere carping. In social life they constitute the main body of malcontents. The original anal characteristic of self-will, can, however, develop in two different directions, as Jones has convincingly shown. In some cases we meet with inaccessibility and stubbornness, that is, with characteristics that are unsocial and unproductive. In others we find perseverance and thoroughness, *i.e.* characteristics of social value as long as they are not pushed to extremes. We must here once more draw attention to the existence of other instinctual sources besides anal erotism which go to reinforce these tendencies.

The opposite type has received very little consideration in psycho-analytical literature. There are certain neurotics who avoid taking any kind of initiative. In ordinary life they want a kind father or attentive mother to be constantly at hand to remove every difficulty out of their way. In psychoanalysis they resent having to give free associations. They would like to lie quite still and let the physician do all the analytical work, or to be questioned by him. The similarity of the facts disclosed by the analysis of these cases enables me to state that these patients used in childhood to resist the act of defæcation demanded of them, and that then they used to be spared this trouble by being given frequent enemas or purges by their mother or father. To them free association is a psychical evacuation, and—just as with bodily evacuation—they dislike being asked to perform it. They are continually expecting that the work should be made easier or done for them altogether. I may recall a reverse form of this resistance, which I have likewise traced back to anal erotic sources in an earlier paper.[6] It concerns those patients who wish to do everything themselves according to their own method in their psycho-analysis, and for this reason refuse to carry out the prescribed free association.

In this paper I do not intend so much to discuss the neurotic symptom-formations arising from repressed anal erotism, as its characterological manifestations. I shall therefore only touch upon the various forms of neurotic inhibition which obviously have to do with a displacement of libido to the anal zone. The fact that avoidance of effort is a frequent feature of the anal character needs further discussion; and we must briefly consider what the state of affairs is in the person with a so-called 'obsessional character'.

If the libido of the male person does not advance in full measure to the stage of genital organization, or if it regresses from the genital to the anal developmental phase, there invariably results a diminution of male activity in every sense of the word. His physiological productiveness is bound up with the genital zone. If his libido regresses to the sadistic-anal phase he loses his productive power, and not only in the purely generative sense. His genital libido should give the first impulse to the procreative act, and therewith to the creation of a new being. If the initiative necessary for this reproductive act is lacking, we invariably find a lack of productivity and initiative in other respects in his behaviour. But the effects go even beyond this.

Together with the man's genital activity there goes a positive feeling-attitude towards his love-object, and this attitude extends to his behaviour towards other objects and is expressed in his capacity for social adaptation, his devotion to certain interests and ideas, etc. In all these respects the character-formation of the sadistic-anal stage is inferior to that of the genital phase. The sadistic element, which in a normal man's emotional life is of great importance once it has undergone appropriate transformation through sublimation, appears with particular strength in the obsessional character, but becomes more or less crippled in consequence of the ambivalence in the instinctual life of such persons. It also contains destructive tendencies hostile to the object, and on account of this cannot become sublimated to a real capacity for devotion to a love-object. For the reaction-formation of too great yieldingness and gentleness which is frequently observed in such people must not be confused with a real transference-love. Those cases in which object-love and genital libido-organization have been attained to a fair extent are more favourable. If the character-trait of over-kindness mentioned above is combined with a partial object-love of this kind, a socially useful 'variety' is produced, which in essential respects is, nevertheless, inferior to full object-love.

In individuals with more or less impaired genitality we regularly find an unconscious tendency to regard the anal function as the productive activity, and to make it appear as if the genital activity were unessential and the anal one far more important. The social behaviour of these persons is accordingly strongly bound up with money. They like to make presents of money or its equivalent, and tend to become patrons of the arts or benefactors of some kind. But their libido remains more or less detached from objects, and so the work they do remains unproductive in the essential sense. They are by no means lacking in perseverance—a frequent mark of the anal character—but their perseverance is largely used in unproductive ways. They expend it, for instance, in the pedantic observance of fixed forms, so that in unfavourable cases their preoccupation with the external form outweighs their interest in the reality of the thing. In considering the various ways in which the anal character impairs male activity we must not forget the tendency, often a very obstinate one, of postponing every action. We are well acquainted with the origin of this tendency. There is often associated with it a tendency to interrupt every activity that has been begun; so that in many cases as soon as a person begins doing anything it can already be predicted that an interruption will occur very soon.

More rarely I have found the reverse conduct. For instance, one of my patients was prevented from writing his doctor's thesis through a long-standing resistance. After several motives for his resistance had come to light we found the following one: he declared that he shrank from beginning his work because when he had once begun he could not leave off again. We are reminded of the behaviour of certain neurotics in regard to their excretions. They retain the contents of the bowel or bladder as long as they possibly can. When finally they yield to the need that has become too strong for them there is no further holding back, and they evacuate the entire contents. A fact to be particularly noted here is that there is a double pleasure, that of holding back the execreta, and that of evacuating it. The essential difference between the two forms of pleasure lies in the protracted nature of the process in the one case, and in its rapid course in the other. As regards the patient just mentioned the long-deferred beginning of the work signified a turning from pleasure in retention to pleasure in evacuation.[7]

A detail from the history of the same patient will show the degree to which a preponderance of anal over genital erotism makes the neurotic inactive and unproductive. During his analysis as well he remained wholly inactive for a long period, and by means of this resistance prevented any alteration taking place in his condition and circumstances. As is often the case in obsessional patients, his sole method of dealing with his external and internal difficulties was to swear violently. These expressions of affect were accompanied by very significant behaviour. Instead of thinking about the success of his work, he used to ponder over the question of what would happen to his curses— whether they reached God or the devil, and what was the fate of sound-waves in general. His intellectual activity was thus replaced by neurotic brooding. It appeared from his associations that the brooding question about the place where noise finally got to referred also to smell, and was in the last instance of anal erotic origin (flatus).

Generally speaking, it may be said that the more male activity and productivity is hindered in neurotics, the more pronounced their interest in possession becomes, and this in a way which departs widely from the normal. In marked cases of anal character-formation almost all relationships in life are brought into the category of having (holding fast) and giving, *i.e.* of proprietorship. It is as though the motto of many of these people were: 'Whoever gives me something is my friend; whoever desires something from me is my enemy'. One patient said that he could not have any friendly feelings towards me during his treatment, and added in explanation: 'So long as I have to pay anybody anything I cannot be friendly towards him'. We find the exact reverse of this behaviour in other neurotics; their friendly feeling towards a person increases in proportion to the help he needs and asks for.

In the first and larger group envy stands out clearly as the main character-trait. The envious person, however, shows not only a desire for the possessions of others, but connects with that desire spiteful impulses against the privileged proprietor. But we will only make a passing reference to the sadistic and anal roots of envy, since both are of minor and auxiliary significance in the production of that character-trait, which originates in the earlier, oral phase of libido-development. One example will suffice to illustrate the connection of envy with anal ideas of possession, and that is the frequent envy of his analyst on the part of the patient. He envies him the position of a 'superior', and continually compares himself with him. A patient once said that the distribution of the rôles in psycho-analysis was too unjust, for it was he who had to make all the sacrifices; he had to visit the physician, produce his associations, and to pay the money into the bargain. The same patient also had the habit of calculating the income of everyone he knew.

We have now come very close to one of the classical traits of the person with an anal character, namely, his special attitude to money, which is usually one of parsimony or avarice. Often as this characteristic has been confirmed in psycho-analytical literature, there are yet a number of features connected with it which have not received much notice, and which I shall therefore proceed to deal with.

There are cases in which the connection between intentional retention of fæces and systematic parsimony is perfectly clear. I may mention the example of a rich banker who again and again impressed on his children that they should retain the contents of the bowels as long as possible, in order to get the benefit of every bit of the expensive food they ate.

Some neurotics limit their parsimony or their avarice to certain kinds of expenditure, while in other respects they spend money with surprising liberality. There is a class of patient who avoids spending any money on 'passing' things. A concert, a journey, a visit to an exhibition, involves expense and nothing permanent is got in return. I knew a person who avoided going to the opera for this reason; nevertheless he bought piano scores of the operas which he had not heard, because in this way he obtained something 'lasting'. Some of these neurotics avoid spending money on food, because it is not retained as a permanent possession. It is significant that there is another type of patient who readily incurs expense for food in which he has an over-great interest. These are the neurotics who are always anxiously watching their bodies, testing their weight, etc. Their interest is concerned with the question of what remains of the material introduced into their body as a lasting possession. It is evident that they identify the content of the body with money.

In other cases we find that the neurotic carries his parsimony into every part of his life; and on certain points he goes to extremes without effecting any appreciable economy. I might mention an eccentric miser who used to go about in his house with the front of his trousers unbuttoned, in order that the button-holes should not wear out too quickly. It is easy to guess that in this instance other impulses were also operative. Nevertheless it is characteristic that these could be concealed behind the anal erotic tendency to save money, and that this motive should be so much emphasized. In some patients we find a parsimony in the special instance of using toilet paper. In this a dislike of soiling a clean thing co-operates as a determining factor.

The displacement of avarice from money or the value of money to time may be observed quite frequently. Time, it may be remembered, is likened to money in a familiar saying. Many neurotics are continually worrying over waste of time. It is only the time which they spend alone or at their work that seems to them well employed. Any disturbance in their work irritates them exceedingly. They hate inactivity, pleasures, etc. These are the people who tend to exhibit the 'Sunday neuroses' described by Ferenczi,[8] *i.e.* who cannot endure an interruption of their work. Just as every neurotically exaggerated purpose often fails to achieve its object, so is this the case here. The patients often save time on a small scale and waste it on a great one.

Such patients frequently undertake two occupations at once in order to save time. They like, for example, to learn, read, or accomplish other tasks during defæcation.[9] I have repeatedly come across people who in order to save time used to put on or take off their coat and waistcoat together, or on going to bed would leave their pants in their trousers in order to put on both garments in one movement in the morning. Examples of this kind could easily be multiplied.

The forms in which pleasure in possession can express itself are very numerous. The stamp-collector who deeply feels the gap in his set of stamps is not so far removed from the miser who, according to popular notion, counts and gloats over his gold pieces. But Jones' work concerning the impulse to collect is so informative that I can add nothing of importance to it.

On the other hand, it seems to me necessary to make a brief allusion to a phenomenon which is closely related to the subject's pleasure in looking at his own possessions. I refer to the pleasure in looking at one's own mental creations, letters, manuscripts, etc., or completed works of all kinds. The prototype of this tendency is looking at one's own fæces, which is an ever-new source of pleasure to many people, and is in some neurotics a form of psychical compulsion.

This fact of a libidinal over-emphasis of possession explains the difficulty our patients have in separating themselves from objects of all kinds, when these have neither practical use nor monetary value. Such people often collect all sorts of broken objects in the attics under the pretext that they might need them later. Then on some occasion or other they will get rid of the whole lot of rubbish at once. Their pleasure in having a mass of material stored up entirely corresponds to pleasure in the retention of fæces. We find in this case that the removal (evacuation) of the material is delayed as long as possible. The same persons collect bits of paper, old envelopes, worn-out pens and similar things, and cannot get rid of these possessions for long periods of time, and then at rare intervals they make a general clearance, which is likewise associated with pleasure. Among business men and clerks I have sometimes come across a particular tendency to preserve carefully quite soiled and torn blotting-paper. In the unconscious of these neurotics the spots of ink are equivalent to the stain of fæces. I might mention that I knew a senile and weak-minded woman with a strong regression of libido to the anal stage who used to put the toilet paper she had used in her pocket and carry it about with her.

The following peculiar habit of a woman who also exhibited unusually pronounced anal traits in other respects shows clearly that throwing away objects is equivalent in the unconscious to evacuating fæces. This woman was unable to throw away objects that had become useless. Nevertheless, she sometimes felt impelled to throw some object of this kind away, and so she had invented a method of tricking herself, as it were. She would go from her house into a neighbouring wood with the object to be removed—perhaps some old clothes—fixed to her back by one corner tucked under her apron-string. On her way through the wood she would 'lose' it and return home another way so that she should not catch sight of the 'lost' object. In order to give up possession of an object, therefore, she had to let it fall from the back part of her body.

People who do not like to get rid of worn-out objects do not as a rule readily take to new ones. They buy new clothes, but do not wear them; they 'keep' them for the future, and only take a real pleasure in them so long as they hang unused in the cupboard.

The disinclination to throw away worn-out or worthless objects frequently leads to a compulsive tendency to make use of even the most trifling thing. A rich man used to cut his empty match-boxes into small strips and give them to his servants to light the fires with. A similar tendency appears in women in the period of involution.

In many cases the person's interest in making use of remnants undergoes an incomplete kind of sublimation; as, for instance, when a neurotic has as his favourite day-dream the utilization of the refuse of a whole town, though no practical result of his reflections may appear. We shall deal later with day-dreams of this nature.

We find a tendency to extravagance less frequent than parsimony in our patients. In an observation communicated to the Berlin Psycho-Analytical Society, Simmel made the parallel between extravagance and neurotic diar-rhœa just as evident as that between avarice and constipation, which has long been clear to us. I can confirm the correctness of his view from my own experience, and indeed I drew attention some years ago to the fact that spending money can represent an equivalent for a longed-for but neurotically inhibited release of libido.[10] I might mention here the inclination some

women have to throw away money. It expresses hostility towards the husband, whose 'means'[11] are taken from him in this way; it concerns, therefore—if we leave out other determinants—an expression of the female
castration complex in the sense of a revenge on the man. We see here again
sadistic motives co-operating with those of anal-erotic origin.

We can quite understand, from their contradictory attitude towards defæcation, the meanness many neurotics show in saving small sums of money
while they will spend largely and generously from time to time. These
persons postpone emptying the bowels as long as possible—often giving
lack of time as a reason—and when they do go to the w.c. only evacuate a
small quantity of fæces. But every now and then they have an evacuation on
a grand scale.

We occasionally come across persons with pronounced anal character
whose libido has turned quite exclusively to the possession of money. A
patient told me that as a boy he did not play at battles with lead soldiers like
other children, but with pieces of money. He got people to give him copper
coins, and these represented ordinary soldiers. Nickel ones were non-commis-
sioned officers of various rank, and silver ones were officers. A silver five-
mark piece was the field-marshal. This officer was secured from all attack in
a special building 'behind the front'. One side took 'prisoners' from the other
in the battle and added them to its own army. In this manner one side
increased its possession of money until the other had nothing left. It is quite
obvious that the 'struggle' in the patient's unconscious was against his 'rich'
father. It is worth noting, however, that money entirely replaced human
beings. And indeed when this patient came to me for treatment he took no
personal interest in other people whatever; only the possession of money and
money values attracted him.

The conduct of our patients with regard to order and cleanliness is just as
contradictory as it is in spending money. This fact is so familiar to every
psycho-analyst that a general reference to it should not be necessary; but
certain particulars in this connection deserve special consideration.

Pleasure in indexing and classifying, in compiling lists and statistical
summaries, in drawing up programmes and regulating work by time-sheets,
is well known to be an expression of the anal character. This tendency is so
marked in many people that the fore-pleasure they get in working out a plan
is stronger than their gratification in its execution, so that they often leave it
undone. I have known a number of patients with a long-standing inhibition in
their work who would draw up a plan of work say every Sunday for the

coming week, and would then fail utterly to put it into practice. It is to be noted that they included not only undecided people but obstinate ones who in their self-opinionated way rejected the proved methods of others and wanted to act according to their own.

Many neurotics remain during life in a particular attitude of ambivalency towards order and cleanliness. There are people who are very well groomed as far as their exterior goes. But whereas their visible costume and linen is irreproachable, their underclothing and the covered parts of their body are exceedingly dirty.[12] These same people tend to preserve scrupulous order in their houses. On the writing table, for instance, every object will have its special place, and the books are placed with great care and regularity in the book-case where they are visible. In the drawers, however, complete disorder reigns, a disorder which is only corrected by a thorough clearance on rare occasions, and then only in a temporary way.

I might mention here that in the unconscious of these neurotics a disordered room, disarranged drawers, etc., represent the bowel filled with fæces. I have repeatedly had occasion to analyse dreams which allude to the bowel in this way. One of my patients brought me a dream in which he climbed up a ladder after his mother in order to get into a lumber-room in the attics. It was an incest-dream with an anal coitus-phantasy in which the anus was represented symbolically as a narrow ladder and the bowel as a lumber-room.

Character-traits connected with orderliness, as, for example, thoroughness and accuracy, are often closely associated with the opposite characteristic. These traits are particularly dealt with in Jones' investigations, and I need not go into them, but I may mention the craving for symmetry and 'fairness' which is often represented in the anal character.

Just as some neurotics count their steps in order to reach their destination with an even number of paces, so they tolerate no asymmetry in other matters. They arrange all their objects symmetrically. They divide everything with minute exactness. A husband will draw up calculations to show his wife that there is no equality between their respective expenditure on clothes, etc.; he will constantly be working out what the one has spent and what the other is therefore entitled to spend to make things even. During the food shortage in the Great War two unmarried brothers kept house together. When the rationed meat for both was put on the table they divided it by weighing each portion on a pair of letter scales. Both were anxious lest the other should go short or feel himself unfairly treated. The perpetual desire to be 'quits' with other people, *i.e.* to be under no obligation, however trifling, is also significant. That other people with pronounced anal character have a tendency to forget their debts (particularly when they are for small sums) may be taken as a symptom of unsublimated anal erotism.

Finally, a discovery of Jones must be discussed which he only mentions by the way, but which obviously is the condensed result of wide experience.

A most interesting result of anal erotism, he writes, 'is the tendency to be occupied with the reverse side of various things and situations. This may manifest itself in many different ways; in marked curiosity about the opposite or back side of objects and places—e.g. in the desire to live on the other side of a hill because it has its back turned to a given place; in the proneness to make numerous mistakes as to right and left, east and west; to reverse words and letters in writing; and so on.'

I could support Jones' view with numerous examples from my own experience. They are of far-reaching importance for understanding certain neurotic symptoms and character-traits. There is no doubt that the displacement of libido from the genital to the anal zone is the prototype of all these 'reversals'. In this connection the conduct of many people who are considered eccentric may be mentioned. Their nature is built up for the most part on anal character-traits. They tend to act in great and small things in a manner opposite to that of other people. They wear clothes that are as dissimilar as possible from the prevailing fashion. They work when others play. If they do work at which others sit, they stand. When others ride, they go on foot; or run while others walk. If people wear warm clothing, they do the opposite. The food they enjoy is opposed to the general taste. The connection between this and the familiar character-trait of obstinacy is unmistakable.

During my student days I knew a young man who was noticeable for his peculiar habits. He lived unsocially, resisted the fashion of the time in an ostentatious manner, and would not conform to the customs of the rest of the students. As I was having a mid-day meal with him one day in a restaurant I noticed that he took the menu in the reverse order, i.e. he commenced with the sweet and ended with the soup. Some years later I was asked by his relatives to see him professionally. I found that he had already developed definite paranoic delusions. If we bear in mind the great significance of anal erotism in the psycho-genesis of paranoia, a significance which Ferenczi has pointed out, we can understand this man's eccentric behaviour as an anal character-formation, and therefore as a precursor of paranoia.

Certain cases of neuroses in women, in which an unusually strong castration complex is expressed, reveal to us best the deeper meaning of such a tendency to reversal. We find in them that it springs from two main motives—

a displacement of libido from 'in front' to 'behind', and the wish for a change of sex. I hope to have something to say concerning this condition of mind in another connection.

I should like to conclude these remarks on anal character-traits with an observation the truth of which I should like others to test. This is that the anal character sometimes seems to stamp itself on the physiognomy of its possessor. It seems particularly to show itself in a morose expression. Persons who are deprived of normal genital gratification tend to surliness [13] as a rule. A constant tension of the line of the nostril together with a slight lifting of the upper lip seem to me significant facial characteristics of such people. In some cases this gives the impression that they are constantly sniffing at something. Probably this feature is traceable to their coprophilic pleasure in smell. In the case of a man who had this kind of facial expression I once remarked that he looked as though he were constantly smelling himself. Someone who knew him quite well said that he really did have the habit of smelling his hands and every object he picked up. I might add that he exhibited the typical anal character-traits in a pronounced form.

I do not claim to have dealt exhaustively with the subject of anal character-traits in this paper. On the contrary, I am conscious how little justice I have done to the richness and variety of the material. In reality I have had in view another object, namely, to increase our knowledge of the pregenital phases of the development of the libido by making some additions to the investigation of the anal character. As I have said at the beginning, this paper is intended to be followed by a study of the manic-depressive states, for the understanding of which a knowledge of the pregenital stages of development is essential.

NOTES

1. 'Anal-erotic Character Traits' (1918).
2. 'Analerotik und Analcharakter' (1910).
3. 'On the Ontogenesis of an Interest in Money' (1916).
4. 'Vom "mittlerem" Kinde' (1921).
5. [*Ed. note:* See Karl Abraham, "The Narcissistic Evaluation of Excretory Processes in Dreams and Neuroses," in *Selected Papers,* vol. 1 (New York: Brunner/Mazel, 1953), chap. 17.]
6. [*Ed. note:* See Karl Abraham, "A Particular Form of Neurotic Resistance against the Psycho-Analytic Method," in *Selected Papers,* vol. 1 (New York: Brunner/Mazel, 1953), chap. 15.]
7. The tendency to retain the fæces represents a special form of adherence to fore-pleasure, and seems to me to merit special consideration. I will only mention one

point concerning it in this place. Recently frequent attempts have been made to set up two opposite 'psychological types' and to bring all individuals into one or other category. We may recall in this connection Jung's 'extraverted' and 'introverted' types. The patient whom I mentioned above was undoubtedly turned in upon himself in the highest degree, but he gave up this attitude of hostility to objects more and more in the course of his analysis. This and many similar experiences go to prove that 'introversion' in Jung's sense is an infantile clinging to the pleasure in retention. We are therefore dealing with an attitude that can be acquired or given up, and not with a manifestation of a rigid psychological type.

8. 'Sunday Neurosis' (1919).

9. For these neurotics the w.c. is the true place of 'production', to which its solitude is an assistance. One patient who showed violent resistance against giving free associations during the analytic hours produced them at home in the w.c., and brought them ready made to the analysis.

10. [*Ed. note:* See Karl Abraham, "The Spending of Money in Anxiety States," in *Selected Papers,* vol. 1 (New York: Brunner/Mazel, 1953), chap. 14.]

11. [The German word *'Vermögen'* = 'means', 'wealth'; also = 'sexual capacity'. —*Trans.*]

12. There is a saying in Berlin regarding such people: *Oben hui, unten pfuil* ['On top all spry, below, oh fie!']. In Bavaria they say more coarsely, *Oben beglissen* [—'shining'], *unten beschissen* [—'beshat']. The contradictions in some people in this respect is a matter, therefore, of common knowledge.

13. Some, it is true, have at their command plentiful narcissistic sources of pleasure, and live in a state of smiling self-satisfaction.

5. Inhibitions, Symptoms, and Anxiety
Sigmund Freud

LET US TURN to the obsessional neuroses in the hope of learning more about the formation of symptoms. The symptoms belonging to this neurosis fall, in general, into two groups, each having an opposite trend. They are either prohibitions, precautions and expiations—that is, negative in character—or they are, on the contrary, substitutive satisfactions which often appear in symbolic disguise. The negative, defensive group of symptoms is the older of the two; but as illness is prolonged, the satisfactions, which scoff at all defensive measures, gain the upper hand. The symptom-formation scores a triumph if it succeeds in combining the prohibition with satisfaction so that what was originally a defensive command or prohibition acquires the significance of a satisfaction as well; and in order to achieve this end it will often make use of the most ingenious associative paths. Such an achievement demonstrates the tendency of the ego to synthesize, which we have already observed. In extreme cases the patient manages to make most of his symptoms acquire, in addition to their original meaning, a directly contrary one. This is a tribute to the power of ambivalence, which, for some unknown reason, plays such a large part in obsessional neuroses. In the crudest instance the symptom is diphasic:[1] an action which carries out a certain injunction is immediately succeeded by another action which stops or undoes the first one even if it does not go quite so far as to carry out its opposite.

Two impressions at once emerge from this brief survey of obsessional symptoms. The first is that a ceaseless struggle is being waged against the repressed, in which the repressing forces steadily lose ground; the second is that the ego and the super-ego have a specially large share in the formation of the symptoms.

Obsessional neurosis is unquestionably the most interesting and repaying subject of analytic research. But as a problem it has not yet been mastered. It must be confessed that, if we endeavour to penetrate more deeply into its

Reprinted by permission of Sigmund Freud Copyrights and W. W. Norton and Co., Inc., from *Inhibitions, Symptoms, and Anxiety* by Sigmund Freud, translated from the German by Alix Strachey, New York, 1959, pp. 112–22. Copyright © by The Institute of Psycho-Analysis.

nature, we still have to rely upon doubtful assumptions and unconfirmed suppositions. Obsessional neurosis originates, no doubt, in the same situation as hysteria, namely, the necessity of fending off the libidinal demands of the Oedipus complex. Indeed, every obsessional neurosis seems to have a substratum of hysterical symptoms that have been formed at a very early stage.[2] But it is subsequently shaped along quite different lines owing to a constitutional factor. The genital organization of the libido turns out to be feeble and insufficiently resistant, so that when the ego begins its defensive efforts the first thing it succeeds in doing is to throw back the genital organization (of the phallic phase), in whole or in part, to the earlier sadistic-anal level. This fact of regression is decisive for all that follows.

Another possibility has to be considered. Perhaps regression is the result not of a constitutional factor but of a time-factor. It may be that regression is rendered possible not because the genital organization of the libido is too feeble but because the opposition of the ego begins too early, while the sadistic phase is at its height. I am not prepared to express a definite opinion on this point, but I may say that analytic observation does not speak in favour of such an assumption. It shows rather that, by the time an obsessional neurosis is entered upon, the phallic stage has already been reached. More-over, the onset of this neurosis belongs to a later time of life than that of hysteria—to the second period of childhood, after the latency period has set in. In a woman patient whose case I was able to study and who was overtaken by this disorder at a very late date, it became clear that the determining cause of her regression and of the emergence of her obsessional neurosis was a real occurrence through which her genital life, which had up till then been intact, lost all its value.[3]

As regards the metapsychological explanation of regression, I am inclined to find it in a 'defusion of instinct', in a detachment of the erotic components which, with the onset of the genital stage, had joined the destructive cathexes belonging to the sadistic phase.[4]

In enforcing regression, the ego scores its first success in its defensive struggle against the demands of the libido. (In this connection it is of advantage to distinguish the more general notion of 'defence' from 'repression'. Repression is only one of the mechanisms which defence makes use of.) It is perhaps in obsessional cases more than in normal or hysterical ones that we can most clearly recognize that the motive force of defence is the castration complex and that what is being fended off are the trends of the Oedipus complex. We are at present dealing with the beginning of the latency period, a period which is characterized by the dissolution of the Oedipus complex, the creation or consolidation of the super-ego and the creation of ethical and aesthetic barriers in the ego. In obsessional neuroses these processes are carried further than is normal. In addition to the destruction of the Oedipus complex a regressive degradation of the libido takes place, the super-ego becomes exceptionally severe and unkind, and the ego, in obedience to the super-ego, produces strong reaction-formations in the shape of conscientiousness, pity and cleanliness. Implacable, though not always on that account successful, severity is shown in condemning the temptation to continue early infantile masturbation, which now attaches itself to regressive (sadistic-anal) ideas but which nevertheless represents the unsubjugated part of the phallic organization. There is an inherent contradiction about this state of affairs, in which, precisely in the interests of masculinity (that is to say, from fear of castration), every activity belonging to masculinity is stopped. But here, too, obsessional neurosis is only overdoing the normal method of getting rid of the Oedipus complex. We once more find here an illustration of the truth that every exaggeration contains the seed of its own undoing. For, under the guise of obsessional acts, the masturbation that has been suppressed approaches ever more closely to satisfaction.

The reaction-formations in the ego of the obsessional neurotic, which we recognize as exaggerations of normal character-formation, should be regarded, I think, as yet another mechanism of defence and placed alongside of regression and repression. They seem to be absent or very much weaker in hysteria. Looking back, we can now get an idea of what is peculiar to the defensive process in hysteria. It seems that in it the process is limited to repression alone. The ego turns away from the disagreeable instinctual impulse, leaves it to pursue its course in the unconscious, and takes no further part in its fortunes. This view cannot be absolutely correct, for we are acquainted with the case in which a hysterical symptom is at the same time a fulfilment of a penalty imposed by the super-ego; but it may describe a general characteristic of the behaviour of the ego in hysteria.

We can either simply accept it as a fact that in obsessional neurosis a super-ego of this severe kind emerges, or we can take the regression of the libido as the fundamental characteristic of the affection and attempt to relate the severity of the super-ego to it. And indeed the super-ego, originating as it does from the id, cannot dissociate itself from the regression and defusion of instinct which have taken place there. We cannot be surprised if it becomes harsher, unkinder and more tormenting than where development has been normal.

The chief task during the latency period seems to be the fending-off of the temptation to masturbate. This struggle produces a series of symptoms which appear in a typical fashion in the most different individuals and which in general have the character of a ceremonial. It is a great pity that no one has as yet collected them and systematically analysed them. Being the earliest products of the neurosis they should best be able to shed light on the mechanisms employed in its symptom-formation. They already exhibit the features which will emerge so disastrously if a serious illness follows. They tend to become attached to activities (which would later be carried out almost automatically) such as going to sleep, washing, dressing and walking about; and they tend also to repetition and waste of time. Why this should be so is at present not at all clear; but the sublimation of anal-crotic components plays an unmistakable part in it.

The advent of puberty opens a decisive chapter in the history of an obsessional neurosis. The genital organization which has been broken off in childhood starts again with great vigour. But, as we know, the sexual development in childhood determines what direction this new start at puberty will take. Not only will the early aggressive impulses be re-awakened; but a greater or lesser proportion of the new libidinal impulses—in bad cases the whole of them—will have to follow the course prescribed for them by regression and will emerge as aggressive and destructive tendencies. In consequence of the erotic trends being disguised in this way and owing to the powerful reaction-formations in the ego, the struggle against sexuality will henceforward be carried on under the banner of ethical principles. The ego will recoil with astonishment from promptings to cruelty and violence which enter consciousness from the id, and it has no notion that in them it is combating erotic wishes, including some to which it would not otherwise have taken exception. The overstrict super-ego insists all the more strongly on the suppression of sexuality, since this has assumed such repellent forms. Thus in obsessional neurosis the conflict is aggravated in two directions: the defensive forces become more intolerant and the forces that are to be fended off become more intolerable. Both effects are due to a single factor, namely, regression of the libido.

A good deal of what has been said may be objected to on the ground that the unpleasant obsessive ideas are themselves quite conscious. But there is no doubt that before becoming conscious they have been through the process of repression. In most of them the actual wording of the aggressive instinctual impulse is altogether unknown to the ego, and it requires a good deal of analytic work to make it conscious. What does penetrate into consciousness is usually only a distorted substitute which is either of a vague, dream-like and indeterminate nature or so travestied as to be unrecognizable. Even where repression has not encroached upon the content of the aggressive impulse it has certainly got rid of its accompanying affective character. As a result, the aggressiveness appears to the ego not to be an impulsion but, as the patients themselves say, merely a 'thought' which awakens no feeling.[5] But the remarkable thing is that this is not the case. What happens is that the affect left out when the obsessional idea is perceived appears in a different place. The super-ego behaves as though repression had not occurred and as though it knew the real wording and full affective character of the aggressive impulse, and it treats the ego accordingly. The ego which, on the one hand, knows that it is innocent is obliged, on the other hand, to be aware of a sense of guilt and to carry a responsibility which it cannot account for. This state of affairs is, however, not so puzzling as it would seem at first sight. The behaviour of the super-ego is perfectly intelligible, and the contradiction in the ego merely shows that it has shut out the id by means of repression while remaining fully accessible to the influence of the super-ego.[6] If it is asked why the ego does not also attempt to withdraw from the tormenting criticism of the super-ego, the answer is that it *does* manage to do so in a great number of instances. There are obsessional neuroses in which no sense of guilt whatever is present. In them, as far as can be seen, the ego has avoided becoming aware of it by instituting a fresh set of symptoms, penances or restrictions of a self-punishing kind. These symptoms, however, represent at the same time a satisfaction of masochistic impulses which, in their turn, have been reinforced by regression.

Obsessional neurosis presents such a vast multiplicity of phenomena that no efforts have yet succeeded in making a coherent synthesis of all its variations. All we can do is to pick out certain typical correlations; but there is always the risk that we may have overlooked other uniformities of a no less important kind.

I have already described the general tendency of symptom-formation in obsessional neurosis. It is to give ever greater room to substitutive satisfaction at the expense of frustration. Symptoms which once stood for a restriction of the ego come later on to represent satisfactions as well, thanks to the ego's inclination to synthesis, and it is quite clear that this second meaning gradually becomes the more important of the two. The result of this process, which approximates more and more to a complete failure of the original purpose of defence, is an extremely restricted ego which is reduced to seeking satisfaction in the symptoms. The displacement of the distribution of forces in favour of satisfaction may have the dreaded final outcome of paralysing the will of the ego, which in every decision it has to make is almost as strongly impelled from the one side as from the other. The over-acute conflict between id and super-ego which has dominated the illness from the very beginning may assume such extensive proportions that the ego, unable to carry out its office of mediator, can undertake nothing which is not drawn into the sphere of that conflict.

In the course of these struggles we come across two activities of the ego which form symptoms and which deserve special attention because they are obviously surrogates of repression and therefore well calculated to illustrate its purpose and technique. The fact that such auxiliary and substitutive techniques emerge may argue that true repression has met with difficulties in its functioning. If one considers how much more the ego is the scene of action of symptom-formation in obsessional neurosis than it is in hysteria and with what tenacity the ego clings to its relations to reality and to consciousness, employing all its intellectual faculties to that end—and indeed how the very process of thinking becomes hypercathected and erotized—then one may perhaps come to a better understanding of these variations of repression.

The two techniques I refer to are *undoing what has been done* and *isolating*.[7] The first of these has a wide range of application and goes back very far. It is, as it were, negative magic, and endeavours, by means of motor symbolism, to 'blow away' not merely the *consequences* of some event (or experience or impression) but the event itself. I choose the term 'blow away' advisedly, so as to remind the reader of the part played by this technique not only in neuroses but in magical acts, popular customs and religious ceremonies as well. In obsessional neurosis the technique of undoing what has been done is first me with in the 'diphasic' symptoms, in which one action is cancelled out by a second, so that it is as though neither action had taken place, whereas, in reality, both have. This aim of undoing is the second underlying motive of obsessional ceremonials, the first being to take precautions in order to prevent the occurrence or recurrence of some particular event. The difference between the two is easily seen: the precautionary measures are rational, while trying to get rid of something by 'making it not to have happened' is irrational and in the nature of magic. It is of course to be suspected that the latter is the earlier motive of the two and proceeds from the animistic attitude towards the environment. This endeavour to undo shades off into normal behaviour in the case in which a person decides to regard an event as not having happened.[8] But whereas he will take no direct steps against the event, and will simply pay no further attention to it or its consequences, the neurotic person will try to make the past itself non-existent. He will try to repress it by motor means. The same purpose may perhaps account for the obsession for *repeating* which is so frequently met with in this neurosis and the carrying out of which serves a number of contradictory intentions at once. When anything has not happened in the desired way it is undone by being repeated in a different way; and thereupon all the motives that exist for lingering over such repetitions come into play as well. As the neurosis proceeds, we often find that the endeavour to undo a traumatic experience is a motive of first-rate importance in the formation of symptoms. We thus unexpectedly discover a new, motor technique of defence, or (as we may say in this case with less inaccuracy) of repression.

The second of these techniques which we are setting out to describe for the first time, that of isolation, is peculiar to obsessional neurosis. It, too, takes place in the motor sphere. When something unpleasant has happened to the subject or when he himself has done something which has a significance for his neurosis, he interpolates an interval during which nothing further must happen—during which he must perceive nothing and do nothing.[9] This behaviour, which seems strange at first sight, is soon seen to have a relation to repression. We know that in hysteria it is possible to cause a traumatic experience to be overtaken by amnesia. In obsessional neurosis this can often not be achieved: the experience is not forgotten, but, instead, it is deprived of its affect, and its associative connections are suppressed or interrupted so that it remains as though isolated and is not reproduced in the ordinary processes of thought. The effect of this isolation is the same as the effect of repression with amnesia. This technique, then, is reproduced in the isolations of obsessional neurosis; and it is at the same time given motor reinforcement for magical purposes. The elements that are held apart in this way are precisely those which belong together associatively. The motor isolation is meant to ensure an interruption of the connection in thought. The normal phenomenon of concentration provides a pretext for this kind of neurotic procedure: what seems to us important in the way of an impression or a piece of work must not be interfered with by the simultaneous claims of any other mental processes or activities. But even a normal person uses concentration to keep away not only what is irrelevant or unimportant, but, above all, what is unsuitable because it is contradictory. He is most disturbed by those elements which once belonged together but which have been torn apart in the course of his development—as, for instance, by manifestations of the ambivalence of his father-complex in his relation to God, or by impulses attached to his excretory organs in his emotions of love. Thus, in the normal course of things, the ego has a great deal of isolating work to do in its function of directing the current of thought. And, as we know, we are obliged, in carrying out our analytic technique, to train it to relinquish that function for the time being, eminently justified as it usually is.

We have all found by experience that it is especially difficult for an obsessional neurotic to carry out the fundamental rule of psycho-analysis. His ego is more watchful and makes sharper isolations, probably because of the high degree of tension due to conflict that exists between his super-ego and his id. While he is engaged in thinking, his ego has to keep off too much—the intrusion of unconscious phantasies and the manifestation of ambivalent trends. It must not relax, but is constantly prepared for a struggle. It fortifies this compulsion to concentrate and to isolate by the help of the magical acts of isolation which, in the form of symptoms, grow to be so noticeable and to have so much practical importance for the patient, but which are, of course, useless in themselves and are in the nature of ceremonials.

But in thus endeavouring to prevent associations and connections of thought, the ego is obeying one of the oldest and most fundamental commands of obsessional neurosis, the taboo on touching. If we ask ourselves why the avoidance of touching, contact or contagion should play such a large part in this neurosis and should become the subject-matter of complicated systems, the answer is that touching and physical contact are the immediate aim of the aggressive as well as the loving object-cathexes.[10] Eros desires contact because it strives to make the ego and the loved object one, to abolish all spatial barriers between them. But destructiveness, too, which (before the invention of long-range weapons) could only take effect at close quarters, must presuppose physical contact, a coming to grips. To 'touch' a woman has become a euphemism for using her as a sexual object. Not to 'touch' one's genitals is the phrase employed for forbidding auto-erotic satisfaction. Since obsessional neurosis begins by persecuting erotic touching and then, after regression has taken place, goes on to persecute touching in the guise of aggressiveness, it follows that nothing is so strongly proscribed in that illness as touching nor so well suited to become the central point of a system of prohibitions. But isolating is removing the possibility of contact; it is a method of withdrawing a thing from being touched in any way. And when a neurotic isolates an impression or an activity by interpolating an interval, he is letting it be understood symbolically that he will not allow his thoughts about that impression or activity to come into associative contact with other thoughts.

NOTES

1. [I.e. occurs in two instalments. Cf. a passage near the end of Lecture XIX of the *Introductory Lectures* (1916–17).]

2. [See the beginning of Section II of Freud's second paper on 'The Neuro-Psychoses of Defence' (1896). An example occurs in the 'Wolf Man' analysis (1918), *Standard Ed.*, **17,** 75.]

3. See my paper on 'The Disposition to Obsessional Neurosis' (1913) [*Standard Ed.*, **12,** 319 f.].

4. [Towards the beginning of Chapter IV of *The Ego and the Id* (1923), Freud had suggested that the advance from the sadistic-anal to the genital phase is conditioned by an accession of erotic components.]

5. [For all of this, see the 'Rat Man' case history (1909), *Standard Ed.*, **10,** 221 ff. and 167 *n.*]

6. Cf. Theodor Reik, Geständniszwang und Strafbedürfnis (Leipzig, Vienna, and Zurich, 1925), 51.

7. [Both these techniques are referred to in the 'Rat Man' analysis (1909), *Standard Ed.*, **10,** 235–6 and 243. The first of them, in German *ungeschehenmachen'*, means literally 'making unhappened'.]

8. [In the original: 'as *"non arrivé"* '.]

9. [Cf. the 'Rat Man', 246.]

10. [Cf. several passages in the second essay in *Totem and Taboo* (1912–13), e.g. *Standard Ed.*, **13,** 27 ff. and 73.]

6. Obsessional Neurosis: A Summary of Psycho-Analytic Views as Presented at the Congress

Anna Freud

INTRODUCTION

Despite the help in summarizing given to me by my three colleagues, Drs K. T. Calder, P. G. Myerson and S. Ritvo, the task of surveying the Congress's views on obsessional neurosis remains a formidable one. Above all, it is not one which can be compressed into a short time and for this I ask the indulgence of an audience, already tired out by listening.

When selecting obsessional neurosis as the main topic of the Congress, the Programme Committee, knowingly or unknowingly, seems to have been guided by two sentences taken from Freud's 'Notes upon a Case of Obsessional Neurosis' (1909). One, that he was puzzled why it is so difficult to understand obsessional neurosis when, after all, the thought processes in it are so near to ours and the mysterious transition from mind to body, met with in hysteria, is not present. Second, that in this respect the concerted effort of a group of people may succeed where the single individual fails.

As regards the first point, some guidance has been offered to us already by one of the papers contributed to the Congress: namely that obsessional neurosis is hard to unravel not in spite of, but because of the pathology being located in the thought processes themselves, thereby attacking the patient's very means of communicating with us as well as our ability to identify with him and the aberrations of his logic and reasoning. As regards the second point, it is left to our interpretation whether what Freud had in mind was concentrated work on obsessional neurosis by many analysts individually, or the deliberate effort in group discussion and interchange of opinion, as we

Reprinted by permission of The Institute of Psycho-Analysis from *International Journal of Psycho-Analysis* 47 (1966): 116–22, by permission of International Universities Press from *Writings of Anna Freud*, vol. 5, *Research at the Hampstead Child Therapy Clinic and Other Papers 1956–1965* (1969), 116–23, and by permission of Mark Paterson and Associates.

have witnessed it during this Congress, an effort the result of which we are now encouraged to assess.

I. THE CONCEPT OF OBSESSIONAL NEUROSIS AS BROUGHT TO THE CONGRESS

I assume that all members of the Congress brought with them to Amsterdam their own definition of the structure of an obsessional neurosis and that they listened to the proceedings with the questions in mind how far this personal conception needed amendment, i.e. to be made more precise; to be extended on the basis of more clinical material; or to be adjusted to accommodate advances in factual knowledge and new theories.

Speaking, thus, as the average individual Congress member, I review in what follows my own picture of obsessional neurosis.

As regards its *range,* in consensus with general opinion, I have viewed it always as a specific kind of mental constellation, extending from the ego syntonic and near normal—during development, in character formation—to the status of an extremely severe neurotic disturbance, bordering occasionally on the schizoid and schizophrenic proper. While, at the former end of the series, the obsessional manifestations prove stabilizing for personality formation, at the extreme latter end they are devastatingly crippling and equally harmful for the internal equilibrium and the external adaptation of the individual.

As regards the *quality of the id content* warded off in obsessional neurosis, my case material never led me to doubt that these are the impulses of the pregenital (i.e., pre-phallic) anal-sadistic stage.

As regards the *ego devices* used for the purpose of warding off from consciousness, what I am familiar with are the following in varying combinations: denial, repression, regression, reaction formation, isolation, undoing, magical thinking, doubting, indecision, intellectualization, rationalization—altogether a formidable array, all of them, with the exception of regression, operating strictly within the area of the thought processes.

As regards the *external clinical picture,* I find this determined above all by the prominence of the reaction formations which provide the impression of stability and immutability; by the intensity of the counter-cathexes which provide the mental strain; and by the profusion of intellectualizations, i.e. the attempt to bind id energies through secondary process thinking. It is the last named factor which ties the occurrence of obsessional neuroses to a particular level of ego development before which other than obsessional solutions of conflict have to be resorted to.

That there is no obsessional neurosis in which reaction formations and intellectualization do not play a large part, helps me also to *differentiate* between obsessions proper and some other manifestations which appear similar on the surface and, for this reason are often confused with them. What I have in mind here are, for one, the repetitive tendencies as they are found in the very young, normally, and in mental defectives, abnormally; they are pre-ego mechanisms arising from the repetition compulsion and have nothing in common with obsession except their monotony. Secondly, what are often wrongly classified as obsessive are the urges which govern the behaviour of addicts, psychopaths, many delinquents, etc.; but, far from being compulsive, i.e. reactive, defensive, these are merely compelling, due to the full force of an id urge, not of an ego device behind them.

As to the *conditions which are favourable* for the formation of an obsessional neurosis, my views of them coincide with the ideas to be found in the analytic literature. There is the suggestion that obsessional defence sets in if the ego matures more quickly than the drives, i.e. in those instances where the anal-sadistic trends come to their height when ego and superego are too far advanced already to be able to tolerate them. There is the typical, and widely accepted, pre-condition also of obsessions arising where the individual regresses libidinally from the phallic to the anal-sadistic level while ego and superego retain their moral and aesthetic standards.

Obsessional outcomes are promoted also by a constitutional increase in the intensity of the anal-sadistic tendencies, or a constitutional preference for the use of defence mechanisms such as reaction formation, intellectualization, isolation etc. Both are found in the children of severely obsessional parents, probably as the result of inheritance combined with parental handling. Traumatic happenings during the anal phase, such as seductions or undue interference by excessively early and strict bowel training, also exert their influence in the same direction.

Finally, to cover all the facts known to us, any satisfactory conception of obsessional neurosis has to go beyond the aspect of intersystemic conflict between id, ego, and superego, and take into account the *intrasystemic contradictions* within the id such as they exist between love-hate, passivity-activity, femininity-masculinity. It is true, of course, that these are present in everybody as the ambivalence and bisexuality inherent in human nature. But, normally, ambivalence is taken care of by fusion between libido and aggression and bisexuality by the synthetic function which deals with opposing strivings as soon as they arise from the unconscious and approach the conscious surface of the mind. Both these functions seem to fail in individuals who are destined to become obsessional; or, to express it better, it is the failure of fusion and synthesis above all which determines the occurrence of an obsessional neurosis. Why this happens is an open question still, although some possible answers are hinted at in the literature: where excessive amounts of aggression are turned inwards against the self, the individual becomes torn within himself and develops a preference for inner strife as opposed to striving for inner harmony. This increases normal ambivalence, and ambivalent strivings are used for the purpose of perpetuating inner conflicts. For the obsessional it is, then, as natural to be at cross purposes with himself as he is invariably at cross purposes with his objects. Aggressive argumentation and hostile attitudes to the environment run parallel with the torturing relationships which exist between his inner agencies.

The *variations in the symptomatology* of the obsessional neurosis seem to me accounted for by the many elements which enter into its causation such as the prominence of either the sadistic or the anal tendencies in the id; the excessive use of any one or of several of the relevant defence mechanisms; the different rate of growth in id and ego; the prominence of either mother or father as the main target of the child's death wishes; the interaction between intersystemic and intrasystemic conflicts, etc. There are so many elements, and the possible combinations between them are so endless, that it needs not an analyst's but a mathematician's mind to calculate their number.

II. QUESTIONS BROUGHT TO THE CONGRESS

Doubtless, the average member of Congress also brought with him an array of open questions, hoping to find answers to them. As it emerged in the discussions, we seem to know more about obsessional neurosis as a completed mental structure and about its impact on character and personality than we know either of its pre-stages or of its future fate. Accordingly, the queries turned very noticeably in two directions: the past and the future of the obsessional neurosis.

As to the past: the question was raised repeatedly of *how early* we can detect the signs that a particular individual is predestined to develop an obsessional neurosis. Can it be seen in the *oral phase* already, or, at any rate, before anal-sadism has achieved phase dominance? If this can be done, in *which areas* of the infant's personality should we expect to find the clues? Will the success or failure of the *mother-infant* relationship be a decisive factor? Or is it the type and rate of *ego* development by which the issue is decided? In other words, is there a *recognisable matrix* within which the ground is prepared for obsessional development?

As to the future: is the adult obsessional neurosis *preceded* always by an infantile one? If not, which other type of neurotic disturbance is its most frequent *forerunner?* Or *vice versa:* is an infantile obsessional neurosis always *followed* by an adult one? If not, what is its further fate? Does experience point to it that an infantile obsessional neurosis can be *outgrown?* If not, what are the most frequent developments in later life, *neurotic* or *psychotic?*

In short, the whole 'natural history' of the obsessional neurosis, past, present and future, was brought into discussion during the Congress, at one time or another.

III. MATERIAL OFFERED TO THE CONGRESS

For the elucidation of the foregoing problems, we were offered two patients and, concerning them three case histories, namely the Rat Man, analysed by Freud, and Frankie treated first by Bornstein and subsequently by Ritvo, the latter presenting the 'Correlation of a Childhood and Adult Neurosis', the main theme of the Congress programme.

That one of the case histories under scrutiny concerned a child was profitable, of course, but also led to some complications. When discussing the diagnosis of Frankie's infantile disturbance and the change-over in his symptomatology from phobic to obsessional, the Congress, I feel, did not acknowledge sufficiently the difference between children and adults so far as diagnosis categorization is concerned. As expressed lately by some authors, the current psychiatric diagnoses do not fit our adult analytic patients. I should like to add that they fit our child cases even less and that the need for their reformulation is urgent to avoid misunderstandings as they occurred in discussing Frankie.

While the adult patient is a person in his own right, his self divided off from the object world and structured inwardly, and while his pathology is more or less static, nothing of this is true for the child. The younger he is, the more undifferentiated is his personality; his self, and later at least his super-ego, merges with the objects; his body merges with his mind, his affects with his intellect. His defence organization is incomplete and his pathology fluid, open to developmental alterations. While passing from one stage to another, he passes also through crises, upheavals, chaotic states for which transient solutions are adopted.

As regards Frankie's change from a predominantly phobic child into a predominantly obsessional adolescent, it did not seem profitable to me therefore that the Congress looked for reasons in the technical handling of the case and discussed the alternative of whether this was due either to drive regression (from phallic genital to anal) or to ego progression (from bodily to purely mental mechanisms). To me it seemed obvious that his symptomatology had to undergo changes since he was certainly not ill enough, and was also helped analytically enough, not to be at a standstill between the ages of 7 and 21. His object world had changed progressively, the mother being replaced by a young female. His drives had changed level, the genital dangers and concerns being added to the previous phallic ones. Since, according to the severity of his infantile disturbance, he remained in precarious mental balance, adult pathology was determined not by the child analyst's influence nor by an either-or of progression versus regression, but by a combination of his progressively intellectual defence organization with a regressive inability to tolerate and maintain genitality and object love. Much valuable Congress time was spent on the discussion.

For the rest, the material offered proved excellent as a clinical basis for much theoretical speculation. From this it seems possible to me to abstract some distinct topics and to outline some contributions made to them by the Congress.

IV. CONGRESS TOPICS

Topic 1: The Matrix of Obsessional Neurosis

To pursue every mental disorder back to its earliest indications in individual life is considered the duty of every analyst and, as such, has loomed large in many of the Congress papers.

In 1909, when Freud published his 'Notes Upon a Case of Obsessional Neurosis', it was a pioneering achievement to look behind the apparent pathogenic importance of recent events, such as the father's death, difficulties in love affairs, etc., and to unearth the upsetting events of the anal-sadistic stage as preceding them. Today, with much analytic interest concentrated on the first year of life, the anal period as the beginning of pathology seems disappointingly late to many authors. Hence, every attempt has been made to antedate the onset of obsessional neuroses.

In fact, almost every element of early infantile life was brought forward in this respect and, especially, the events within the early mother-infant relationship were named as relevant pathogenic factors. Weight was given to the consequences of the mother's failure to cathect the infant or the infant's failure to relate to her; to the mother's influence on normal body-mind interaction; her failure to act as comforter and protector against anxiety; her assistance or lack of it in the infant's task of joining up part objects and establishing whole object relationships; her role for determining the later difference between the neurotic and the schizoid type of obsessional neurotics, the former operating within the area of object love, the latter falling back on more primitive narcissistic positions. Equal weight was given by other authors to the experience of object loss and this particular factor was transposed back also and inserted into the history of the Rat Man via the early death of his beloved sister.

Important as all these points are in general, it must have struck many listeners, as it struck me, that here the Congress failed to distinguish adequately between the specific and the non-specific, since only some of the suggestions quoted represent elements of the first kind. Lack of a healthy earliest relationship to the mother has its consequences, certainly, for the infant's interest in and cathexis of the environment; leads to delayed or defective unfolding of many ego functions; damages the building up of a defence organization, of drive- and anxiety-control. But, and this seems to me a compelling argument, the resulting faulty personality development can serve equally well as basis for any other neurotic or psychotic disorder or disturbance of adaptation. If we want to restrict ourselves to those factors in the mother-child relationship which are truly specific for obsessional neurosis, then we are left with a few only, such as damage done to the synthetic function, to the capacity for fusion of love and hate, to the ability to maintain object love as contrasted with self-love. Also, where early object loss is concerned, we have to think in less global terms. Losing a love object in early life (through rejection, withdrawal, neglect, separation, death) is an experience which can initiate a variety of disturbances. What is significant for obsessional neurosis is not the event as such but the child's belief that it is the result of his own death wishes and the feelings of guilt attached to this interpretation.

We should take into account also that an excellent early relationship to the mother may promote rapid ego growth and instead of safeguarding the individual this may be instrumental in creating the very precocity of superego functions which we have met as one of the preconditions of obsessional neurosis.

Topic 2: The Instinctual Background of Obsessional Neurosis

Not all the contributors to the topic were ready to accept the classical view that it is the id content of the anal-sadistic phase which is warded off by means of the obsessional symptomatology; and some rival claims were raised, especially for the tendencies towards oral incorporation of the object and for voyeurism. There was even one attempt to disconnect obsessional neurosis altogether from any specific instinctual content and to consider its symptomatology instead as wholly determined by the ego mechanisms which are characteristic for it, whatever the nature of the warded-off material. What speaks against this opinion is the fact that in clinical work we always uncover anal-sadistic material when we undo defences such as reaction formations, isolation, undoing, i.e. the obsessional ones *par excellence,* while other id material is found to have been dealt with by other mechanisms and to produce different symptoms.

What I missed in this particular area of the discussion was a more detailed investigation into the events and trends of the anal-sadistic phase itself. Little was said about the distinction between anal passivity and anal aggression as the source of danger, although the difference between these two eventualities is decisive for the type of obsessional symptomatology which is produced. Neither was there mention of how difficult it is to decide in the analysis of an obsessional patient whether his excessive anal passivity is a direct instinctual expression or a reaction against his anal sadism, or, *vice versa,* whether his aggression is a direct id urge or reactively heightened to ward off passive fantasies. Another aspect hardly touched on was the economic one, i.e. the question of relative quantity in the instinctual endowment of obsessional individuals.

On the other hand, differences were brought out sharply and argued closely with regard to the role of drive regression. For all authors operating within the classical theory, the step backwards from the phallic-oedipal level to anal-sadism is a *sine qua non* for the formation of an obsessional neurosis. For many others this seems to be an expendable pathogenic factor.

Topic 3: A Possible Link between Matrix and Anal-Sadism

Personally, I could not help waiting for the mention of a specific factor which might bridge the gap between the relevance of the early mother-infant relationship and that of the later anal-sadistic stage. I had met with this in a case and wondered whether other analysts had had similar experiences.

In the instance I have in mind, a boy in his anal phase (2–3 years) exasperated his mother by being a persistent soiler. Resisting all her efforts to make him defaecate at the appointed time and place, he dirtied himself all over as soon as he was left on his own. This remained unexplained until, one day, he was overheard actually to talk to his excrement and call on it to come and keep him company. It emerged then that he had been exposed to traumatic separations from his mother in his first year, had suffered neglect from care-taking strangers, bewildering changes of environment, etc. and that, in the course of these events, his libido had withdrawn from the object world and turned to the body product, thereby producing this particular exacerbation of anal concerns.

Links of this kind between failure in object relations and heightened anality may be more common than we realize. If that should be the case, the repercussions for later defence against anality may be significant. However that may be, no instance of this type was mentioned at the Congress.

Topic 4: The Ego in Obsessional Neurosis

According to the trends of the time, the contributions to this topic were numerous and left few areas unexplored.

One innovation, brought more or less independently by a number of authors, was the notion of a general cognitive and perceptive style of the ego. This implies an extension of the concepts of defensive devices, defence mechanisms, defence organization, to include besides the ego's dealings with danger, anxiety, affects, etc., also its everyday functioning such as perceiving, thinking, abstracting, conceptualizing. An ego style, in this sense, is linked with the concept of defence but by no means identical with it. It represents an attempt to embrace the area of conflict as well as the conflict-free area of secondary process functioning.

The authors claim that some of these 'ego styles' are more relevant for the obsessional type of defence than others. Since they assume that ego styles are adopted fairly early in infantile life, and remain permanent, they conclude that detailed examination of ego functioning in this respect may enable the observer to predict the individual's later choice of neurosis.

With regard to early and transient obsessional symptomatology, stress was laid by some authors on its signal function for the ego's affect and energy control, as opposed to the later function of obsessional symptoms as static and limiting compromise formations.

No new defence mechanisms were added to those with which we are familiar.

Topic 5: Mutual Influences between Id and Ego in Obsessional Neurosis

Although the interactions between id and ego are central for the problem of obsessional neurosis, only two of the main topics are singled out here as having played a prominent part in individual papers and group discussions.

The relations between drive and defence.

Several possibilities were offered to the audience in this respect:

(a) that for warding off id content, the ego is limited to employing the mechanisms available to it according to its level of development. This is a chronological view according to which early instinctual trends are dealt with inevitably by the most primitive early defence mechanisms and drive and defence are interlinked according to the time of their emergence;

(b) that instinctual level and ego defence level do not always coincide owing to id and ego progressing occasionally at different speeds; that accordingly, for example, obsessional defences may appear in the ego before the individual has reached the anal phase;

(c) that every instinctual trend evokes a defence mechanism specific to it, and that defences change for developmental reasons in conformity with changes of the id content;

(d) that, at an early date, under the influence of the id, the ego develops a style which from then onward remains permanent, irrespective of developmental changes.

It must have been obvious to the audience that some of these theoretical suggestions are incompatible with each other and that a choice will have to be made between them on the basis of further clinical observations.

The relations between drive regression and ego regression in the
obsessional neurosis.

By those authors who regard regression as an indispensable element in the
build up of an obsessional neurosis, a number of valuable suggestions,
amendments and additions to existing theory were brought forward such as
the following:

(a) that the term regression with regard to its occurrence in the obsessional
    neurosis should not be used in a global way, but that careful distinction
    should be made between regression on the instinctual side and on the
    ego side, including the interactions between them;
(b) that if drive regression is followed by ego regression, distinction
    should be made between structural regression (i.e. lowering of stan-
    dards, demands, etc.) and functional regression (i.e. return to magical,
    wishful, primary process thinking, lessening of reality testing, of the
    synthetic function, etc.);
(c) that regression in id or ego should be considered from the aspects of
    depth, spread, irreversibility, etc.

Topic 6: Obsessional Neurosis versus Phobic

Based on the case of Frankie, great interest was expressed in the change of
pathology from a phobic to a predominantly obsessional illness. The phenomenon was discussed from a number of angles, such as the following:

(a) as a step of defence by motor action and body language to defence
    by thought manipulation, possibly representing an advance in ego
    maturation;
(b) as a general phenomenon within the body-mind problem: while in
    hysteria the body behaves as if on its own, the mind does the same in
    obsessional neurosis;
(c) from the aspect of counter-cathexis: while in a phobia, representation
    of danger may be compressed successfully into a single material
    object, locus, etc., which is then avoided, obsessional symptoms have
    the tendency to spread and a greater and more constant expenditure of
    counter-cathexis is needed to hold them in check;
(d) from the aspect of analytic therapy: during the analysis of adult obses-
    sionals, earlier phobic states re-appear slowly, which is a favourable

prognostic sign. In child analysis on the other hand, where obsessional defence may dissolve quickly, uncontrolled impulsive behaviour appears instead, a difference which is unexplained so far.

Topic 7: Attempts at Avoiding Obsessional Pathology

During the discussion of the Frankie case, certain elements were mentioned as part of his obsessional neurosis which, I believe, permit a different classification.

His 'couldn't care less' attitude, his depersonalization of the analyst, his insolence in the transference are, to my mind, items of pathological behaviour aimed at playing down his own feelings as well as devaluating the object world. They are on a par with the 'computer ideal' of some individuals, i.e. the conception of themselves as a mind without body, or an intellect without feelings. Such attitudes are defensive, not in the sense of warding off or immobilizing a particular instinctual trend, but more generally in the sense of trying to do away with sources of danger altogether. Where they are successful, the need for further defence activity is eliminated at the expense of a character or behaviour change, and no obsessional neurosis proper is organized.

The well-known sexualization and consequent play with anxiety serves the same purpose. If a potential danger situation is turned into a source of masochistic pleasure, no further symptom formation is necessary.

Topic 8: Beneficial and Harmful Effects, Successes, Failures, and Limits of Obsessional Neurosis

It remains to summarize the opinions expressed concerning the impact of obsessional development on personality growth, on character formation and, more generally, on the maintenance or loss of mental equilibrium.

Repeated mention was made of the *beneficial* aspect of the defences characteristic for obsessional neurosis, namely of their serving as safeguards against impulsive behaviour, delinquency, or schizophrenic breakdown, in short of their stabilizing effect. Under the same heading, obsessional symptomatology was described as halting regression from proceeding below the anal phase, and preventing thereby further spread of pathology.

In connexion with the Rat Man and Frankie their *harmful* effect on ego activity and the distorting effect on the personality as a whole were discussed.

Frankie was used also as an example to demonstrate the partial *failure* of obsessional defence, his doubts about his intellectual capacity being regarded as a return of the repressed castration fantasies, as well as, in general, the return of the warded off self-awareness of defect. Similar doubts of obsessional patients about their own intactness whether intellectual, emotional, aesthetic or moral, are well known and, I believe, indicate always that the obsessional symptoms have failed, partially at least, to accomplish their objective.

Finally, the *limits* of obsessional neurosis were outlined clearly. As shown in Frankie's case, death wishes against love objects, fantasies of drowning in a sea of defaecation, passive feminine trends, etc., are held in check successfully by denial, repression, reaction formation, intellectualization, etc., in short by an obsessional neurosis. On the other hand, tendencies towards merging with the object, primary identification, loss of personal identity are beyond the scope of the obsessional devices. Since they demand stronger measures such as splitting of the ego, projection, etc., they expose the patient to the danger of paranoid or perverse solutions.

CONCLUSION

The Programme Committee's endeavour to crystallize the interest of Congress members around a main topic seems successful on the whole. To say the least, it has presented us with a vivid picture of analytic problem-solving, with its painstaking back and forth between observation of clinical data, abstraction and generalization, and reapplication of theoretical thinking to the further elucidation of our patients' material.

7. Psychoanalytically Oriented Short-Term Dynamic or Anxiety-Provoking Psychotherapy for Mild Obsessional Neuroses

Peter E. Sifneos

OBSESSIVE-COMPULSIVE NEUROTICS are traditionally considered difficult to treat. Some severe cases have been treated by psychoanalysis with good results, others have failed to respond to any type of psychotherapy. There are, however, patients who suffer from mild obsessional-compulsive neuroses of sudden onset who not only respond well to psychoanalytically oriented, short-term, dynamic, or anxiety-provoking, psychotherapy, but also, in follow-up interviews, seem to have maintained their improvement.

In the psychoanalytic literature there is a consensus that, because of predispositions from childhood, the regression from the phallic-Oedipal situation to the anal-sadistic level of the personality organization is the main pattern encountered in obsessive-compulsive neurotics, and it is because of this that they are more difficult to treat than patients with anxiety hysteria. Severe obsessional neurotics have usually been suffering from incapacitating symptoms for a long time, yet they continue to postpone consulting a psychiatrist or analyst. They are superstitious and narcissistic individuals, with a tendency to distort their thought processes as dreams are distorted, and to use omnipotent and magical thinking. They evidence a punitive super-ego. They are persons whose whole relationships with other people are colored by a most marked ambivalence between love and hate, which leads to a "partial paralysis of will, an incapacity to come to any decision," and a strong "compulsion of doubt."[3] The use of regression, reaction formation, avoidance, undoing, and isolation as defenses is prevalent, with a resulting lack of affect. These well-known characteristics of the obsessional neurotics are, to an extreme degree, formidable barriers even to psychoanalytic treatment.

Reprinted by permission of Human Sciences Press, Inc., from *Psychiatric Quarterly* 40 (1966): 271–82.

As with any other condition, however, there are degrees of neurotic involvement. The questions, therefore, that must be raised are: How serious are these various characteristics in each individual patient? How serious is the childhood predisposition, the early fixation, the ambivalence, and, above all, the regression?

In a psychiatric clinic population one encounters patients whose adult interpersonal relations are colored by Oedipal conflicts and who may regress temporarily to pre-Oedipal conflicts and who may regress temporarily to pre-Oedipal states of organization, to avoid the anxieties they are faced with. These are persons who have made good psychological adjustments to life up to the regression point but, faced with hazardous environmental situations—such as a recent engagement, a sexual relationship, marriage, or separation from a loved one—have developed anxiety. A precipitating environmental factor—a fight with another man, the admission to a husband by his wife that she had had premarital sexual relations, or criticism from a person in authority, such as a supervisor at work—intensifies anxiety, and these persons find themselves in a state of "emotional crisis"[9] which is defined here as a "painful state requiring alleviation or solution for better or for worse." At this point they seem to utilize all sorts of inappropriate defense mechanisms to overcome their painful crises, but they are unsuccessful. Sooner or later these inappropriate defenses lead, in turn, to the formation of psychiatric symptoms. Regression, reaction formation, isolation, and undoing are used at times by some of these patients, and the resulting symptoms are unmistakably obsessive-compulsive in nature.

One is struck, however, by a general state of "fluidity" that seems to be generally apparent. The defensive pattern is unmistakably present, but it does not seem to have solidified along rigid lines; the neurosis does not appear to be crystallized into the patterns of the classic chronic obsessional neurotic illness. Anxiety seems to be present more often than one would expect, and it gives rise to considerable suffering which, in turn, motivates these patients to seek help early in order to try to get rid of the disturbing and ego-alien symptoms. Presented with such a picture, one cannot fail to see not only the danger of the development of a chronic obsessive-compulsive neurosis, but also the potential of a therapeutic intervention, with a good promise of possible reversal of the whole state of affairs.

It could be argued, of course, that what is described is not an obsessive-compulsive neurotic patient at all. Yet, unless one wants to confine the term obsessive-compulsive to describe only the severe long-standing conditions, the difference dynamically is in a matter of degree alone.

It is obvious, therefore, that the assessment of the basic nature of the original childhood neurosis is of prognostic importance in differentiating between these two groups of patients. In an effort, therefore, to evaluate clinic patients specific criteria have been used for selecting individuals to receive short-term dynamic psychotherapy. Some of these happened to be mildly obsessive-compulsive, yet they were accepted for treatment rather than being referred for psychoanalysis. These patients were seen in the Psychiatry Clinic of the Massachusetts General Hospital.

The following are the criteria used: (1) an acute onset of obsessive-compulsive symptoms in a fairly well-adjusted patient facing an emotional crisis; (2) a general fluidity of the defenses utilized, with evidence of anxiety and suffering; (3) a good motivation for help; (4) intelligence above average; (5) a history of at least one meaningful relation with another person and ability to interact well with the evaluating psychiatrist and express some affect during his interview.[1]

Here is an example: A 21-year-old woman student came to the clinic because of anxiety from indecision about two conflicting wishes—to enter a convent and to marry her boyfriend. "I am in an emotionally critical period of my development where a false move could ruin my life," she said. She associated her symptoms with difficulties with her religious father (whom she admired and feared) which began as far back as she could remember. She said that the onset of this paralyzing indecision had lasted for six weeks, after she had been told by her mother that she should officially announce her engagement to her boyfriend. Following the announcement, she was frightened every time her boyfriend came to visit her, and after each visit she would pray to her favorite saint for forgiveness. Unable to sleep at night, she would be preoccupied with the constant thought that if she were to be married, she would be "damned forever," and it was at those times that she would experience the need to enter the convent. On other occasions after seeing her fiance, she felt unworthy and dirty. She became anxious; but she realized how nonsensical these thoughts were; and she emphasized how completely immobilized she had felt by her "inability to think straight." She described this feeling at length as "her constant torment." When her father talked to her about the religious aspects of the wedding ceremony, she felt anxious but, nevertheless, went to consult a priest about the situation. The priest told her to be married to her boyfriend as soon as possible. As a result, she felt panicky and grew very angry at the priest. Her indecision became more acute, and she was unable to sleep that night. The interview turned out to be the precipitating factor that brought her to the hospital, for it was following this that she reluctantly decided to consult a psychiatrist and came self-referred to the psychiatric clinic for assistance. She was an intelligent young woman who appeared to be anxious. She related reasonably well and was able to give her history clearly; but she asked for reassurance as to whether psychotherapy would help.

Another patient, a 24-year-old graduate student from a nearby university, came to the psychiatric clinic complaining of inability to decide whether he should enroll for a Ph.D. degree or enter his father's business in New York. He went to New York five times in one month, but felt unable to make up his mind. The last time he made the trip his mother recommended that he see a psychiatrist, and following this he became anxious. He noticed that his hands were unusually dry, and had the urge to wash them repeatedly. This compulsion persisted and made him unable to work. Upon his return to Boston he came to the clinic for help.

A 35-year-old man, after he found out casually in the sixth year of his marriage that his wife had had premarital sexual relations with another man, came to the clinic complaining of the sudden onset of obsessive thoughts of wanting to kill his wife which were countered by a wish to kill himself. He missed work on several occasions, and his wife became very angry with him.

The complaints and symptoms presented by these patients were severely incapacitating to them and radiated distress to the close members of their families.

Patients meeting the criteria already enumerated then had special goal-setting interviews with the director of the clinic, during which final attempts were made to assess motivation for psychotherapy by asking questions regarding their expectations of the results of the short-term therapy.

The aim of short-term dynamic psychotherapy is to be anxiety-provoking and to focus in a specific area of emotional conflict underlying the patient's symptoms. By accomplishing this it helps the patient understand the defense mechanisms that he uses to handle his anxiety, and teaches him new ways of dealing with it.[1, 2]

THE TECHNIQUE OF SHORT-TERM DYNAMIC OR ANXIETY-PROVOKING PSYCHOTHERAPY FOR MILD OBSESSIONAL NEUROTICS

1. Early Utilization of the Positive Transference

As mentioned, the ability of these patients to relate to the interviewer in their evaluation interviews was considered an important prognostic guide as to their ability to develop a positive transference during their psychotherapy. At this point one should attempt to distinguish between the terms "transference" and "transference neurosis." Freud[3] says that "the transference occurs outside of the analysis," and adds that "if someone's need for love is not entirely satisfied by the reality, he is bound to approach every new person whom he meets with libidinal anticipatory ideas." Glover[4] also thinks of it as "a normal affective phenomenon governed by unconscious mechanisms of displacement and promoting social adaptation." Transference is defined as "an emotional interaction between two people, having both conscious and unconscious aspects."[1]

"Transference neurosis," on the other hand, is defined as "the transfer of all conscious and unconscious fantasies, emotions, attitudes of people in the past onto the therapist during the psychoanalytic treatment."[1] Glover[4] puts it as follows: "Everything that takes place during the analytic session, every thought, action, gesture with reference to the external thought and action, every inhibition or thought or action relates to the transference situation between the patient and his analyst." The difference between the two terms is only a matter of degree, but it is helpful to keep them apart for practical reasons as far as the technique of the psychotherapeutic process is concerned.

The early transference, of course, varies with each individual, and the therapist must deal with it as it appears in each case. More or less, however, the nature of the transference of our obsessional patients is ambivalent to a certain extent, but the positive features predominate early in the treatment and the therapist capitalizes on this to establish a therapeutic alliance and uses it as the main tool of psychotherapy. For example, as soon as the first evidence of resistance may appear—and it usually does appear very early, even in the third or fourth interview—it is taken up by the therapist. He focuses on this by emphasizing that positive feelings seemed to prevail up to that particular time and contrasts them with the sudden appearance of resistance. The therapist also helps the patient become aware very early that his feelings for the therapist are duplications of his feelings toward people in the past. What F. Deutsch[5] calls "the correct use of the doctor-patient relationship" has, in the author's opinion, a great deal to do with the correct use of these early manifestations of the patient's positive transference as contrasted with the early appearance of resistances.

2. Concentration in Areas of Unresolved Conflicts

The second technical point of short-term dynamic psychotherapy involves concentration in the area of understanding the defenses used to avoid the anxiety which is related to the unresolved Oedipal conflict and underlies the obsessional symptoms which represent a regressive compromise. The therapist attempts to demonstrate this pattern repeatedly to the patient, even if this tends to make the patient more anxious. He uses as often as possible clear-cut examples arising from the transference relationship, and at times preferably quotes verbatim from the patient's interview material. Thus, the therapist helps the patient to re-examine the pattern of his Oedipal conflicts. He helps him to understand his regression and to realize that the problems in his present-day interpersonal relations are related to these past neurotic difficulties.

3. Active Avoidance of Characterological Complication

"The optimal level of positive feeling in the patient which is conducive for effective psychotherapeutic work," as Knight[6] puts it, "and maintains the proper emotional distance between patient and therapist," can be achieved, in the author's opinion, only if the psychiatrist actively avoids deep-seated characterological problems. This active intervention on the part of the therapist is an important technical point of short-term psychotherapy. It tends to delay the appearance of the transference neurosis, which, if "allowed to reach great intensity," can "impair the therapy," as Alexander[7] claims. When, for example, the patient, in order to avoid talking about his antagonistic and competitive feelings for authority figures, starts to bring up longings and wishes to be taken care of by women, the therapist, rather than listening at length, may point out that he is avoiding his competitive and aggressive feelings for male figures. This again tends to make the patient more anxious.

4. Avoidance of the Development of a Transference Neurosis

The most important technical feature of short-term psychotherapy has to do with taking advantage of the time lag in the appearance of the transference neurosis.[2] As time goes by, the therapy will be colored more and more by the appearance of the transference neurosis which the patient will invariably develop in one form or another; but the delay of its appearance is evidence of the patient's strength of character and ability to test reality. On a once-a-week face-to-face interview, a therapist does not have access to all the patient's unconscious fantasies, and he cannot analyze the transference neurosis as one does in psychoanalysis; thus, theoretically and technically, the psychotherapy may end in an impasse. Time is of the essence, therefore, and it is crucial, then, to know when to stop.[1,2]

5. Repeated Demonstration of Ambivalence

The repeated demonstration of the ambivalent nature of the transference situations and the constant emphasis that the patient's difficulties in his interpersonal relations are the result of his attitudes stemming from Oedipal situations, seem finally to lead to changes in the patient's attitudes. A general "loosening up" seems to take place. At these times the patient may make such remarks as, "Where do we go from here?" or, "I feel better," or "I understand myself more." Although this may signify some resistance, usually it is evidence that some new learning has taken place. This is what the author assumes Alexander[7] means by "interpretative learning" and Freud by "the process of re-education." Sooner or later there are signs of striking improvement in the patient's relationship to people around him and in his ability to work. The time, then, has come when therapy must stop.

6. Early Termination of Treatment

The therapist's attitude about early termination is also of crucial importance.[1] At times, due to his own intellectual curiosity about the eventual outcome or because of his idea that the patient would not be able to function without him, his counter-transference is prejudiced against termination. Young residents who want to be amateur psychoanalysts are inclined to prolong the psychotherapy. Some analysts, having abandoned psychotherapy long ago, tend to think of it as being of little use. As supervisors of residents, they are likely to encourage the prolongation of the treatment. Many a patient who shows evidence of early improvement is treated for years without further progress being achieved. Glover[4] gives an example of an obsessive patient who improved after being treated for only a few months. In a casual accidental follow-up 30 years later, the improvement had been maintained with no evidence of any returning symptoms. Fenichel[8] also emphasizes that some patients with obsessive-compulsive symptoms of short duration can improve rapidly. This is indeed the case from the present findings. What is striking is that their improvement is still in evidence long after the termination of treatment.

The following case report illustrates briefly some of the technical points already discussed. A 32-year-old man, while on his honeymoon, developed a sudden onset of acute obsessive-compulsive symptoms consisting of a need to pick up papers or pieces of metal from the floor or from the street. He had the urge to make sure he had had picked up everything and to know that everything was clean. He was also tormented by the preoccupying thought that he might have been in some way responsible for his father's death, although he realized the absurdity of such thoughts. He was intelligent, related very well, had a good work history and fairly good relations with other people. He responded well during the evaluation interview, and was eager for help because his symptoms interfered with his marriage and his work. His father had died six months before the treatment was started. He said that although he cried during his father's funeral, he had noticed on other similar occasions an inappropriate tendency to laugh. Soon after his father's death he met a young woman, fell in love with her, and, after a courtship of four months which involved satisfactory sexual relations, they decided to be married. While on their honeymoon, his wife received a wedding present. She hurriedly opened the package, and in her delight at its contents, she forgot to gather up the wrappings that were strewn all over the floor of the hotel room. When the patient saw them he meticulously started to pick them up and experienced a feeling of intense anger as he did so.

He always came early for his interviews, related well to his therapist, and made a genuine effort to understand himself. At the fourth interview, he arrived ten minutes late and was silent when the therapist pointed it out. After a moment, he turned to him angrily and said, "You're blaming me for being late." The therapist emphasized that that was not his intention, at which the patient apologized, was silent for a while, and then said that an entirely irrelevant episode from his childhood had crossed his mind. He was encouraged to talk about it, and as he reminisced he said that when he was 12 years old he liked to go fishing with his father. On one occasion he dropped his fishing rod accidentally and as he tried to retrieve it he almost overturned the boat. His father was very angry at him and said, "You are always so careful. How can you be so careless now? I could have drowned!" He said he remembered being angry at that time and that this irrelevant thought had entered his mind: "How can my dad be so sloppy and leave his desk in such a mess!" He again became silent. When asked what he was thinking he said he had noticed several sheets of paper lying on the psychiatrist's desk. Upon being asked what this reminded him of, he answered, "Dad did not give up. He called me to his study and kept on lecturing to me about safety. I didn't care. The only thing I could think about was the sheets of paper strewn all over his desk," and then, with a smile, he added, "You have a cute secretary."

At the next interview the patient was 15 minutes late. He said that his compulsive symptom had been very bothersome for the whole week. He then announced that he had an irrelevant urge to take the wastepaper basket and strew its contents all over the doctor's desk. At this point he became visibly anxious, his hands started to shake, and he associated that this thought was in a way connected with the fear that he was somehow responsible for his father's death. As the therapist drew a parallel between his attitude toward him and his attitude toward his father, the patient admitted having the fantasy that he wished the therapist would drop dead suddenly. "Then I can sleep with your secretary," he added. The patient was on time for the next appointment, and related the following dream: He had gone hunting with a girlfriend when, suddenly, a huge ostrich appeared and started chasing him. Although he wanted to kill the bird to impress his girlfriend, he was unable to do so because his gun "would not fire." He woke up feeling somewhat relieved. When asked about his association to the dream, he remembered that when he was six years old he tried to peek at his older sister while she was taking a shower and felt vaguely that this was a wrong thing to do. Later on during the interview he remembered his father returning from fishing. He had caught several fish and they were all lying on the kitchen table. What had impressed him most was a rainbow trout that appeared to have been decapitated accidentally. He shuddered at the idea and was visibly shaken. In the next few interviews he talked a great deal about his relations with women. He loved to give parties, and women were very much attracted to him, but he had a tendency to disregard his own date and flirt with his best friend's girl. He said that his mother always liked to give dinner parties when his father was on fishing trips. His father disapproved of this. For those dinner parties, he remembered, his sister always dressed seductively. He remembered having dreams of being married to his sister, but always woke up feeling very anxious because a dark figure would invariably threaten him. He also noted that his wife looked very much like his sister.

The psychodynamics of this case are obvious. The therapist brought together repeatedly the attitude of the patient toward his father and the therapist, and his associations with the fishing episode, the decapitated rainbow trout, his father's death, and his anger at the therapist and his wish that he would drop dead. His attitude toward his sister, his marriage after his father's death, and his wishes for the psychiatrist's secretary were also linked together. As a result of the interviews, the patient's symptoms improved dramatically and soon disappeared. Therapy was discontinued after the sixteenth interview. Three years later he was asymptomatic.

The author has reported in two other papers the results of short-term dynamic psychotherapy.[1,2] Although the symptomatic relief is not the most outstanding finding, the patients' attitudes toward their symptoms seem to have changed and they are no longer bothered by them as much as they were before. In addition, there is considerable improvement of their self-esteem, and evidence that a "new learning experience" has taken place. The patient who had the obsessive fear of wanting to kill his wife put it as follows: "I discovered something new. I hadn't been satisfied because I couldn't find the right answers for what happened around me. Now, in my treatment, I learn to look into the past to find out where these urges of mine originate. It was difficult at first, but I got used to it; and now, although at times the thought that I might kill my wife still crosses my mind, I am not bothered by it. Some of my nervousness still exists, but it is nothing in comparison with the past. I found a better way to figure things out for myself."

Although no basic characterological changes seem to occur, there is some evidence that dynamic changes have taken place. In follow-up interviews the patients have overcome their emotional crises and show new adaptive and new learning patterns. They are able to figure out their emotional difficulties even after termination of treatment. Thus, although their symptoms may not be entirely eliminated, these patients can work, contribute more, and relate better to people around them. In sum, they are happier human beings.

SUMMARY

Patients who, unable to overcome emotional crises,[9] became anxious and developed mild obsessive-compulsive neuroses of sudden onset were treated by psychoanalytic psychotherapy of short duration. In this paper, criteria for selection of such patients from a psychiatric clinic population are listed. The technique of short-term dynamic psychotherapy or anxiety-provoking treatment, is described. Special emphasis is placed on the utilization of the positive transference, the avoidance of a transference neurosis, and early termination of treatment. Brief case reports are presented. In the follow-up interviews, although no basic characterological changes have been achieved, there is evidence of new learning and over-all improvement.

REFERENCES

1. *Sifneos, P. E.: Dynamic psychotherapy in a psychiatric clinic. In:* Current Psychiatric Therapies. *J. Masserman, editor. Grune & Stratton. New York. 1961.*

2. ———: *Seven years experience with short-term dynamic psychotherapy. In:* Proceedings of the Sixth International Congress of Psychotherapy, *London, England. August 1964. Selected Lectures, pp. 127–135. S. Karger. Basel. 1965.*
3. *Freud, S.: The dynamics of transference. On transference love, On beginning treatment. In:* The Complete Psychological Works of Sigmund Freud. *Vol. XII. Hogarth. London. 1958.*
4. *Glover, E.:* The Technique of Psychoanalysis. *International Universities Press. New York. 1955.*
5. *Deutsch, F., and Murphy, W.:* The Clinical Interview. *Vol. I. International Universities Press. New York. 1954.*
6. *Knight, R., and Friedman, C.:* Psychoanalytic Psychiatry and Psychology. *International Universities Press. New York. 1954.*
7. *Alexander, F., and French, T.:* Psychoanalytic Psychotherapy. *Norton. New York. 1945.*
8. *Fenichel, O.:* Psychoanalytic Theory of Neurosis. *Norton. New York. 1945.*
9. *Sifneos, P. E.: A concept of emotional crisis.* Ment. Hyg., *44: 2, April 1960.*

8. Therapy of the Obsessive Personality

Leonard Salzman

THE PROBLEMS implicit in the therapy of obsessional states all derive from their characteristic defenses which in most regards are antithetical to the therapeutic task. These defensive tactics are such that they militate against the very essence and requirements of the therapeutic process. The psychotherapy of emotional disorders, as initiated and expanded by the work of Sigmund Freud and the schools of psychoanalytic psychodynamic therapies that followed, requires basic agreements with the patient in order for the process to proceed. Many of these requirements are inimical to the obsessional defensive structure—which tends, therefore, to make the process of therapy difficult, arduous, tedious, and sometimes unrewarding. On the other hand, the intricacies and extraordinary variety of tactics that characterize the human brain are all played out in this disorder, and it is a fascinating and rewarding encounter if one is willing to be free, flexible, and open to the intricacies of these maneuvers, in order to effectively counter them. Consequently, treatment of the obsessional is a difficult but rewarding endeavor.

The essential task in the therapy of the obsessive-compulsive disorders or in dealing with the obsessional dynamisms in other personality disorders is that of conveying insight and initiating learning and change without getting caught in the *obsessional tug-of-war.* This term describes obsessional behavior which in all its varied aspects attempts to limit learning from experience and to maintain a rigid style of functioning that avoids novelty and change. Many of these tactics stimulate hostility in others and prevent the collaborative efforts needed in the psychotherapeutic enterprise.

As with all neurotic difficulties, the work lies in the identification, clarification, and, finally, alteration of the defensive patterns which maintain the neurosis. Such progress becomes possible when the patient's self-esteem or ego strength becomes sufficiently strengthened to withstand the major as-

Reprinted by permission of Jason Aronson from *Treatment of the Obsessive Personality* by Leonard Salzman, New York, 1980, 179–215.

saults against his defenses. While the problems that brought about the obsessional defenses are comparatively easy to uncover, the defensive structure which develops around these issues is most difficult to unravel. At times the particular issues of the patient are obvious and are plainly stated in his obsessional ruminations or his compulsive rituals. For example, a ritualistic avoidance of knives may be a clear statement within the awareness of the patient that he has some uneasiness about losing control of his hostile impulses. Thus, the identification of the problem—which is the fear of loss of control of his hostile impulses—is simple enough. However, it is soon evident that it is not a fear only of injuring someone else that is involved but rather a generalized uneasiness and uncertainty about the possibility of losing control in general or of being unable to control oneself at all times. The fear of loss of control is the central conflict, which gets displaced onto a variety of issues—hostility being an obvious one, since it is difficult to understand how tenderness, if uncontrolled, may produce dangerous or threatening situations. Such a development is more subtle, complex, and irrational.

It is paradoxical that in the attempts to clarify an obsessional's life, the issues become more complicated and confused. Ordinarily, increasing one's knowledge of a particular problem helps to focus on the relevant components. In dealing with the obsessional, however, new issues and qualifications of the old ones tend to broaden the inquiry. It often appears as though the patient were deliberately confusing the situation by introducing new issues when there is a real danger of clarifying something. By introducing more details and qualifications he wants to assure greater accuracy; he is trying to be precise and to avoid making errors. The additional factors are generally raised as he gets close to seeing his responsibility or failure in some activity. Before he is ready to accept an observation about some matter in which he played a responsible role, he tries to involve every possibility outside himself. Therefore, it looks as if he does this purposefully, as these new factors often lead the investigation into a cul-de-sac from which no fruitful return is possible.

In order to obtain some value from such a development once it has occurred, the therapist must go back to the beginning of the exchange and retrace it carefully, noting where the extraneous or vaguely relevant matters were introduced by the patient. It is only rarely that this sort of unraveling can take place outside of therapy. Ordinarily, one is left with a feeling of hopelessness and helplessness when one gets caught in a conversation which appears to be moving in one direction and suddenly shifts just as one approaches the destination. Attempts to retrace the path generally lead to further digression. Usually, the other party simply withdraws altogether. It is this activity that causes the obsessional to be referred to as "slippery" or "elusive"—it is so hard to pin him down.

In therapy it is imperative that such communication entanglements be worked through so that the patient can see exactly what he does and how he defeats attempts at understanding. He must recognize that while he may not do this deliberately, it nevertheless occurs frequently and regularly. The therapist must retrace the conversation and point out every new digression as it develops. He must resist all temptations to follow every lead an every rationalization; he must stick to the point in following through this particular gambit. Recording sessions can be very useful in this regard, but the compulsiveness of the therapist may outweigh the advantages gained by the patient, who can hear just how he frustrates clarity even while he is searching for clarification.

It is inevitable that the therapist will occasionally get caught in the flypaper of the obsessional's way of life, and he must recognize it as quickly as possible so as to avoid as much of it as he can. The patient gets a sense of power out of these exchanges, in which his verbal gymnastics serve to frustrate the therapist.

The situation just considered is illustrated by the following vignette: A patient expressed irritation at her husband because he became abusive about the driver in front of him. Her husband countered by saying that the driver was a poor one who was endangering himself as well as others. Besides, he asked, why did she always defend the other person and attack him? She stated that her concern was with his behavior because he was her husband. He charged her with being an appeaser and with failing to criticize others even when it was deserved. He referred to another occasion when, at a party, she had agreed with a guest who was obviously wrong in order to avoid a heated argument. She replied that she didn't want the party to break up—she was not just being an appeaser, she was just more socially adept than he was. At this he accused her of being a phony and of going overboard to be nice to others when she didn't really mean it. The issue had now moved from his irritable, egocentric behavior to her passive, compliant tendencies, and, if it did not get interrupted either by tantrums or sullen withdrawal by either of them, could extend far into the night, ranging from attack to counterattack as each one's sensitivities got touched upon. The ludicrousness of such an argument is more easily noted by an observer than by the participants.

It is clear in the preceding account that the subject was changed in the course of the exchange. At the outset, the husband was criticized, but when he counterattacked she was left defending herself. Generally, the patient's emotions are running so high and the need to win and overwhelm the other is so great that there is little chance of a logical or clear semantic analysis of the situation. When the partner also has some obsessional problems, the stickiness is compounded and only havoc can result. One can see how each step gets the original issue mixed in with additional issues until it is simply lost sight of.

It is necessary to face this aspect of the obsessional's difficulties early in the therapeutic work. The most effective way of countering it is by a slow, step-by-step unraveling process, as indicated above, wherein the actual side-stepping techniques are uncovered and brought to the patient's attention. The obfuscating tendencies can then be recognized and acknowledged. The fly-paper entanglements refer to the tendency to get caught up in every distracting movement of the obsessional without recognizing its purpose at the same time. Only when the therapist discovers that he is now far removed from the original communication or report of an anxiety experience of great relevance does he experience the quality of being entangled and unable to extricate himself. All efforts to do so produce more engulfments and accusations of being defensive, confused, or incompetent. It leaves the therapist feeling impotent and helpless.

THERAPEUTIC ALLIANCE

The patient must have a minimum of trust in the therapist and a willingness to accept the role of patient for the process to begin. The readiness to admit the need for help does not mean a total acceptance of another's ability to provide such help. The obsessional's excessive standards for himself and others coupled with his contempt and disdain for anything but the best require an idealized image of the therapist and the process, which is impossible to fulfill. To overcome the initial uneasiness the therapist must be fantasized as perfect, infallible, and free from anxiety or deficiency. Unless this romanticized and exaggerated notion is exposed, it will soon perish in a disappointed recognition of the therapist's humanity.

The therapist must also be alert to his expectations of the patient and his capacity to fulfill the therapeutic contract. While there are many formal requirements for the doctor-patient relationship, such as keeping appointments, paying the fees, and saying whatever comes to mind—all of which can be agreed upon in advance—there are some requirements which cannot be met so easily, in view of the nature of the neurotic or psychotic process. The obsessional patient will try to follow the formal requirements scrupulously. However, the more pervasive tendencies of omniscience and omnipotence, the characteristic doubts, the grandiose contempt, and the tendencies to distract will play havoc with the therapeutic process unless these matters are always kept in the forefront of the therapist's attention.

This type of patient does not deliberately sabotage the therapy; he is merely behaving as an obsessional. His behavior is not resistance, nor is it a need to defeat either the therapist or the therapy; it is merely another manifestation of obsessional behavior. The therapist cannot assume or take for granted that the patient will suddenly change and stop behaving like an obsessional simply because he has agreed to enter into therapy. It would be naive to expect that a neurotic who has difficulty in coming to grips with an issue or who procrastinates and is given to indecisiveness will be able to commit himself quickly to a process that demands total commitment and involvement.

It will be a long time before he will be able to verbalize his doubts about himself, the therapist, and the process. It is essential that he hold himself aloof and free of entanglement and commitment so that he can avoid being hurt and humiliated. He will need to know his therapist and experience a number of incidents with him before the more subtle safeguards can be dropped and the beginnings of trust can take place. It is inevitable that a person who must know everything and never be deficient or fallible will react to treatment as a challenge or a threat. In order to learn one must be receptive as well as motivated, which means to be free of the obstacles which interfere with learning. One must be able to listen with an open mind, without immediate denial or derogation of the material presented. Therapy is a learning process which requires the active interest and participation of the patient, and this is true whether one views the dynamics of cure as the result of insight, genetic reconstruction, resolution of transference neurosis, reconditioning, corrective emotional experience, or simple relearning. Therefore, not only is it necessary to motivate the patient to explore his way of living in order to discover the inappropriate patterns of behavior and their sources, but it is also necessary to interest and encourage him to take steps to change his way of life. This requires a therapist who can demand participation without challenging or stirring up the patient's opposition. The patient must acquire sufficient trust, self-esteem, and readiness to take some risks and face the possibility of failure.

UTILIZING INSIGHTS

All of the above-mentioned therapeutic requirements pose particular difficulties for the obsessional. In addition to his learning problems, he faces often insurmountable obstacles in attempting to try out new ways of functioning. Since most of the obsessional patterns of behavior arise from feelings of powerlessness and uncertainty, the patient finds it particularly threatening to try out new solutions unless he can have some guarantees and expectations of success. In spite of their unsatisfactory results, the old patterns are more familiar. There must be strong incentives to attempt new solutions.

Understanding that the obsessional needs to control and that the nature of the therapeutic relationship puts him in a dependent role, the therapist must acknowledge the patient's defiance and discomfort as a natural outcome of his neurotic demands. Because of these dependency problems, the therapeutic relationship should not be of an authoritarian type if it is to succeed. However, the very structure of the psychoanalytic situation tends to encourage a development in which the therapist is the leader, the teacher, and the person who has an "in" on what's happening. The patient is the pupil who is forced to depend on the ministrations of the magic man who sets the rules of the game. Such an atmosphere may tend to produce an outwardly compliant attitude with an inwardly resistive and negativistic defense.

The obsessional ordinarily proceeds only by being forced—by either circumstances or strong pressures—to overcome his indecisive ruminations. While he needs pushing, he nevertheless resents it and insists that he be allowed to act on his own, free from compulsion. Therefore, the therapist may be caught in a double bind if he takes a strong hand to forestall the controlling tendencies of the patient while allowing sufficient space for maneuvering so that the patient is permitted to decide on matters for himself. For any useful work to grow out of the therapeutic relationship, the prevailing atmosphere must be one of freedom—with a lack of compulsion and authority, with a minimum of rules and rituals, and with a maximum of exchange, in which the rights and limits of both parties are clearly understood. For the patient to perceive clearly his patterns of operation, the therapeutic atmosphere must not parallel the life experiences of the obsessional. In every respect the treatment behavior of the obsessional must be understood in its contradictory aspects, in order to maintain the cooperation and participation of the patient.

The patient must not be viewed as a stubborn ingrate who is arrogant and contemptuous, and if only he would behave right, all would be well. The understanding that the compulsive behavior is beyond his control and therefore not available to volitional change must limit the therapist's expectation that knowledge will undo the compulsion. At the same time the patient must make efforts to understand the reasons for his continued need for guarantees and certainty that interferes with attempts to change his behavioral patterns. This paradoxical and contradictory situation must be fully explored in the therapy.

The ultimate goal in therapy is to effect a change in the patient's living, not merely to induce insight. Insight is only the prelude to change; it provides the tools for the alteration in one's patterns of living. But the therapist must also assist the patient in utilizing his new understandings. This demands an approach which is less rigid and less tied up in traditional methodology. The therapist must feel free to be of active assistance in the process. Obsessional patterns which are heavily involved with ritualistic forms of behavior cannot be resolved by therapeutic measures which are just as overloaded with ritual. The therapist must be flexible enough to try novel approaches and techniques.

The process of therapy, therefore, can only be described in general terms that leave room for considerable variation and flexibility in specific instances. Broad tendencies and characteristic maneuvers of both the patient and therapist can be discussed because the nature of the obsessional defense produces particular technical problems. However, detailed exchanges and specific interventions will vary with each patient and therapist.

Not every obsessional patient will present all the characteristics. Some elements will be more obvious and will play a more important role in one patient or be of secondary importance in another. It is the therapist's job to recognize the main themes in each case, as well as the subsidiary themes. Therapeutic emphasis must be placed on the major mechanisms but at the same time should not minimize the lesser patterns.

GENERAL PRINCIPLES

Since the therapist should not have a preconceived program but rather some general open hypotheses, his reaction to the patient must avoid stereotypical attitudes or responses. For example, if one hypothesizes that obsessional behavior controls hostile or aggressive impulses, it follows that the expression of such feelings should be encouraged. The therapist in noting instances of hostile feelings or attitudes might insist on the verbalizations of these feelings. At times, this technique may be unsuccessful, but at other times it may produce strong negative responses with a stubborn insistence that the patient does not feel hostile. At other times the therapist may interpret friendly responses as reaction-formations, insisting that the patient become aware of the true underlying feelings. Such exchanges often lead to contention and power plays in which one or the other must yield—most often the patient in his concern about not alienating the therapist. At times the therapist may become annoyed or, if he does not feel irritated, pretend to be in order to stir up manifest expressions of hostility.

While role-playing may be valid under certain conditions, it is not useful and may be dangerous in the therapy of obsessional states. A prior decision to avoid all intellectual discussions in therapy is also unwise, since it resembles so closely the obsessional's tendency to make resolutions or plans to replace spontaneous responses. Such a decision should come out of the experiences in the process of therapy.

The patient's persistent intellectualization which the therapist knows is not the salient issue cannot artificially or prematurely be avoided until the relationship will sustain the therapist's attempts to do so. One cannot say, "It's all too intellectual. Tell me how you feel about your wife (or someone else)." The patient will become annoyed and will respond with a sharp reply that he is doing the best he can and besides he has no feelings toward his wife. Instead, one approaches the matter by suggesting that while his descriptions are useful and accurate, they leave out a major dimension—that is, how he felt about it all.

A spontaneous bit of irritation or anger in response to a specific event can meaningfully advance the therapy. But a prescription for the therapist to express hostility in order to encourage the patient's hostile feelings or a program of provocative silence to stimulate the patient's anger may be quite detrimental. Such controlled responses are easily identified by the patient and seen as a contrived attempt to test his reactions. He may respond in a way which is expected to win approval or he may become discouraged because he feels manipulated and "on trial" instead of being engaged in a collaborative enterprise.

The obsessional person has considerable difficulty in being spontaneous or direct in the expression of his feelings. A spontaneously provoked response by the therapist can be very efficacious in stimulating the patient's spontaneity, although this type of approach requires a highly responsive therapist and a greater involvement and participation by him in the process. It means that the therapist must take some risks with regard to exposing some of his own weaknesses and deficiencies. As well as being able to maintain some objectivity and separateness, he must respond in human terms to the interpersonal exchanges to demonstrate to the patient that being human, fallible, and admitting to deficiencies need not result in rejection or humiliation. Instead of rejecting the therapist, the patient may have heightened respect for him—which can be an important learning experience for the patient and may encourage him to try it too. Such an approach to a patient is both difficult and uncomfortable for the therapist, but it is more interesting and fruitful for both therapist and patient.

The use of humor and sarcasm in the therapy of the obsessional can be most effective too; it requires becoming involved with the patient's tendencies toward extremes and his difficulty in dealing lightly with any issues. A most effective technique in this respect is to highlight the patient's extreme positions by pressing still further, which has the effect of slapstick exaggeration and often points up the pretentiousness of the patient's superstandards. Exclamations such as "God, did you really do that or say that?" or "how could you?" in a good-humored way can quickly mobilize patient participation. Such exclamations are viewed as friendly and empathic and create closeness and cooperation.

When the patient demands that every detail be precisely accurate or that impossible goals be achieved, one can agree that this might be possible if the patient were indeed a combination of God, Einstein, Shakespeare, and General MacArthur. The effective use of this type of sarcasm may be more successful than hours of patient explanation and clarification. The obsessional's latent sense of humor is one of his unused capacities and to bring it out into the open and help him use it can be a most rewarding experience. The use of humor and spontaneous laughter can often break through a communication impasse.

The therapist's attempts at humor, however, are not invariably met with warm acceptance. The patient may just as frequently counter the therapist's efforts with condescending jibes and contemptuous ridicule. He may deprecate the humor and derogate the therapist's intelligence and skill by insisting that "making light of serious matters" displays an immature mind. A defensive therapist may become annoyed or hurt, but the patient's reactions can be seen as further evidence of the patient's intense seriousness and inability to touch lightly on many matters which are not actually crucial to his existence. It is a laboratory demonstration of how the patient does react to attempts to make life more fun.

THE THERAPIST

While it is generally agreed that the sex of the therapist is not a significant factor in the therapy of obsessionals, the age, experience, and background are quite relevant and at times very significant. One factor is crucial: The therapist must not be so obsessional himself that he will inevitably get caught in a *folie à deux,* which can prolong therapy indefinitely if it manages to survive at all. A degree of obsessionalism can be an asset in all therapeutic endeavors. It encourages attentive concern and intellectual curiosity. When recognized by the therapist, his own obsessional qualities can enhance his ability to discover it in his patient. However, if too severe or unnoticed it can be an insurmountable handicap and is undoubtedly one of the major issues that prolong therapy in these disorders. This tendency is often coupled with passivity, which can only encourage the patient's passive resistances and indecisiveness. Passivity as a technical tool is too often viewed as the model for the ideal psychoanalyst. However useful it might be on other occasions, for the treatment of the obsessional it can be counterproductive.

A therapist who cannot get unlocked from the patient's struggles to control because he himself must always be in control either traps his patient into passive compliance and endless analysis or drives him away early by stirring up a great deal of hostility. Under such circumstances the patient and therapist may get into an obsessive bind in which the needs of each one may be satisfied at the high cost of permanent invalidism of the patient. While the obsessional patient will prefer a therapist who is older and very experienced, he will often end up with the opposite, a younger and less experienced therapist who is less of a threat to his omniscience and whom he thinks is more likely to be controlled and subdued.

To proceed successfully with the therapy of the obsessional, the therapist must be active, directive, and closely tuned to irrelevant communications so that they can be turned off as quickly as possible.

These distracting activities often occupy the bulk of therapy if allowed to continue and must be identified early in the work. How can the therapist know what is relevant and what is irrelevant? Except in the extremes, this is a difficult and complicated problem. The recipe for a cake, the number of cracks in the office ceiling, or the detailed description of occupational tasks can readily be identified as irrelevant to the therapeutic task at hand. The preoccupation with endless detail about one's early years, the school build-ings, teachers, and empty accounts of earlier events may seem relevant but may well turn out to be evasive devices to forestall the examination of one's feelings and attitudes toward the teacher or other significant individuals.

One might say, "That is very interesting, but what happened between you and the teacher?" We now know enough about personality development and certain characterological disorders to be sure that certain matters are entirely irrelevant, others are relevant, and most are open to question. It is in this in-between area that the skill, intuition, and experience of the therapist are called upon in order to make judgments about the relevance of the communication.

The relevance of certain communications will, of course, be determined by the particular theoretical predilictions of the therapist. Some therapists consider all communication about the patient's earlier years as relevant, while others feel that such a focus is not always useful. Some insist that any reality concerns are out of place in analysis, considering useful only data that concern the transference. There are wide differences in viewpoints, depending on the therapist's theoretical position. However, it is universally agreed that the encouragement of certain details or topics tends to convey to the patient that some matters are of greater interest to the therapist, thereby encouraging their presentation.

Whatever the theoretical preference, certain issues are clearly irrelevant when they fail to advance the understanding of either the origin or the development of the personality defenses which characterize the disorder. Therefore, what is clearly relevant in all theoretical persuasions is material that touches on the dynamics of the obsessional state and the defense tactics which are an intrinsic part of it. Material which relates to anxieties (past or present), attempts at control, and preoccupations with guarantees and certainty is always pertinent and needs to be encouraged. The patient's evasive and defensive tactics must be brought into the open.

Material with emotional content usually has some degree of relevance in the therapeutic situation. However, the difficulty in deciding what is relevant should not allow the therapist to encourage undirected free association, which, in the obsessional, has a tendency to veer away from pertinent data. Neither should the notion that "everything is relevant" permit the therapist to allow treatment to continue endlessly because he is unwilling to narrow down the patient's communications. In a sense, everything can be shown to have a degree of relevance to everything else. However, it is no longer necessary to allow every therapeutic involvement to become a research project designed to prove such notions as determinism and unconscious motivation. Therapy is a practical contract directed at illuminating and alleviating behavioral disorders. Increasing knowledge of these disorders has enabled us to localize our inquiries, thereby giving us some clues as to what is pertinent and what is not. What may appear relevant during one session may be irrelevant in another. It is a judgment which can only be made in terms of material to be dealt with at a particular time; it must be decided upon in a specific situation.

In discouraging certain communications at particular times, one must be careful not to discourage it altogether. When the obsessive recital of dreams may, at one time, be avoiding currently unpleasant issues, this avoidance needs to be made known. Yet it should not be done in a way that would be entirely discouraging.

As suggested above, the obsessional has a great capacity to confuse the therapeutic process by producing irrelevant free associations or by constantly changing the subject or by having a sticky inability to change the subject. Great skill is called for on the part of the therapist to direct or control these tendencies. The therapist must be able to intervene actively and draw the focus of attention back to the significant matters. The defensive maneuvers may require frequent and repeated attention.

The therapist must always be aware of the limits of his patient's capacities to tolerate certain interpretations or observations; he must stop short lest he increase the anxiety and the defenses which ordinarily protect the patient against anxiety. This will limit the patient's capacities to observe and acknowledge the therapist's interpretations. When interpretations are seen as criticisms or as deflating the patient's esteem, the patient will react with even more elaborate defenses. On the other hand, the therapist's observations must not be too bland or else they may be easily overlooked.

Activity on the part of the therapist is an absolute essential from the beginning of the therapy to the end. Even a meager understanding of the dynamics of the obsessional state requires that the therapist not permit the techniques which defeat communication to continue for too long a time, although the therapist's activities must never be so intense as to overwhelm the patient or make him feel that the therapy is being run by the therapist. It does mean that the therapist must understand the obsessional's defense mechanisms of maintaining anxiety at a minimum, in order to facilitate learning and ultimately to resolve the obsessional patterns. Consequently, free association as well as the tendency toward endless detail and circumstantiality in the obsessive accounts must be controlled by the therapist. Passivity in the therapist can only lead to interminable analyses in an atmosphere that becomes more clouded and confused—often the reason for the long, fruitless analyses which characterized an early stage in the development of the methodology of psychoanalytic treatment of the obsessional.

TRANSFERENCE AND COUNTERTRANSFERENCE

The therapist is universally viewed as an authoritative figure who expects and demands maximum and perfect behavior. The patient feels that these demands are unreasonable and irrational and that the demands are more than he is capable of. The therapist clearly represents one parental figure who is more striking than the other and with whom there had been a relationship of some perverseness in terms of exaggerated expectations from the patient (which the patient felt to be far beyond his capacities). Often, both parents may be involved.

The therapist is seen as a critical, judging individual, with no respect for human frailties, who is sitting in judgment on every action of the patient. He is viewed as an unfriendly antagonist who must be overcome and exposed. At the same time, however, he must be impressed with the patient's skill and talents. These notions exist alongside those which aggrandize and idealize the therapist. He is put on a pedestal as being perfect and infallible and a model of controlled, spontaneous, passionate, and detached objectivity. He conforms to all the stereotypes and Hollywood versions of the romanticized psychoanalyst who is all-wise and all-understanding. Both these views put the patient at a distance and require him to behave properly and adequately.

It is only comparatively late in therapy that the patient can experience a collaborative interest on the part of the therapist and see him as a friendly helper rather than a caustic critic. Until then there is an ever-present atmosphere of suspicious uncertainty on the part of the patient and a readiness to hostility, which is generally well disguised in a superficially friendly and respectful demeanor. Such an atmosphere is easily punctured at the slightest rise of tension. This often makes the patient uneasy, so that he will strive to undo any damage that might have resulted from his anger and irritation. He tends to attribute to the therapist every deficiency which he despises in himself. His charges will range from his feeling that the therapist is a perfectionist, a procrastinator, and an indecisive person to ideas that he is a hypocrite and phony, whose standards are so flexible that they lack integrity. One can get a very clear view as to what ails the patient by examining his distorted views of the therapist.

Generally, the traits and attitudes attributed to the therapist are largely irrational and unjustified, but some of the characterizations may be more or less true. The therapeutic atmosphere may very well be one of an irrational authority who expects the rules to be followed simply because they exist and who demands certain behavior because it is good for the patient. The silent, passive, unseen therapist can easily exaggerate the authoritative atmosphere of the therapeutic setting and unnecessarily aggravate or rationally confirm the patient's defenses. Some of the elements of the classical techniques tended to do this very thing. The patient was put in an inferior, reclining role and was forced, by the rules of the game, to take over and proceed with the job. He received few, if any, answers to questions that might disturb him, and he was faced with a totally unreal situation in which he either accepted the rules or left.

Problems in the therapeutic situation are often crystallized in the rules for payment and absences, whether or not they are announced long in advance. Some therapists require a fixed contract in which all hours are paid for regardless of illness, occupational crises or vacation requirements. No accommodation is made for accidents, job requirements, or unexpected critical demands on the patient. This arrangement is rationalized on the grounds that the analyst has only a limited amount of time and that the patient must guarantee to fill it whether or not he can be present. This is not to say that the patient must not accept responsibility for the appointment; he must not absent himself for frivolous, escapist, or trivial reasons. However, in the treatment of an obsessional, a flexible, open attitude must prevail, and arrangements about cancellation and absences must be open to discussion and compromise, taking into account the therapist's needs and the patient's rights.

If flexibility is not part of the therapeutic atmosphere, the obsessional can easily accommodate to the rules and incorporate them into his rituals.

Therapy can thus become another ritual for the obsessional, rather than an experience in undoing his ritualistic symptoms. By following the rules rigidly and precisely and cooperating with every requirement of the process, the patient can often reinforce his neurosis, producing insuperable obstacles to its clarification and resolution. This can frequently result in the patient's achieving considerable insight but failing to gain any change in behavior or character structure as a result of the insight.

The therapist must be constantly aware that the obsessional's skill in deceiving himself and others and his secret demands for perfection, omniscience, and omnipotence reflect themselves in the relationship with him. Patients' apparent cordiality and conviviality in the face of an exchange in which they feel derogated must always be scrutinized, especially when the therapist is forced to make explanations or defenses of his interpretations. The cordiality is a thin veneer, and the underlying irritation and resentment must be brought into the open.

The *countertransference* phenomenon, or the reaction of the therapist to the patient, will vary considerably from therapist to therapist. The responses of the therapist, however, are of invaluable significance in the elucidation of the obsessional's way of life. The increased utilization of the countertransference phenomenon is one of the contributions of the post-Freudian psychoanalysts (this has been dealt with at length in my earlier book, *Developments in Psychoanalysis* [New York: Grune and Stratton, 1963]).

The need for the therapist constantly to examine and occasionally to comment on his own feelings in response to some communication or the patient's behavior can bring the whole matter of emotions into the forefront of the work. The therapist may have some reaction to the patient's characteristic obsessional devices which can be identified or to some covert process in which the therapist has unwittingly been drawn into a defensive role. In the latter situation, he may feel particularly irritated at his own failure to be observant, a feeling which could be brought into the sessions. The way the therapist uses his reactions can be of great influence in the outcome of therapy. When he can be uninvolved in the sense of observing the patient's characteristic behavioral traits and identifying them, he can help the patient see what effect such behavior might have on others. At such times, the observations should be descriptive rather than critical and should convey goodwill and warm interest.

On the other hand, when the patient's behavior is irritating and particularly annoying or when it puts the therapist in a bind and stimulates his own anxieties about his deficiencies, the therapist's open responses will not be useful to the patient unless the therapist can acknowledge his own limitations and show the patient how the latter succeeded in drawing the therapist into his own neurotic net. In such an instance the therapist must be prepared to acknowledge his own defensive needs and his own tendency to justify himself and to be correct. He must also be able to express irritation and annoyance at the patient's undercover derogating and deriding activities. To be useful to the patient, such a procedure must be done in an atmosphere in which the emphasis is on the therapist's limitations and humanness, rather than on the patient's hostilities.

The tendency to focus on the hostile behavior of the patient serves only to distract the therapeutic process from its real task of investigating the sources of the patient's uncertainties and his need for guarantees in living. The therapist can always turn the discussion onto these matters when the patient is hostile, by expressing some curiosity about what the patient feels is being endangered that requires this hostile attack. In this way the hostility is seen only as a defense and not as a cause. It takes the focus off the hostility issue.

It is unfortunate that some psychodynamic theories stress the role of hostility as the etiology of obsessional behavior. This not only focuses on anger, but also gives permission for the therapist to be forever discovering the hostile elements in obsessional behavior, overlooking other key issues such as grandiosity, omniscient and omnipotent requirements, and anxieties about commitment, trust, and security. Too often, the therapist interprets the effect of the obsessional's behavior on others as its intent, thereby failing to indentify cause and consequence and encouraging more, rather than less, compliant and appeasing behavior. To tell a patient that he is hostile is to criticize, condemn, moralize, and implore him to behave better. To indicate that a patient's behavior produces a feeling of being attacked, demeaned, or deprecated suggests that the patient may be unaware of his hostility or that his efforts at communication misfire and stimulate reactions that are not intended. Such an attitude is more likely to encourage introspection than correction, with feelings of guilt and condemnation. Therapy must go beyond encouraging a patient to express his unexpressed hostile feelings or thoughts. It must discover the origin and adaptive purposes of such reactions if, in fact, they are present. Hostile attitudes are often defensive, rather than primal, and the therapist must go beyond the anger to look for the anxieties of being hurt, abandoned, or destroyed.

The therapist can use his reactions to initiate and accelerate insights by pointing out how the patient's behavior seems phony, hypocritical, or grandiose. Again, these reactions must be presented as an observation, rather than as a personal grievance or criticism. This can be done by wondering out loud whether others might not react in a similar way in response to many aspects of the patient's behavior. The use of a sharp or caustic comment or the single, well-intoned phrase can often simulate greater emotional response than the well-phrased intellectual formulation, which usually stirs up a defensive counterattack. The emphasis must be on comments or exclamations which will stir up feelings without humiliating the patient. The production of humiliation will sidetrack the inquiry. Sullivan employed his reactions with great skill in his work with obsessionals, and this undoubtedly accounted for much of his success with them.

The need for the active participation of the therapist has already been stressed. It must be emphasized that the possibility of involvement, exchange, and participation of the therapist can stimulate the patient to commit himself and make known his real feelings and attitudes. It can supply the needed experience in risking a relationship with a figure who will not be punitive or rejecting. The more involved the patient gets in the therapy, the clearer will his subtle and most closely guarded techniques come out into the open and be available for study. The more gross and obvious techniques will become evident early in therapy and will make it possible for changes to be made. However, the more elusive and intricate neurotic patterns which closely resemble nonneurotic behavior can become clear only in the intricacies of a relationship in which the patient allows himself some freedom to relax and let go. The best setting for such discoveries lies in the reactions of the therapist—usually called countertransference feelings—to the patient's behavior. The training of the therapist permits him to recognize these maneuvers and to bring them to the patient's attention, thus helping the patient to eliminate them from his living.

One must clearly distinguish between becoming truly involved and getting into arguments in order to win. Getting entangled in the flypaper tactics of the obsessional is not necessarily becoming more intimate or more involved. Any involvements or interactions of the patient and therapist should always be with regard to the therapeutic task. While quarreling indicates some involvement, it has no real place in the therapeutic process. The therapist must be aware that when he becomes active, certain safeguards must be applied so that activity does not turn into a repetition of the malevolent, authoritarian relationship which the patient had to deal with through his early experiencing.

The interaction characterized by the one-upmanship maneuver to maintain control of the therapeutic work can illustrate dramatically some of the pitfalls of an unaware or unsophisticated therapist. What is designed as a collaborative adventure can be changed into a struggle for control and position, and the therapeutic process can be viewed by some as a state of warfare. While it may be a struggle, it is not a war; the goal is not to win a battle but to communicate meaning and understanding to another, in order to help him deal with his problems in living. Transactional Analysis emphasizes these therapeutic gambits and can be very effective in resolving some of these problems if they do not get embedded in the win-or-lose portions intrinsic to many of the "games" that are played. An aware and skillful therapist can avoid these traps or, if he falls into them, can extricate himself by a skillful review of the tactics employed in the game.

If the therapist is unable to identify the patient's tactics of using double binds, semantic paradoxes, and verbal assaults—all devices used by obsessionals—therapy can very well develop into a state of war. The therapist must not lose sight of the fact that his job is to expose the tactics, not to beat the patient at his own game. Double binds are common occurrences in the obsessional's developmental history and in his own functioning, and one can easily be caught up in the game if one is not constantly on guard.

PAST VERSUS FUTURE

The obsessional is oriented toward the future, in order to guarantee that his living will be free of anxiety. Therefore, his interest in the past is generally meager, if not absent. At best, his recollection of his early years is distorted, and this period is frequently seen as a time when he was mistreated by one or both parents in a hypercritical and demanding fashion. His recollections of the more recent past are generally seen as a succession of occasions when he was taken advantage of and pushed around or was the object of discrimination by disrespectful people. Quite often, the therapist is fooled into thinking he is hearing a detailed and accurate review of some earlier historical event. The recollection seems so clear and lucid that it may be accepted in toto—as a fact. One needs to be very cautious in this regard and assume that every recollection has at least suffered some distortion, exaggeration, or convenient reconstruction.

The obsessional's tendency to distort the past as mentioned earlier, produced the crisis in Freud's theorizing that ultimately resulted in his greatest discovery. On the basis of the accounts of his obsessional patients—who described passive sexual assaults in their early years—Freud postulated that the obsessive disorder was caused by such sexual assaults. When, however, he attempted to validate these accounts, he discovered that they were untrue and were fantasies of the patient. He was then forced to acknowledge that either his theories were based on lies or he needed to explain such fantasized accounts in other ways. Freud resolved this difficulty when he recognized the power and significance of the imagination and the effect that thinking has on an individual's behavior. It became clear not only that actual events could produce widespread consequences but also that the person's imaginings or fantasies were capable of influencing his psychological history and behavior. Thus, the recollections of an individual may not be a major concern, as they are very likely to be distorted.

The obsessional's ability to reconstruct his early years is quite limited, as he has little interest in the past. His present behavior is related not only to his past experiences but also to the variety of defenses erected in the early years. The obsessional may have learned very little from his past experiences because his defenses prevented him from drawing any reasonable deductions from them. As a result, a successful experience or performance does not prevent anxiety about the next occasion. He approaches it with the same uneasiness and uncertainties, as though it had never happened before. Each occasion is a new trial in which he must prove himself over and over again.

Psychoanalytic therapy originally emphasized the need for a genetic reconstruction of the person's life, with emphasis on his libidinal development. It was assumed that the reconstructions would undo the repressions, which were the basis of the neurotic symptoms. However, much of the research on the therapeutic process and the ego psychological theories of personality development have raised doubts about the validity of this view. Whichever view may be correct, the possibility of an adequate or accurate genetic reconstruction of an obsessional's early life is highly questionable. Therefore, an emphasis on the past and the problem of the obsessional's distorted recollections make the usefulness of this aspect of therapy highly uncertain.

The most effective approach seems to be in the examination of recent events—particularly those events that occur in the ongoing relationship with the therapist. In this sense the transference and countertransference phenomena play their unique roles in advancing the therapeutic process by occurring in the actual moments of interaction of patient and therapist. They are therefore available for immediate examination. The emphasis on the *here and now* by many post-Freudian theorists finds its greatest reward in the treatment of obsessional disorders. The more recent conceptions of mental illness do not focus exclusively on the genesis of these disorders as libidinal deformations, nor do they conceive of the beginnings in relation to any specific trauma. The developments are seen as occurring in an atmosphere in which repeated experiences produce effects on the person in obvious or subtle ways. Therefore, discovering the actual origin or beginning of a symptom or personality characteristic seems of less value than a general recognition of the milieu or atmosphere of the household or the general attitudes of the parents.

In the ultimate development of the behavioral disorder, the conditioning effect of repeated experiences plays a major role, in addition to that of the initiating cause. In the adult years one deals with a problem the origin of which is only a single element in its continuation; the persistence of the faulty pattern is related to the process of conditioning and habit. Therapy must unravel the detailed and widespread defensive techniques which develop and penetrate into every aspect of the obsessional's life, as well as search for the origins of the symptoms. This requires a knowledge of the patient's present living in order that the therapist may see the subtleties and intricacies of his defensive processes. This is a most difficult task and comprises the bulk of the work in the therapeutic process. To achieve this the therapist must be prepared for a long and arduous job of repeating the same observations and interpretations frequently before they are truly recognized by the patient. It requires patience and understanding of the tenacious and persistent nature of the obsessional process.

One may find that the patient avoids present failures or recognized deficiencies, as they tend to expose too much of his feelings. In contrast, past angers can be described and experienced calmly, so that the actual value of their assessment in the therapeutic process is sharply reduced. Present emotional responses must be faced, and, as they are impinging on other responses, they can be usefully explored. As the exploration of such emotional experience is crucial to any useful work, stress on the here and now serves this purpose very well.

PROBLEMS OF CONTROL

Therapy requires a free, uncontrolling attitude toward one's thoughts and the ability to say aloud whatever may come to mind. Ordinarily, the obsessional tries to examine, appraise, and screen every thought before he utters it, in order to avoid exposing himself unfavorably. Thus, on the one hand his impulse is to censor anything that might make him appear in an unflattering light, while on the other hand he has a need to follow the therapist's instruction meticulously. In trying to do the latter he gets hung up on endless, detailed elaborations of each thought, which may unwittingly expose too much. The free flow of associations is also impeded by his difficulty in getting off a subject once it is started, thereby dwelling on what is no longer associative data but merely detailed bits of data. Any idea, thought, or attitude that happens to come to mind is simply worked to death. Both of these tendencies may succeed in controlling the content of the psychoanalytic hour.

The patient may frequently bring to the session a written or memorized agenda, which rigidly controls the content of the session and guarantees that nothing is left out and that nothing is inadvertently added. Fringe thoughts or ideas which occur in the course of the session are generally not permitted to interrupt or alter the prearranged presentation. The patient may unconsciously select and censor his thoughts in order to control the content of the interview. This must be brought to his attention—not as an aspect of his deceitfulness or failure to cooperate but as an impediment in the therapeutic process.

A patient who early in his therapy manifested overt and covert tendencies to try to run the therapeutic sessions by having an unwritten agenda wanted to take over the role of therapist. On one occasion, while this patient was deciding what was relevant to discuss, I pointed out that this was his method of controlling the sessions and that it would be preferable if he did not decide for himself unless the matter concerned something unquestionably irrelevant. He agreed and then went to the other extreme. He stated that he would therefore make no judgments of relevance at all; he wanted me to make the decision, so that he would not be accused of censoring any material. However, this could allow *him* to criticize or discount any judgments I might make. He was in effect saying, "Fine, I'll do what you say. But I'm letting you know that unless I run the show, I'll criticize it, or else take no responsibility for the consequences."

While insisting that he should not be asked to decide about the relevance of certain matters until he was much better informed, he still tried to run the process. I was trying to say that he should not control the process, but he was attempting to control it more effectively.

The tendency of some patients to stay rigidly on a topic and avoid fringe thoughts or associations might seem to indicate their efforts to avoid distraction. While this may be the case, it is also a way of avoiding unplanned or spontaneous reactions. That is, as one cannot predict the consequences of such reactions it is safer not to evoke them at all.

The problem of an agenda and the rigid adherence to a plan was exemplified in the behavior of an obsessional who became preoccupied prior to each session with concerns about *not* bringing an agenda to insure that he would freely present whatever came to mind. This was particularly true with regard to his concerns about his grandiose fantasies. If he were consciously concerned about some important matter, he could *not* bring it up as this would be preplanning. Therefore, important material would be postponed for long periods of time until it would be accidentally revealed.

Control of a situation can be direct or indirect, subtle and unwitting or calculated and obvious. The controlling tactics used by an obsessional, however, are rarely obvious to him, even though they may seem blatant and unmistakable to others. One image the obsessional has of himself is of someone who is under the influence of others, pushed and pulled by them. He sees himself a passive victim of the demands and requirements of others, and he feels himself to be helpless in the face of forces he must overcome. While he may see his helplessness, he generally does not recognize his defensive, controlling tactics and the striving for power involved in them. These elements must be drawn to his attention in the therapeutic process. To become aware of how he appears to others can help him understand why others react to him as they generally do.

One of the most effective techniques for controlling others is to put oneself entirely at the other's disposal and to abandon all pretense and plans for directing one's own life. While this appears to be a state of total dependency and can result in rejection, it may succeed in getting the other person to focus entirely on fulfilling the obsessional's needs. The risk of failure is present, but it is fairly safe to assume that in a middle-class Western culture such a display of total incapacity will stir up sympathy and help rather than open rejection. While it may overtly convey a total lack of control of the universe, covertly it serves to manipulate others through the emotional influence of helplessness. This type of "no control" is often a most effective device for exerting maximum control over others.

This personality trait manifests itself in the seemingly self-effacing, compliant person who presumes to do exactly what you want him to do. He follows all rules and procedures precisely. In therapy he will free-associate and will not withhold anything, following all instructions scrupulously. He will say anything and everything that comes to mind, including stock quotations, the number of cracks in the ceiling, the voluminous details of an exchange with the florist about how to care for African violets, and every last detail—inning by inning—of the baseball game. The overconforming literalness of this type of response tends to sabotage and interfere with the therapeutic process because it wastes so much time on what is clearly irrelevant and serves to distract from the relevant. When this is called to the patient's attention, he may respond with, "You told me to say everything that comes to my mind and not to censor any of it." In fact, these are the instructions he received. He is afraid not to say everything lest he leave out something important. If anything might be significant, his devotion to the total truth as well as his rigidity about the rules justify such detail.

The therapist must therefore be alert to who is controlling the interview and the therapy. It must always be very clear as to who is the doctor and who is the patient.

TUG-OF-WAR

In his relationships the obsessional invariably becomes involved in a tug-of-war when he attempts to one-up others, both in therapy and out. Since his security rests upon his always being right, even the most trivial exchange becomes a duel which he must win. In therapy he may have to have the last word with a routine question or comment, even if it may undo the whole hour's work or may cast doubt on the entire exchange. This is the effect of the familiar closing comment of many obsessional—namely. "How am I doing?" or "Do you think I'm getting any better?" It is essential not to be drawn into answering the question but to indicate instead, while exiting from the office, that it should be discussed at the next session. It is most important to raise it at the next session if the patient forgets to, and it would not be surprising if he did forget. At another time the patient may challenge the therapist's capability in an attempt to put him on the defensive. This puts the therapist in an inferior role and requires him to explain his actions to another person who sits in judgment upon him. This technique is used in other personality configurations as well, but it is particularly common in obsessional relationships.

In the tug-of-war the patient tries to gain control by raising doubts about the validity of the process, the theory which underlies it, or the capacity of the therapist to utilize both. The patient not only may raise doubts about the concept of the unconscious or the validity of introspection but also may begin to attack psychotherapy as a pseudoscience and the practitioners as dupes or quacks. He may bring in the latest magazine, book, or newspaper attack on psychiatry or quote the prevailing detractor or antagonist to the psychotherapeutic methodology, whether it be valid or not. These attacks are generally timed to deal with the patient's feelings that the therapeutic situation is a hostile one and that the therapist is criticizing him and putting him in his place. The patient feels that he must counterattack and reassert his position. It is important at such times that the therapist does not get caught up with the patient's hostility and view it as if it were the primary issue. The patient is trying to establish some parity in a situation in which he feels himself to be inferior, and his hostility is a defensive device to overcome this supposed inferiority.

Hostile and aggressive feelings are often responsible for a great many of the obsessional's difficulties. However, the need to establish parity or even superiority may or may not involve feelings of hostility toward others. If his sense of control is endangered, as in a therapeutic situation in which he is forced to recognize his fallibility, the patient may very well react with anger and irritation and attack the therapist. The basis for such an attack can be clearly understood in terms of a need to control rather than as a reflection of some underlying "hostile core." The patient has great concerns about controlling his hostile impulses, as well as everything else, and it is therefore necessary to understand the causes of his hostility. In spite of the prevalence of hostile feelings in the obsessional, he has more difficulty in dealing with his tender impulses and his fear that they may get out of control and that he might be overly kind or loving. These reactions are even more dangerous than his hostile feelings because he sees them as weak, as giving up, and as losing the tug-of-war. Being tender means being a sucker or being taken advantage of; this feeling is untenable for him.

The struggle to be on top in the therapeutic situation may extend over long periods of time. Occasionally, it can be resolved early in therapy, but because it reflects the totality of the obsessional's character structure, it generally weaves in and out of the therapeutic process from beginning to end.

A patient spent several weeks exploring his objections to a statement I made and finally appeared with evidence to prove that I was wrong. He had difficulty understanding that I might have accepted his objections at the time I made the statement and that he need not have spent so much time re-searching his challenge. He felt I would defend my statement to death, just as he would have; he therefore needed support for his attack. In the interval, while he was accumulating data to counter my statement, he was subtly contemptuous of me, buoyed up by the knowledge that he had won the argument.

A comfortable capacity to admit errors and fallibility without any pretense of humility or virtue is an important quality in the therapist—not only to avoid the tug-of-war but also to demonstrate the possibility that one can be wrong and can survive without humiliation or anguish. There are many such opportunities in the course of therapy, and the therapist should not pass up any occasion to admit his error when he turns out to be wrong. Staging such an event, however, in order to give the patient such an experience, may create an atmosphere of trickery with regard to the therapist as well as to the process as a whole. One can be sure that enough situations will occur spontaneously, so that the therapist need not search for such opportunities.

It is obvious that the therapist cannot enter into the tug-of-war in order to overcome his "opponent." There are more significant issues involved which concern the elucidation and demonstration of the patient's insistent need to win or to be on top. He must be helped to see how this interferes with learning and relating effectively with people. To win in an immediate sense may often mean gaining control, but such control can be useless and ineffec-tive. The tug-of-war, when it occurs in therapy, provides an opportunity for the obsessional patient to see in microscopic proportions how he functions in the world at large. Winning, which may supersede all other values for him, can be more costly than it is worth. Therefore, the tug-of-war is a most effective therapeutic tool if the therapist can use it skillfully. He should not avoid a challenge on the assumption that the patient may convert it into a battle but should grasp the chance to enlighten the patient about this tendency. If the therapist evades the challenge, he encourages the grandiose fantasies of the patient and strengthens his neurotic defenses. Intelligent confrontation and involvement—in which the therapist stands firm while yielding at opportune moments—can provide great enlightenment to the patient.

PROBLEMS OF PERFECTION

The desire to be perfect leads to a variety of complications in the therapeutic process, as therapy is basically a learning situation and the obsessive is unable to admit to deficiencies.

In order to learn, one must initially accept the premise that there is something to be learned. If the obsessional assumes a perfection and refuses to acknowledge gaps in his understanding, learning is extraordinarily difficult. His security rests on a presumed invulnerability based on his feelings of perfection and omniscience. He has the illusion that he can meet any challenge and can therefore be certain about his existence. An interpretation or observation which is unexpected, unfamiliar, or novel and which might challenge this conviction is denied, repressed, or overlooked. If it cannot be bypassed in these ways it is either minimized or rationalized as reflecting the therapist's jealousy or critical unfriendliness. At these times the patient views therapy as a battle; he feels he must defend himself against attack. This will occur in spite of his awareness of the need for therapy. He may even be aware of his unreasonable tendency to react as though attacked, yet he must still defend himself to maintain his illusion of perfection.

Such contradictory behavior is comprehensible when one recognizes that the obsessional's neurotic integration rests on the need to deny any deficiency or lack of knowledge about himself and the universe. Therefore he must resist or parry every observation which reflects on this matter. He may produce new data to cast doubt on the truth of any such observation made by the therapist. He will raise insignificant exceptions to question the validity of the interpretation. If the therapist's interpretation is convincing and cannot be evaded, the patient minimizes its value in order to make it more palatable and to reduce the shame of having to admit that he did not already know about the matter. Although he may accept the interpretation, he will move on quickly to other matters which, he says, are more important. Thus, the impact is reduced. At other times, while ostensibly agreeing with the interpretation, he will set up a barrage of highly intellectualized counterattacks to undermine or undo the interpretation.

After many qualifications and clarifications he may finally accept the interpretation but not without some belligerent counterattack. He may charge the therapist with running him down or with trying to destroy his self-esteem. Such an attack may put the therapist on the defensive and serve to tone down the interpretation, so that the real issue is evaded.

The patient may, at times, deny the observation only to discover it himself as a fresh and novel idea in succeeding hours. He will behave as if he figured it out all alone and will present it as a fascinating discovery. In doing this he can salvage the notion of his perfection and maintain the fiction of his flexibility. The patient's need to be perfect pushes him to present the most precise and extensive account of every event to be certain that nothing is left out. This produces an enumeration of the most minute details and accounts of minor and insignificant events. He will ramble on endlessly in his need to clarify and qualify every statement. Such endless detail may be rationalized as accurate reporting. One gets a clear impression, however, that the patient has no capacity to separate the relevant from the irrelevant. While this type of communication outside of therapy may be only boring and irritating, it is most important that in therapy the patient note the effect of such tendencies.

The patient attempts to retain the illusion of perfection by being doubtful or inattentive to interpretations. Since interpretations are the only way to advance a real understanding of the obsessional defenses, the patient's tendency to maintain his neurotic esteem and avoid what he considers a humiliating acceptance of shortcomings may prevent any movement in therapy. The undoing process often occurs even while the therapist is speaking. As he listens, the patient is already preparing his defenses, justifications, or counterattacks and is thus only partly paying attention to the therapist's statement. He may even feel superior by deciding that the interpretation does not go far enough and that the therapist is not so bright after all. Some patients literally hear nothing of what is said. They may often be able to identify exactly when they stopped hearing and began ruminating about some irrelevancy unconnected with the immediate exchange. This must be dealt with summarily, or valid and valuable exchanges can take place without any noticeable effect on the patient. The most brilliant observations or formulations can be wasted unless they are attended to; this requires that the therapist present them in a palatable fashion. The therapist's skill is manifested most clearly in his capacity to deal with this particular problem.

A particularly bright professor could identify exactly the moment that he would turn off listening and start preparing his offensive. On one occasion when he was describing his concerns about the worthiness of his lecture because he had failed to mention some unessential but interesting details, I suggested that he was again demanding the impossible of himself. I then focused on how this issue had appeared time and again and reminded him of his intolerance to forgetting names, even those he didn't care to remember. At this point he began to detail covertly, while I continued to talk, the names of all the people he had run into in the past week. It was an examination and he was testing his performance. He heard no more of what I was saying until a few moments later when he could tell me exactly what had happened.

The emphasis on intellectuality is another means of avoiding the potential humiliation of not being perfect. It prevents real involvements in any emotional exchange and thereby sidetracks the possibility of being influenced or affected by the therapist's interpretation or observation. Intellectualizing and philosophizing about life is a most successful device to avoid participating in it. The obsessional exhibits great skill in avoiding any involvement with the therapist, although he may talk extensively about involvement and the problems of transference and countertransference. He will even talk about feelings and emotions. However, it will be a succession of words drawn from an intellectual comprehension of the issues involved, devoid of any real emotional response. It is therefore necessary to focus on real feelings and to limit, as much as possible, such intellectual discussions. Obviously, they cannot be avoided entirely, but they can and should be minimized; and, whenever possible, their true function should be demonstrated to the patient.

Extremes

An aspect of perfection which poses innumerable therapeutic problems is the obsessional's tendency to think and live in extremes. For him, it is not a matter of being correct but of being perfect. His living is secure only when he can be assured of absolute safety, infallible prediction, and absolute certainty about his status—absolutes demanding superhuman attributes. The reaction to any discovery of inadequacy in therapy is one of extreme despair, discouragement, and feeling of failure.

Any attempt, therefore, to highlight these extreme demands in therapy and to portray the impossibility of fulfilling them may result in a countercharge that the therapist is supporting the opposite extreme and is trying to make the patient into an ordinary or mediocre person. Each time the therapist tries to point out that the demands for perfection are unachievable and only lead to despair and disappointment, he may be accused of having standards which are too low and of being too easily satisfied. At the beginning of therapy it is impossible for the patient to take a middle ground—that is, to do the best he can or to utilize the skills which he does have. He insists that this is not enough. As long as he must have absolute guarantees he cannot be satisfied with human uncertainties. He cannot see that to accept one's human limitations is an act of strength that accounts for some of man's great achievements. The need to reassert this constantly in the therapeutic exchanges results in the charge that therapy is attempting to reduce the patient's performance to a minimum. It is hard for the patient to accept the fact that being human does not mean being satisfied with the least output, or the utilization of only a fraction of one's capacities. The therapist must regularly interpret and demonstrate that the insistence on perfection produces the very results the patient abhors. Mediocrity is *not* the alternative to the superhuman expectations of the obsessional, although this is the only way he can see it. He sees the world in extremes because he lives that way and feels that unless he is pushed to act he will not perform at all. Therefore, when he is encouraged to relax or to limit his demands, he interprets this as encouragement to slacken his standards.

The tendency to see the world in extremes is the reason that some obsessionals fear to drink or take drugs. They feel that they would be unable to control themselves and would go to extremes; that is, they fear they would become alcoholics or drug addicts. They therefore go to the opposite extreme and never take a drink or use drugs, even aspirin. The drug issue also involves not wanting or needing outside help in filling some need—they can do it themselves. This often delays their visits to physicians when the situation justifiably requires it.

The therapist must help the obsessional patient to recognize that doing the best one is capable of is neither mediocre nor ordinary, but richly productive. To help the patient strive for a realizable goal which utilizes his highest skills and capacities is not a matter of compromise. One is not either a God or a shameful mortal. One can be proud and productive even while being restrained by human limitations.

If security is attainable only by being king, one cannot accept the role of prime minister, which is just as unsafe as being an ordinary citizen. This is the essence of the problem of extremes in the obsessional, and no amount of reassurance about the value of being second-best will suffice. Since the excessive demands owe to compulsive requirements, an intellectual clarification of the problem does not serve to reduce it, even though it paves the way for eventual change.

The dilemma of the extremes and the contradictory behavior resulting from them are reflected in the obsessional's inconsistent attitudes toward his need for others and his need to present himself as entirely independent and self-sufficient. The contradiction between his dependent and independent needs creates innumerable therapeutic crises and impasses, which need to be clarified by frequent interpretation and repetition. This is particularly highlighted in the phobic states when the obsessional requires the presence of another person in order to function at all. Although he insists on total independence, his phobia requires and therefore justifies his dependence. The independent and self-reliant behavior is preferred by the obsessional, as it helps sustain the illusion of a perfect, infallible, omniscient being. Total independence, however, cannot be achieved; the obsessional is forced to rely on others—for example, to marry or to go to a doctor. This reflects itself in the therapeutic process when the obsessional grudgingly admits that he is in need of treatment or insists that he is doing it for someone else. By going to a psychotherapist he is satisfying someone else's needs. He frequently reminds the therapist that while the therapy may be useful, it is not really necessary for him. But, he adds, since he is in treatment, why has it not overcome all the problems which he refuses to admit he had in the first place?

Whatever his reasons for being in therapy, what he really wants from therapy, on one level, is to become more perfect and to overcome the deficiencies which interfere with his achieving perfection. Being forced to acknowledge his deficiencies because of some crisis or unfortunate circumstance, he expects that therapy will now overcome them and will make him totally independent. However, he wants the therapy and the therapist to accomplish this. He is willing to acknowledge the expertness of the psychiatrist, to pay his fees, and to follow all the necessary instructions. In return, he expects the doctor to resolve the difficulties. The concepts of relationship, mutual endeavor, and collaboration are alien to him. As he doesn't really feel that he needs the therapist, he has no need to develop any relationship with him.

The obsessional is particularly incompetent in the area of interpersonal relationship. Relationship involves participation, which, in turn, implies some need or dependency as well as commitment and exchange that grow out of some trust in the relationship. The demand for self-sufficiency obviates and complicates all his attempts at forming relationships, and this becomes more aggravated as he grows older. Intimacy, either sexual or nonsexual, is largely foreign to him because he has had such limited experience with it, and nonsexual intimacy is what the therapeutic relationship requires.

Helping the obsessional gain insight into how he actually behaves requires not only the clear recollection of a recent event but also the elimination of the patient's doubts and uncertainties about such events. This does not mean a perfect reconstruction. It requires only enough recall to be able to illuminate the basis for the anxiety which stimulates obsessional processes. The here-and-now experience enables the therapist to pin down the facts of an event and the patient's feelings about it. His reaction to an event and his way of dealing with his anxieties are more easily ascertained when one explores a recent event that is uncluttered by the distortions, denials, or sheer forgetting permitted by the passage of time. For the obsessional, past events and hazy recollections are ideal opportunities to use powers of verbal manipulation and distortion. The patient finds it easier to restrict his communication to the past. It is easier for him to discuss angers, frustrations, or difficulties that occurred years ago. Because the emotional elements in the obsessional's life are generally constrained and under control, it is imperative that they be brought into focus with regard to his present attitudes and relationships, thereby forcing him to acknowledge the relevance to his present behavior and his responsibility for its effect on his present living.

PROBLEMS OF OMNISCIENCE

If the patient expects to know everything, he feels utterly humiliated when he is forced to acknowledge a new piece of information. The obsessional must accept new insights and points of view about his past and present living, and he must come to recognize that his preconceptions and distortions restrict and prejudice his present experiences. He must learn that he is not viewing the environment with fresh and open eyes. He must see that he cannot really learn unless he is able to observe what is actually happening. He must learn to learn by becoming aware of his tendency to see everything in the light of what he expects to find in the first place—that is, in light of the concept of the self-fulfilling prophecy, which plays a vital role in all neurotic processes. When one expects or anticipates rejection, hostility, or criticism, one can misconstrue or misinterpret a situation in this light. Consequently, one reacts by withdrawn irritation or outright hostility, thereby angering the other person and fulfilling the anticipated rebuff. If one is anxious and uneasy, an atmosphere of tension can be created, putting other individuals into an anxious or uncomfortable state. The obsessional can then interpret the other person's behavior as unfriendly. The uneasy expectation prevents him from actually discovering how the other person feels, and the tense atmosphere is interpreted as a rejection.

The inability to acknowledge limitations makes every observation, interpretation, or clarification a criticism and a challenge to the obsessional's omniscience. He cannot admit that there are things he does not know. He must challenge each observation at length, even while he may be aware that it is correct and useful. Most often, the patient's behavior is out of his awareness, and he automatically defends his position. His defensiveness may be manifested by his going on the offensive and saying that the interpretation is wrong or, if right, that it is too strong, poorly timed, and badly done because it came through as criticism and derogation rather than as a simple observation. He is on the attack and tries to embarrass the therapist and put him on the defensive. His need to be critical has enabled him to develop his skills in finding the weak and vulnerable areas in his opponent. Such maneuvers not only tend to weaken the therapist's observations but also serve to shift the focus from the patient's deficiencies to the therapist's weaknesses.

To minimize the patient's resistances to learning, the therapist's interpretations should not be presented as if they were obvious. Instead, they should be presented as curious and interesting observations on which the patient himself can elaborate. One should avoid saying, "From what you have said about the event, it is clear that your competitive need to excel must alienate others." Instead, it would be preferable to say, "What effect did you think your pushing John aside might have had on him?" or "How would you react in the face of a competitor who was pressing hard to beat you?" One should pose interpretations in the form of riddles in which the necessary ingredients for a solution can be supplied by the patient. In this way the patient makes the discovery which leads to some useful interpretations, and he does not have to resist the information. While this works very effectively for a while, the patient may soon catch on to the device and feel that it is an attempt to trick him. But even when discovered, it turns out to be more palatable than other techniques. As suggested previously, the patient may at other times hear an interpretation, deny it, and return several weeks later to announce that he has just discovered it himself. One cannot force or hurry understanding in such patients; one needs to repeat, over and over again. To make it more likely that the interpretation will take hold, the therapist must hold it back until the patient's life experiences are so clear and almost self-evident that the patient is ready to have the insight himself. Above all, the interpretation must not be made in an attacking or critical vein, such as, "How come you didn't see it?" (implying "You must have been stupid not to notice it!"). Often a preliminary statement noting why it would have been difficult for the patient to recognize it sooner can make a strong interpretation more palatable. Yet no amount of skill and maneuver can make an interpretation easy for the obsessional to take. He has to discover that he does not know everything, and this stirs up much resentment.

Some obsessionals who are able to limit the range of their interests may become bright, well informed, and highly proficient in their professional fields. Others, however, may have a superficial knowledge of many matters.

Because they are aware of a lack of depth in many areas of knowledge, they avoid detailed discussions and prefer to keep matters on a surface level. If challenged in discussions, they make extreme and dogmatic statements in an effort to overwhelm their opponents and thereby terminate the discussion. Thus, they frequently take extreme positions which are difficult to defend, and they often find themselves supporting a point of view in which they do not believe. These complications generally arise when they are unwilling to admit to a lack of knowledge or an error and become entangled in a web of indefensible rationalizations.

This happens regularly in therapy when the obsessional faces someone who is better informed than he is on at least one subject. The therapist will have many opportunities to demonstrate such complications; because of their need to know everything, obsessionals will invariably stick their necks out, and the consequences can be quite humiliating to them. The therapist must exert great care not to get involved to the point of humiliation, but to interrupt the patient before he goes too far. Past experiences, both inside and outside of therapy sessions, can be used to document the therapist's presentation, instead of allowing the present situation to unfold completely. In this way the emotional encounter with the therapist can be used to advance the therapeutic process without stirring up too much resistance.

The patient may sometimes be eager to accept the therapist's observation and demonstrate his understanding, but he may leave no time for the amplification of the interpretation. He conveys the notion that he knew it all the time so "let's get on with it." He may, at times, even proceed to a statement about the therapist's great memory or his cleverness in understanding human behavior. This not only changes the focus of the exchange but also serves to stimulate the therapist's goodwill toward the patient. It is necessary on such occasions to examine this maneuver as well as the interpretation. The therapist must show the patient that the latter's readiness to receive the interpretation was intended as flattery to the therapist as well as evidence of the patient's own cleverness. The remark can then be seen as a maneuver in which the patient is actually shifting the focus from his behavior to the therapist's behavior.

In his omniscient strivings the patient may try to become informed about psychiatry in general and the therapist's professional orientation in particular. This fulfills the patient's need to know everything and also supplies him with ammunition to flatter or attack the therapist when a suitable occasion arises. As psychotherapy is still a young, growing science, it has many schisms and factions. Both organizationally and scientifically there are opposing points of view and, at times, bitter factional disputes. The patient may take advantage of this situation and adopt a superior attitude toward "petty, quarrelsome scientists who haven't been able to put their own houses in order." On the other hand, the patient may become an active partisan or proselyte of his own therapist's persuasion.

As he becomes well informed about the particular orientation of his therapist, the patient may color his observations and experiences, emphasizing those aspects he assumes to be of interest to his therapist and minimizing others. He soon learns that his therapist is particularly interested in sex or dreams, or recent versus past experiences. He may unwittingly slant his presentation to suit these interests. While this occurs more or less in all patients, it is particularly evident in the obsessional, who places great emphasis on intellectual skill and one-upmanship. In these situations, the omniscient strivings serve many purposes.

The emphasis on knowing also allows the patient to deal with the therapeutic process by the use of psychoanalytic jargon, which can result in an intellectual exercise that makes therapy an examination of psychoanalytic theory rather than of the patient's behavior: The patient attempts to deal with the therapist by impressing him with his brilliant observations—to be looked at in terms of theory rather than in terms of his own life. Too often, the therapist himself is guilty of substituting psychoanalytic jargon for comprehensible language. The obsessional patient can become quite expert in using this terminology to enter the "club," but it serves to evade a meaningful confrontation with his attitudes and behavior. Freud had this type of person in mind when he advised his patients against reading or becoming too familiar with psychoanalytic literature. He wished to avoid as much as possible any slanting of a patient's productions which would be stimulated by reading. He also wanted to forestall discussions about psychoanalysis that might be stimulated by such reading. Although this injunction still remains useful, it has become impractical because most patients have already become acquainted with psychoanalytic writings, either in popularized or professional forms.

In the service of pleasing the therapist and fortifying his theories, a patient may avoid discoveries or observations which he thinks may negate these theories. In his own search for certainty and in his skill at accumulating knowledge, the patient may not want to disturb the therapist's established systems. He needs to view the therapist as an idealized figure, in order to put his trust in him. To preserve this image, the patient may forego criticism and intellectual disagreement. He may even seek out evidence or distort observations in order to fortify the therapist's analytic orientation. Such activity must be dealt with by the therapist with dispatch and in a forthright fashion if the therapy is not to become a technical course or a mutual admiration society.

If the therapist is himself obsessional and requires such idealization, the therapeutic process reaches a stalemate. It may appear to be progressing well with few complications, but little therapeutic progress will be noted, and therapy may become an interminable process.

PROBLEMS OF GRANDIOSITY

The obsessional's grandiosity is often manifested in his arrogant and contemptuous behavior, even though it may be dressed in a cloak of modesty and humbleness. He may expose his snobbishness and haughty behavior by slips of the tongue, accidental oversights, or deliberate deletions.

One patient, while standing in a cafeteria line with his wife, had ordered two rare roast beef sandwiches. One turned out to be less rare than the other. The patient insisted that the less rare one was his wife's. This resulted in a rather heated argument about the restaurant and its defects. After he related the story during a therapeutic session, I asked him how he knew that the less rare sandwich (the least desirable one) was his wife's, since he had picked them both off the counter. He suddenly became silent and was dumbfounded when he realized that he had automatically taken it for granted that the better one was naturally for him. It was also striking that his wife did not make this observation but instead got into an argument about the restaurant and the poor service. The patient operated under the assumption that he was a privileged and special person whose desires were to be catered to at all times.

To maintain the illusion of superiority and to protect his grandiose conception of himself, the obsessional may limit his socializing to inferiors or to occasions when his superior feelings will go unchallenged. He may feel marked envy and anxiety in the presence of realistic status differences, and while he may yearn for relationships with higher-status individuals, he will either derogate them or discover some deficiency in them that allows him to eliminate them as potential friends. If they are rich, they may not be intelligent enough. If they are intelligent, he will insist that they are phony or pretentious. However, resolving the dilemma by limiting his relationships to inferiors leaves great areas of dissatisfaction because his own status is not sufficiently acknowledged by associating with such people.

In therapy, grandiosity manifests itself in a variety of ways; it needs to be identified whenever it appears. This issue often accounts for the aloofness and the failure to become involved in a relationship with the therapist. The patient remains distant but proper and does the job as it is outlined to him. Secretly, he feels superior and contemptuous of the therapist; he is "on" to what is happening. He feels smug and "above it all." He may catalog the therapist's deficiencies, storing them for use at a proper time. He may, for example, keep track of the time the sessions start, watching to see that he gets all the time he is entitled to and storing up evidence of the therapist's oversight. Such stored-up grievances are usually held as secret weapons and are revealed only under sufficient provocation. Meanwhile, they may be used to maintain secret feelings of superiority in his relationship to the therapist.

Such feelings may seriously interfere with the therapeutic work, not only because they are secret but also because they are used to discount or discard any formulations which the patient doesn't like. They help the patient remain on the outside, looking in. By feeling superior to what is going on, the patient remains uninvolved while he is supposedly participating in a mutual exchange. If the therapist fails to bring this into the open, documenting it well, it will seriously hamper the progress of therapy. If the therapist succeeds in exposing this technique to the patient, it will enhance the patient's respect for the therapist.

In this connection, a patient related an incident concerning his pregnant wife, who awakened in the middle of the night with a cramp and proceeded to wake him up. He became furious with her for awakening him, showing no concern about her pregnancy and suggesting that if she could not control her wakefulness she should sleep in another room. The following morning he recognized the arrogance of his attitude and felt quite remorseful. However, while relating the incident, he also reported his fantasy of how he thought I might behave under similar circumstances. In his fantasy he assumed that I allowed my wife to push me around, and he felt contempt for me because of this. When I called attention to the difficulties he had in making his tenderness for his wife evident, he fantasized that I was a softy who couldn't stick up for my rights. He was certainly remorseful about what he could recognize as arrogant behavior toward his wife, but he was unaware of his arrogance toward me during this exchange. I called his attention to this behavior and to how he felt toward me because he thought that I was taking his wife's side. He could then see his arrogance as it was expressed in various relationships.

The obsessional's grandiosity leads him to expect magical leaps and massive advances in therapy. He is impatient with small gains and expects every meaningful interpretation to be followed by great advances or total cure.

There is often a profound disappointment when an illuminating exchange is followed by a repetition of the old pattern. When this happens, the patient criticizes the therapist and the psychotherapeutic theory as well as himself because he feels that he has failed to live up to his own grandiose expectations. As he can accept only total and complete restoration of his grandiose self through therapy, he cannot abide the slow, gradual process of learning and changing. This leads him to the frequent charge that the therapy is doing no good: "Nothing has changed" or "It's been a waste of time and money."

After acknowledging some advance when the patient recognizes that his somatic preoccupation is a way of dealing with doubts about his acceptability as a clever and creative person, he may begin to derogate himself for needing still to utilize obsessional techniques. He should be beyond that. His grandiosity, which requires automatic acknowledgment from others as to his brilliance, prevents him from appreciating the advances he is making in resolving his obsessional tendencies. The therapist must avoid trying to justify his work or blaming events on the patient's lack of cooperation. When progress is slow or absent, the therapist should not put the blame on the patient's resistance or resort to the concept of the negative therapeutic response. While many factors may be at work in the negative therapeutic reaction, it is clear that many therapeutic impasses or failures are also caused by the therapist's inadequate handling of the obsessional defense; this the therapist must face and take responsibility for. Therefore, failure cannot be said to be exclusively the fault of either the patient or the therapist. However, understanding of undue expectation, a need for magical solutions, and feelings of despair and disappointment when immediate success is not forthcoming is of particular significance in the treatment of obsessionals.

The therapist must show interest in the patient's charges that the work is not going well or that little progress is being made. He should not act as though such charges are entirely unjustified and as if he were always above reproach. Generally, one can find both rational and irrational elements in a patient's complaints, and when dealt with seriously, they offer an opportunity for the patient to examine his grandiose expectations and for the therapist to explore his own deficiencies. An admission of the slowness of the process and the limited success it has produced presents the patient with a view of the therapist's realistic goals in contrast to the patient's extravagant expectations. It may even be useful for the patient to recognize that because of the comparatively youthful state of the science of psychotherapy, the therapist is bound by limitations imposed by the science itself. This is a valuable learning experience for someone whose major difficulty lies in his reluctance to acknowledge any limitations caused by nature or biology. To have this acknowledged in a matter-of-fact way, without apologies, may be of great help in getting the patient to accept some limitations in his own existence. Such an exchange may well serve to increase the patient's respect for the therapist's honesty and integrity.

The obsessional's hope that psychotherapy will enable him to become perfect and invulnerable is an aspect of his expectations which often overshadows all of his goals. He hopes that psychotherapy will build up his resources so that he will never need to be dependent upon anyone and that it will strengthen his esteem so that he will never again need to be beholden. He hopes therapy will provide him with sufficient placidity and detachment that he need not be upset or distressed under any circumstances, even unfavorable ones. In short, he secretly hopes to repair his deficiencies and overcome his weaknesses and be made perfect—all as a result of therapy. When he discovers that, instead of making him a superman, therapy attempts to strengthen his humanness and get him to accept his imperfections, he is both angry and disappointed. Instead of an anxiety-free existence in a state of perfect living, he discovers that therapy will only help him to live with anxiety in an imperfect world in which he will have no ultimate control over his destiny. Such goals are so alien to him that he considers himself a failure for even approaching them. This produces the typical obsessional dilemma: As he becomes emotionally and psychologically more mature, he seems to feel that he is getting worse. However, as therapy progresses, he comes to realize that in the long run to accept his humanness will provide a more valid source of security. At this time, the patient's complaint that he is getting worse is often evidence of improvement—particularly when it is clear that getting worse means becoming less dependent upon his neurotic patterns. It is crucial that these factors be clearly explained to the patient, so that he can tolerate some temporary discomforts in order to gain the ultimate increase in his security.

PART II

Psychological Research

9. The 'Obsessional': On the Psychological Classification of Obsessional Character Traits and Symptoms

Joseph Sandler and Anandi Hazari

THE TERM 'obsessional' has a wide number of rather different usages. It is employed to denote a well-recognized clinical condition (as in 'obsessional neurosis' or 'obsessional state'), as a descriptive label applied to single symptoms, as an indication of a type of character in both normal and disturbed subjects, and as a term of abuse or approbation used to describe one's friends or colleagues (often depending on whether one finds their behaviour irksome or not).

A great many definitions of obsession and compulsion are recorded in the literature (e.g. Freud, 1895; Fenichel, 1945; Masserman, 1946; Bennet, 1949; Glover, 1949; Noyes, 1949; Curran & Guttman, 1951; Henderson & Gillespie, 1951; Mayer-Gross, Slater & Roth, 1954; Laughlin, 1956). The implication of all these definitions is that an *obsession* is an unwanted but repetitive thought which forces itself insistently into consciousness and recurs against the conscious desires of the person concerned. Such thoughts may include intrusive doubts, wishes, fears, impulses, prohibitions, warnings and commands. Neither reason nor logic can influence these pointless, repugnant, insistent and absurd thoughts, and they persist so tenaciously that they cannot be dispelled by conscious effort. On the whole they are recognized by their owners as largely irrelevant and irrational. A *compulsion,* in addition to having many qualities in common with obsessions, is generally thought of as expressed in action. It can be regarded as a morbid, intrusive, insistent and repetitive urge to perform some stereotyped act—apparently trifling and meaningless—which is contrary to the patient's ordinary conscious wishes or standards. Failure to perform the compulsive act usually results in anxiety,

Reprinted by permission of the British Psychological Society from the *British Journal of Medical Psychology* 33 (1960): 113–22.

while once it has been carried out, there usually occurs some temporary subjective lessening of tension.

Many authors (e.g. Freud, 1907; Fenichel, 1945; Masserman, 1946; Bennet, 1949; Noyes, 1949; Laughlin, 1956) maintain that obsessions and compulsions are related phenomena and that an obsessional act is an expression of an obsessional thought. Freud (1907) classed compulsive acts and ceremonials with obsessive thoughts and ideas. He regarded the two types as forming a definite clinical entity, and in his view compulsions could be seen as defensive behavioural reactions to obsessional thoughts and impulses. Henderson & Gillespie (1951) also take the view that both obsessive-ruminative and obsessive-compulsive states can be included in the obsessive psychoneurosis, but they do point to a clinical differentiation between patients who perform compulsive acts and those in whom the ruminations do not lead to such activity. Many writers regard the difference between obsession and compulsion as a superficial one and hold that they both serve the same purpose of defence against anxiety and do it in much the same way. As both phenomena are frequently found in the same person, the term obsessive-compulsive neurosis is in common use, though the term 'obsessional neurosis', which includes the performance of compulsive acts as well, is perhaps more current.

In discussing 'The predisposition to obsessional neurosis' (1913), Freud noted a distinction between the neurosis proper and a type of character which corresponded to it. Whereas in the neurosis there is a failure of repression with the emergence or threatened emergence into consciousness of the repressed material, in the formation of the corresponding character-traits, the repression is more successful and it easily attains its aim by replacing the repressed with reaction formations and sublimations. Thus Freud observed a distinction between obsessional (anal) character-traits and obsessional neurosis. In his essay on 'Character and anal erotism' (1908) he had described the traits of orderliness, parsimony and obstinacy as constituting the cardinal triad of the anal character. Later this difference between symptoms and traits was elaborated by Jones (1918) and Abraham (1921), and others.

THE RELATION BETWEEN OBSESSIVE-COMPULSIVE SYMPTOMS AND CHARACTER-TRAITS

The essential nature of the obsessive-compulsive symptom seems to lie in its appearance as a mental content, an idea, image, affect, impulse or act with a subjective sense of compulsion overriding an internal resistance. The symptom is usually recognized by the patient as alien to his personality and something to be combated.

Certain character-traits to which the term 'obsessional' is often applied tend, however, not to arouse anxiety and seem to be ego-syntonic in nature. They are seldom felt to be irrational or absurd, nor do they seem to the subject to be an intolerable load which he would willingly forgo. On the contrary, the possession of such traits is often considered to be subjectively and socially worth while. Thus the excessively tidy person may be described as having an obsessional character, but he must be contrasted with the person who cannot bear, for example, to touch certain objects without feeling compelled to wash his hands. It seems to follow that a distinction can be made between obsessional and compulsive traits which are not considered alien to the personality, and those which are similar in form to the symptoms of obsessional neurosis, though quantitatively insufficient to cause a gross impairment of normal mental functioning and which do not lead their possessor to seek psychiatric help.

Some authors hold that the difference between an obsessional character-trait of any sort and an obsessional neurosis is purely one of degree. Thus Masserman (1946) and Noyes (1949) assert that an obsessive-compulsive neurosis appears when the defensive thoughts and acts of the person with an obsessional character become disrupted, or when obsessive-compulsive behaviour becomes too widely pervasive and deviant. Reich (1949) considered that there are fluid transitions from compulsive symptoms to the corresponding character attitudes. Michaels & Porter (1949) are of the opinion that obsessional neurosis represents a pathological exaggeration of normal character variants, and that a certain degree of compulsiveness may be regarded as an asset, within the range of normal personality variation. Such compulsive tendencies are represented by a normal concern with cleanliness, orderliness, responsibility and law-abidance which may hardly be considered pathological in a civilized society. Rapaport (1948) holds that the breakdown of the obsessional character is inevitably followed by the development of obsessional neurosis. Against this, certain authors (e.g. Mayer-Gross *et al.* 1954) assert that the obsessional neurosis does not represent a further breakdown of the obsessional character. Should the person with an obsessional character suffer a nervous breakdown, there is no evidence (according to these authors) to suggest that he will necessarily or even frequently become an obsessional neurotic. They point out that other pathological reactions such as depression, excessive anxiety and paranoia also develop in obsessional personalities.

Some investigators believe that obsessional character-traits are developed simultaneously with compulsive symptoms as part of an obsessive-compulsive neurosis, while others hold that the development of the obsessional character structure wards off definite obsessive-compulsive symptoms. In Fenichel's opinion (1945) both types occur.

Rado, in his chapter on 'Obsessive behaviour' in the *American Handbook of Psychiatry* (1959) differentiates 'obsessive attacks' from 'obsessive traits', but goes on to discuss both as reflections of obsessive behaviour, occurring together in the same person.

THE PRESENT STUDY

It is the purpose of the research reported here to investigate certain character-traits and neurotic symptoms which can be designated 'obsessional' or 'compulsive'. We have attempted to attack the problem of whether these can be conveniently classified in a way which is meaningful both psychologically and statistically. To this end we have made use of the responses of a group of neurotic subjects to a psychological inventory (Sandler, 1954) and have employed a classificatory technique which has proved of value in investigations of a similar sort (Sandler & Pollock, 1954a–c; Kanter & Sandler, 1955; Sandler & Rakoff, 1955; Dixon, de Monchaux & Sandler, 1957a,b; Sandler, de Monchaux & Dixon, 1958; Sandler, 1958; Taçon, 1958; Bishop, 1958).

The raw data of this study consist of the responses made by 100 patients attending the Tavistock Clinic (50 men and 50 women) to the items of the Tavistock Self-Assessment Inventory. This research instrument has been described elsewhere (Sandler, 1954). It contains 867 items, and a subject can record, in response to each item, his own assessment of whether the statement contained in each item is predominantly true or false in respect of himself. For any one item we therefore have a set of scores which can be expressed in dichotomous form.

Forty of the items in the Inventory relate to obsessive and compulsive character-traits and symptoms, and these were selected for the present study. They are listed in Table 9.1.

Subjects

One hundred patients, 50 men and 50 women, have been used in this investigation. They were all neurotics in the sense that each one had some sort of psychological problem which had caused him to seek medical aid.

Table 9.1. The 40 Test Items

1. I tend to get very worried over relatively minor matters.
2. I dislike 'doing things by halves'.
3. I frequently find that a thought or a tune keeps recurring in my head for a long time.
4. I tend to worry for a long time over humiliating experiences.
5. I often ask myself, 'have I done right?'
6. I try to be perfect in my work.
7. I get furious with people who leave the lavatory in a filthy state.
8. I hate dirt or dirty things.
9. I am a punctual sort of person.
10. I dislike making hurried decisions.
11. I often find myself getting behind with things in general.
12. I often have to check up to see whether I have closed a door or switched off a light.
13. When I describe something I feel I must use exactly the right words.
14. I am usually consistent in my behaviour, going about my work in the same way, following the same routes, etc.
15. I tend to brood for a long time over a single idea.
16. I have a passion for being thorough in most things I do.
17. I usually find it difficult to get started on things I have to do.
18. I find it very difficult to make up my mind, even about unimportant things.
19. I am often inwardly compelled to do certain things even though my reason tells me it is not necessary.
20. I spend most of my time worrying about small details.
21. I am slow in deciding on a course of action.
22. I find that a well-ordered mode of life with regular hours and an established routine suits me very well.
23. I sometimes feel inwardly compelled to do things even though I do not really want to do them.
24. I am the sort of person who pays a great deal of attention to detail.
25. I find it hard to interrupt a task before I have finished it.
26. I am 'fussy' about keeping my hands clean.
27. I find I have sometimes to memorize numbers or count things that are not important.
28. I am very systematic and methodical in my daily life.
29. I take great care in hanging or folding my clothes at night.
30. If something I like becomes soiled or damaged it is completely 'spoiled' for me.
31. At times I feel the compulsion to count things.
32. I take pride in having a neat and tidy handwriting.
33. I sometimes find myself compelled to walk or step over cracks in the pavement in a special way.
34. I usually do things slowly and deliberately.
35. I have higher standards of cleanliness than the average person.
36. I find I have to stop and think before doing even the smallest thing.
37. I am troubled by bad and dirty thoughts.
38. There are some things which I feel I have to touch whenever I see them.
39. I sometimes get bad words in my mind and find it difficult to get rid of them.
40. I cannot get to sleep if I have not done certain things in a special order.

These adults were referred to the Tavistock Clinic either by a general medical practitioner or by some social agency. The Tavistock Clinic is an out-patient clinic which admits, for diagnosis and treatment, patients suffering mainly from various psychoneuroses. Psychotic patients, and those suffering from severe organic disturbances are generally not referred to this clinic. Keeping in view the type of patient admitted, it can be assumed that the population under investigation was composed of adult neurotics, although the possibility that some suffered from mild psychotic illnesses cannot be excluded. The ages of these patients ranged from 16 to 54, with a mean age of 30 years.

These patients were admitted to the Tavistock Clinic, London, over a period of 2 years. No patient who did not complete all the six booklets of the Self-Assessment Inventory was included in this study. No subjective criteria were used as the basis of selection. The population studied consisted of the first 50 men and the first 50 women to complete the Inventory.

Procedure

In order to find a basis for the classification of the responses of the subjects to the 40 items used, it was decided to subject the data to factor analysis, using Thurstone's Centroid Method (1947). The items were intercorrelated using phi-coefficients (point product-moment coefficients). The rationale of this procedure has been given by Sandler & Pollock (1954a, Appendix 1).

The resultant 40×40 correlation matrix was factored into two common factors, accounting for 14.95 and 7.61% of the total variance respectively.[1]

The factor saturations are listed in Table 9.2. It will be seen that the

Table 9.2. The Centroid Factor Saturations

Item	Factor I	Factor II	Item	Factor I	Factor II
1	0.49	0.09	21	0.28	0.34
2	0.27	−0.29	22	0.23	−0.27
3	0.42	0.22	23	0.60	0.16
4	0.48	0.38	24	0.43	−0.39
5	0.44	0.24	25	0.27	−0.21
6	0.28	−0.19	26	0.40	−0.36
7	0.20	−0.28	27	0.42	0.25
8	0.37	−0.41	28	0.35	−0.50
9	0.12	−0.28	29	0.46	−0.39
10	0.35	0.20	30	0.41	0.09
11	0.31	0.44	31	0.49	0.21
12	0.45	0.31	32	0.26	−0.37
13	0.33	−0.16	33	0.46	0.26
14	0.25	−0.16	34	0.22	−0.12
15	0.52	0.28	35	0.33	−0.14
16	0.32	−0.43	36	0.45	0.23
17	0.31	0.28	37	0.35	0.26
18	0.49	0.26	38	0.25	−0.09
19	0.62	0.28	39	0.32	0.23
20	0.43	0.04	40	0.42	0.06

Table 9.3 Items with High Projections on Vector A

29. I take great care in hanging or folding my clothes at night.	with regular hours and an established routine suits me very well.
28. I am very systematic and methodical in my daily life.	13. When I describe something I feel I must use exactly the right words.
24. I am the sort of person who pays a great deal of attention to detail.	7. I get furious with people who leave the lavatory in a filthy state.
8. I hate dirt or dirty things.	25. I find it hard to interrupt a task before I have finished it.
26. I am 'fussy' about keeping my hands clean.	6. I try to be perfect in my work.
16. I have a passion for being thorough in most things I do.	35. I have higher standards of cleanliness than the average person.
32. I take pride in having a neat and tidy handwriting.	14. I am usually consistent in my behaviour, going about my work in the same way, following the same routes, etc.
2. I dislike 'doing things by halves'.	
22. I find that a well-ordered mode of life	9. I am a punctual sort of person.

saturations of the items with Factor I are all positive. Factor II is bipolar, having both positive and negative saturations (a consequence of the Centroid method). Full details of the procedures used have been given elsewhere (Hazari, 1957).

In order to assist interpretation of the relative position of the items in the two-factor space, they have been plotted graphically in the usual way (Fig. 9.1). For purposes of identification, each item has been given a short title consisting of a single word or phrase. The full text of each item may be found by reference to Table 9.1.

A distinct clustering of the items can be seen to occur, and after a careful examination of the findings, it was decided to relate the positions of the points denoting the test items to two reference vectors, A and B, as shown in Fig. 9.1. These were obtained through a formal rotation of the Centroid factor axes through 45° (a slightly 'better' fit could be found by departing slightly from 45°, but as the differentiation between the items is so gross, no psychological refinement of the results would occur from its use).

Reference to the items differentiated by the factor analysis shows an immediate and striking classification of our 'obsessional' items into two main, more-or-less independent tendencies, represented by the vectors A and B in Fig. 9.1. The items with the highest projection on vector A are shown in Table 9.3, and those with the highest projections on vector B, in Table 9.4. (Items 1, 20, 23, 30, 34, 38 and 40 do not fall so clearly into the two groups in Fig. 9.1, and are thus not included in Tables 9.3 and 9.4.)

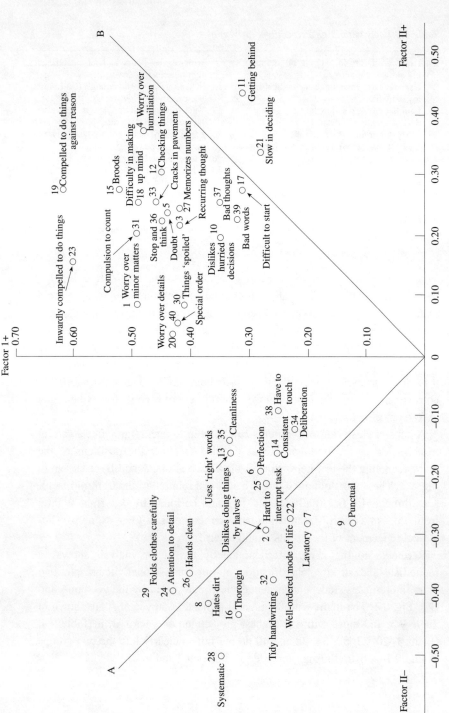

Figure 9.1. The distribution of items in the two-factor space

Table 9.4. Items with High Projections on Vector B

19. I am often inwardly compelled to do certain things even though my reason tells me it is not necessary.
4. I tend to worry for a long time over humiliating experiences.
15. I tend to brood for a long time over a single idea.
12. I often have to check up to see whether I have closed a door or switched off a light.
18. I find it very difficult to make up my mind, even about unimportant things.
11. I often find myself getting behind with things in general.
33. I sometimes find myself compelled to walk or step over cracks in the pavement in a special way.
31. At times I feel the compulsion to count things.
36. I find I have to stop and think before doing even the smallest thing.
5. I often ask myself, 'have I done right?'
27. I find I have sometimes to memorize numbers or count things that are not important.
3. I frequently find that a thought or a tune keeps recurring in my head for a long time.
21. I am slow in deciding on a course of action.
37. I am troubled by bad and dirty thoughts.
17. I usually find it difficult to get started on things I have to do.
10. I dislike making hurried decisions.
39. I sometimes get bad words in my mind and find it difficult to get rid of them.

Discussion of Results

The distinction between the two groups of items is at once impressive and meaningful. A patient who reports an item of the 'A' type will have a greater-than-chance tendency to report other items of the same type, and little more than a chance likelihood of giving a positive response to the items of group 'B', and vice versa. We seem to have two tendencies which, in their appearance in this group of patients, appear to be more or less unrelated.

The A-Type

The items in Table 9.3 present a picture of an exceedingly systematic, methodical and thorough person, who likes a well-ordered mode of life, is consistent, punctual and meticulous in his use of words. He dislikes half-done tasks, and finds interruptions irksome. He pays much attention to detail and has a strong aversion to dirt. The picture we get is very similar to that which has been described by many authors as the 'obsessional' character, and corresponds, in certain aspects, to the anal-reactive character depicted in the psycho-analytic literature. Rado (1959) describes the person with an obsessional character as 'overconscientious in his own particular way. What he is mostly concerned with are the minutiae, the inconsequential details, the meticulous observance of minor rules and petty formalities'.

Although the term 'obsessional' has frequently been applied to this constellation of character traits, it is clear that they bear no relation, as far as occurrence and distribution are concerned, to the items in group 'B', which resemble qualitatively far more the symptoms of obsessional neurosis. It is the supposed correlation between the two groups which has led to the use of the descriptive label 'obsessional' for this type of character structure, and the results of the present investigation give reason for seriously questioning the suitability of this description.

What distinguishes the items in this group from those in group B is the fact that they appear to be well-integrated into the personality, a source of pride and self-esteem rather than of the anxiety and tension—the 'worry'—which we usually associate with obsessional symptoms, and which is so marked a characteristic of group 'B'. They represent traits of character which are ego-syntonic (or rather self-syntonic), and which conform to their possessor's ideal standards for himself—standards which are rather more demanding than those of the average person. From the point of view of pathology, these traits may also be taken to represent reaction formations against unconscious and unwanted and smearing and dirtying impulses. Freud has pointed out (1914) that conformity to one's ego-ideal is a source of raised self-esteem, of narcissistic gain, and in view of this a suitable, though tentative, designation for the character pattern described here might be *reactive-narcissistic*.

The B-Type

The items in Table 9.4 all resemble, to a greater or lesser degree, the symptoms of an obsessional neurosis. We have here a person whose daily life is disturbed through the intrusion of unwanted thoughts and impulses into his conscious experience. Thus he is compelled to do things which his reason tells him are unnecessary, to perform certain rituals as part of his everyday behaviour, to memorize trivia, and to struggle with persistent 'bad' thoughts. He tends to worry over his past actions, to brood over ideas, and finds himself getting behind with things. He has difficulty in making up his mind, and he has inner resistance to commencing work.

In spite of the obvious description of the items in this group as 'symptoms', one may wonder whether, in mild form, the pattern found here exists in patients who do not break down with an obsessional neurosis. We are all familiar with the 'chronic worrier', and it seems likely that a personality type exists which presents this picture in a form which does not yet deserve the title 'obsessional neurosis' or 'obsessional state'. If the picture presented here represents a personality type, which in exaggerated form might appear as obsessional neurosis, then it would seem legitimate to apply the description *obsessional personality* to this type of person.

The Distinction between Types

This description of two 'pure' types, isolated on a statistical basis from our Inventory data, does not at all imply that the types are mutually exclusive; the notion of 'independence' of types in this context is a statistical one. Most subjects who show the attributes indicated by the items will show a mixture of both types, and relatively few will be representative of the 'pure' forms. What the research does indicate is that the items *within* a group will tend to be positively associated, but that the association of *reactive-narcissistic* with true *obsessional* features is more or less at random.

The distinction we have made is descriptive, and it does not follow at all that the two do not share, to some extent, a common pathology (for example, conflicts centred around 'anal' urges). Even if both types share common conflicts, the mode of resolution of these conflicts is quite different in both, and it would be incorrect, as some authors have tended to do, to minimize the differences between the two.

CONCLUSIONS

The findings of the present investigation are consistent with the view that the term 'obsessional' has at least two distinct connotations, embracing two relatively independent constellations, which we have referred to as the *reactive-narcissistic character* and the true *obsessional* picture. This latter constellation might possibly represent a continuum ranging from the *obsessional personality* on the one hand to *obsessional neurosis* or *obsessional state* on the other.

On the basis of these results a number of questions can be poised.

1. What symptoms are presented by patients with a *reactive-narcissistic* character which lead them to seek treatment?
2. Do the patients with an *obsessional* personality ask help for obsessional symptoms, or do they present other psychiatric states as well?
3. What are the further correlates of the two constellations described? Is, for example, the *obsessional* personality only part of a much wider personality disturbance?

4. What sex differences are evident in the distribution of the two constellations and their correlates?

In an attempt to provide at least partial answers to these questions, a further investigation has been undertaken. This will be reported in a subsequent paper.

NOTE

1. The amount of variance accounted for by the common factors is usually low when phi-coefficients are factored. Some investigators make use of tetrachoric correlation coefficients in order to obtain higher common factor variances, but this is at the expense of accuracy, as the calculation of tetrachoric coefficients produces serious distortions in the correlation matrix.

REFERENCES

Abraham, K. 1921. Contribution to the theory of the anal character. In Selected Papers on Psychoanalysis (1948). London: Hogarth.
Bennet, E. A. 1949. The neuroses. In Modern Practice in Psychological Medicine. Ed. by J. R. Rees. London: Butterworth.
Bishop, J. S. 1958. A study of schizoid personality traits in adult psychiatric patients. Ph.D. Thesis. London: University of London Library.
Curran, D. & Guttman, E. 1951. Psychological Medicine. Edinburgh: Livingstone.
Dixon, J. J., de Monchaux, C. & Sandler, J. 1957a. Patterns of anxiety: the phobias. Brit. J. Med. Psychol. 30, 34.
———. 1957b. Patterns of anxiety: an analysis of social anxieties. Brit. J. Med. Psychol. 30, 107.
Fenichel, O. 1945. The Psychoanalytic Theory of Neurosis. New York: Norton.
Freud, S. 1895. Obsessions and phobias—their psychical mechanism and their aetiology. In Collected Papers, 1 (1948). London: Hogarth.
———. 1907. Obsessive acts and religious practices. In Collected Papers, 2 (1948). London: Hogarth.
———. 1908. Character and anal erotism. In Collected Papers, 2 (1948). London: Hogarth.
———. 1913. The Predisposition to obsessional neurosis. In Collected Papers, 2 (1948). London: Hogarth.
———. 1914. On Narcissism: an introduction. In Standard Edition, Vol. 14 (1957). London: Hogarth.
Glover, E. 1949. Psychoanalysis. New York: Staples.
Hazari, A. 1957. An investigation of obsessive-compulsive character-traits and symptoms in adult neurotics. Ph.D. Thesis. London: University of London Library.

Henderson, D. K. & Gillespie, R. D. 1951. A Text-Book of Psychiatry. *London: Oxford University Press.*

Jones, E. 1918. Anal erotic character traits. In Papers on Psychoanalysis *(1938). London: Ballière, Tindall and Cox.*

Kanter, V. B. & Sandler, J. 1955. Studies in psychopathology using a self-assessment inventory. V. Anxiety, functional dyspepsia and duodenal ulcer: an investigation. Brit. J. Med. Psychol. **28,** *157.*

Laughlin, N. P. 1956. The Neuroses in Clinical Practice. *London and Philadelphia: W. B. Saunders.*

Masserman, J. H. 1946. Principles of Dynamic Psychiatry. *London and Philadelphia: W. B. Saunders.*

Mayer-Gross, W., Slater, E. & Roth, M. 1954. Clinical Psychiatry. *London: Cassell.*

Michaels, J. J. & Porter, R. T. 1949. Psychiatric and social implications of contrasts between psychopathic personality and obsessive-compulsive neurosis. J. Nerv. Ment. Dis. **109,** *122.*

Noyes, A. P. 1949. Modern Clinical Psychiatry. *London and Philadelphia: W. B. Saunders.*

Rado, S. 1959. Obsessive behavior. In American Handbook of Psychiatry. *New York: Basic Books.*

Rapaport, D. 1948. Diagnostic Psychological Testing, *Vol. 2. Chicago: Year Book.*

Reich, W. 1949. Character Analysis. *New York: Orgone Institute Press.*

Sandler, J. 1954. Studies in psychopathology using a self-assessment inventory. I. The development and construction of the inventory. Brit. J. Med. Psychol. **27,** *142.*

——. *1958. The use of the Tavistock Self-assessment Inventory in Psychosomatic Research.* Proc. Roy. Soc. Med. **51,** *948.*

Sandler, J., de Monchaux, C. & Dixon, J. J. 1958. Patterns of anxiety: The correlates of social anxieties. Brit. J. Med. Psychol. **31,** *24.*

Sandler, J. & Pollock, A. B. 1954a. Studies in psychopathology using a self-assessment inventory. II. Some neurotic gastro-intestinal symptoms: functional dyspepsia in men. Brit. J. Med. Psychol. **27,** *146.*

——. *1954b. Studies in psychopathology using a self-assessment inventory. III. Some neurotic gastro-intestinal symptoms: functional dyspepsia in women.* Brit. J. Med. Psychol. **27,** *235.*

——. *1954c. Studies in psychopathology using a self-assessment inventory. IV. Some neurotic gastro-intestinal symptoms: defaecatory difficulty in men and women.* Brit. J. Med. Psychol. **27,** *241.*

Sandler, J. & Rakoff, V. 1955. Blushing. World Science Review, *November. (Abstract of paper to Brit. Assoc. for Advancement of Science.)*

Taçon, S. F. 1958. An investigation of some psychosomatic symptoms in adult neurotic patients. Ph.D. Thesis. London: University of London Library.

Thurstone, L. L. 1947. Multiple Factor Analysis. *Chicago: University of Chicago Press.*

10. Obsessive Compulsive Neurosis in Children

Lewis L. Judd

For the purposes of this paper the symptoms of obsession and compulsion will be defined and identified separately. The term obsession will refer to an unwanted repetitive thought, which insistently forces itself into consciousness and recurs against the wishes of the patient. It may include ideas, images, affects, or impulses, which neither reason, logic, nor conscious effort are able to influence. A compulsion has many qualities in common with an obsession, but it is expressed in action and is described as a repetitive, stereotyped, and often trivial motor act. Failure to perform the compulsive act results in increasing anxiety, but once performed there is usually a temporary subjective reduction of tension. The essential nature of the obsessive compulsive symptoms, as opposed to similar personality traits, is that they are recognized by the patient as being incongruous and alien to his personality and are, therefore, always combated and resisted.

An interest in the obsessive compulsive neurosis in children was first generated by seeing two patients, ages 7 and 10, who both presented the unmistakable features of this reaction. A search of the literature, to learn of others' experiences with children who had this syndrome, was quite unrewarding. It was surprising to learn that very little has been written about the occurrence of this neurosis in childhood and much of what has been written is contradictory or inconclusive. It is also interesting that each author, who has added to the scanty literature on this subject, commented on the vagueness and lack of specific information of former articles.

It was noticeable that very few studies made contributions to clarify any of the factors related to the natural history of this disease in children.

Stimulated by this, a study focusing solely on the descriptive characteristics of the neurosis was undertaken, using case material from the Child Psychiatry Service at the UCLA Neuropsychiatric Institute. The concentration was on

Reprinted by permission of the American Medical Association from *Archives of General Psychiatry* 12 (1965): 136–43.

observable factors and characteristics, in an attempt to collect and catalogue more descriptive information.

By design, psychodynamics were not formally dealt with and when they appear it will be only by implication or as a part of a patient's history.

It was anticipated that by using a descriptive approach in combination with a sufficient number of cases it would be possible to make some statistically valid, definitive statements about this neurotic reaction in childhood.

LITERATURE REVIEW

The inconclusiveness of the literature is forcibly represented by the basic disagreement as to whether this condition does or does not exist in children. Several of the general textbooks of child psychiatry indicate that the onset of this illness is very rare before puberty. Kanner[33] in his text refers to many analytic authors who in reporting adult analyses indicate some obsessive symptoms can be traced into childhood. He also states that children are rarely brought in for treatment of obsessive compulsive neuroses before 14 years of age. Benjamin[4] along with Bakwin and Bakwin[2] in their texts, both agree that obsessive ideas and compulsive actions are common in children, but are relatively innocuous and not neurotic.

Further inquiry reveals that other authors, usually reporting from specific clinical data, give evidence that this reaction can occur during childhood. One of the first references to disabling compulsive symptoms in a child was recorded by Freud[17] in his description of the laborious ritualization undertaken by an 11-year-old boy before he could sleep. In the paper "The Predisposition to Obsessional Neurosis"[21] published in 1913, he also stated that the neurosis shows its first symptoms between the ages of 6 and 8.

In 1935, Muriel Hall[28] reported obsessive compulsive neuroses in two 12-year-old children. Her conclusions were that this diagnosis was valid when the intensity and permanence of the obsessive compulsive symptoms are severe enough to interfere with the child's functioning. Her cases had an insidious onset (with symptoms occurring two to five years before treatment); the patients had good insight into their symptoms; were timid; imaginative and very moralistic, and had a family history of obsessive compulsive tendencies.

Five years later Bender and Schilder[3] described a syndrome they called Impulsions, which was closely allied to an obsessive compulsive reaction. The children, usually males, were pathologically preoccupied with very specific interests, upon which they fixed their total attention to the exclusion of other activities. These interests were so impelling and engrossing as to interfere with normal social adaption. In contrast to obsessions and compulsions, which the patient characteristically protests and resists, these interests or Impulsions were pursued with great satisfaction. It was these authors' opinion that a significant percentage of the cases of obsessive compulsive neuroses formerly reported fell into the Impulsion category and that the neurosis was rare under the age of 10.

In his article, in 1942, Leo Berman[6] reviewed 3,050 cases admitted to the Children's Services at Bellevue and the Bradley Home during a four-year period (1935–1939). Of this total, 62 were diagnosed as having obsessive compulsive neuroses. More careful scrutiny of the record eliminated all but six which were considered unequivocally typical of the syndrome. The average age symptoms were noticed was 11½ with a range of 10 to 12 years. He emphasized that most of his cases had enormously aggressive feelings to the parent of the same sex. Plus the majority of the children had exhibited long standing behavior problems and neurotic tendencies. Included was a three- to five-year follow-up; two cases developed early signs of schizophrenia, one settled into a chronic obsessional state, and the remaining three, although symptom-free, were still mildly disturbed.

Four years ago, reporting in the Scandinavian literature, Elis Regner[47] outlined two typical cases of obsessive compulsive neurosis in 10-year-old children. His conclusions were very general, stating that there was an uncertain hereditary factor and that the symptoms appeared as a part of an anxiety-aggression neurosis. He also indicated that this diagnosis in children is not uncommon and that most cases were resistant to psychotherapy.

A still unresolved controversy is the relationship of this neurosis to schizophrenia. Bleuler,[7] Wooley,[53,54] Diethelm[13] and others indicate an intimate relationship and imply that obsessive compulsive neurosis is a latent schizophrenic reaction. Aubrey Lewis,[34] reporting on a large number of adult obsessive compulsive neurotics, states that they rarely become schizophrenic, although he admits that schizophrenia in adolescents may be ushered in by obsessional symptoms. Maudsley,[37] on the other hand, felt it was a latent affective psychosis. Louise Despert,[14] the one child psychiatrist who comments on this specific problem, reports a definite difference between obsessive compulsive neurosis and childhood schizophrenia. She states that in the neurosis, anxiety, panic, and fantasies may temporarily distract the child's attention from the environment, but his reality testing is not impaired. There is no interference with the ability to abstract and no other thought disorder is present. The neurotic child also experiences his pathological mental contents as incongruous and foreign; this is not characteristic of the psychotic child.

A totally different consideration from the identification with psychosis is this neurosis' relationship to normal behavior. A fascinating observation, mentioned by all authors, is the well-documented existence of compulsive ritualization which is inherent in the normal development of children. Piaget[45] has identified this phenomenon in infants. Gesell[24-26] mentions the ages 2 to 3 years as a specifically prominent period of time for the development of complicated ritualistic systems. He states, "ritualization is like a restatement of the situation, a method of defining, and perhaps of improving new abilities, but it is itself a general ability and product of growth."

It is not only seen in earlier development but the normal play of all children is replete with evidence of ritualistic and compulsive behavior. Anyone who has observed a child meticulously stepping or not stepping on sidewalk cracks, tapping a stick back and forth along a fence, touching each street light they pass, etc.—the examples are endless—cannot help but be impressed with the obvious compulsive quality to this activity.

But the relationship of normal compulsive ritualization seen in children to the crippling neurotic reaction, both having outward resemblances to each other, has not been formally dealt with in the literature. Little mention has been made about the question, when is compulsive behavior a transitory representation of normal development and when is it a neurotic symptom? For many clinicians this factor has added further to the confusion and to the reluctance in making the diagnosis in children.

Thus, the obsessive compulsive neurosis of childhood is in the unique position of being closely associated with normal behavior and yet, at the same time, being implicated, by some, as an ominous forerunner of a psychotic process.

After reviewing the literature, it seems that the normal occurrence of compulsivity and ritualization along with the scarcity of case material have contributed more to the nebulous descriptions of this syndrome in children than any other factors.

METHOD OF STUDY

Children 12 years old and under who had been evaluated or treated on either the Psychiatric In- or Out-Patient Services since 1959 were screened using data from statistical forms which are completed on every patient. They were screened both for the diagnosis of obsessive compulsive neurosis and separately for the symptoms of obsessions or excessive compulsivity. The

Table 10.1. Incidence of Obsessive Compulsive Neurosis

	No. children/adults since 1959	No. children with diagnosis of ob comp neurosis	% Total
Incidence in children	405	5	1.2%
Incidence in adults	1,625	21	1.2%

same screening technique was used for the adult psychiatric patients (16 years and older), seen since 1959 on either the In- or Out-Patient Services, to obtain data to compare the incidence of the neurosis in our adult and child patients. Since the purpose was only to provide information for comparison, the adult data will not be reported in detail, but the incidence figures will be included later in the results.

Out of a total of 405 children seen since 1959, 34 were registered as either obsessive compulsive neurotics or had these symptoms. These charts were then reviewed and only those cases which met the following criteria were studied further: first, the patient had to have a well-defined constellation of obsessive compulsive symptoms; second, and most important, these symptoms had to be the most prominent evidence of psychopathology in the patient's clinical picture; and third, this symptomatology had to be severe enough to interfere with the child's general functioning.

Only four cases completely met the criteria outlined; one case was included which satisfied the requirements, but it also had some resemblance to the Impulsion syndrome of Bender and Schilder. (Of the 29 patients who were screened out, 25 were schizophrenic and four were organically brain damaged children.) Therefore, five of the 405 children seen could be considered as meeting this definition of obsessive compulsive neurosis.

The records of these cases were then much more carefully evaluated and the data from the charts supplemented by interviews with the children's therapists. This information was analyzed for various factors consisting of general descriptive facts, symptoms, and any observable factors postulated as to etiology. Our own cases were compared to elicit any consistencies and these, in turn, were compared with observations and conclusions reported in the literature.

In addition, over the past year, 20 children in this age group were informally interviewed regarding their compulsive behavior and rituals. Some of these children were patients who had no obsessive compulsive symptoms and some were normal children. Since this in no way could be considered a formal study, the results will not be recorded but will be included later in the paper as a partial source in discussing the differentiation between normal compulsivity and the neurotic symptoms.

RESULTS

The average age of illness onset was 7½ years with a range of 6 years 4 months to 10 years 2 months. There were three boys and two girls. This made up the total of five. The patients were seen for a varying number of hours, being seen respectively for a total of 1, 8, 25, 70, and 75 hours. The longest period of continued observation for any one case was 18 months.

In outlining the rest of the information, only those characteristics which were either present or absent in at least three or more of the children are offered for further consideration. The more ambiguous characteristics will be accompanied by a quoted example, from the records, of what is being described.

The following eight characteristics were found in all five of the cases that were reviewed:

1. The onset of the illness was sudden and often quite dramatic.
2. The level of intelligence was clinically estimated to be above normal and the three cases psychometrically measured were scored in the superior to very superior range. (IQ range 125–145.)
3. The obsessive and compulsive symptoms were encountered in combination and never separately. The most common compulsions were hand washing, touch compulsions, and extensive bedtime rituals. The obsessions were usually concerned with germs and contamination; right (good) and wrong (evil); and fears about potential harm or danger.
4. A significant number of symptoms were disruptive to the environment and invariably put the child in conflict with it.

Example: 7-year-old boy (therapist), "He was very preoccupied with sexual questions which he directed to his parents. . . . He also expressed concern that he had fecal material on his hands that he was unable to remove by washing. . . . He was unhappy and frequently cried at school."

Six-year-old girl (therapist), "She was unable to stop repeating obscene words. . . . She stood up in school and talked about stealing pencils and pointers from her class. . . . She could not stop thinking and speaking about burglars or stealing."

5. There were persistent, frequently verbalized guilt feelings about various thoughts and actions.

Example: 7-year-old boy (therapist), "He tells of how naughty he feels all the time and in spite of many people saying he isn't, he is unable to feel any differently. He told his mother that although she considered him to be a nice boy he was really quite naughty."

6. When first seen, they possessed a rigid, absolute, adult-like moral code, more rigorously active than one would expect for children of this age group.

Example: 8-year-old boy (therapist), "He is an exceedingly virtuous boy. During his early life he developed a strong sense of right and wrong. He was never able to break any rules and was even very angered and frustrated when other children would cheat at games."

7. The fantasy life of the children was not constricted but considered to be very active.
8. The children were never considered psychotic, nor were there evidences noted of any psychotic process.

The following six characteristics were found in four of the five cases reviewed:

1. Prior to the illness' onset the children appeared to function normally and were not considered disturbed. The only consistent evidence of compulsive tendencies were overcompliance and excessive concern with rules.
2. There was a history of significant psychopathology in the parents or near relatives, very often with prominent obsessive compulsive traits or symptoms.
3. The bowel training was nonpunitive, uneventful, and accomplished in the normal time range without any regressions.
4. An identifiable precipitating event appeared to be present. There were no consistencies as to the events themselves, which ranged from the death of an ambivalently regarded grandmother to a talk on sex.

Example: 10-year-old girl (therapist), ". . . as her mother was talking to her about the facts of life she became very disturbed screaming, 'Don't tell me those awful things. I'll kill myself if I have a baby.' Immediately after she began washing her hands every five minutes and would not touch doorknobs unless she had a kleenex in her hand."

5. Transient phobic phenomena were frequently observed in these children. Characteristic of this behavior is that the object of the phobia is changed often and avoided for only short periods of time.

Example: 10-year-old girl (Mother), "She was terrified of her capri pants, saying that someone had spit on them, but the next day this didn't worry her as she wore them out to play. That night she was afraid to sleep on her pillow, but this didn't last too long either. Yesterday she was afraid to touch her notebook because some boy had done something to it, but I guess she forgot about it as she took it to school with her today."

6. There was excessive ambivalence and marked openly aggressive feelings toward one or both parents.

Example: 6-year-old girl who is very dependent on her mother (therapist), "She constantly stated that her mother didn't love her . . . that she wanted to kill her mother . . . she wishes her mother would die."

The following characteristics were found in three of the five cases reviewed:

1. The home was one in which religion played an important role and strict adherence to religious principle was emphasized (two Jewish, one Catholic, one Methodist, and one no religion).
2. The discipline administered by the parents was noticeably inconsistent and erratic.

Three of the five cases were seen in treatment. All improved, but there is some evidence that mild to moderate disturbances are still present. The other two children were removed from treatment by their mothers because, in the opinion of the therapists, the child's treatment resulted in symptoms of psychological decompensation in both mothers. The follow-up revealed that neither of these two children have overt obsessive compulsive symptoms at present.

Masturbation played a significant role in two of the cases, but according to the information available, was not implicated in the others.

The following are characteristics which have been reported in the literature as either being frequently present or etiologically significant in this neurosis. They were found in none or possibly one of the cases reviewed:

1. Pathologically willful or obstinate
2. Pathologically envious
3. Frequent bouts of constipation
4. A history of sexual trauma
5. Feelings of depersonalization

COMMENT

Before discussing the results, qualifications about the information received should be stated. The wide range in the number of hours each patient was seen creates unevenness and a lack of uniformity in the reliability of the data. Information obtained from a one hour consultation certainly cannot be equated with that obtained after 75 hours of observation. Secondly, our paucity of cases is reminiscent of the experience of former workers, most notably Berman,[6] who after reviewing 3,050 cases culled out only six with this diagnosis. Our small number of cases made statistical analysis unfeasible, consequently the factors encountered with some consistency are offered only as possible trends or as factors of interest without statistical confirmation.

It is conceivable that some of the consistencies reported may be the result of certain selection procedures inherent in any social institution rather than representing a valid consistency in the syndrome itself. This possibility cannot be fully answered, but despite this, aspects of the cases reported were homogeneous and deserve further comment.

It seems apparent that obsessive compulsive neurosis does occur in children and that the age of symptom onset may be earlier than has been generally described. The fact that it occurred in both adult and child patients in the identical percentage of 1.2% is interesting and somewhat startling. Although our adult percentage does run lower than usual, as in most large surveys, obsessive compulsive neurotics make up 2%–3% of the adult psychiatric population.

The generally higher levels of intelligence of these patients; the family history of significant psychopathology often with obsessive features; the excessive ambivalence and marked aggressive feelings to the parents; the rigid adult-like moral code; the unvarying presence of guilt reactions, all have been frequently described in the literature and were confirmed by our findings.

The sudden onset of symptoms in what appeared to be a relatively uncompulsive normal child which typifies the early course of our patients, is unusual and has not been reported as typical. This factor in turn may have had some influence on the higher frequency with which a precipitating event was reported in our cases, as a sudden onset in any illness invariably promotes observers to impute causal significance to the events that occurred just prior to the appearance of symptoms. No one incident is solely responsible for the appearance of this neurosis, but in our cases the identified precipitating factors were often events viewed by the children themselves as symbolic of a major area of chronic conflict and maladjustment.

Most child psychiatric services report that children are brought in for treatment when symptoms occur which have created irritation and anxiety in the environment. Our findings coincided with this; none of the children were so-called silent sufferers. They all had some symptoms that were disruptive, frightening, and annoying to the adults and peers they had contact with.

The transient phobic episodes seen frequently in obsessive compulsive childhood neuroses are different from the classically described phobic reactions. In a true phobia, the specific phobic object or situation is constant (relatively); this alone is able to initiate the avoidance behavior. Each reencounter with the object of the phobia results in the same avoidance reaction. In the phenomenon described here, the phobic object is not constant; it is frequently changed, and if reencountered does not initiate phobic behavior. All of the transient phobias in our cases appeared to have specific obsessions as a basic underlying constituent. Because the obsessions were with the patient constantly, regardless of the surroundings, they operated continuously, creating out of neutral events and objects things to be feared and avoided. With reference to the example given, the phobic object was changed three times in 48 hours, from capri pants, to a pillow, to a notebook. There is little outward consistency of these objects, but what did appear to be a constant was the patient's obsession with being contaminated.

There was a distinct lack of reported difficulties and adverse conditions associated with toilet training. This is unusual, although the articles which identified a significant relationship between bowel training and predisposition to obsessive compulsive neurosis have all been intensive studies of single cases. It is possible this type of information may not be as readily available to the style of this study. It also is possible that the true picture of the child's experience may have been distorted, consciously or unconsciously, when it was reported by the parents.

In previous writings there has been some speculation about strict religious adherence and its relationship to this illness. Another idea, postulated by Woolley,[52] is that severely inconsistent parental discipline predisposes children to this neurosis. Both of these factors were present in three of the five children, but diametrically opposite factors were observed in the other two cases, making further theoretical expansion very tenuous.

Authors differentiating diagnostically between normal childhood compulsions and the neurotic symptoms agree that the neurosis is quite resistant to treatment. This is supported by our treated cases, who although improved, are reported to have disturbances still present. The two untreated patients, no longer exhibiting obsessive compulsive symptoms, may have converted into "silent sufferers," as the children's physicians believe that severe problems continue to exist. Definitive statements about the long-term course of the illness and the prognosis are not possible because no case was observed longer than 18 months.

Finally, the observations obtained from the small informal survey previously referred to will be tentatively outlined to help establish some criteria for differentiating normal compulsivity and ritualization from pathological behavior. The compulsive behavior inherent in normal development and play was never experienced by the children as something alien or incongruous. They reported no internal need to combat or resist it. Under mild external pressures, they were able to abandon their ritualistic activities without experiencing any apparent anxiety. This type of ritualism was invariably perceived by the child as pleasant and enjoyable. It was always performed eagerly, was usually short-lived, was never disruptive, and did not interfere with the child's general efficiency or normal functioning. Each of these characteristics is distinctly opposite from those describing the neurotic symptoms.

SUMMARY

The purpose of the study was to gather descriptive information about the obsessive compulsive neurosis from cases seen on the Children's Service at the UCLA Neuropsychiatric Institute. Five cases, of 405 children 12 and under, met criteria defined to approximate as closely as possible the obsessive compulsive reaction. These cases were evaluated for general information and to determine what, if any, consistencies appeared.

It was found that this disease made up 1.2% of both the childrens' and adult case loads. There was no sex predilection and the average age of symptom onset was 7½ years.

Those consistencies that were found are offered as possible trends and not as definitive statements. This tentativeness is made necessary by the relatively few cases studied and the number of uncontrolled variables that were present.

In our cases, the neurosis occurred in brighter than average children who previous to this were not obviously disturbed. The onset was sudden and often linked with a symbolically significant precipitating event. They presented with a combination of obsessive and compulsive symptoms that were disruptive to both the children and their environment. Guilt feelings were prevalent as were transient phobias. They had ambivalent and aggressive feelings toward their parents, who were themselves usually disturbed, often having similar traits and symptoms. The children, although difficult treatment cases, could be treated effectively with psychotherapy.

Lastly, some very general criteria were outlined to help clinical differentiation between normal and neurotic compulsivity in children.

REFERENCES

1. *Abraham, K.: "Contributions to Theory of Anal Character (1921)," in* Selected Papers on Psychoanalysis, *New York: Basic Books, Inc., Publishers, 1960.*
2. *Bakwin, H., and Bakwin, R. M.:* Behavior Disorders in Children, *Philadelphia: W. B. Saunders Company, 1953.*
3. *Bender, L., and Schilder, P.: Impulsions, Specific Disorder of Children,* Arch Neurol Psychiat *44: 990–1005, 1940.*
4. *Benjamin, E., et al:* Lehrbuch der Psychopathologie des Kindersalters, *Zurich and Leipzig: Rotapfel Verlag, 1938.*
5. *Bennett, L.:* Delinquent and Neurotic Children, *London: Tavistock, 1960.*
6. *Berman, L.: Obsessive, Compulsive Neurosis in Children,* J Nerv Ment Dis *95: 26–39, 1942.*
7. *Bleuler, E.:* Dementia Praecox or Group of Schizophrenias, New York: International Universities Press, 1955.
8. *Bornstein, B.: "Fragments of Analysis of Obsessional Child: First Six Months of Analysis,"* in Psychoanalytic Study of the Child, *New York: International Universities Press, 1950, vol 7.*
9. *Burr, C. W.: Neuroses of Childhood,* Arch Pediat *30: 416–423, 1913.*
10. *Chatterji, N. N.: Psychology of Obsession and Compulsion,* Indian J Psychol *29: 175–179, 1954.*
11. *Clancy, J., and Norris, A.: Differentiating Variables: Obsessive-Compulsive Neurosis and Anorexia Nervosa,* Amer J Psychiat *118: 58–61, 1961.*
12. *Dai, B.: "Obsessive-Compulsive Disorder in Chinese Culture," in* Culture and Mental Health, *Opler, ed., New York: The Macmillan Co., 1951.*
13. *Diethelm, O.:* Treatment in Psychiatry, *ed 3, Springfield, Ill: Charles C Thomas, Publisher, 1955.*
14. *Despert, L.: "Differential Diagnosis Between Obsessive-Compulsive Neurosis and Schizophrenia in Children," in* Psychopathology of Childhood, *P. H. Hoch and J. Zubin, ed., New York: Grune & Stratton, Inc., 1955.*
15. *Dorcus, R. M., and Shafer, G. W.:* Textbook of Abnormal Psychology, *Baltimore: The Williams & Wilkins Co., 1950.*

16. *Fenichel, O.:* Psychoanalytic Theory of Neurosis, *New York: W. W. Norton & Company, 1945.*

17. *Freud, S.: "Obsessions and Phobias: Their Psychical Mechanisms and Their Etiology (1896),"* in Collected Papers, *New York: Basic Books, In., Publishers, 1959, vol 1.*

18. *Freud, S.: "Obsessive Acts and Religious Practices (1907),"* in Collected Papers, *New York: Basic Books, Inc., Publishes, 1959, vol 2.*

19. *Freud, S.: "Character and Anal Eroticism (1908),"* in Collected Paper, *New York: Basic Books, Inc., Publishes, 1959, vol 2.*

20. *Freud, S.: "Notes on Case of Obsessional Neuroses (1909),"* in Collected Papers, *New York: Basic Books, Inc., Publishers, 1959, vol 3.*

21. *Freud, S.: "Predisposition to Obsessional Neurosis (1913),"* in Collected Papers, *New York: Basic Books, Inc., Publishers, 1959, vol 2.*

22. *Freud, S.: "Inhibitions, Symptoms and Anxiety (1926),"* in Collected Papers, *New York: Basic Books, Inc., Publishers, 1959, vol 20.*

23. *Freud, S.:* General Introduction to Psychoanalysis, *New York: Garden City Pub. Co., Inc., 1946.*

24. *Gesell, A. L.:* Mental Growth of Pre-School Child, *New York: The Macmillan Co., 1925.*

25. *Gesell, A. L.:* Guidance of Mental Growth in Infant and Child, *New York: The Macmillan Co., 1930.*

26. *Gesell, A. L.:* First Five Years of Life, *New York: Harper Brothers, 1940.*

27. *Greenacre, P.: Study of Mechanism of Obsessive-Compulsive Conditions,* Amer J Psychiat *79: 527–538, 1923.*

28. *Hall, M. B.: Obsessive-Compulsive States in Childhood: Their Treatment,* Arch Dis Child *10: 49–59, 1935.*

29. *Hastings, D. W.: Follow-Up Results in Psychiatric Illness,* Amer J Psychiat *114: 1057–1066, 1958.*

30. *Heuyer, G., et al: Syndrome Obsessional chez un Enfant de Dix Ans,* Rev Neuropsychiat Infant *6: 343–348, 1958.*

31. *Ingram, I. M., and McAdam, W. A.: EEG, Obsessional Illness and Obsessional Personality,* J Ment Sci *106: 616–691, 1960.*

32. *Ingram, I. M.: Obsessional Personality and Obsessional Illness,* Amer J Personality *117: 1016–1019, 1961.*

33. *Kanner, L.:* Child Psychiatry, *ed 3, Springfield, Ill: Charles C Thomas, Publisher, 1957.*

34. *Lewis, A.: Problems of Obsessional Illness,* Proc Roy Soc Med *29: 325–335, 1936.*

35. *Lowenfeld, M. F: New Approach to Problem of Psycho-Neurosis in Childhood,* Brit J Med Psychol *11: 194–226, 1931–32.*

36. *Luria, A. S.:* Nature of Human Conflicts, *New York: Liveright Publishing Corporation, 1932.*

37. *Maudsley, H.:* Pathology of Mind, *London: Macmillan & Co., 1879.*

38. *Mayer-Gross, W.; Slater, E.; and Roth, M.:* Clinical Psychiatry, *Baltimore: The Williams & Wilkins Co., 1960.*

39. *Mowrer, O. H., and Keehn, J. D.: How Are Intertrial Avoidance Responses Reinforced?* Psychol Rev *65: 209–221, 1958.*

40. *Mowrer, O. H.:* Learning Theory and Behavior. *New York: John Wiley & Sons, 1960.*

41. *Noyes, A., and Kolb, L.:* Modern Clinical Psychiatry, *ed 5, Philadelphia: W. B. Saunders Company, 1960.*

42. *Pavlov, I. P.: Attempt at Physiological Interpretation of Obsessional Neurosis and Paranoia,* J Ment Sci *80: 187–197, 1934.*

43. *Pearson, G.: Case of Compulsion Neurosis in Eleven-Year-Old Boy,* Amer J Orthopsychiat *10: 136–151, 1940.*

44. *Pearson, G. H. J.:* Emotional Disorders of Children, *New York: W. W. Norton & Company, Inc., 1949.*

45. *Piaget, J.:* Construction of Reality in Child, *New York: Basic Books, Inc., Publishes, 1954.*

46. *Pollett, J. D.: Natural History Studies in Mental Illness—Based on Pilot Study of Obsessional States,* J Ment Sci *106: 93–112, 1960.*

47. *Regner, E. G.: Obsessive Compulsive Neuroses in Children,* Acta Psych Neuro Scand *34: 110–125, 1959.*

48. *Rado, S.: "Obsessive Behavior"* in American Handbook of Psychiatry, *S. Arieti, ed., New York: Basic Books, Inc., Publishers, 1959.*

49. *Sandler, J., and Hazari, A.: 'Obsessional': On Psychological Classification of Obsessional Character Traits and Symptoms,* Brit J Med Psychol *30: 113–122, 1960.*

50. *Vandicks, H. V.: Clinical Study of Obsessions,* Brit J Med Psychol *11: 234–250, 1931–1932.*

51. *Werner, H.:* Comparative Psychology of Mental Development, *New York: Science Editions, 1961.*

52. *Woolley, L. F.: Studies in Obsessive Ruminative Tension States: III. The Effect of Erratic Discipline in Childhood Emotional Tensions,* Psychoanal Quart *11: 237–252, 1937.*

53. *Woolley, L. F.: Studies in Obsessive Ruminative Tension States: IV. Psychasthenia, Definition and Delimitation,* Psychoanal Quart *11: 465–480, 1937.*

54. *Woolley, L. F.: Studies in Obsessive Ruminative Tension States: V. Etiology, Dynamics and Genesis,* Psychoanal Quart *11: 654–676, 1937.*

55. *Yaskin, J. C.: Psychoneuroses and Neuroses,* Amer J Psychiat *93: 107–125, 1936.*

56. *Ziegler, L. H.: Compulsions, Obsessions and Feelings of Unreality,* Hum Biol *1: 514–527, 1929.*

11. An Experimental Contribution to the Psychology of Obsessive-Compulsive Neurosis

(On Remembering Completed and Uncompleted Tasks)

Heinz Hartmann

THE QUESTION as to whether and how completion or interruption of tasks, wishes, and thoughts influences their recall has been discussed for some time in the special area of the psychology of dreams. W. Robert wrote in 1886: "The causes [of dreams] are always the same: the resumption of sensory impressions which have not been worked through intellectually or an uncompleted mental activity.... Dreams are precipitations of thoughts nipped in the bud.... Something that has been fully thought through never produces dreams; only something that dwells unfinished on someone's mind or passes casually through one's mind can do so." The author interprets his observations in terms of a theory which ascribes to dreams a tension-reducing function: dreams have healing power, they are a safety valve of the mind; "... a human being deprived of the possibility to dream would have to become mentally disturbed after some time because large amounts of unfinished and undigested thoughts and of shallow impressions would accumulate in his brain. Under their impact, whatever must be incorporated into memory in a finished and completed form would be smothered."

Y. Delage (1891) places even stronger emphasis on this very viewpoint. He bases his theory on the following observations: "As a rule, ideas which occupied the mind during waking do not come back in dreams"; and "An impression can produce a dream only if the mind has turned away from that impression almost immediately after having received it or due to absent-mindedness at the moment of perception. This distraction of the mind may assume such an extent that the perception was completely unconscious to the

---

Reprinted by permission of Hogarth Press and Random House UK, Ltd., from *Essays on Ego Psychology* by Heinz Hartmann, London, 1933, pp. 404–18.

point where it left no trace in memory. It is understandable that in that case the dream appears to be entirely a spontaneous formation."

Delage presents the following theoretical constructs for the classification of these findings: "Every sensation, every idea contains a certain amount of energy which it spends in investing the thought. When our attention is diverted from it the energy consumption stops; the smaller this consumption, the more energy remains available. During sleep attention is neither directed by the will nor diverted by new sensations, and we are left to our old impressions which arise from a state of temporary inhibition, and each one with its remaining amount of energy tends to resume its interrupted development." The unresolved impressions form "set springs" (*"des ressorts tendus"*) and "there can be more force in a little tightened spring than in a bigger one which has almost resumed its position of inertia. . . . In short, our impressions are accumulators of energy." From this statement the author derives a piece of advice concerning the avoidance of nightmares: "If you fear their flow, it is wise to discharge them before falling asleep."

We present an example from Delage's work which is of special interest for our further considerations because in this illustration the "incompleteness" is represented by an obsessive fear: "One of my cousins, a young man with a very nervous temperament, frequently goes hunting with his younger brother. Sometimes a vivid impression crosses his mind like a bolt of lightning at the moment of pulling the trigger: isn't his brother in his line of fire? But since his brother is right at his side, safe, and in no danger, the thought disappears immediately. At night he often dreams that he killed him while hunting. Once the danger was real, not for the brother but for an old woman whom the hunter had not seen. The shot passed right above her head. This time the emotion was terrible. All day long he did not stop thinking of it, and in the evening they spoke about nothing else at home. That incident he never saw in a dream."

It is known that Freud (1900) partially corroborated the observations underlying the above theoretical constructs and wove them into his theory of dreams. He mentioned Robert as well as Delage. To be sure, in the over-all structure of Freud's theory of dreams the aforementioned observations play a minor and not a central part. Thus we read in *The Interpretation of Dreams:* "The unconscious prefers to weave its connections round preconscious impressions and ideas which are either indifferent and have thus had no attention paid to them, or have been rejected and have thus had attention promptly withdrawn from them" (p. 563). And a few pages earlier: "There is no need to underestimate the importance of the psychical intensities which are introduced into the state of sleep by these residues of daytime life, and particularly of those in the group of unsolved problems. It is certain that these excitations continue to struggle for expression during the night; and we may assume with equal certainty that the state of sleep makes it impossible for the excitatory process to be pursued in the habitual manner in the preconscious and brought to an end by becoming conscious" (p. 554f.). But in order to enter a dream any waking thought must connect itself with a repressed infantile wish. Freud states in relation to the question whether unresolved wishes can have the function of instigating dreams: ". . . children's dreams prove beyond a doubt that a wish that has not been dealt with during the day can act as a dream-instigator. But it must not be forgotten that it is a *child's* wish, a wishful impulse of the strength proper to children. I think it is highly doubtful whether in the case of an adult a wish that has not been fulfilled during the day would be strong enough to produce a dream" (p. 552).

We cannot pursue this thought any further here. It must suffice for our purposes to have indicated what importance contemporary dream theory attributes to the reproduction of uncompleted material.

Pötzl (1917) conducted tachistoscopic experiments in which he exposed pictures at speeds of 1/100 seconds. He was able to demonstrate in the majority of cases (for nine out of twelve subjects) that these pictures pre-sented during the day exerted a clear-cut influence on the formation of the manifest dream of the following night. Immediately after the pictures were exposed, everything the subjects could indicate with reference to their percep-tions was recorded. A second protocol contained the corresponding associa-tions of the day. A comparison with the dreams of the following night showed that those elements of the pictures which were not contained in the protocols appeared faithfully reproduced in their details and clearly recognizable in the dream—in other words, those which apparently remained entirely unnoticed during the tachistoscopic exposure and which also had not occurred to the subjects afterwards. Pötzl "found that there exists a relationship of exclusion, owing to which whatever has been mentally formed as a Gestalt is excluded from subsequent development so that only parts of the original excitation can develop and whatever has developed into a Gestalt loses the power to act further" (p. 117).

Malamud and Linder (1931) later reported similar experiments using par-tially modified hypotheses. These authors proceeded from the following train of thought. When elements of a situation are not perceived or are forgotten and when these same elements can then be shown to be associated with specific repressed excitations appearing in the dreams of the following night, the mechanism of this kind of forgetting or nonperceiving can then be understood. The results of the experiments showed that some elements of the pictures appeared which had been omitted in the description of what had been perceived during the exposures. These elements which had been omitted in the protocols seemed to stand in some specific relationship to former experiences and frequently to the subjects' central conflicts. But it appears that experiences of the day preceding the dream can influence the results in so far as these experiences connect with complex elements.

Allers and Teler's work (1924) touches also to some degree upon our problem. These authors were looking for an answer through experimentation to the question whether "unnoticed" material could be demonstrated to have an influence on our conscious thought processes. Their experimental method was the following: the tachistoscopic exposure of pictures was 4/100 sec., which was considerably longer than in Pötzl's experiments; protocols about the subjects' perceptions and association tests were obtained on the following day; besides neutral stimulus words the list contained words which referred to those elements in the pictures which did not appear in the protocols. "The results of these experiments are: under the influence of suitable stimulus words, pictorial 'representations' appear in the interval between stimulus and response word; although not mentioned in the description given by the subject immediately after the exposure, and not recognized either then or thereafter as having been seen earlier, i.e., as having been components of the originally exposed pictures, these 'representations' are nevertheless elements of the perceptual manifold presented" (p. 141). In the opinion of the authors, the selection of what is perceived is determined by the factor of 'word-nearness," the nameability of individual components, because in view of the experimental instructions the subjects are set to reproduce them.

Contrary to Pötzl's dream experiments, the clearly perceived elements of the pictures always stood out in the reports of these subjects. I shall not discuss to what degree this may be related to the peculiarities of the process of dreaming. Allers and Teler believe that the difference in results may be attributed to the difference in exposure time.[1]

Zeigarnik (1927) dealt with the problem of the effect of current needlike tensions on certain forms of recall. This research was part of a more extensive series of experiments conducted by Kurt Lewin concerning the psychology of action and emotion. An answer was sought to the question how recall of activities interrupted before their completion is related to recall of completed tasks. Each subject was given some tasks to be completed and some which were interrupted before completion. To exclude possible differences due to the characteristics of any given task, the tasks were distributed among the subjects in such a way that each task was interrupted as often as it was completed.

The ratio of the retained uncompleted (RU) to the retained completed (RC) activities is a measure of the preference of one of these groups in retention over the other. Lewin and Zeigarnik demonstrated that, on the average, the uncompleted tasks were recalled about 90 per cent better than the completed ones; i.e., the arithmetic mean of RU/RC is 1.9.

The authors gave the following theoretical explanations of their findings: "At the time when a subject forms the intention to execute the task on the basis of the instructions a quasi need is produced which by itself strives for the completion of the task. Dynamically speaking, this process corresponds to the genesis of a tension system which aims at relaxation. Completion of the task then means discharge of the system, relaxation of the quasi need. When a task is interrupted there remains a tension residue; the quasi need is not satisfied." The reason for better recall of unfinished activities thus lies in the continuation of a "quasi need." Recall here plays the role of an indicator of the needlike tension.

This theoretical formulation of the facts reminds us of the dynamic-energetic concepts of psychoanalysis and of the "set springs" referred to by Yves Delage. Zeigarnik writes: "How such tensions will express themselves in the apparently quite different process of recall can be derived only from a general theory of psychic dynamics, which would first of all have to decide whether the process of recall is concerned simultaneously with the discharge of individual tensions." Such a general psychodynamic theory exists—the psychoanalytic one—which can explain the dynamic relationship between certain classes of experiences and recall. Freud (1920) proceeds from the observation that the dreams of persons with traumatic neuroses lead them again and again back to the situation of the accident. This fact obviously contradicts the pleasure-seeking and unpleasure-avoiding tendency, which is otherwise a useful guide of far-reaching applicability for the explanation of psychic relationships. We are dealing here with a result of what Freud called repetition compulsion. The traumatic neurosis is understood to be the consequence of a breach in the stimulus barrier, and the dreams of those suffering from traumatic neurosis "are endeavouring to master the stimulus retrospectively, by developing the anxiety whose omission [at the time of the trauma] was the cause of the traumatic neurosis" (1920, p. 32). The repetition factor in children's play must be understood from the same point of view. Here too recall serves the mastery of experiences. Children's play is a "process of assimilation through repetition" (Waelder, 1932). These two examples demonstrate cogently how the process of recall can operate in the service of tension discharge. However, we must not forget that the psychoanalytic concept of repetition compulsion does not include every repetition in the psychic realm.

Zeigarnik's experiments further demonstrated that differences in the interpretation of the request for recall influence the will to recall and thereby also the ratio of RU to RC. Moreover, subjects who can be considered to have a relatively impulsive character showed a particularly high predominance of RU over RC. The RU/RC ratio is higher in children than in adults. "The more uncontrolled a person's needs are, the less he can renounce need gratification; the more 'childlike' and natural he is in the experiment, the stronger is his tendency to a preponderance of uncompleted actions." The RU/RC ratio remains very constant in individual subjects. Finally, the decisive issue concerning the ratio of recall is the internal completion of the task and not its external termination.

Schlote (1930) has rechecked Zeigarnik's experiments. He found that "the unfinished activities assumed a preferred position in relation to the finished tasks in so far as the activity which corresponds to an uncompleted task shows a tendency to return to consciousness when an opportunity arises; and this return occurs much faster and with greater certainty than is the case with completed tasks. Naturally this preferred position must express itself also in better retention due to the effectiveness of such a tendency." Schlote, who closely follows the psychological formulations of Ach, recognizes only the effectiveness of the determining tendencies directed toward goal realization as the cause of better retention of incompleted tasks. I cannot discuss here Schlote's objections to Lewin's concept of quasi needs, and to his method, and in part to the results of Zeigarnik's experiments.

The subject matter of the experiments reported below is the recall of completed and uncompleted activities by obsessive-compulsive neurotics. For several reasons, it seemed to me of interest to investigate the behavior of obsessive-compulsive neurotics with respect to this question. Various authors have correctly emphasized that incompleteness or inability of closure is characteristic of the thinking of obsessive-compulsive neurotics. This quality of their thought processes in particular gave rise to the expectation that the "tension systems" might in their case act differently from the way in which they act in normals, and that this difference might be verified experimentally. Thus some light might be thrown also on the tendency toward repetition, which is a well-known but not yet fully understood characteristic of obsessional neurosis. Recently Federn (1930) correctly pointed out that this tendency toward repetition occurs—I should like to add the qualification: in part—on this side and not beyond the pleasure principle, and that it must therefore not be equated with the repetition compulsion as this term is commonly used in psychoanalysis. Yet the effect of true repetition compulsion is unmistakable in obsessional neurosis.

The method follows that reported by Zeigarnik (1927). The subjects were given the following tasks: (1) to write down a poem; (2) to model a head from plasticine; (3) to draw a flower vase; (4) to write an address in printed letters; (5) to draw a plan of Vienna; (6) to combine pairs of cardboard triangles from among a larger number of such triangles into quadrangles; (7) to prick holes at a given distance inside a square; (8) to cross out all letters "l" and "n" in a sentence; (9) to compose a meaningful sentence of four words; (10) to count backwards from 90 to 49; (11) to multiply 5457×6337; (12) to write down ten cities whose names begin with "L"; (13) to solve a matchstick problem; (14) to cut out a spiral from a piece of paper; (15) to make a package; (16) to write down three names each beginning with the letter "k" of famous men, works of art, cities, animals, and plants; (17) to solve a puzzle; (18) to draw a cube which stands on one corner; (19) to continue a started honeycomb pattern; (20) to put together a postcard cut into pieces; (21) to pick out needles of a specific kind from a larger quantity; (22) to arrange strips of paper according to length; (23) to braid; (24) to write down ten nouns without either "e" or "r."

One half of the tasks were carried out to completion; during the other tasks the subject was interrupted before completion. Tasks completed by the first subject were interrupted for the next subject, etc. Only spontaneously recalled tasks were used for the calculation of the results (for the reasons for this procedure, see Zeigarnik, p. 39).

First the experiments were carried through with a control group of five healthy subjects. I could confirm in all cases Zeigarnik's findings of a preponderance of RU over RC. The ratio RU/RC was 1.75, 1.50, 1.43, 1.25, 1.50 for the five healthy subjects respectively, with a mean of 1.48. Yet these scores are considerably lower than those reported by Zeigarnik. I do not know what is responsible for this difference of our results in general. But perhaps it may be of interest to point out that subject IV who scored lowest has a somewhat autistic personality and a character which is close to the compulsive type. If this subject is disregarded in the calculation, the mean is raised to 1.55.

The same experiments were then made with nine obsessive-compulsive neurotics. The results are summarized in Table 11.1.

Whereas we obtained a mean RU/RC ratio of 1.48 with the healthy

Table 11.1.

Subject	RU	RC	$\dfrac{RU}{RC}$
I	9	10	.90
II	8	8	1.00
III	4	4	1.00
IV	7	5	1.40
V	8	8	1.00
VI	9	7	1.28
VII	6	7	.86
VIII	3	7	.43
IX	4	2	2.00
Mean	6.4	6.4	1.10*

$$*M\,\frac{RU}{RC} \neq M\,\frac{RU}{RC}$$

subjects, we obtained a mean of 1.10 with the obsessive-compulsive subjects. *Obsessive-compulsive neurotics recall uncompleted activities hardly better than completed ones.*

The extraordinarily high ratio score obtained by subject IX stands out in this series, but this subject's behavior during and after the experiment did not provide an explanation. One may wonder whether the idea the subject formed concerning the subsequent enumeration of the tasks played a role. Zeigarnik's experiments demonstrated that subjects for whom the enumeration means a mere narration obtain generally a higher RU/RC ratio than those who consider the enumeration a memory test. Subject IX belongs, however, to the latter group—a circumstance giving the appearance of irregularity with regard not only to the ratio but also the small number of remembered tasks (RU + RC = 6). Subjects I, V, and VIII also belong to this type who considers the enumeration as a memory test. For them, the sums of RU and RC are 19, 16, and 10 respectively, with a mean of 15. If subject IX, however, is included, a mean of 12.9 is obtained as compared to a mean of 13 for the representatives of the other type (both means for RU + RC). In this case, there is then little difference between the mean RU/RC ratios (1.08 as compared to 1.11).

Thus the two groups differ less from each other than in Zeigarnik's experiments with normal subjects; evidently the interpretation of the enumeration as a memory test does not, for the obsessive-compulsive neurotics, play a significant role in the framework of their total attitude toward the experiments. We must also remember that, according to Zeigarnik, the difference of

RU/RC for the two groups arises mainly as a result of differences in the RC scores which approach the RU scores more in one case than in the other (see p. 37). On the other hand, our obsessive-compulsive subjects did (on the average) not obtain very different RU and RC scores.

All subjects regarded the experiment as an intelligence, aptitude, or diagnostic test. They believed it served to determine "whether my mind has suffered" (subject II); "whether I am normal" (subject IV); "you doubt my intelligence!" (subject III); "it is like fingerprints for criminals" (subject VI); "it is like at an employment agency" (subject VIII); "it has to do with a psychotechnical test" (subject VII). Subjects I, V, and IX said: "Intelligence test."

Subjects I, II, IV, V, and VII stated spontaneously that the investigation made them "nervous." Subject V said: "I am so excited. I have feelings of anxiety and my heart beats faster as if it would jump out of my body from all that fear."

Zeigarnik found that the "excited" subjects in her group of healthy individuals did not have better recall of uncompleted tasks. Our obsessive-compulsive subjects who obviously "became nervous" during (and because of) the experiment did not show any—or more correctly, any significant—decrease in the RU/RC ratio. The ratio is 1.03 for our "nervous" subjects as compared to 1.18 for those subjects who did not show or report any "nervousness" in this sense during or after the experiment. In view of the difficulties involved in delineating somewhat reliably this factor of "becoming nervous," I am not attributing any great significance to the difference between Zeigarnik's and our results.

The majority of our subjects spontaneously reported afterwards that they had the feeling of having performed poorly, or of having been generally incapable, or that they doubted the correctness of their solutions of the tasks (subjects II, III, VII, VIII, IX). Subject VIII said: "I am never sure the first time . . . surely I did not do well!" and subject IX: "I have the feeling I should have done better!" and subject VII: "Did I do it right? It is certainly all wrong!" Such remarks were also made after the individual tasks. Occasionally the subjects voiced the intention to resume the task.

Zeigarnik's investigations showed that a number of subjects experienced certain tasks as unfinished, although they were "objectively" completed; furthermore, that some subjects were dissatisfied with their performances even on subjectively completed tasks. These tasks were *better retained* than the remainder of finished tasks. We have seen that such behavior constitutes the rule among obsessive-compulsive subjects. These findings would thus agree with the fact that the RU and RC scores of obsessive-compulsive neurotics differ less from each other than those of normals. However, if we compare those subjects who reported dissatisfaction with their performance with the rest of the group, no significant differences appear (1.06 and 1.14, respectively). Of course, it is easily possible that such criteria as "dissatisfaction with the performance" were not adequately expressed in the reports of our subjects. Zeigarnik explains the fact that completed tasks with which her subjects were dissatisfied were better retained than other completed tasks by saying that "the subject is subjectively in a situation similar to that of having been interrupted. The need to repeat the task develops in the subject." I want to emphasize that subjective incompletion of a task and the tendency for repetition must be recognized as influences upon recall.

What is the situation concerning this "need to repeat" with respect to our subjects? With this question we return to the psychology of obsessive-compulsive neurosis. The tendency to repeat plays an important role in the symptomatology of the majority of our subjects: the compulsion to rip open again what has been sewn (subject I), always to turn around in the street (subject II), to do everything twice (subject IV) etc.; other symptoms were obsessional doubt and indecision. I do not want to enter here upon the remainder of the symptoms. If the cases in which these symptoms played a predominant role (they are only partially identical with those who reported dissatisfaction with their performance) are compared with others in which these symptoms are less evident, the first group shows a considerably lower value for the investigated ratio than does the latter group (.93 as compared to 1.43). It clearly is large enough to deserve our attention. It clearly speaks in favor of the tendency to repeat and of the subjective sense of incompletion influencing recall.

It was particularly Friedmann (1920) who placed the factor of incompleteness of or inability to complete a thought process in the center of a theory of obsessive-compulsive neurosis. Obsessional thoughts, according to his theory, are supposed to be the consequence of the logical impossibility of completing doubts, worries, expectations.

Because of Freud we know today more about the structure and genesis of obsessive-compulsive neurosis, though this disease is still "unconquered as a problem" (Freud). We also have better insight into the nature of compulsive repetitions. The part played by the "repetition compulsion" (in its narrow sense) in obsessive-compulsive neurosis is obscure; but here we must disregard also the little we know so far about its role as a fixating factor in repression and its relationship to the destructive drives, which move so strongly into the foreground in obsessive-compulsive neurosis (Federn, 1930). I do not want to discuss here the psychoanalytic theory of obsessional thinking and of obsessive-compulsive neurosis in general, and refer the reader to two recently published, excellent books which treat this subject in detail (Nunberg, 1932; Fenichel, 1931). I mention only some of the well-established findings which are closely related to our subject matter. We can understand the compulsion to execute two opposed actions immediately after each other (diphasic symptoms) on the basis of what many analyses have taught us: one of these actions represents a drive gratification and the other a defense against the drive impulse. The obsessive-compulsive neurotic's belief in magical "omnipotence of thought" explains (together with our knowledge about the drive structure of these neurotics) his inhibition of thought; the magic procedure of "undoing," which is characteristic of this disease, enables us partly to understand compulsive repetitions. The tendency to undo "may perhaps account for the obsession for *repeating* which is so frequently met with in this neurosis and the carrying out of which serves a number of contradictory intentions at once. When anything has not happened in the desired way it is undone by being repeated in a different way; and thereupon all the motives that exist for lingering over such repetitions come into play as well. As the neurosis proceeds, we often find that the endeavour to undo a traumatic experience is a motive of first-rate importance in the formation of symptoms" (Freud, 1926, p. 120). The repetition is aimed at weakening or canceling the magical significance of an action. If, however, the obsessive-compulsive neurotic's strict superego was not satisfied with the details of the repetition, then further repetitions follow. The magical world of the obsessional neurotic and his hypercathexis of thought processes—which are related to his typical regression and to the restriction of his activities (activity equals destruction)—also are responsible for his endeavor to blur the differences between what actually happened and what possibly might have happened, between what has been done and what he has thought.

Now we understand why, for the obsessive-compulsive neurotic, the character of "completedness" of an action remains subjectively relative, and where the "need to repeat" originates. This is also the source to which the peculiarity of the results obtained with the obsessive-compulsive subjects can be attributed. Here we see the factors which find their expression in the altered structure of their "quasi needs."

We are now confronted with the question in which way we have to think of "quasi needs" as dependent on *true needs*. Obviously for any general psychodynamic theory it will be decisive to what degree its concepts can do justice to the *dynamically decisive* driving forces. It seems to me that my investigations demonstrate that Lewin's dynamics is in need of—and is capable of—being complemented by a more comprehensive theory of drives. In view of the manifold correspondences of concepts and content, I consider it very promising to make the attempt to base Lewin's psychology upon psychoanalytic dynamics of drives and affects. However, to prove in detail the fruitfulness of this attempt would mean to go beyond the scope of this paper.

NOTE

1. Recent research has considerably advanced the study of some of the problems touched upon in the introduction to this paper.

REFERENCES

Allers, R. & Teler, J. (1924), On the Utilization of Unnoticed Impressions in Associations. In: Preconscious Stimulation in Dreams, Associations, and Images. Psychological Issues, Monogr. 7. New York: International Universities Press, 1960.

Delage, Y. (1891), Essai sur la théorie du rêve. Rev. Scientifique, 48.

Federn, P. (1930), The Reality of the Death Instinct, Especially in Melancholia. Remarks on Freud's book Civilization and Its Discontents. Psychoanal. Rev., 19, 1932.

Fenichel, O. (1931), Hysterien und Zwangsneurosen. Vienna: Internationaler psychoanalytischer Verlag.

Freud, S. (1900), The Interpretation of Dreams. Standard Edition, 4 & 5.

——— (1920), Beyond the Pleasure Principle. Standard Edition, 18.

——— (1926), Inhibitions, Symptoms and Anxiety. Standard Edition, 20.

Friedmann, M. (1920), Über die Natur der Zwangsvorstellungen und ibre Beziehungen zum Willensproblem. Wiesbaden: Bergmann.

Malamud, W. & Linder, F. E. (1931), Dreams and Their Relationship to Recent Impressions. Arch. Neurol. & Psychiat., 25.

Nunberg, H. (1932), Principles of Psychoanalysis. New York: International Universities Press, 1955.

Pötzl, O. (1917), The Relationship Between Experimentally Induced Dream Images and Indirect Vision. In: Preconscious Stimulation in Dreams, Associations, and Images. Psychological Issues, Monogr. 7. New York: International Universities Press, 1960.

Robert, W. (1886), Der Traum als Naturnotwendigkeit erklärt. Hamburg: H. Seippel.

Schlote, W. (1930), Über die Bevorzugung unvollendeter Handlungen. Z. Psychol.,
117.

Waelder, R. (1932), The Psychoanalytical Theory of Play. Psychoanal. Quart., 2, 1933.

Zeigarnik, B. (1927), Über das Behalten von erledigten und unerledigten Handlungen.
Psychol. Forsch., *9.*

12. The Treatment of Chronic Obsessive-Compulsive Neurosis

Stanley Rachman, Ray Hodgson, and Isaac M. Marks

CHRONIC OBSESSIVE-COMPULSIVE neurosis is a distressing and often crippling disorder which is resistant to treatment. Despite a few successes (Meyer, 1966; Stern, 1970), behavioural and other treatments have been disappointing (Bailey and Atchinson, 1969; Marks *et al.*, 1969; Furst and Cooper, 1970). This paper reports encouraging results in the treatment of this condition with newer behavioural techniques which were given in a controlled investigation.

We made 2 major comparisons—between behavioural and control treatment (relaxation), and between the two behavioural methods of 'modelling' (imitation learning) and 'flooding'. Modelling was based on the experimental work of Bandura (1969) and its recent application to handicapped obsessive patients (e.g. Rachman *et al.*, 1970). Flooding was tried because of its successful results in phobic patients (Boulougouris *et al.*, 1971). The behavioural techniques were also derived in part from those of Meyer (1966).

THE PATIENTS

Ten patients were selected who were at least moderately incapacitated by a chronic obsessive-compulsive disorder. Compulsions had to be present for entry into the trial, and patients complaining only of ruminations were excluded. Each patient had been ill for at least one year and had already received other psychiatric treatment. Six of the patients were unable to work. Two others were severely hampered and two moderately hampered in their capacity to work. Leucotomy had been considered in five of the ten cases. In addition to these ten, another seven patients were interviewed but excluded; in two the disorder was only mild, two mothers of young children were

Reprinted by permission of Pergamon Press, Elsevier Science, from *Behavior Research and Therapy* 9 (1971): 237–47.

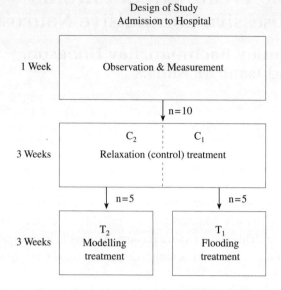

Figure 12.1. Experimental design

unable to accept a seven-week period in hospital, one reluctant patient discharged herself within 12 hr of admission, one patient became depressed before entering the trial, one had no compulsions. Three other referrals were excluded without interview because their disorders were primarily ruminative.

The mean age of the treated patients was 35 years, mean symptom duration 10 years. Five had had previous inpatient psychiatric treatment. Seven had had depression at some stage, 3 had received ECT. Three had associated phobias. Five patients had been treated by tricyclic drugs. In 6 patients the obsessive-compulsive illness created striking handicaps and extraordinary ramifications in the family, e.g. one affectionate mother was unable to touch her 3 children for fear of contamination; another girded her daughter with intolerable restrictions of movement, forced her family to join her in evacuating the 'contaminated' home, and did not allow them to wear shoes indoors. Other patients forced their spouses to wash excessively like themselves. A precis of each patient's illness appears in the Appendix.

Experimental design (Fig. 12.1). All patients were told that they would have new forms of treatment which would probably help them. They were admitted for a minimum of 7 weeks: the first week was devoted to evaluation, and the next 6 weeks to experimental treatment, with one session lasting 40–60 min every weekday. In the first 3 weeks all patients had 15 sessions of control relaxation treatment. Over the second 3 weeks patients were assigned at random to 15 sessions either of modelling or of flooding. After this 6-week experimental period, patients were followed up and treatment was continued when necessary.

All patients were taken off drugs throughout the experimental period, except one who had been on amitriptyline for months beforehand and remained on it during the trial.

THE TREATMENTS

I. Relaxation control (C_{1+2}).

Each session began with general enquiries about the patient's health and mood. He was then given tape-recorded relaxation instructions followed by a request to think about one of his obsessive worries during the final 10 min of each session.

II. Flooding in vivo (T_1).

A hierarchical list constructed as with modelling. The patient was then encouraged and persuaded, not forced, to enter the most disturbing situation first. The therapist did not act as a model for imitation but was calming and reassuring throughout the session. At the end of each session, which lasted 40–60 min, the patient was encouraged to maintain any contamination and refrain from carrying out his rituals for increasing periods. Similarly, reassurance and support were given throughout the course of treatment but virtually no supervision was provided between sessions.

As an example of flooding treatment, in managing the patient who feared contamination from animals, a hierarchy was constructed. During the first session she was encouraged to touch items from the top of her hierarchy (i.e. hamster and dog). The hamster was the set free to run around her bed, towel, cloths and personal belongings. It was placed in her handbag for a few minutes and also in her hair. This almost total contamination of her environment was accomplished during the first session and repeated daily. Several times throughout the treatment she was encouraged to stroke a dog and then to contaminate her clothes, hair and face.

III. Modelling in vivo (T_2).

The patient and therapist constructed a hierarchical list of situations which caused distress and produced avoidance and compulsive rituals (e.g. touching dirt, walking near to children, etc.). The patient was then encouraged to gradually enter each of the provoking situations, commencing with the least upsetting and graduating to increasingly disturbing ones. Each step was first demonstrated to the patient by a calm and reassuring therapist and the patient then 'shadowed' his therapist's actions. Each step was repeated until the patient completed the sequence without assistance. At the end of each treatment session, which lasted from 40 to 60 min, the patient was encouraged to maintain any contamination and refrain from carrying out his compulsive acts (e.g. checking, washing his hands, etc.) for steadily increasing periods of time. Hardly any supervision was provided between treatment sessions. This method resembles *in vivo* desensitisation (Wolpe, 1958) supplemented by modelling and encouragement not to engage in compulsive acts after each session.

As an example of modelling treatment, in a patient with fear of contamination from hospitals the following hierarchy was constructed: 1. bandage, 2. dirty lint; 3. medicine; 4. kidney bowl; 5. hypodermic syringe; 6. faked T.B. sample; 7. approaching a hospital; 8. touching ambulances; 9. entering a hospital casualty waiting room; 10. walking around a hospital and touching walls, door knobs, etc.

The first session began with the lowest item from the hierarchy. The therapist repeatedly touched a bandage on his clothes, hair and face; the patient was then asked to imitate the therapist's actions. Throughout the three weeks of modelling all items in the hierarchy were dealt with in the same way, e.g. towards the top of the hierarchy the patient watched the therapist walk up to the hospital entrance and touch an ambulance. She then copied the therapist's actions.

After the 3-week experimental period, patients were reassessed and discharged if a substantial reduction in obsessive symptoms had occurred. If the patient reported problems at home, the therapist visited the home and gave appropriate further treatment; e.g. the patient just described was troubled by 'contaminated' objects at home (e.g. old clothes, children's toys) so in three modelling sessions the therapist and then the patient touched these objects in the home.

Preliminary research (Rachman, Hodgson and Marzillier, 1970) had indicated that the endless requests for reassurance of certain patients were comparable to the more obviously compulsive rituals such as handwashing. Consequently all reassurance was withheld from patients during the second 3 weeks of the experimental treatment period. All attendants, relations and friends were advised to refuse requests for reassurance, e.g. if a patient asked, "will the child I passed in the garden survive?", he received the answer, "I am afraid that I cannot answer that sort of question".

MEASURES

These were taken just before treatment, after 3 weeks of relaxation control treatment, after a further 3 weeks of either modelling or flooding, and after 3 months followup.

1. Clinical Ratings Scales

These were modified from those of Gelder and Marks (1966) and Watson *et al.* (1971a). Each patient and a "blind" medical assessor rated each of the patient's 5 main obsessions for 'phobic anxiety' and for 'phobic avoidance'. These scales were previously found to be reliable across raters (Watson *et al.*, 1971a) reliability being 0.82 for individual scale scores and 0.89 for the totals of 5 scales together. Patient and assessor also rated free-floating anxiety, panics, depression and depersonalisation. In addition, the assessor rated social adjustment on the following scales—work, leisure, sex, family relationships and other relationships.

2. Attitude Scales

Attitude was measured to 4 concepts—2 control concepts (GOD, DEVIL) and 2 concepts concerning the patient's obsessions (e.g. TOUCHING GUINEA PIGS, TOUCHING MY TROUSER ZIP). Each concept was rated on 10 semantic differential scales from 4 dimensions—evaluation (pleasant–unpleasant, good–bad, nice–nasty), danger (safe–dangerous, harmful–harmless, secure–risky), dirt (filthy–spotless, clean–dirty, pure–contaminated), and wrongness (right–wrong). Each of the scales was scored 0–6, and 'factor scores' were obtained by summing scales within each dimension. Twenty-four hr retest reliability for the factor scores was 0.98 for evaluation and for dirt, 0.91 for danger and 0.94 for wrongness.

3. Avoidance Test

Patients were asked to undertake a variety of activities which they usually avoided because of their obsessions, e.g. one patient was asked to sit on a chair without checking it for broken glass beforehand, another was asked to touch rubbish, etc. Each patient was given about 10 tasks, and the avoidance score was the percentage of items failed. For two patients appropriate avoidance tests could not be constructed—both later fell into the modelling group.

4. Fear Thermometer

This was the amount of anxiety the patient felt while trying to carry out the most difficult of the avoidance tasks. The patient rated this on a 0–100 scale. On the second and subsequent assessments anxiety was rated during the same task as that used during the initial assessment.

5. Leyton Inventory (Cooper, 1970)

This is a measure of obsessive-compulsive phenomena which provides 4 scores—trait, symptom, resistance, interference.

6. P.E.N.

This provides 3 scores—psychoticism, extraversion and neuroticism.

RESULTS

The following comparisons were made by 2-way analyses of variance:

1. Modelling and Flooding Combined (T_{1+2}) vs. Relaxation Control (C_{1+2}) (n = 10, see Figs. 12.2–12.4, Table 12.1)

Modelling/flooding proved significantly superior to the control treatment on the following measures: total 5 obsessions, assessor's rating for phobic anxiety $(p < 0.001)$ and phobic avoidance $(p < 0.001)$; total 5 obsessions, patient's rating for phobic anxiety $(p < 0.001)$ and phobic avoidance $(p < 0.002)$; total 5 obsessions, both raters and both scales combined $(p < 0.001)$; fear thermometer $(p < 0.001)$; avoidance $(p < 0.001)$; obsessive attitude, evaluative factor $(p < 0.05)$; depression, assessor's rating $(p < 0.05)$; free floating anxiety, patient's rating $(p < 0.05)$.

The fact that control treatment always preceded modelling/flooding was unlikely to be responsible for these effects, as in crossover designs it is the first treatment which is usually associated with more powerful effects, not the second (Boulougouris et al., 1971; Watson et al., 1971b).

Attitude change

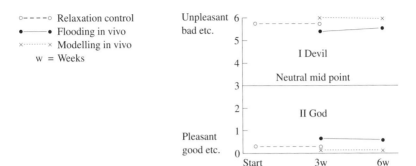

Obsessive concepts

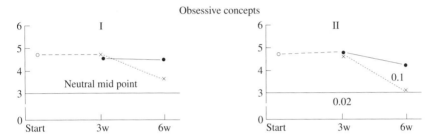

Figures 12.2–12.4. Main changes during 6 weeks of experimental treatment. The numbers 0.001, 0.002 etc. are *p* values for difference between flooding and modelling combined vs. relaxation control (*n*=10). Underlined numbers 0.05, 0.01 etc. are *p* values for difference between flooding or modelling alone vs. relaxation control (*n*=5).

2. Flooding *in Vivo* Alone (T_1) vs. Relaxation Control (C_1) $(n = 5)$

Flooding *in vivo* produced significantly more improvement than relaxation control on the following variables: total 5 obsessions, assessor's rating for phobic anxiety ($p < 0.05$) and phobic avoidance ($p < 0.02$); total 5 obsessions, both raters and both scales ($p < 0.05$); fear thermometer ($p < 0.01$); avoidance ($p < 0.01$).

3. Modelling *in Vivo* alone (T_2) vs. Relaxation Control (T_2) $(n = 5)$

Modelling produced significantly more improvement than did relaxation control on the following variables: total 5 obsessions, assessor's rating for

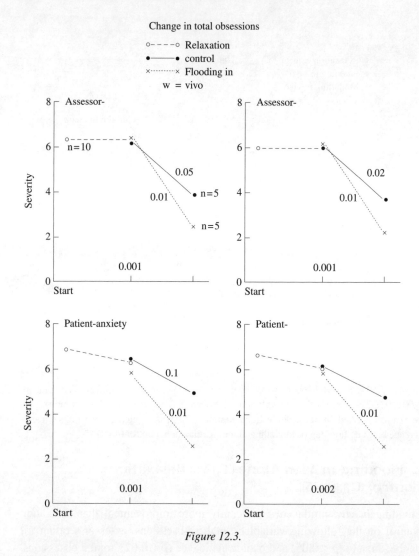

Figure 12.3.

phobic anxiety ($p<0.01$) and phobic avoidance ($p<0.01$); total 5 obsessions, patients rating for phobic anxiety ($p<0.01$) and phobic avoidance ($p<0.01$); total 5 obsessions, both raters and both scales combined ($p<0.01$); fear thermometer ($p<0.01$); depression, assessor's rating ($p<0.05$); anxiety, patient's rating ($p<0.05$).

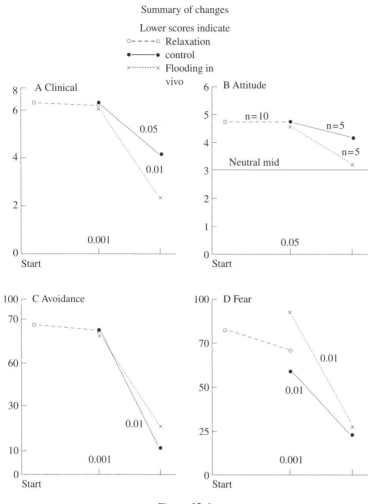

Figure 12.4.

4. Flooding *in Vivo* Alone (T_1) vs. Modelling *in Vivo* Alone (T_2) (n = 5)

There were no significant differences in the effects on obsessions of the two methods, both of which produced significant improvement. The modelling group rated themselves as significantly less anxious in general after treatment than patients in the flooding group ($p < 0.05$).

Table 12.1. Significant Differences between the 3 Treatments (Relaxation Control, Flooding, Modelling)

	1. C_{1+2} vs. T_{1+2} ($n=10$)		2. C_1 vs. T_1 ($n=5$)		3. C_2 vs. T_2 ($n=5$)		4. T_1 vs. T_2 ($n=5$)	
	Anx	Avoid	Anx	Avoid	Anx	Avoid	Anx	Avoid
Obsession 1—								
Assessor	0.01	0.001						
Patient	0.01	0.001						
Obsession 2—								
Assessor	0.01	0.001						
Patient	0.01	0.01						
Obsession 3—								
Assessor	0.02	0.001						
Patient	0.02	0.001						
Obsession 4—								
Assessor	0.01	0.05						
Patient	0.001	0.05						
Obsession 5—								
Assessor	0.001	0.05						
Patient	0.001	0.01						
Total obsessions—								
Assessor	0.001	0.001	0.05	0.02	0.01	0.01	ns	ns
Patient	0.001	0.002	0.1	ns	0.01	0.01	ns	ns
Assessor + patient anx + avoid	0.001		0.05		0.01		ns	
Attitude (2 obsessive concepts, evaluative factor)	0.05		ns		ns		ns	
Fear thermometer	0.001		0.01		0.01		ns	
Avoidance	0.001		0.01					
Depression, assessor	0.05		ns		0.05		ns	
Anxiety, patient	0.05		ns		0.05		0.05 (T_2 better)	

C_1 = relaxation control patients who subsequently had flooding.
C_2 = relaxation control patients who subsequently had modelling.
T_1 = flooding in vivo.
T_2 = modelling in vivo.
Anx = 'phobic anxiety' scale.
Avoid = 'phobic avoidance' scale.
ns = not significant.
All significance levels favour flooding/modelling.
Scales not shown yielded no significant differences.

Depression.

Five patients experienced mild to moderate depression during treatment— 4 during modelling and one during flooding. On occasion this threatened to disrupt treatment.

Prognostic factors.

Twenty-one variables at the start of treatment were correlated with out-come on 5 criteria. No clearcut pattern emerged. Only 3 significant correlations were obtained, which might be expected any way by chance from 105 correlations.

The 2 patients who responded most quickly (patient 4 to flooding and patient 8 to modelling) had the most circumscribed compulsions linked to highly specific situations. The more varied the rituals and their ramifications in the patients' lives the more difficult it seemed to be to reduce them. In two patients improvement in rituals carried out in hospital did not generalise to other rituals at home.

Motivation was important as it facilitated the cooperation necessary in treatment for improvement to occur. However, some patients failed to im-prove despite high motivation and full cooperation, while others benefited from treatment despite poor motivation and cooperation.

Agreement among outcome criteria.

This was satisfactory. Change in the 'total obsessions' clinical score corre-lated 0.02 ($p < 8.01$) with change in attitude and 0.80 ($p < 0.01$) with change on the fear thermometer. Change on the fear thermometer correlated 0.71 ($p < 0.05$) with change in attitude and 0.75 ($p < 0.05$) with change in avoid-ance scores.

Followup.

Three patients received no further treatment after the experimental period. Two received more than 20 additional sessions in hospital and at home and the other five patients received a mean of 5 extra sessions during followup. On clinical scales the 10 patients improved a further 0.3 scale points during the first 3 months followup, compared to 3 scale points during the 6-week experimental period. Improvement in attitude to obsessive concepts was also maintained. The effects of modelling and flooding thus persisted, so these techniques are of potential clinical value. Longer followup is in progress and will be the subject of a separate report.

DISCUSSION

Subject to the limitations imposed by the size of our sample, the investigation showed that both flooding and modelling had therapeutic value in at least some obsessive-compulsive patients. The outcome measures—subjective reports, independent assessments and behaviour-avoidance tests—were reassuringly consistent. They all showed improvement after flooding and modelling, both of which were significantly superior to relaxation control treatment. Improvement has been maintained so far to 3 months followup.

The absence of significant differences between flooding and modelling raises interesting questions. An obvious possibility is that both methods act through a common factor which might also be present in Meyer's (1966) technique. In all 3 techniques the patients are exposed, in the therapist's presence, to *in vivo* situations which evoke discomfort and/or anxiety and are then discouraged or prevented from "undoing" the exposure. These common features suggest that improvement occurs through habituation (Lader and Wing, 1966; Rachman, 1968; Rachman, 1970) to the discomfiting situations, but more evidence is needed to confirm this. The tacit prevention of rituals might also play a vital role. Our treatments clearly contain several components and these can only be clarified by further research.

The speed of action of the treatments varied greatly. Two patients with circumscribed obsessions were relieved within 10 days, one by modelling and one by flooding, but two were unchanged after 3 weeks. Further treatment after the experimental period helped to extend improvement, and in 3 patients treatment was carried out for brief periods at home as well as in hospital.

Home treatment greatly facilitated generalization of improvement in patients with extensive rituals, and such patients are not worth treating in hospital unless home treatment is guaranteed later. Unlike Meyer (1966) we did not provide 24-hr supervision to prevent all rituals. This was not necessary in 4 of our patients, who improved greatly without supervision. However, our impression is that improvement would have speeded up in 4 others had constant supervision been available. In one patient this would probably not have helped as she did not change at all despite full cooperation. This was puzzling, as her rituals were fairly limited. Home supervision requires major organisation of treatment personnel, and is feasible in few centres at present. Without such supervision, uncooperative patients may respond poorly to treatment. In addition the families of chronic obsessives often need much support. Obsessions and compulsions can have major social repercussions and these have to be dealt with. Relatives have to be taught not to be involved in patients' rituals and how to respond to patients' demands on them. As patients stop their rituals, time becomes available for alternative constructive activities, and they need encouragement to develop a normal social life.

It is surprising that more patients appeared clinically depressed during modelling than during flooding, but ratings did not reflect this. Our flooding treatment during the experimental period put much less pressure on patients than did the flooding treatments of Boulougouris et al., (1971) and Watson et al. (1971a). Had more pressure been exerted to stop their rituals patients might have improved even more and showed greater depression. During followup when more pressure was exerted on one patient to cease washing and hoarding she became depressed for 2 days but recovered rapidly and improved further in her compulsions. The role of support and praise was clear in her—she bluntly said at one point "I hoped you'd pat me on the back for throwing those things away". Improvement with flooding seemed to take longer in these obsessive patients than it does in phobics, and it is clear that phobic and obsessive-compulsive behaviour differ in important ways.

Like Meyer's work, our study suggests that newer psychological treatments can be helpful for certain chronic obsessives, especially as improvement has been consolidated during 3 months followup. As obsessive-compulsive disorders are so distressing to patients and their families involved in the rituals these results are encouraging. However, many problems remain. Effective treatment components need to be isolated, other procedures like thoughtstopping, satiation and flooding in fantasy require investigation, and a service context for treatment has to be worked out, as well as methods to treat patients with obsessive ideas but no rituals.

REFERENCES

Bailey, J., and Atchinson, T. (1969). The treatment of compulsive handwashing using reinforcement principles. Behav. Res. & Therapy 7, 323–326.

Bandura, A. (1969). The Principles of Behavior Modification. Holt, Rinehart & Winston, New York.

Boulougouris, J., Marset, P., and Marks I. M. (1971). Superiority of flooding (implosion) to desensitization for reducing pathological fear. Behav. Res. & Therapy 9, 7–16.

Cooper, J. (1970). The Leyton Obsessional Inventory. Psychol. Med. 1, 48–64.

Furst, J., and Cooper, A. (1970). Failure of systematic desensitization in two cases of obsessional-compulsive disorders. Behav. Res. & Therapy 8, 203–206.

Gelder, M. G., and Marks, I. M. (1966). A controlled prospective trial of behaviour therapy. Br. J. Psychiat. 112, 309–319.

Lader, M., and Wing, L. (1966). Physiological Measures: Sedative Drugs and Morbid Anxiety. Maudsley Monograph, Oxford Univ. Press, Oxford.

Marks, I. M., Crowe, M., Drewe, E., Young, J., and Dewhurst, W. G. (1969). Obsessional compulsive neurosis in identical twins. Br. J. Psychiat. 115, 991–998.

Meyer, V. (1966). Modification of expectations in cases with obsessional rituals. Behav. Res. & Therapy 4, 273–280.

Rachman, S. (1968). Phobias: Their Nature and Control. Thomas, Springfield.

────── (1970). Verhaltenstherapie bei Phobien (Trans. J. Bergold). Urban and Schwarzenburg, Munchen.

Rachman, S., Hodgson, R., and Marzillier, J. (1970). Treatment of an obsessional compulsive disorder by modelling. Behav. Res. & Therapy 8, 385–392.

Stern, R. S. (1970). Treatment of a case of obsessional neurosis using thought-stopping technique. Br. J. Psychiat. 117, 441–442.

Watson, J., Gaind, R., and Marks, I. M. (1971a). Prolonged exposure treatment of phobias. Br. Med. J. 13–15.

Watson, J., Gaind, R., and Marks, I. M. (1971b). Relevant and irrelevant fear in flooding: a cross-over study of phobic patients. Behaviour Therapy 2 (in press).

Wolpe, J. (1958). Psychotherapy by Reciprocal Inhibition. Stanford Univ. Press, Stanford.

APPENDIX: THE PATIENTS

Flooding Treatment Group

Patient 1, aged 25, had for 8 years had extensive checking rituals related to intense fears of glass or of being alone. She found the flooding sessions upsetting but made steady progress. On discharge she was substantially better and able to find normal employment.

Patient 2, aged 25, had for 3 years been compelled to retain objects in their original positions and/or straighten them (e.g. bedding, carpets). Her compulsions were so crippling that her husband and child were obliged to join her in evacuating their house. She was very tense, resisted treatment, and made but slight progress.

Patient 3, aged 47, had washing and hoarding rituals for 28 years and was pre-occupied with dirt. She cooperated moderately well in flooding, and her washing was reduced. The hoarding, which was not treated, did not change.

Patient 4, aged 46, had for 5 years displayed a handwashing compulsion coupled with a fear of animal contamination. She cooperated well and was free of compulsions after less than 10 hr of flooding treatment.

Patient 5, aged 37, had for 8 years feared contamination in the water supply, avoided toilets and washed compulsively, She cooperated fully but failed to improve.

Modelling Treatment Group

Patient 6, aged 31, was a compulsive handwasher of 5 years standing who feared dirt, disease and the possibility of harming her child. She resisted treatment but still improved.

Patient 7, aged 37, had for 8 years been fearful of harming people and was unable to be alone. She responded well and resumed normal employment.

Patient 8, aged 45, had for 28 years been a compulsive handwasher who feared urine, semen and dirt. He became free of his compulsions within 10 hr of treatment.

Patient 9, aged 26, had for 5 years been a compulsive handwasher who feared sexual contamination. She was extremely uncooperative and failed to improve.

Patient 10, aged 36, was a compulsive handwasher of 12 years standing who was frightened of cancer, hospitals and doctors. She made substantial progress during treatment.

13. Obsessional-Compulsive Problems: A Cognitive-Behavioural Analysis

Paul M. Salkovskis

THE RECENT EXPLOSION of cognitive-behavioural approaches to clinical conditions has been matched by an increasing interest in the experimental validation of the underlying theoretical formulations. Teasdale (1982) has suggested that clinically useful strategies tend to arise from the availability of new paradigms, that is, well-elaborated sources of potential hypotheses and methodology. In these terms, cognitive models of emotional disorders have attained paradigmatic status and are beginning to make major contributions to the development of empirically based psychological therapies. In particular, Beck's cognitive model (Beck, 1967, 1976) has provided a coherent theoretical explanation of the basis of a variety of clinical conditions and normal mood states with important implications for treatment. It is particularly important that this model has also served to generate a considerable amount of experimental work testing predictions regarding, for instance, depression (Clark and Teasdale, 1982) and anxiety (Butler and Mathews, 1983).

Although the cognitive model has provided useful information on the nature and treatment of depression and anxiety disorders in general, it has so far failed to offer a comprehensive approach to the understanding and treatment of obsessional disorders. This is particularly surprising as it could be argued that obsessional thinking is the archetypal example of a cognitive disorder in the neuroses. A cognitive explanation of obsessional-compulsive problems is proposed by Beck (1976). However, this account of obsessional thoughts appears to be based solely on the view that the content of obsessions is related to thoughts of danger in the form of doubt or warning. There is no discussion of the difference between these and the thoughts of danger or risk subsequently shown to be specific to anxiety (e.g. Sewitch and Kirsch, 1984), although one might expect this distinction to be necessary for any cognitive

Reprinted by permission of Pergamon Press, Elsevier Science, from *Behavior Research and Therapy* 23 (1985): 571–83.

view specific to the psychopathology of obsessions. Indeed, a number of the examples identified by Beck (1976, Chap. 7) as being anxiety- and fear-related cognitions appear to involve major elements of doubt or warning.

A differently orientated attempt at a cognitive-behavioural conceptualization of obsessive-compulsive disorder was made by McFall and Wollersheim (1979). However, this is directed at 'bridging the gap' between behavioural and psychoanalytic theory, and carries with it many of the problems associated with such an enterprise (Yates, 1983). Throughout there is a heavy dependence on the presence of preconscious and unconscious cognitions, which, compared to the psychoanalytic formulation, are said to be 'closer to the individual's awareness' as unacceptable ideas and feelings. No serious attempt is made to elaborate the processes involved in the direct cognitive and behavioural manifestations of these processes, other than mention of an undue belief in 'magical rituals'. Drawing heavily on Carr (1974) the main mediating processes are considered to be 'deficits' in primary and secondary appraisal—unfortunately, they are unable to distinguish between inaccuracies of cognitively mediated threat appraisals in obsessional patients and those in other patients. This lack of specificity must surely be a key issue and one which will probably only be resolved by a careful analysis of the *psychological processes* involved in intrusive phenomena rather than description of the characteristics of individuals experiencing obsessions. Furthermore, it is hard to see what benefits will arise from adopting psychodynamic concepts in an area where so much effort has been directed towards psychoanalytic treatment with such conspicuously poor outcome (Cawley, 1974), irrespective of the elaborate theoretical basis of this approach.

Previous attempts at cognitive *intervention* have concentrated on largely atheoretical techniques such as thought-stopping (e.g. Stern, Lipsedge and Marks, 1973) and have been mostly unsuccessful. Rachman and Hodgson (1980) have discussed distraction and dismissal procedures; however, convincing empirical evidence of the utility of such approaches has yet to be reported. It is important to consider the possibility that such procedures may be counter therapeutic, either by virtue of becoming 'neutralizing' in themselves, or by interfering with functional CS exposure (Borkovec, 1982).

Clearly, any attempt to conceptualize obsessions in cognitive terms must, as a first step, specify the position of obsessions within an hypothesized framework of cognitive phenomena such as that proposed by Beck (Beck, Epstein and Harrison, 1983). The relationship between 'negative automatic thoughts' and obsessions initially appears promising. Certainly, both can be regarded as subsets of Rachman's (1981) group of unpleasant intrusive cognitions. However, Beck (1976) clearly states that automatic thoughts are "not the typical repetitive thoughts reported by patients with obsessional neurosis" (p. 37), although he does not go on to discuss what the important differences are. There are three major reasons why it is important to clarify the relationship between automatic and obsessional thoughts and hence place intrusions firmly within the context of cognitive theory:

1. The integration of the concept of unpleasant intrusive cognitions with cognitive theory seems particularly important now that there is evidence supporting the view that such intrusions or obsessions are part of "normal experience" (Rachman and de Silva, 1978; Salkovskis and Harrison, 1984). It is now possible to entertain the view that obsessional thoughts, previously regarded as pathological, may be on a continuum with normality, in the same fashion as mood states such as anxiety and depression, together with their associated cognitions.

2. It has been suggested by workers such as Rachman (1983a) that the link between depressed mood states and clinical worsening of obsessions (as well as resistance to behavioural treatments) could be accounted for in terms of the growing evidence of increased accessibility of negatively valenced cognitions in depressed mood states (Teasdale, 1983). For such an account to be fully useful, obsessional phenomena need to be integrated into cognitive theory so that more specific predictions about the putative mechanism of this interaction can be made with confidence, allowing the direct testing of propositions from both areas of work.

3. The development of specific cognitive techniques for the treatment of obsessional-compulsive problems could augment behavioural treatments in general and perhaps allow new approaches to 'treatment failures' as described by Foa (1979), Foa, Steketee, Grayson and Doppelt (1983) and Rachman (1983b) in whom cognitive factors (especially depressed mood and overvalued ideation) appear to be crucial.

Interesting comparisons may be made between the separate literatures on obsessions (including unwanted intrusive thoughts) and negative automatic thoughts. Rachman (1981, p. 89) defines intrusive unwanted thoughts as "repetitive thoughts, images or impulses that are unacceptable and/or unwanted" and goes on to specify the necessary and sufficient conditions for identification of a thought, image or impulse as intrusive as "the subjective report that it is interrupting an ongoing activity; the thought, image or impulse is attributed to an internal origin, and is difficult to control."

Negative automatic thoughts, on the other hand, are defined by Beck, *et al.*

Table 13.1. Comparison of Obsessional Thoughts (Rachman and Hodgson, 1980) and Automatic Thoughts Described by Beck (1976)

Characteristic	Obsessional thoughts	Negative automatic thoughts
Relationship to 'stream of consciousness'	Intrude into	Run parallel to
Accessibility	Very easy	Can be difficult even with training
Perceived intrusiveness (irrelevance of interruption)	High	Low
Perceived rationality	Irrational	Rational
Relation to belief system	Inconsistent (ego dystonic)	Consistent (ego syntonic)
Relationship to external stimuli	Partial	Partial
Attributed source	Internal	Internal
Modalities affected	Linguistic, images and impulses	Linguistic and images
Content	Idiosyncratic	Idiosyncratic

(1983) as "elicited by stimuli (actual external events *or* thoughts about events)" and "*plausible* or reasonable, although they may have seemed far-fetched to somebody else. The patients accepted their validity without question and without testing out their reality or logic." (Beck, 1976, p. 36)

Further careful examination of the literature allows us to derive the comparison illustrated in Table 13.1. The major differences between these negative automatic thoughts and obsessions seem to lie in the perceived intrusiveness, immediate accessibility to consciousness and the extent to which they are seen as being consistent with the individual's belief system. This last difference is particularly important, insofar as Beck's view of cognitions producing affective disturbance rests on their perceived *realistic* and *plausible* nature, and their acceptance by the individual experiencing them. By contrast, obsessions are unacceptable, irrational and implausible. Obsessions are incongruent with the individuals belief system, unlike negative automatic thoughts which are an expression of it.

If we are not able to regard obsessions as being a type of negative automatic thought, where do they fit into a cognitive model of psychopathology? Rachman (1971, 1976) has suggested that obsessional thoughts are noxious conditioned stimuli which have failed to habituate, and which are maintained by the mechanisms involved in two-process learning. Adopting this view and attempting to consider obsessional problems from a cognitive standpoint, I would like to argue that obsessional thoughts function as stimuli which may provoke a particular type of automatic thought. The evidence is

222 PAUL M. SALKOVSKIS

that disturbing *intrusions* occur frequently in normal individuals without leading to serious disturbance of mood or coping. It seems likely that they may become a persistent source of mood disturbance only when they result in negative automatic thoughts through interaction between the unacceptable intrusions and the individuals belief system, i.e. in some kind of adverse evaluation ('this is a bad thing to be thinking'). This process is very similar to one frequently considered to produce affective disturbance in depressed patients when making global judgements of self in relation to behaviour, viz. 'if I get angry with the children that means I'm a bad mother'; 'if I have thoughts like this that means that I'm an evil person', 'thinking this is as bad as doing it' (Fennell, 1984). The intrusions will only be expected to produce distress when they have some (idiosyncratic) meaning or salience to the individual experiencing them (i.e. strong adverse personal implications). This is consistent with the findings of Parkinson and Rachman (1981), who report finding that, for normal Ss, intrusions high on unacceptability were 'worse in all respects' than intrusions of low acceptability, i.e. less dismissable, controllable, produced more discomfort, anxiety, stress, resistance and were of longer duration. In terms of Beck's model intrusions may, for some individuals on some occasions, activate pre-existing dysfunctional schemata and hence result in unpleasant automatic thoughts. Such automatic thoughts in response to intrusions appear to relate specifically to ideas of being responsible for damage or harm coming to oneself or to others, or associated imagery of a similar nature (see below and Table 13.4). That is, obsession-provoked automatic thoughts or images revolve around personal responsibility, the possibility that if things go wrong it might well be the persons' own fault. Such responsibility may be indirect as well as direct, so that the possibility of preventing harm caused by external agents is equally potent. Clearly, such ideas of responsibility would lead to self-condemnation in vulnerable individuals to the extent that such responsibility (or failure to avoid culpability) is abhorrent to them. Such ideas of responsibility can extend to having had the thought itself; that is, if the person believes that they are responsible for their own thoughts (Borkovec, Robinson, Pruzinsky and DePree, 1983; Borkovec, 1984), the content of which is abhorrent to them, then they presumably regard themselves as being responsible for being a bad or evil person unless they take steps to ensure their blamelessness. The affective disturbance usually described as arising from the obsession or intrusion actually arises from such automatic thoughts about the intrusion rather than from the intrusion itself. As depression primes concepts of self-blame this may be used to account for the increased distress experienced by obsessionals when depressed.

The prominence of a clearly identifiable and extremely obvious cognition (i.e. the intrusion) has probably served to prevent the closer examination of cognitions associated with obsessions, despite the adoption of Lang's (1970) three-systems model. The doubting described by Beck as typical of the ideation of obsessionals appears to be characteristic of the initial intrusion. The ideation from which the emotional disturbance arises is a cognitive response to this, and relates to responsibility or possibility of blame for some kind of personally salient harm (cf. Turner, Steketee and Foa, 1979). Impulses are similarly not particularly disturbing unless there is some belief in the possibility that they might be carried through, and blame being likely to fall on the individual as a result of failing to control the impulse.

Neutralization, either as compulsive behaviour or cognitive strategies (e.g. thinking a 'good thought' after having a 'bad thought') can be understood easily in this context as attempts to put things right, and avert the possibility of being blamed by self or others. Active attempts at such rectification are more likely against the background of thoughts of direct responsibility for harm, especially amongst those described by Rachman as being of 'tender conscience'. Clearly, if it is possible to rectify something that one may be responsible for, then any possible consequences cease to be a worry. The persistent seeking after reassurance, particularly from those in authority, displayed by many obsessionals also makes much more sense when viewed in this context and can be seen as a way of spreading the responsibility. Thus, the patient who has thoughts of harming other may somewhat diminish their feelings of responsibility by making sure that others know, often in great detail, the content of their worries or even carry out actions for them. So, if the doctor, psychologist or relative knows that the patient has touched a potential source of disease and then something likely to be touched by others, then they share the responsibility to some extent. This may also help account for the differences in the ability of different individuals to provide 'valid' reassurance. [See Foa (1979, p. 173) for a particularly interesting illustration of the power of reassurance in obsessionals with 'overvalued ideas'.] Some clinicians regard such reassurance seeking as a form of neutralization, but often the connection is unclear; for instance, in contamination fears where washing is the usual form of neutralization involved, but in addition reassurance is persistently (and often irritatingly) sought. Assessment and formulation based on ideas of responsibility or blame for disaster related to the effects of contamination and not washing may have greater explanatory value in the functional analysis of individual patients than fears of contamination *per se*. The implications for treatment are also important. Whereas some writers (Marks, 1981, p. 84) have stressed the importance of not providing reassurance during treatment, more often this important topic is given little prominence in descriptions of behavioural treatments. Where it is discussed, reassurance is, at best, defined very narrowly indeed, usually in terms of direct verbal requests. Frequently, reassurance seeking adopts subtle guises, and may not be recognized as a form of neutralization by patient or therapist. At worst, active provision of reassurance is recommended as a way of decreasing discomfort and improving compliance, with little regard for potential detrimental effects (Warwick and Salkovskis, 1985). These authors highlight the important difference between effective transmission of new information relevant to the patient's problems as opposed to repetitive provision of old information as a way of producing a temporary reduction in anxiety in response to doubts (i.e. intrusive thoughts) expressed by the patient. A further important implication is for the *way* in which treatment is carried out. That is, therapist-directed exposure could, under some circumstances, act to provide inappropriate reassurance and hence unwittingly lead to failure of response prevention. Examples of this include repeated unnecessary therapist modelling and excessive use of specific instructions without a shift in the emphasis towards self-directed exposure. In such circumstances, a careful analysis of the individual case with such a possibility in mind could be coupled with a strong emphasis on homework and self-programmed generalization. For the same reason, care also needs to be exercised in the use of spouse as therapist. In cases where there is a failure to generalize outside therapist-directed sessions, careful examination of this possibility is indicated, and programmed exposure to responsibility for their own programme is often useful. Some evidence for this view is provided by Roper and Rachman (1976), who demonstrated that it is difficult to elicit urges to check in the presence of the experimenter, and that urges to check elicited in the absence of the experimenter were significantly stronger than if the experimenter were present. In fact, they account for this phenomenon in terms of the transfer of responsibility to the experimenter or therapist, although they do not explain why this should have such an effect.

Neutralization can therefore be regarded as attempts to avoid or reduce the possibility of being responsible for harm to oneself or others. Frequently, the effort required for neutralization is slight when compared to the awful consequences of failure to neutralize, at least in the early stages of the disorder. Certainty of blamelessness is extremely difficult to achieve, how-ever, and if the consequences of being to blame are particularly unpalatable to the individual concerned then the availability heuristic might be expected to come into operation, in a similar way to that suggested in anxiety by Butler and Mathews (1983). It is possible to go on to argue that the cognitive distortion involved in obsessional-compulsive problems relates to an inflated belief in the probability of *being the cause* of serious harm to others or self, or failing to avert harm where this may have been possible rather than an increased belief in the probability of harm *per se.* Related to this is Rach-man's (1983a) view that close clinical and theoretical attention needs to be paid to cognitions in which the informational content is "recent representa-tive, personally salient (and) vivid" (p. 76). Frequently occurring *thoughts* regarding unacceptable actions (or possible failures to 'put right' where this may have been possible) may seem to the patient to be representative of the actions (or failure to act) themselves, in the light of their beliefs regarding the connection between thought and action (Borkovec *et al.,* 1983). This could equally apply to thoughts of having made a mistake. Clearly such thoughts are likely to be salient both in terms of their implications for possible unpleasant outcomes such as blame or criticism by others (Turner *et al.,* 1979), and in terms of their implications for action (neutralizing).

This view allows the explanation of a previously problematic clinical observation, the occurrence of intrusions without consequence discomfort. The presence or absence of dysphoric mood or salient belief appears to be an important determinant of whether discomfort follows such intrusions or not. Beck (1976) argues that negative automatic thoughts become more prominent when disturbed mood is present; thus, the intrusions are likely to cause more affective disturbance in the dysphoric individual due to the increased accessibility of *specific types* of negative automatic thoughts (Teasdale, 1983). This is not to say that pre-existing dysphoria is necessary for such affective disturbance; clearly, a particularly salient or vivid intrusion could provoke discomfort in the absence of generalized disturbed mood state rather in the way that failure experiences can provoke depressed mood whatever the initial state, but are more likely to when there is a pre-existing mood distur-bance. Themes of danger (as in anxiety) and loss (as in depression) are both frequently present in the content of obsessional compulsive ideation, so that, for instance, it could appear very likely (dangerous) that something terrible (constituting a loss) *will* happen, and the individual concerned be responsible to some degree for this. Some degree of responsibility is assumed by the obsessional as similar to being fully responsible. This model would predict that increased accessibility of such concerns (as occurs in heightened anxiety and depression) would result in clinical worsening of obsessions.

The formulation outlined above was arrived at as a result of careful consideration of a large number of obsessional patients, and is illustrated below by two examples of quite different patients. Both patients were interviewed about the content of their intrusive thoughts, and then asked to try and focus on any thoughts subsequent to the intrusions as they occurred, particularly if these were associated with discomfort.

Case 1

Patient J.F. had recently qualified as a medical doctor, and was referred just prior to starting her house jobs and getting married. She was displaying compulsive behaviour related to ideas that she might become contaminated by substances such as cosmetics which could have become transformed by sunlight or heat into carcinogens; also that she might catch warts from her fiancee. She was well aware of the extremely unlikely nature of her intrusion, but was disturbed by the possibility to the extent that she spent most of the day protecting cosmetics, soap powder and the like from sunlight and heat, and avoided contact with anything which might be contaminated by such combinations. She avoided any consumer goods which might be 'different' or 'untested' for carcinogens, to the point of dismantling enormous shop displays to find an unflawed packet. She reported intrusions regarding the possibility of things having become carcinogenic, and the safety standards used ("have they tested handcream with this particular brand of toothpaste *and* when it has all been in the sun?"). She reported that when discomfort was provoked by these stimuli, it was accompanied by a vivid image of herself with her face disfigured by skin

Table 13.2. Intrusions and Automatic Thoughts for Patient J.F.: Health Concerns

Intrusion	Automatic thought	Consequence
This hand cream may be contaminated as a result of mixing with sunlight, and some chemical inter-action	I'll get cancer and it'll be my own fault (plus im-age of her face horribly disfigured by a growth)	Seeks reassurance, refuses to use cosmetics
Some contaminated hand-cream may still be on my hands	No-one will want to know me not even my fiance, because I'll have made myself rot away	Rinses hands repeatedly
This damaged packet of food might have become contaminated by some (unknown) chemical and have become carcino-genic	If I don't find a perfect packet I'll have been re-sponsible for Peter and myself getting cancer	Asks assistant, doesn't buy it, tries to find a packet without any flaws

Table 13.3. Intrusions and Automatic Thoughts for Patient E.C.: Social Evaluative

Intrusion	Automatic thought	Consequence
(When closing a building) I might not have switched the light off	I'll get into dreadful trouble; I'll be disgraced or lose my job because of this carelessness on my part	Checks light repeatedly
(Shakes hands having touched an unidentified substance on a desk) I've given this girl a disease, perhaps poisoned her	I'll have caused terrible harm to her, might even have caused her death	Makes sure she isn't ill
(Made an unwitting comment to class about headmaster) someone will tell him I was rude about him	My thoughtlessness will result in my getting the sack, or at least into terrible trouble	Tells class he didn't mean what he said in that way
(Took some drawing pins from work to use at church) someone will find out about this	I'll be described as a thief. I'll be in terrible disgrace because of what I have done	Hides drawing pins

cancer, or the thought that if she did get cancer that her fiancee would certainly be so revolted that he would abandon her. Also, she reported that the thing that made it worst of all was the idea that *it would all be her fault because she had not done enough to prevent such an occurrence.* When she experienced intrusions which were not accompanied by these throughts and images and the idea of blame, they did not particularly upset her and compulsive behaviour did not follow. Table 13.2 shows the intrusions and associated automatic thoughts for this patient.

This patient clearly illustrates thoughts of being responsible for physical harm, mainly to herself. The second example is quite different, insofar as the range of intrusions is much more varied, and the ideation is related to social-evaluative concerns.

Case 2

Patient E.C. was a 50-yr-old schoolteacher, and had been referred as a result of an acute worsening of long-standing problems. At the time of referral he was checking excessively, showing clear depressive symptoms which he attributed to the severity of the obsessional symptoms. His obsessions took the form of 'unfinished business', in that he could not leave the topics concerned alone until he was sure that he had not been "responsible for something resulting in terrible disgrace" (his words). He was convinced of the stupidity of the checking, but had no doubts about the certainty of disgrace if the intrusion were true. Table 13.3 shows the intrusions and ideation for this patient.

A series of patients seen by the author were reviewed prior to detailing the specific model outlined above, and the results of these investigations (based on interviews) are given in Table 13.4.

Table 13.4. Obsessions and Their Associated Ideation

Sex	Duration (yr)	Type of intrusion	Ideation	Behaviour
F	5	Blasphemous thoughts	I won't be forgiven for these thoughts; I have sinned by having them	Avoids churches, prays
F	7	Thoughts of having picked up someone's money, or set fire or made them lose their purse	I might have done something which will make me a thief; the thought might mean I want to be a thief	Asks if people have their purse, seeks reassurance, avoids tills, purses
F	14	Thoughts of harming her children; images of strangling them, them dead by her hand	This means that I want to do these things; having such thoughts means I am evil; having the picture may make it happen	Avoids being on her own with children, tries to think good thoughts
F	2	Thoughts of having contaminated others, especially her children by touching them	I will have caused people/my children to get cancer, they'll get sick because of me	Avoids touching anything which others may touch, washes, checks, seeks reassurance
M	6	Thoughts of having made a serious mistake at work (architect), of having left some vital detail out	I'll be blamed for having made an expensive or injurious mistake through carelessness; I'll lose my job	Checks work repeatedly, asks others for advice, avoids finishing work
F	8	Thoughts of things being out of place, untidy	People will regard me as a bad wife person because of my behaviour	Cleans, reassurance
F	4	Thoughts of harm coming to her dog	It'll be me that hurt the dog	Tries to think good thoughts
F	7	Doubts about having turned off the gas, etc.	My flat will explode, my neighbours will die because I didn't check	Repeated checking
M	13	Thoughts of getting a sexually transmitted disease, of leaving the gas (and other things) turned on	I'll be ill because I neglected my health, things will go wrong because I was neglectful	Checks genitals, seeks reassurance, checks gas
F	3	Thoughts of wishing harm on friends and family	Having these thoughts might make these things happen. I'll have harmed people I love	Tries to think of people alive and well
F	4	Thoughts of being very overweight, thoughts of ghosts coming into the house (as she does things, e.g. closing door)	If I do things while having such awful thoughts, these things might happen because of this	Thinks of herself as underweight, pictures an angel as she repeats
M	8	Thoughts of having herpes or other disease	I may transmit disease to my family; if I don't show the doctor, he'll not make the right diagnosis	Avoid contact with family, goes repeatedly to clinic
F	2	Thoughts of harming others by contamination, carelessness, fire and other things	If I cause harm to other people then I will not go to heaven	Checks, washes, gets other to do things for her
M	10	Thoughts about not having locked the door, ruminating about 'floaters' in his eyes	If I don't get rid of these thoughts I won't be able to enjoy myself	Checks, deliberately distracts himself

A COMPREHENSIVE COGNITIVE-BEHAVIOURAL MODEL OF OBSESSIONS

The account of obsessions described here clearly owes much to the previous 'anatomy of obsessions' proposed by Rachman (1978), and makes many of the same assumptions, specifically that obsessional symptoms should be conceptualized along the lines of a three-systems model, and that intrusions *per se* are a normal phenomenon.

Figure 13.1 illustrates the main elements of the proposed model, including the mechanisms by which resonating responses are maintained, and the gating mechanisms affecting the probability of particular sequences. The environment is full of a wide range of potential triggering stimuli for intrusive thoughts. However, most obsessional patients will take steps to avoid encountering such stimuli as much as possible (Robertson, Wendiggenson and Kaplan, 1983). This avoidance may be overt or covert—that is, it may involve keeping out of particular environments and not allowing contact with particular stimuli, or may involve attempts to steer their thoughts off particular topics. This type of behaviour will be indistinguishable from that seen in phobics, with the intention being identical. Clearly such strategies may fail (or even be counter-productive, so that the avoidance behaviour itself begins to trigger the thoughts it is intended to prevent), in which case triggering stimuli are encountered. Such stimuli may be external (e.g. the sight of sharp knives), or may be other thoughts related or unrelated to the obsession. It seems likely that they may include the performance or even the satisfactory termination of a neutralizing response. There is no reason to believe that the processes governing the triggering of unpleasant intrusive thoughts are different from those involved in any other type of thought.

The intrusive thought triggered at this stage is, by definition, ego dystonic—that is, the content is experienced as inconsistent with the individual's belief system, and is perceived as objectively irrational. The reaction of the individual experiencing this intrusion (stimulus) will therefore be determined by the extent to when its occurrence is salient for the person concerned. If they believe that odd thoughts with an unpleasant content can occur and have no further implications, then the sequence will terminate here. If, on the other hand, they believe that thoughts of this kind might have important implications, then automatic thoughts would be expected to arise as a function of the strength of the beliefs concerned, which in turn will be affected by pre-existing mood state (Teasdale, 1983). The kinds of belief involved are probably best summarized in terms of Beck's (1976) concept of 'dysfunctional

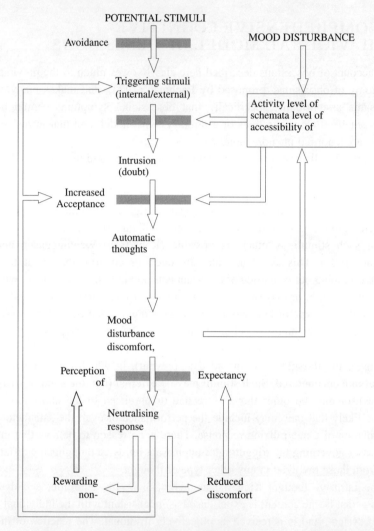

Figure 13.1. Mechanisms and Modulating Influences in Obsessional Thoughts and Behaviour

assumptions'. Dysfunctional assumptions most likely to interact with intrusive thoughts include:

(1) having a thought about an action is like performing the action;
(2) failing to prevent (or failing to try and prevent) harm to self or others is the same as having caused the harm in the first place;
(3) responsibility is not attenuated by other factors (e.g. low probability of occurrence);

(4) not neutralizing when an intrusion has occurred is similar or equivalent to seeking or wanting the harm involved in that intrusion to happen;

(5) one should (and can) exercise control over one's thoughts.

The assumptions involved in each case will vary considerably, but in each case an element of responsibility, blame or control will be involved in a way which interacts with the content of intrusive thoughts to produce automatic thoughts concerning some combination of blame, threat and loss. As already discussed, such automatic thoughts will, by definition, be ego syntonic.

Mood disturbance will result from the automatic thought, and this in turn is likely to lead to neutralizing responses. The likelihood of occurrence of neutralizing responses will depend on previous experience in terms of the extent to which relief is expected as a result of their performance (including schedule effects). Also important is the extent to which their non-performance is salient to the beliefs described above (i.e. perceived responsibility).

There are three main consequences of neutralizing, each of which have further implications for the process described. Firstly, neutralizing usually results in reduced discomfort (Hodgson and Rachman, 1972; Roper, Rachman and Hodgson, 1973) which allows the development of obsessional behaviour as a strategy for coping with stress. This not only increases the probability of subsequent neutralizing, but may also result in generalization of this strategy for anxiety reduction to other circumstances (see below). Secondly, neutralization will be consistently followed by non-punishment. Rewarding non-punishment is a powerful reinforcement in its own right (Gray, 1975) and will also be expected to have an effect on the perceived validity of the beliefs described above. These would act along the lines of 'I acted on my belief and felt better, therefore the belief must have some basis in truth' and 'the disaster I attempted to forestall has not come about, which may mean that my neutralization was a reasonable and effective thing to do'. Finally, the performance or completion of neutralizing will be, in itself a powerful and unavoidable triggering stimulus.

Pre-existing mood disturbance, although not central to the model proposed, can act at several levels. It could, for example, lead to resonation of the system in the absence of specific triggering stimuli if it were strong enough, insofar as in predisposed individuals specific cognitions relating to responsibility would become available as a result of severe dysphoria (Teasdale, 1983). Mood disturbance would widen the range of stimuli which provoke intrusions in the first place, the range of intrusions which lead to negative automatic thoughts, and the activity level of pre-existing dysfunctional schemata. If the intrusion serves as a stimulus resulting in a negative automatic thought, then the consequent mood disturbance will feed back to increase accessibility of further negative automatic thoughts. Specifically it can be predicted that increases in anxiety will result in more frequent intrusions, while depression will result in an increased probability of negative automatic thoughts and hence discomfort.

Clearly, if the automatic thoughts arising from the intrusion do not include the possibility of being in some way responsible (either actively or passively), then neutralizing is very unlikely to take place, and the result is likely to be heightened anxiety or depression rather than an obsessional problem. It could also be added that rapid extinction of affective responses would also be predicted in these circumstances, as in the stress-induced intrusions reported by Horowitz (1975). Thus, for the obsessional patient threat and loss are to be avoided, but responsibility more so.

For the model to be useful, a number of important observations need to be encompassed within the framework offered here, leading to specific modifications in particular circumstances. It should be added that these observations are problematic for most current theoretical models of obsessive-compulsive disorder, and the ways in which this model deals with them are, in the main part, not markedly different from other related formulations such as that proposed by Rachman (1978).

(1) Clinically, compulsions which appear to be fundamentally 'senseless' and not specifically related to thoughts of blame or responsibility may be encountered (de Silva, 1984). It is even possible to encounter individuals who actually find the performance of rituals pleasurable, although such individuals seldom present for treatment entirely of their own accord.

The key to this issue appears to be the presence of extremely well-elaborated and above all, effective, neutralization. This can be in the form of covert or overt compulsive behaviour. In each of the cases drawn to my attention, the compulsion has assumed considerable stereotypy, and most commonly has been present for a considerable period of time. For instance, a colleague allowed me to interview a girl (who had been referred for a psychosomatic condition), who found rearranging objects in exact lines, sometimes for many hours, a relaxing and pleasurable activity. She also reported strong urges to perform such activity during times of stress. When interviewed, she was able to date the onset of this behaviour to her early teens, at which time she recalled feeling that if she did not line things up harm would come to her parents. She did not recall these thoughts having diminished, but was emphatic that they had not been present for some years. It would appear that completely effective avoidance may lead to the disappearance of the automatic thoughts (and anxiety) in a way similar to that described by Solomon (Rescorla and Solomon, 1967). In avoidance experiments, dogs learned to shuttle so effectively that they did not encounter any aversive stimuli. They also ceased to show any signs of fear, although preventing the avoidance response resulted in the reinstatement of fear responses. It is interesting to note that Beck (1976) makes a similar observation, noting that consistent avoidance in phobics is related to lack of awareness of 'maladaptive ideation' (i.e. negative automatic thoughts), adding that being forced into the avoided situation leads to activation of such ideation, and consequent easy identification. In obsessions, this situation would be expected to occur in individuals for whom the neutralization is fully effective and can be carried out on every occasion. In such cases, the obsession would cease to elicit the negative automatic thoughts, as the thoughts of blame would not apply if 'putting things right' were immediately and consistently possible. It is also possible that the neutralizing response would come to have the kind of reinforcing properties associated with a strong safety signal (Rachman, 1984), and may occur independently of intrusions, as described in the case above. In cognitive terms, the neutralizing response could come to elicit *positive* automatic thoughts, although this need not necessarily happen. From this analysis, a number of testable predictions can be made about obsessions for which no thoughts of blame or responsibility can be found: (i) a highly effective neutralizing response will always be present; (ii) thoughts of blame or responsibility will have been present at the onset of the obsession; (iii) the obsession will tend to be of very long duration or of early onset; (iv) little or no resistance to the obsession will be present for most of the time; (v) little or no subjective or psychophysiological disturbance will accompany the performance of the neutralizing behaviour, although response prevention will tend to produce both; and (vi) the neutralizing response will tend to be very stereotyped. Such patients are relatively rare, but these predictions have been borne out in the five such cases the author has been able to interview.

(2) Thoughts of blame or responsibility are not prominent in many 'normal' obsessions, in the absence of compulsive behaviour.

In a sense, this may well be a key strength of the present formulation. It does appear that thoughts of blame and responsibility are not present in some normal Ss. This is particularly the case for individuals who report that they do not engage in any neutralizing activity. The explanation for this can be found in the previously described distinction between automatic thoughts and intrusions. Normal Ss experiencing intrusions with weak or no negative automatic thoughts of blame are almost certain not to attempt neutralizing, as this would clearly serve no function whatsoever. Parkinson and Rachman (1980) report, in a study of habituation of 'normal' obsessional thoughts, that eliciting the thought stimulated the urge to neutralize in only 1 of 60 Ss. This is in very marked contrast with studies on clinical obsessions, in which the urge to neutralize is consistently elicited in such circumstances. This, then, appears to be a major difference between 'normal' and clinical obsessions, and can be easily explained within the framework offered here. Hence, it is argued that 'normal' obsessions, in most circumstances, do not elicit negative automatic thoughts of blame. They may not elicit any response at all, or they may elicit negative automatic thoughts unrelated to blame or responsibility (such as thoughts related to threat or loss), produce discomfort without neutralizing, and simply habituate with repetition. Predictions from this aspect of the model would be: (i) there will be a strong association between neutralization and thoughts of blame in normal obsessions; (ii) normal and abnormal obsessions will differ in terms of the likelihood of thoughts of blame being present; (iii) when thoughts of blame are present in normal obsessions, the belief in such thoughts will be considerably less than in a clinical population even when the effect of frequency of intrusive thoughts is partialled out; (iv) the content of intrusive thoughts is likely to be more variable over time in a normal compared to a clinical sample; and (v) when neutralization takes place frequently in a normal obsession, the scope of this will closely parallel clinical obsessions.

(3) While the relationship between mood and obsessions is easily explained where obsessions increase as a result of mood disturbance, there is a small identifiable subsample ('losers') for whom depression results in a decrease and sometimes complete remission of obsessional symptoms (Gittelson, 1966). Such individuals show a return of obsessional symptoms once the depression lifts. The explanation for this phenomenon may be found in the content of the cognitions involved in these patients when they become depressed. In depression two relatively distinct sets of cognitions may be involved; self-blame and guilt feelings as opposed to overwhelming feelings of helplessness and hopelessness. The belief that things are going (or have gone) wrong as a result of the patient's own actions as opposed to the belief that nothing one does makes any difference at all, now or ever, would have quite different effects on the assumptions described as underlying obsessional problems. Ideas of self-blame and guilt should amplify any pre-existing obsessional thoughts ('gainers'), while hopelessness and helplessness would invalidate those already present ('losers'). Predictions from this would be: (i)

'gaining' and 'losing' should relate to the interactions between obsessional beliefs and depressive beliefs such that hopelessness specific to obsessional content will inversely correlate with worsening of obsessions; (ii) 'losing' should be confined to depression (particularly retarded depression), and should not be seen in anxiety states without severe depression or hopelessness; and (iii) for such patients the intrusive thoughts will still occur in depression but will be regarded as 'not mattering'.

The therapeutic implications of this model are largely consistent with those of the behavioural model, with some particular additions. It would be predicted that attempts at cognitive modification of obsessions should concentrate not on modification of intrusions, which would be unlikely to have other than a transient effect on the belief system of the individual, but on the automatic thoughts consequent on the intrusions, and the beliefs which give rise to these. Clearly, exposure and response prevention are vital in the context of this model in terms of their effect on the resonating circuits in the later stages of the sequence described here. These procedures, together with related techniques such as modelling, would also function in the same way as the behavioural experiments currently employed in cognitive therapy for depression and anxiety (Beck, Rush, Shaw and Emery, 1979; Beck and Emery, 1979). Such an approach provides the opportunity to challenge automatic thoughts by thinking and behaving differently, in ways which may often be more effective than purely cognitive manoeuvres alone (Rachman, 1983a). If some modification of the occurrence, nature or impact of automatic thoughts concerning responsibility were possible in tandem with such procedures, then the subjective discomfort and psychophysiological disturbance could be reduced as well (de Silva and Rachman, 1981) with important implications for compliance. Likewise, if it were possible to alter the assumptions associated with the obsession, presumably the possibility of any resonance being set up would be removed and habituation enhanced accordingly. Another major application of cognitive techniques would be with individuals who may present difficulties in exposure, such as those who fear contamination by stimuli which it would be unwise to allow direct exposure (e.g. poisons) or in whom the predicted disasters arising from failure to perform the obsessions are remote in time, such as fears of contamination by potential carcinogens.

It is important to stress that attempts to act on the intrusion itself by means of direct argument would probably be unsuccessful between sessions and would, at worst, be most akin to providing reassurance and hence serve to strengthen the dysfunctional schemata. If the intrusion is regarded as the stimulus resulting in particular automatic thoughts rather than the cognitive basis of the discomfort itself thus is clearer; reassurance is simply providing a further means of avoiding the stimulus. Another possibility for therapy relates to the use of cognitive intervention in depressed obsessionals, for whom there is now considerable evidence or failure to respond to behavioural treatments (Rachman, 1983b; Foa, 1979). If a cognitive approach is employed with such patients, then particular attention would need to be paid to dealing with thoughts of guilt or overwhelming responsibility; within-session habituation to exposure would then be expected to proceed, this probably being a necessary condition for clinical improvement (Foa, 1979).

Clearly, further validation of the view expounded here is required, and a study to provide this is under way. Preliminary single-case experiments evaluating the value of an approach of this kind with a variety of problems are also being carried out (Salkovskis and Warwick, 1985b). A case study which raises further questions of the type discussed here and illustrates the use of a cognitive intervention in a depressed obsessional who developed overvalued ideation has been completed (Salkovskis and Warwick, 1985a). Ultimately, the utility of such a model must rest on its ability to make a contribution to the clinical assessment and treatment of obsessional patients.

REFERENCES

Beck A. T. (1967) Depression: Clinical, Experimental and Theoretical Aspects. (Republished as Depression: Causes and Treatment. Univ. of Pennsylvania Press, Philadelphia, Penn., 1972.)

Beck A. T. (1976) Cognitive Therapy and the Emotional Disorders. International Univ. Press, New York.

Beck A. T., and Emery, G. (1979) Cognitive therapy of anxiety and the phobic disorders. Unpublished manuscript, Center for Cognitive Therapy, Univ. of Pennsylvania, Philadelphia, Penn.

Beck A. T., Epstein N. and Harrison R. (1983) Cognitions, attitudes and personality dimensions in depression. Br. J. cog. Psychother. 1, 1–16.

Beck A. T., Rush A. J., Shaw B. F., and Emery G. (1979) Cognitive Therapy of Depression. Guilford Press, New York.

Borkovec T. G. (1982) Facilitation and inhibition of functional CS exposure in the treatment of phobias. In Learning Theory Approaches to Psychiatry (Edited by Boulougouris, J.), pp. 95–102. Wiley, New York.

Borkovec T. G. (1984) Worry: physiological and cognitive processes. Paper presented at the 14th A. Congr. European Association for Behaviour Therapy, Brussels.

Borkovec T. G., Robinson E., Pruzinsky T., and DePress J. A. (1983) Preliminary *exploration of worry: some characteristics and processes.* Behav. Res. Ther. **21,** 9–16.

Butler G., and Mathews A. (1983) *Cognitive processes in anxiety.* Adv. Behav. Res. Ther. **5,** 51–62.

Carr A. T. (1974) *Compulsive neurosis: a review of the literature.* Psychol. Bull. **81,** 311–318.

Cawley R. (1974) *Psychotherapy and obsessional disorders. In* Obsessional States *(Edited by Beech, H. R.), pp. 259–290. Methuen, London.*

Clark D. M., and Teasdale J. D. (1982) *Diurnal variation in clinical depression and accessibility of memories of positive and negative experiences.* J. abnorm. Psychol. **91,** 87–95.

Fennell M. J. V. (1984). *Personal communication.*

Foa E. B. (1979) Failures in treating obsessive-compulsives. Behav. Res. Ther. **17,** 169–176.

Foa E. B., Steketee G., Grayson J. B., and Doppelt H. G. (1983) *Treatment of obsessive-compulsives: when do we fail?* In Failures in Behaviour Therapy *(Edited by Foa, E. B., and Emmelkamp, P. M. G.), pp. 10–34. Wiley, New York.*

Gittelson N. (1966) *The fate of obsessions in depressive psychosis.* Br. J. Psychiat. **112,** 705–708.

Gray J. A. (1975) Elements of a Two-process Theory of Learning. *Academic Press, London.*

Hodgson R. J. and Rachman S. J. (1972) *The effects of contamination and washing in obsessional patients.* Behav. Res. Ther. **10,** 111–117.

Horowitz M. (1975) *Intrusive and repetitive thoughts after experimental stress.* Archs gen. Psychiat. **32,** 1457–1463.

Lang P. J. (1970) *Stimulus control, response control and the desensitization of fear. In* Learning Approaches to Therapeutic Behaviour *(Edited by Levis D. J.). Aldine, Chicago, Ill.*

Marks I. M. (1981) Cure and Care of Neurosis. *Wiley, New York.*

McFall M. E. and Wollersheim J. P. (1979) *Obsessive-compulsive neurosis: a cognitive-behavioural formulation and approach to treatment.* Cog. Ther. Res. **3,** 333–348.

Parkinson L., and Rachman S. J. (1980) *Are intrusive thoughts subject to habituation?* Behav. Res. Ther. **18,** 409–418.

Parkinson L. and Rachman S. J. (1981) *The nature of intrusive thoughts.* Adv. Behav. Res. Ther. **3,** 101–110.

Rachman S. J. (1971) *Obsessional ruminations.* Behav. Res. Ther. **9,** 229–235.

Rachman S. J. (1974) *Some similarities and differences between obsessional ruminations and morbid preoccupations.* Can. psychol. Ass. J. **18,** 71–73.

Rachman S. J. (1976) *The modification of obsessions: a new formulation.* Behav. Res. Ther. **14,** 437–444.

Rachman S. J. (1978) *An anatomy of obsessions.* Behav. Analysis Modif. **2,** 253–278.

Rachman S. J. (1981) *Special issue on unwanted intrusive cognitions.* Adv. Behav. Ther. **3,** 87–123.

Rachman S. J (1983a) *Irrational thinking with special reference to cognitive therapy.* Adv. Behav. Res. Ther. **5,** 63–88.

Rachman S. J. (1983b) Obstacles to the successful treatment of obsessions. In Failures in Behaviour Therapy (Edited by Foa E. B. and Emmelkamp P. M. G.), pp. 35–57. Wiley, New York.

Rachman S. J. (1984) Agoraphobia—a safety-signal perspective. Behav. Res. Ther. 22, 59–70.

Rachman S. J. and Hodgson R. J. (1980) Obsessions and Compulsions. Prentice-Hall, Englewood Cliffs, N.J.

Rachman S. J. and de Silva P. (1978) Abnormal and normal obsessions. Behav. Res. Ther. 16, 233–248.

Rescorla R. A. and Solomon R. L. (1967) Two process learning theory: relationships between Pavlovian conditioning and instrumental learning. Psychol. Rev. 74, 151–182.

Robertson, J. Wendiggenson P. and Kaplan I. (1983) Towards a comprehensive treatment of obsessional thoughts. Behav. Res. Ther. 21, 347–356.

Roper G. and Rachman S. J. (1976) Obsessional-compulsive checking: experimental replication and development. Behav. Res. Ther. 14, 25–32.

Roper G., Rachman, S. J. and Hodgson, R. (1973) An experiment on obsessional checking. Behav. Res. Ther. 11, 271–277.

Salkovskis P. M. and Harrison J. (1984). Abnormal and normal obsessions: a replication. Behav. Res. Ther. 22, 549–552.

Salkovskis P. M. and Warwick H. M. C. (1985a) Cognitive therapy of obsessional-compulsive disorder: treating treatment failures. Behav. Psychother. 13, 243–255.

Salkovskis P. M., and Warwick H. M. C. (1985b) Morbid pre-occupations, health anxiety and reassurance. Submitted for publication.

Sewitch T. S. and Kirsch I. (1984) The cognitive content of anxiety: naturalistic evidence for the predominance of threat-related thoughts. Cog. Ther. Res. 8, 49–58.

de Silva P. (1984) Personal communication.

de Silva P. and Rachman S. J. (1981) Is exposure a necessary condition for fear reduction? Behav. Res. Ther. 19, 227–232.

Stern R. S., Lipsedge M. S., and Marks I. M. (1973) Obsessive ruminations: a controlled trial of thought-stopping. Behav. Res. Ther. 11, 659–662.

Teasdale J. D. (1982) What kind of theory will improve psychological treatment? In Learning Theory Approaches to Psychiatry (Edited by Boulougouris J.), pp. 57–66. Wiley, New York.

Teasdale J. D. (1983) Negative thinking in depression: cause, effect or reciprocal relationship? Adv. Behav. Res. Ther. 5, 3–25.

Turner S. M., Steketee G. and Foa E. B. (1979) Fear of criticism in washers, checkers and phobics. Behav. Res. Ther. 17, 79–80.

Warwick H. M. C. and Salkovskis P. M. (1985) Reassurance. Br. med. J. 290, 1028.

Yates A. J. (1983) Behaviour therapy and psychodynamic psychotherapy: basic conflict or reconciliation and integration? Br. J. clin. Psychol. 22, 107–126.

PART III

Neuropsychiatric Approaches

14. The Organic Background of Obsessions and Compulsions

Paul Schilder

Obsessions and compulsions have been repeatedly observed in epidemic encephalitis. Such may occur in acute cases as in the observation of Mayer-Gross and Steiner. The majority of cases are either sub-acute or chronic (*cf.* for instance Hermann, Bürger, Bromberg, Jelliffe, L. Bender). Of particular interest are the obsessions and compulsions observed in cases with oculogyric crisis (Stern, Stengel, Jelliffe). Jelliffe has not only collected the whole literature on the subject but has also added valuable observations of his own and has especially pointed to the personality factors which determine, in connection with the encephalitic process, the oculogyric crisis and the contents of the obsessions and compulsions in these cases. The subject has lately been reviewed by Wexberg. It is obvious that the organic disease of the central nervous system is an indispensable factor in the genesis of the psychic symptoms, which have been mentioned. If one reviews the cases in the literature carefully and compares them with one's own experiences, one sees that although infantile experiences and situations have created a pattern, it finds its expression in compulsions on the basis of the organic processes involved. Such a statement cannot fully be substantiated since no reliable methods are available at the moment by which we are able to predict the consequences of infantile patterns. Comparative studies of analyzed cases of obsession neurosis and obsessions and compulsions on an encephalitic basis have led me to the conclusion I have formulated.

The encephalitic process liberates motor impulses and motor innervations. Release phenomena of this kind are for instance the oculomotor spasms, the palilalia, the tic-like movements, the choreic and choreiform phenomena and finally all the impulse phenomena which are comprised under the heading of hyperkinesis. Forced movements of any type even when they occur on a purely somatic basis represent increased innervation and increased activity

Reprinted by permission of the American Psychiatric Press from *American Journal of Psychiatry* 94 (1938): 1397–1416.

and have their reflection in the psychic sphere as increase of impulses which reinforces sadistic attitudes. This is true concerning epileptic attacks (which do not concern us here) as well as for oculogyric crises. Akinetic states and rigidities which restrict impulses and movements dam up impulses which may originate in other levels. These dammed up impulses will finally break through with great violence. Impulsive actions of more or less sadistic character are common in these cases. When they are checked, compulsive phenomena may result. Hyperkinetic phenomena of all levels may lead to compulsions and obsessions. However, akinetic phenomena may lead indirectly to the same result. Compulsions may so originate from motor sources in the widest sense. It is necessary to keep in mind that there exists a direct connection between compulsions (the urge to actions towards which the individual resists) and obsessions (thoughts and representations which maintain themselves in the consciousness of the individual contrary to his intention). A Polish Jew of my observation felt the urge when crossing a street to call out that he is an illegitimate child. He suppressed this impulse and was afterwards tortured by the obsession that he had done so. The obsessive thought substituted the repressed impulse.

I have observed postencephalitic cases in which obsessions had a different genesis. In these cases the patients experienced a change in the state of consciousness in which thoughts and representations were going through their minds and persisted against their wishes. The change in consciousness during oculogyric crisis is a factor which has to be considered for the genesis of compulsions and obsessions observed in these states. Stengel has proved that the vestibular function is changed during the oculogyric crisis. The vestibular function influences the tone and the motor impulses. Studies of Hoff and myself have shown that the change in the function of the vestibular apparatus changes the state of consciousness. There exists therefore a close interrelation between the impulses, the tone, the vestibular apparatus, oculomotor mechanism and the consciousness. Such considerations may lead to the better understanding of a postencephalitic case in which the patient complained that she saw dirt everywhere. She said that everywhere there were dark spots. She had to clean her house continually although she was rather convinced that there was no dirt. She felt particularly uneasy when she saw regular patterns on the pavement or somewhere else and dizziness followed. There was a similar uneasiness when confronted with any complicated optic situation. When she was turned around on a swivel chair she saw more and more dirt. Irrigation of the ear had no specific effect. The patient showed a mild akinesis and rigidity but a particular difficulty in her eye movements. She improved under fever therapy but came back later complaining that everything was glittering before her eyes so that she felt dazzled.

The following case may illustrate the relation between impulses originating from encephalitis and compulsion phenomena.

Case 1

Yvette R., 30 years old, complained that she is compelled to think the whole day. "It is not true that I am lazy—it is not true that nothing interests me. It keeps repeating in my mind. I keep on telling to myself the cockeyed world can go to hell. I have to count the pin holes in everything I see. When I look at something I say how many pin holes are there?" The patient complained that she asks herself concerning every object of how many pin holes it consists. However, she does not try to count.

The patient had a typical encephalitis when she was 15 years old. She was sick for six weeks. A slight rigidity and akinesis remained. She married five years ago. She was worrisome all her life, even before the encephalitis. About three years ago she gave birth to a boy. During her pregnancy she worried she wouldn't be able to take care of the baby. When she came home from the hospital she was so upset that she tried to kill herself with roach poison. She was then sent to a sanitarium. There she developed the fear she might go crazy. She blamed herself that she was the most selfish person in the world. At this time, one of her sisters B told her that she had been lazy all her life. An older sister E admonished her that she should have more interest in the world. Immediately after that the compulsions to say "it is not true that I was lazy all my life and it is not true that nothing interests me" developed. When she complained to her husband he said that she should send the whole cockeyed world to hell. This led to the other compulsion. Several months later she accidentally stuck a pin through the bed sheet in her child's crib. She developed immediately after that the compulsion to count the pin holes. It turned out that she was afraid she might stick a pin in the body of her child.

When the obsessions came she started also to repeat words and short orders again and again. Her appetite disappeared and she didn't sleep well.

During the discussions she talked in terms of exaggerated affection for her husband and for her child, of whom she speaks as honey and darling. She likes also to call the analyst to whom she clings darling. She shows a very outspoken palilalia. This becomes particularly manifest when she reports about her obsessions. She repeats sometimes the beginning of the text but more often the end. She also repeats orders she gives to her baby, especially when they are short. She reports that she gave up religion when she married since her husband is now her God. She declares that she loves her child and husband dearly and that she loves everybody. "I love the whole world." She complains that she is slow in her movements and that she remains sometimes for a long time in frozen attitudes.

The somatic examination shows that the patient has a typical Parkinsonism of medium degree. The rigidity of the face is outspoken. The palilalia is severe. There are no other somatic findings.

The psychoanalytic approach was difficult but a strong attachment to the father going back in early childhood came to the foreground. She was his favorite child and worried very much about his diabetes to which he succumbed when the patient was 13. She was occasionally spanked by her mother whom she disobeyed often. She had little contact with two brothers and a sister much older than herself. She had many fights with her sister E who is four years older and her sister B who is four years younger. She slept with B in one bed. She would often hit her sister B when she didn't obey her.

One of her earliest remembrances is that her sister E wanted to cut off the finger of B and was spanked by her mother. She was also often hit by her sister E. In one of her dreams, one of her nieces wanted to marry a girl. One of the patient's girl friends appears continually in her dreams which are filled with activity. There are also dreams of being held against her will. In one of her dreams she says to her sister E "the whole cockeyed world can go to hell and you too." E kicked her out of the house and told her not to come back again. Her early history is filled with accidents. At three the stick of a lollypop pierced her lips. She burned herself with hot tea and ripped her behind when she slid down a staircase. She hurt her head when she was five. The patient thinks that she was wonderful before the baby arrived. There were frequent worries about money at the beginning of her marriage.

The patient was a lively and aggressive child. We have reason to believe that there were homosexual trends present in her relation to her sisters. A great amount of hostility was in her before she acquired encephalitis and before she gave birth to her child. The hostility against her child was obvious in the pregnancy to which the patient answered by self accusation and depression. After the birth it finally led to a suicidal attempt. It is probable that the akinesis was present before her pregnancy. Her fear of laziness and inactivity comes into appearance with childbirth. There is an increase of impulses in the speech function which leads immediately into the compulsions which express directly and indirectly hostilities against her sisters and her child. She overcompensates her hostilities against others by praising them beyond measure. She heaps all the blame upon herself. Psychotherapy and benzedrine did not cure the patient but she learned to send the cockeyed world to hell with greater ease.

It is easy to see in this case the relation of the change in the motility to the expression of hostile impulses and compulsion. The connection between compulsion and obsession and the motor impulses is not always so clear, but more careful examination of these cases shows very often an intimate relation between impulses and the compulsion.

In spite of the fact that such an obvious connection exists between the impulse disturbance on an organic basis and compulsions, the question rarely has been raised whether it isn't possible to find an organic background for obsession neurosis cases in general. Naturally in the majority of cases there is no history of epidemic encephalitis. If one examines a large material of obsession neurosis cases, one finds not so rarely organic symptoms identical with those found in chronic encephalitis. In the comparatively short time of about two years I have seen seven cases in which slight organic signs could be found in careful examination and in two other cases there was at least some clinical evidence that impulse disturbances on an organic basis were present. The symptoms which are of particular importance in this connection are the following ones: 1. Rigidity of the face and mask-like facies. It is true that an objective appreciation of the mobility of the face is not always easy. When two independent observers agree on this point one might use this symptom if it is not isolated as corroborative evidence. 2. Evidence of flexor rigidity in the arms. We shall generally not expect that cases of this type will show a very outspoken Parkinsonism. Even the cogwheel phenomenon may not be present. Hoff and I have described the so-called convergence phenomenon of the arms. The phenomenon has to be tested as follows: The arms are out-stretched parallel to each other and the patient is ordered to keep his eyes closed. The sign is positive if the hands come nearer to each other. This sign is due to a flexion in the elbow. When merely one arm is tested, the flexion is present too. If both arms are tested one has to take into consideration that the arms diverge in the normal subject. The normal divergence and the convergence on the basis of flexor rigidity may compensate each other. The sign is a reliable help in detecting slight Parkinsonian features and points to an organic lesion of those parts of the brain which are affected in Parkinsonism, and Parkinson. The sign is present in alcoholics when in the state of an acute intoxication and may disappear with the recovery. Although it is very often combined with tremor it may be present without tremor, and tremor may be present without convergence. 3. Tremor of an organic type is an important symptom, even if the tremor is slight. 4. If the convergence of the eyes is impaired (when exophoria is not present) further evidence for an organic process is hardly necessary. However, in the majority of the cases studied here, a decided evidence of impaired convergence could not be given. 5. Great urge to talk and propulsive features in speech are of paramount importance. 6. Hyperactivity and motor urges of higher degree should be considered as confirmatory evidence. Also the history of hyperactivity in childhood should not be neglected. 7. Outspoken rigidities, propulsion and retropulsion, higher degrees of akinesis and catalepsy can hardly be expected in cases of this type. Persistence of tone described by Hoff and myself has not been observed in any one of these cases.

I have observed seven cases of obsession neurosis in which organic signs of the type described here were present. Only a few of these cases will be discussed in detail.

Case 2

Emanuel P., 26 years old, came with the complaint that he is afraid of dogs and cats. They instill awe and disgust in him. Since the age of five he is afraid that dogs might come near him and bite him. He is particularly afraid that his penis might be hurt. By the mere contact with dogs his skin might become like the skin of a dog. His fear of cats is less intensive as the fear of dogs. For many years he cannot eat food when his mother tasted it first before serving. The food might be infected by the saliva of the mother. Furthermore, he is continually plagued with the idea that he might not be clean enough and spends hours in the bathroom, washing his hands again and again. Fears of this type go back to the age of 14.

The patient is small, almost dwarfed. His movements are quick and jerky. He talks incessantly with a loud voice and in a propulsive manner. He repeats very often what he has said but this is not a palilalia. He salivates and spits a little while talking. His face is a little rigid. There is a slight tremor of the head and of the fingers. There is no convergence of arms. The eye convergence is good. The pupils react at the present time but during an examination three years prior the pupils were found slightly irregular and almost stiff. When the patient was 12 years old he suffered from a period of sleepiness and was called "sleepy head" and "dopey" in school. A tentative diagnosis of encephalitis was made but not definitely substantiated. As the later discussion will show he was at that time in a particular psychic strain. He complains often about a pain in his left side, about headache and dizziness. A careful checkup showed that there was no somatic basis for these complaints.

The patient lives with his family the social status of which is rather low. He has two younger sisters who work. The father is often unemployed. The patient himself worked for only a short time during his life as a messenger boy. He lives in constant conflict with his family. For years he was treated in different out-patient departments and was for several months in Central Islip, a state hospital.

As mentioned, he stays in the bathroom for a long time and cannot stand any interruption. He cannot defecate thoroughly when someone is near the bathroom. He washes very carefully and is in fear of being contaminated by germs. When the process of washing is interrupted he begins all over again. When his mother tastes the food she is cooking and puts the spoon again into the food he cannot eat it. He is afraid of being poisoned by the germs which might be contained in the saliva of his mother. He is very sensitive. He feels continually attacked by everybody. People on the street say to him "Hey Red." He is afraid they might beat him. He is also continually afraid that the analyst may make fun of him. He is also afraid that the other patients might laugh at him. He comes to his appointments mostly late and reacts with a great anger if the physician is not able to see him when he comes three or four hours late. He left the treatment in great anger. During the treatment, which lasted several months, his ambivalence was very outspoken. Love to the analyst was combined with fear and violent outbursts of hate when he felt rejected. It was always difficult to finish a session since he clung to the analyst asking question after question and demanding that the answers should be repeated again and again. The patient repeated everything he said several times insisting that he had to repeat in order not to be misunderstood. He liked to write and wrote a long autobiography and long reports in which repititions occurred very frequently.

I quote a few sentences in a report he wrote about an encounter with a cat. "I opened the door and the cat ran out and when I saw the cat run out I ran also because I was very much afraid that the cat is after me and will attack me if I do not run. Then I saw the cat run away from me. I ran after the cat so that the cat will not be at the building where I live, so as not to come into the building where I live. Then I felt my legs shaking and I felt my legs weak." It speaks for the deep-sitting character of his tendencies to repetition that the patient repeatedly dreamed the same dream twice in one night. I do not hesitate to consider the motility and the impulses of this patient as organically determined. However, the ambivalence reinforces many of his motor trends, his doubts and his tendencies to questioning.

His whole sex interest centers around the anal region. He is particularly interested in the anus as such and in the region between the buttocks. This attitude can be traced back to his fourth year when he had scarlet fever and got an enema from his mother. He could not urinate at that time and an onion was put on his penis. When he came to the hospital at 11 because of functional heart trouble he was greatly interested when he saw the nurses give enemas to other children. He liked to fancy himself in the same situation and got sexual pleasure out of such fantasies. Since his 14th year he masturbates thinking of a teacher's rectum, "associating her rectum with a female rectum who gave a child an enema which I had observed." He also had a fantasy of a female giving him an enema. He felt that the "rectum" of females is broader and by getting an enema his rectum would become broader too and like the rectum of a female. He would be so transformed himself into a female. He is extremely interested in seeing these parts of women. He is also interested in smelling the places where women have been sitting. This interest goes back to his fifth year. He has often wishes and fantasies that his father should insert his penis into his rectum. Many dreams and fantasies make it clear that the muzzle of the dog, the dog itself, the penis and feces are equivalent in his mind. He therefore tends to be passive towards his father and his sex organ and towards women who are endowed with a symbolic penis (the nozzle of the enema).

He reports that he loved his father very much when he was small and that his father was very good to him. He occasionally has sexual dreams about his father as spilling semen on the chest of his father. Around his fifth year the father became a menace to him. He is afraid of his father's looks and when his father is angry he is afraid that his father may bite his penis off. The patient reports this with decided gusto and even reports that he has voluptuous sensations in his sex organ when threatened by his father or anybody else. Even the repetition of the story gives him sexual pleasure. He very often has the wish to attack his father with an axe from behind and kill him. Sometimes he wants to choke his father and is afraid his father might choke him. He also has hostile impulses against his mother and sisters. His fear of dogs goes back to his 4th year. He says that dogs have a grim expression in their faces and uses in a description of dogs the same words as he uses in describing his father. He is also afraid of being infected by dogs and to become like a dog if he touches one.

The patient is conscious of his being short, weak and helpless. His autobiography begins "when I was born I was told by my mother and father that I was a short baby." "I used to throw my feet up and down nervously and make nervous motions with a rattle."

The parents obviously were very conscious of the size and weakness of the child and later on became annoyed by his hyperkinetic aggressiveness. Around the fifth year of the patient the counter aggression of the parents was in full swing. At this critical age a scarlatina occurred which led to the handling of the penis and of the anus of the patient by his mother. The passive attitude of the patient mingled immediately with anal and especially sexual motives and the definite pattern was established. The persistent hyperkinesis sharpened the conflicts with the parents. The sexual problems reawakened in connection with hospital experiences before puberty, the anal pattern was reinforced and sexual excitement and masturbation led to preoccupation and sleepiness. His present attitude towards dogs runs parallel to his attitude towards his parents. An early love for a white dog was substituted by the fear of brown dogs. He is now in a world which continually threatens him. The threats coming from father and mother are the threats that he might be cut to pieces and dismembered and especially that he might be deprived of his sex organs. He is furthermore threatened by the saliva of his mother which is poisonous and contains germs. Uncleanliness becomes the general expression of threats coming from excretions of any other person's body. Semen and feces also become formidable. Animals are a combination of the danger coming from direct attack and secretion. They bite and are unclean.

It is obvious that in this psychological development the increase in the motor impulses is of paramount importance. However, the body configuration of the patient in its effect upon the parents and the attitudes of the parents in general are of decisive influence on the further development of this severe neurosis. This is the only case of this group in which the therapeutic effort was without any result.

The obsessional neurotic patient who complained of being too small, mentioned in my paper on ideologies, who had compulsions to curse God and make at the same time movements with his feet, showed a rigid face, a propulsive speech, a slight tremor of the hands and especially of the eyelids. His cursing was obviously in connection with strong motor impulses, not only concerning his speech but also his feet. In his early history, consciousness of his smallness, homosexual attachment to his father and fight against the father play an outstanding part. He makes the movements with his toes three times. He has the urge to touch everything, especially the female breast. There are compulsions to use obscene words. The verbal attack is obviously the precursor of a physical attack which ends in the anal intercourse with the defeated love object.

The 33-year-old Frank M. suffers from severe anxiety states. He had been analyzed for about 2½ years by other physicians. He has compulsions to cut women into pieces, to tear out their sex parts and to devour them either in parts or as a whole. He has similar impulses towards the analyst. He has a compulsion to count. "I count and think in my mind. Also Napoleon has counted windows. I count the corners and borders of every piece of paper. Then I count the planes and break everything in my thoughts. I would like to smash everybody to pieces and urinate upon them." Counting means for the patient to tear and to break into small pieces. This means also a destruction of the human body. The patient has a rigid face, and an enormous urge to talk. In his childhood he was exposed to the attacks of older brothers. He was weak and continually threatened. In addition, he was an hyperactive child and came continually in conflict with his mother.

The 34-year-old Archibald B. has the urge to assault women and kill his wife. Sometimes he wants to assault the women sexually. The idea of killing appeared at first four years ago in a dream. The patient has a slight quick tremor in his left hand which has also a tendency to convergence. There is also a tremor of the eyelids.

Frank B., 30 years old, complains about slight depersonalization symptoms. He complains that he has to count his footsteps. He cannot decide in what direction to walk. He has the urge to explain his symptoms continually to the doctor whom he imagines. Physical examination showed a tremor of the hands and a decrease in the associated movements of the right arm. There is some stiffness in the posture and in the face. The convergence of the left eye is decreased. His speech is slurred and propulsive and there is a staring look in his face. There is no history of encephalitis. This case has not been fully investigated from a psycho-genetic point of view. There are merely slight compulsion symptoms (counting of steps) obviously in connection with an impairment of the motor function. The patient complains bitterly that he has to give constant attention to his staring and to his stiffness. This case reacts obviously to the impairment of the motor function with a compulsive attention to this function.

Alfred R., 30 years old, had the compulsive thought that he is an illegitimate child and that his mother had sex relations with another man whom he identi-

fied. He had the compulsion to kill his mother. The borderline from compulsion
to delusion was not sharp. There was a slight tic movement of the head which
disappeared. At the present time he feels the urge to move his head in this
direction without giving in. The patient has a rigid face. The right side of the
face is particularly akinetic.

Edward T., 21 years old, has an outspoken compulsion to wash. He has a
rigid face, a tremor of the outstretched hands, a marked degree of akinesis,
paralysis agitans posture without rigidities but a slight convergence of the arms.
In the early history anal and sadistic trends were outspoken. It was not possible
in the comparatively short observation to establish a psychological connection
between organic impulse disturbances and the washing compulsion.

In all the seven cases quoted, organic signs are present pointing to organic
lesions of the brain, partially identical in localization with the symptoms of
encephalitis. Four of the cases show evidence of an increase in impulses
which is in obvious connection with the psychological determinants of the
compulsion. In two of the other cases, the self observation of disturbances in
motor impulses forms the basis for obsessive self observation. However, the
connection with impulse disturbances and obsessional symptoms is not as
obvious as in the other cases. In the seventh case, no definite psychological
connection could be made between the motor disturbance and the obsessive
picture.

If one studies the characteristics of these cases in which organic signs are
obvious, one sees in many other cases clinical and psychological characteristics which make it at least probable that a similar impulse disturbance on an
organic basis is at work.

Case 3

Ruth S., 32 years of age, had been in analysis for more than five years before
she came to my observation. She suffers from a fear that she may have killed
others with poison. She thinks she may have gone without her knowledge into
a drug store or into the bathroom and may have mixed there the drugs. When
she passes a drug store she is not sure whether she had not gone in. She is also
haunted by the obsessional fear that she may have kicked automobiles and
automobile drivers causing terrible accidents. Furthermore, she believes that
she has kicked persons in manholes and has destroyed gas pipes and electric
wires by her action. The obsessions go back to her 18th year. She often has
death wishes against her husband, the relatives of her husband and her mother.
She is also otherwise a good hater. In connection with her obsessions she
suffers from time to time an undescribable pain which is localized in the
abdomen but different from somatic pain and is comparable to a feeling of
terrible emptiness. She experienced this pain for the first time when she was

six years old and looked into a garden. The world appeared to her so beautiful that she wanted to take it in as a whole. She would like to die but is afraid to kill herself because she may kill others in the act of killing. In early recollections, blood poisoning of her brother who is two years younger, plays an important part. She feels that this was caused by her and that she had scratched the arm of her brother. She feels that she was mistreated by her mother in her early childhood. There was a strong affection for the father who died of general paresis when she was 12 years old. She was an extremely lively, active and outgoing child. At the age of 12, one of her teachers obviously seduced by her tried to make love to her, however there was merely petting. Her strong sex wishes are only incompletely satisfied by the husband. Her extramarital experiences were few and disturbed by repressions. She is extremely gifted as a writer and is full of activity if not too much hemmed in by her obsessions.

The physical examination was negative. However, her motility is exaggerated. She is continually in movement, doesn't sit still for a minute and is afraid that with every movement she may have kicked something or may have spilled poisons.

The therapeutic result of a therapy which showed the connection of her impulses and drives with her motility was very satisfactory and the obsessions came more and more into the background without disappearing completely.

Her brother who is two years younger shows an excessive sex urge and an excessive potency. He lives his sex urges out without any inhibition. He is an extremely severe alcoholic and was analyzed for more than three years in Germany with no therapeutic results. He has a slight diabetes. He was under observation in Bellevue Hospital and was only seen for a short time.

The history makes it at least probable that we deal with an impulse disturbance in the sense of hyperactivity based on organic factors. The possibility cannot be denied that the brother's and sister's sex urges may be increased too. The repression of these urges by Ruth may be a contributing factor in the structure of her obsessional neurosis. It is interesting that the symptomatology of this case is specifically based on motor impulses which find their psychic fulfillment by contracting the space and bringing the objects which are merely in sight in the reach of her immediate action.

Case 4

Marvin B., 12 years old, suffered from obsessions for more than two years. A letter had arrived from the sister of his mother inviting them to Europe. He pictured Europe vividly, thought how nice it would be to play with other children there and finally could not get rid of this thought. He was so bothered by this continuous desire that he hit himself four times on the left arm, telling himself that he would die if he would continue to think of Europe. An obsessional fear of death set in. He had to hit himself four times on the shin bone with his leg before crossing the street because he thought he might get killed otherwise. When walking on the street he felt an extreme pain when he was by chance touched by passers by. He was afraid that they might wish his death and infect him by their touch. The patient had a severe infection of his arm one year after his obsession had started. When he asked questions he had to repeat them four times. Four is an even number which has something restful about it. Three has something unfinished about it according to his opinion.

There are no organic signs.

Psychoanalysis, which was partially conducted in the group, showed that he had always been an aggressive and violent child who was often hit by father and mother. At six or seven he stole repeatedly and was severely punished. At the age of five he played with other boys on the street and tortured cats, tying them, pressing their muzzles together, pinching them, and pulling their tails. However, he protested when another boy was treated in a similar way by his friends. During the night he had often nightmares that an enormous cat was sitting on his chest. When such happened he went into the bed of his mother. He likes to fight with his older sister. When she made him angry he felt like killing her and wished her death. He acted similarly to his friends with whom he still likes to wrestle. When he wrestles with them he is not afraid to be touched, has no pain and no fears of infection and death. He started to mastur-bate before 10 and just before the outbreak of the obsession neurosis he felt that he might harm himself and tried to stop masturbation without success. He is particularly afraid that the loss of semen which occurred lately during masturbation might do him irreparable harm. There is at the present time a strong sex curiosity and sex urge.

After three months of treatment, the patient is completely free of symptoms, however, the treatment is continued.

The parents are obviously of an aggressive type. The mother has been so during several interviews. A five year older brother has been in the hospital with the diagnosis of schizophrenia. He is at the present time under treatment. He started around his 12th year with a complicated obsessional picture in which obsessional thoughts about vampires were paramount. At the present time he complains about a vibrating sensation near to his heart which reacts especially to noises. The observation is far from being finished. I am at the present time more inclined to believe that one deals with a complicated obsession neurosis. The face of the patient is decidedly rigid. There are no other neurological signs.

Also in this case violent aggression is in the foreground. There is a tendency to actions and to repetitions in which the number 4 and the counting plays an important part. Aggression and fear of infection go hand in hand. The child is lively and very active. I am also in this case inclined to believe that one deals with an organic motor factor. It is remarkable that obsessional features are also present in the brother, although the aggressiveness of the brother expresses itself in fantastic fears and preoccupations.

In a short paper dealing with the psychoanalysis of geometry, arithmetic and physics, I reported two cases of obsession neurosis which do not show any organic signs but show a particular relation to numbers and react to symmetry and asymmetry and to specific numbers with actions which restore the symmetry or remove the danger by motor actions which are repeated five times. I came to the conclusion that obsessional counting and counting in general is an action of an aggressive type. Counting and dividing into parts have a very close relation. To divide into parts means tearing and destruction. Activity and aggression combine very often with oral and anal tendencies. The relation to genital tendencies is not as close. The aggression is obviously not merely derived from oral and anal tendencies. It serves the orientation and self assertion in the world. The intake of food (and its excretion) and the erotism connected with it is merely a part of the self preservation and of the adaptation to the world. Whereas numbers serve as preliminary points of orientation in an almost amorphous world, geometry comes to life in other compulsions. Symmetry and asymmetry in the surroundings provoke, as is well known, changes in the posture and attitude of the individual. Asymmetry is a definite threat and threat to the body, acts on the inner organs and sensations and on the sexual functions. Symmetry and balance are motor phenomena which ask for definite moral attitudes which express themselves in the muscular system (ego) but influence also the intestinal system (libido). There is no doubt that counting, the reaction to symmetry, asymmetry and gravity belong to the fundamental functions of the ego. The functions of the ego are connected with activity and aggressiveness. They do not serve only the maintenance of the equilibrium, the defense against hostile attacks and the possessiveness but also oral and genital tendencies.

I am inclined to believe that in many cases of obsession neurosis, organic factors are at work which influence these fundamental functions of the ego. In a great number of cases a direct proof can be produced that the impulse disturbances are in connection with organic changes in the brain. In other cases, probabilities can be offered. It can be shown that the organic impulse disturbances lead to a specific compulsive symptomatology. The inference may be drawn that in cases which show an identical structure of compulsions are based on motor impulses of the same type. We have reason to believe that there are cases in which psychogenetic factors as commonly defined are at the basis of the impulse disturbance.

I come, therefore, to the conclusion that there exists a group of obsession neurosis cases in which the motor impulses are disturbed. Compulsions are in the foreground of these cases. There is repetition, counting, and a special relation to symmetry and asymmetry. There is a distortion of space. Only Erwin Straus has so far drawn the attention to the space disturbances in the symptomatology of obsession neurosis. I want to be more specific in so far as I endeavor to elucidate the relation of space, geometry, arithmetic and physics to a specific organic apparatus. I want to emphasize that these remarks point to a specific group of compulsions. Obsessional neuroses exist in which such mechanisms are not present. From a psychoanalytic point of view, it has to be emphasized that one deals primarily with changes in the ego functions. These ego function disturbances are in intricate relation to libidinous structures. The details of this problem cannot be discussed in the frame of this clinical paper. Wexberg has also, starting from the experiences of encephalitis cases, come to the conclusion of an organic nucleus in obsession neurosis. I point to a more specific mechanism of a specific group. There may be other organic mechanisms in obsession neurosis cases. Goldstein remarks that there is a symptomatic similarity between the basic tendencies of the obsession neurosis and a striopallidar case which he has observed. He sees the common factor in a tendency to persistence. Our observations do not substantiate this mechanism.

However, I do not think that the organic factor found in the group of obsession neurosis cases described is the only factor which can be observed in obsession neurosis cases. In many obsession neurosis cases, the state of consciousness changes when the obsession occurs. The pictures which represent the obsession become plastic and exceptionally clear. I once heard Dr. Kauders characterize this state of the obsession neurotic case very aptly as visionary state. Such was the case in one of our observations which Dr. Curran has used in a paper on bromide intoxications. This patient, an elderly Italian lady, was forced to think continually of the sex parts of her daughters on whom she wanted to perform cunnilingus. The patient finally took on her own counsel a great amount of bromides and developed a bromide psychosis, in which there was deep clouding of the consciousness. She heard voices and saw her daughters killed. With the disappearance of the bromide psychosis, the obsessions had disappeared completely, and the patient remained well in the subsequent observation of several months. We shall need patient observation and a collection of large material before we can appreciate whether we deal in such cases with organic factors regulating the state of consciousness.

It is difficult to appreciate the number of obsession neurosis cases in which organic motor factors are of importance. Preliminary impressions let me believe that organic signs can be found in about one-third of the cases. In another third the symptomatology arouses the suspicion of an organic background, and in the last third of the cases merely psychogenetic factors as commonly defined are of importance. This statement does not pertain to the general question of the constitution of the obsession neurotic case but merely to definite neurological mechanisms. In the majority of our positive cases we do not deal with sequelae of epidemic encephalitis but with organic changes similar to those observed in encephalitis but of different origin. They may be constitutional or they may be due to lesions in the fetal life, to birth traumas or to toxic and infectious processes of unknown origin.

It is worthwhile mentioning that with the exception of Case 1, satisfactory therapeutic results were obtained, when the patient was either taught in individual analysis or in group psychotherapy which the connections were between his motor drives, his compulsions and his libidinous structure.

SUMMARY

1. Seven cases of obsession neurosis are presented in which definite organic signs were disclosed by neurological examination. These signs remind one of symptoms observed in epidemic encephalitis. However, it is not probable that one deals in these cases with mild encephalitis of the epidemic type. They may be due to constitutional factors and to early traumatic toxic and infectious processes.

2. In two cases, the type of motility and activity hinted to similar organic factors. In other cases, the psychic symptomatology pointed to an underlying motor impulse disturbance.

3. Compulsion neurosis cases of this type show a particular relation to numbers and counting. There is the tendency to iteration and compulsions based upon it. The attitude towards space is changed. The motor drives are in close relation to sadistic attitudes.

4. Similar disturbances and a similar psychic symptomatology are present in the obsessions and compulsions observed in post encephalitic cases in which the organic change in the motor impulses is obvious.

5. Organic factors influencing the state of consciousness may have an influence in some obsession neurotic cases.

6. Psychotherapy has to consider the importance of the motor factors in compulsions and their relations to sadistic attitudes. They have to be appreciated in connection with the libidinous situation. In the majority of the cases treated, good results were obtained.

256   PAUL SCHILDER

BIBLIOGRAPHY

Bender, Lauretta: Anatom. pathol. data on personality function. American Journal of Psychiatry, *92, No. 2, p. 325–357, Sept. 1935.*

Bromberg, W.: Mental symptoms in chronic encephalitis. Psychiatric Quarterly, *4: 537–566, 1930.*

Bürger, H., u. Mayer-Gross: Über Zwangssymptome bein Encephalitis lethargica und über die Struktur der Zwangserscheinungen überhaupt. Z. Neur., *116: 647, 1928.*

Goldstein, Kurt: Über die gleichartige funktionelle Bedingtheit der Symptome bein organischen und psychischen Krankheiten; im besonderen uber den funktionellen Mechanismus der Zwangsvorgänge. Monatsschrift f. Psych. u. Neurol., *57: 191–209, 1924.*

Hermann, G.: Zwangsdenken und andere Zwangserscheinungen bei Erkrankung des striären Systems. Monat. Psych. u. Neurol., *52: 324, 1922.*

Hoff, H., and Schilder, P.: Die Lage reflexe des Menschen. *Vienna, Springer, 1927.*

⸻*: Zur Kenntnis der Symptomatologie vestibulärer Erkrankungen.* Deutsche Zeit. f. Nervenheilkunde, *103: 145, 1928.*

Jelliffe, Smith Ely: Psychopathology of forced movements in oculogyric crises. Nervous and Mental Diseases Monograph Series, *55: 1–219, 1932. (With complete bibliography.)*

Mayer-Gross, W., and Steiner, G.: Encephalitis lethargica in der Selbstbeobachtung. Z. Neur., *73: 1921.*

Schilder, P.: Zur Psychoanalyse der Geometrie, Arithmetik und Physik. Int. Zeit. f. Psychoanalyse, *22: 4, 390–395, 1936.*

⸻*: Psycho-analysis of space.* Int. J. of Psychoanalysis, *16: 274–295 (July), 1935.*

⸻*: Convergence reactions, especially in alcoholics.* J. Nerv. and Ment. Dis., *71: 1, 1930.*

⸻*: Zur Kenntnis der Psychosen bei chronischer Encephalitis epidemica, Nebst Bemerkungen über die Beziehung organischer Strukturen zu den psychischen Vorgängen.* Zeit. f. d. ges. Neur. u. Psych., *118: 3, 327–345, 1929.*

⸻*: The analysis of ideologies as a psychotherapeutic method.* Amer. Jour. Psychiat., *93, No. 3, 601–619, Nov. 1936.*

Stengel, Erwin: Zur Kenntnis der Triebstörungen und der Abwehrreaktionen des Ichs bei Ilirnkranken. Int. Zeit. f. Psych., *21: 4, 544, 560, 1935.*

⸻*: Zur Klinik und Pathologie des postencephalitischen Blickkrampfes.* Monats. f. Psych. u. Neurol., *70: 305, 1928.*

⸻*: Weitere Beiträege zur Kenntnis des postencephalitischen Blickkrampfes.* Zeit. Neur., *127: 441, 1930.*

⸻*: Über psychische Zwangsphenomene bei Hirn kranken.* Jahrbücher f. Neurologie und Psychiatric, *52: 236–248, 1935.*

Stern, Felix: Die Epidemische Encephalitis. *Berlin, Springer, 1928. 2nd edition. Monographien. No. 30.*

Strauss, Erwin: Die Formen des Raümlichen. Nervenarzt., *3. H. 11, 1930.*

Wexberg, Erwin: Remarks on the psychopathology of oculogyric crises in epidemic encephalitis. Jour. Nerv. and Ment. Dis., *85: 56, 1937.*

⸻*: Die Grundstörung der Zwangsneurose.* Z. Neur., *121: 236, 1929.*

DISCUSSION

Dr. HAROLD F. CORSON (Stockbridge, Mass.).—Dr. Schilder brings to our attention a group of cases which are notable because of the presence of both an encephalitic condition and an obsessional compulsive state. He states that although infantile experiences and situations have created a pattern, it finds its expression in compulsions on the basis of the organic processes involved.

The cases presented show evidence that has been interpreted as indication of an encephalitis residual.

The thesis, as I understand it, is that a very definite group of the obsessive-compulsive states has as an important etiological factor certain basic lesions associated with encephalitis. The nature of these lesions is not indicated nor are they differentiated from those that produce any of the infinite variety of mental or emotional changes that may simulate almost any form of psychoses or neuroses.

The various epidemics of encephalitis and the various forms of encephalitis have had a varied mortality and the sequelæ have been somewhat different at times. There are several outstanding groups of cases resulting from the epidemic encephalitis, such as the Parkinsonian type, the choreo-athetosis syndrome and the so-called Apache children whose conduct is so manifestly antisocial. The literature is not lacking in reports of schizophrenic reactions, delirium-like states, Korsakoff's syndromes, paranoid psychoses and depressive states with marked suicidal tendencies associated with the after-results of epidemic encephalitis.

These heterogeneous types of reactions would appear to depend not only on a variety of lesions, either in location or extent, but also on the different individualities of the persons affected.

It has been often observed that when this region of the brain is subject of a pathological lesion the attempt to correlate the lesion with disturbances of function is especially difficult. For one thing the lesions are apt to be multiple or diffuse, or both. The question as to whether we deal with the positive or negative effect must be considered. The time relationship between the lesion and the symptomatology should be of significance.

The possibility that these cases would respond in some way to symptomatic drug treatment such as atropine, stramonium, hyoscine or scopolamine, might be a point for discussion.

The significance of the excellent results reported in these very difficult cases is not clear and the question may be raised as to the possible factors—for example, does a chronic infectious process finally burn itself out? A second factor may be that the patient through treatment learns the most proficient use of an injured central nervous system and is able to make an adjustment by accepting the limitations thus imposed.

It is evident though a constitutional or organic factor is postulated in a large number of the obsessive compulsive states, that Dr. Schilder does not join this with any therapeutic nihilism, but rather the reverse. In calling our attention to the means of detecting the less evident signs of encephalitis, there should result a growth in the number of cases available for study.

The psychoanalytical formulation of the psychological factors will not be especially commented on. A psychobiological organization of the material might well throw into better perspective a number of factors that are overshadowed by the emphasis on the psychosexual. From the description and dynamic point of view, the cases appear to be absolutely typical of the obsessive-compulsive state. In short, the organic process does not appear to have modified or distorted the reaction type.

It also appears to follow that if an organic lesion either dams up energy, releases it without the usual brakes, or if it escapes through unusual channels, either the individual or the community is presented with a problem which can be met in a variety of ways. The Apache or antisocial child who has suffered from epidemic encephalitis finds himself in conflict with his community which is apt to treat him with increasing hostility. That inner conflict in the form of obsessive-compulsive states should result in some instances seems well substantiated in the most interesting group of cases presented by Dr. Schilder.

DR. ERWIN WEXBERG (New Orleans, La.).—I was particularly interested by Dr. Schilder's excellent paper, particularly because about ten years ago I made similar statements in a paper about the basic disturbance in compulsory neurosis in Germany. I have not very much to add as a criticism, but some points which Dr. Schilder certainly knows and which he might as well have mentioned as a support of these ideas.

First is the well known relation between compulsory systems and tic. The tic neurosis is not definitely separated from compulsory neurosis at all and there are definite forms of compulsory neurosis in which compulsory movements can be considered as well as tic movements, and other cases of definite tic neurosis in which the tic seems primary, to be merely a neurological condition, seems to assume a certain psychological meaning so that it slightly turns towards the compulsory movements. I remember a case in which the relation between the tic neurosis and compulsory ideas was in some way familiar, the case of a severe compulsory neurotic whose father had suffered from tic for a long time.

Another point which I made in that first paper on this subject was the relation which seems to me to be rather interesting between compulsory neurosis and stuttering. In some way stuttering seems to be related to compulsory neurosis, and particularly the factor of reiteration, of repetition compulsion which is obvious in the cases of stuttering. I wouldn't claim, therefore, that every stammerer or stutterer would be a compulsory neurotic, but there seems to be some relation.

A slight criticism I would make on this point: Dr. Schilder believes that the motor fact behind compulsory neurosis is to be defined merely as release or tremendous increase of impulses. I don't believe such a quantitative definition will do. I rather believe, as I stated ten years ago, there must be something basically wrong in what might be called the rhythmical function, the higher rhythmical coordination of motor factor, of motor function, which is essential for every motor activity in general. It is a higher function which, for instance, has something to do with building up and finishing a certain coordinated activity, not a movement but an activity.

I refer, for instance, to those cases of obsessional neurosis or compulsory neurosis who are unable to finish something. The case described at that time in my paper was a man who was entirely unable to go to sleep at night. It took him until three, four, even five o'clock in the morning, and once he was unable to go to sleep until nine-thirty in the morning. This came on time and again. It seems to me to be some kind of inability or insufficiency of psychomotor rhythm. This is to be seen in the unjustified repetition, reiteration and perseveration present in practically all cases of compulsion neurosis, particularly the fact that they cannot get away from some point, some idea, and that they stick to it and cannot go on.

Another point which I want to make finally is the following: I think it is well known that compulsory neurosis is rather frequently combined with a state of mental deficiency. Of course this applies to the small minority of cases; but in a comparative survey you will find that whereas neuroses of other kinds are rather rare in cases mentally deficient, compulsory symptoms combined with mental deficiency occur rather often.

Another support for the idea which has been brought forward by Dr. Schilder is that there is some organic background in a certain group of compulsory neuroses.

I wanted to refer also to the feature of aggression, which is obvious in practically every case of compulsory neurosis. It may be in some way described as negativism, such as is particularly obvious in those not very frequent cases in which compulsory symptoms start very early in life, and are mostly referred to such motor functions as bowel movement. In this way the whole complex is related to the Freudian conception of anal erotism. So I would question the libidinous character of the whole mechanism.

DR. PAUL SCHILDER.—I want to make only one point clear. I have observed, as others, obsession neurotic features in cases which are from a clinical point of view epidemic encephalitis cases; but the main group in which I was interested are cases in which with the ordinary neurological examination, the neurological findings might have been neglected. I would furthermore like to say that in these cases the process is not known. The evidence speaks very much against an epidemic encephalitis. It is either something on the constitutional basis or it is some unknown process acquired probably before birth.

About Dr. Corson's remarks, for which I am grateful, I want only to say that the treatment in these cases, which are the main group of my discussion, is a psychological treatment but it is a psychological treatment which with the help of psychoanalytic methods tries also to show to the patient the motor nucleus in his aggressiveness, and this method has proved to be successful, as far as I can judge.

As to Dr. Wexberg's remarks, I can perfectly agree with him, and his two interesting studies on this subject were known to me. I was particularly interested to point to objective neurological findings in these cases. It was furthermore particularly interesting to show in detail how a specific symptomatology concerning space, symmetry, asymmetry, accounting and geometry, is connected with motor impulses. Of course, what has been discussed is in no way the whole psychopathology of obsessional neurosis but only one small part. I am, of course, completely in agreement with Dr. Wexberg that we shall need very many more studies on the organic problems involved in these cases and in other cases, too. In this group the factors seem to be particularly obvious.

15. Obsessive-Compulsive Disorder: Is It Basal Ganglia Dysfunction?

Steven P. Wise and Judith L. Rapoport

WE PRESENT HERE a hypothesis that selective basal ganglia dysfunction underlies obsessive-compulsive disorder (OCD). At the basis of our hypothesis are neuroanatomical, neuropharmacological, and behavioral studies indicating a complex perceptual and cognitive role for the basal ganglia in addition to its more well-accepted motor functions. The hypothesis is also based on case reports suggesting increased obsessive-compulsive symptomatology in certain syndromes associated with basal ganglia disease, response to psychosurgery, and brain-imaging studies. As part of our hypothesis, we present a neural model in which the striatum acts to trigger behavior, and posit that permissive failure of such a system (i.e., the inappropriate triggering of genetically stored and learned behaviors) is the primary cause of OCD.

BASAL GANGLIA DISEASE AND OCD

Tourette's Syndrome and Tics

In his original 1885 description of basal ganglia–associated syndrome that today bears his name, Gilles de la Tourette (1885) reported an association between recurrent motor and phonic tics and obsessive-compulsive behavior. He described a patient who suffered from tics and vocalizations, as well as tormenting, obsessive thoughts: "The more revolting these explosions are, the more tormented she becomes by the fear she will say them again; and this obsession forces these words into her mind and to the top of her tongue." The association between Tourette's syndrome and OCD had since been clarified and expanded. There is a strong genetic link between the multiple motor-verbal tics of Tourette's syndrome and OCD (Pauls et al. 1986). The disorders occur together in the same families, but not necessarily (although frequently)

Reprinted by permission of the American Psychiatric Press from *Obsessive-Compulsive Disorder in Children and Adolescents,* edited by Judith L. Rapoport, Washington, D.C., 1989, 327–44.

in the same individuals. In fact, from 15 to 80 percent of patients with Tourette's syndrome are described as having at least some abnormal obsessive-compulsive symptoms, a rate greatly in excess of the 2 percent lifetime prevalence of OCD in the general population (Karno et al., 1988). Conversely, tics occur in childhood OCD far more frequently than would be expected by chance (Dr. S. Swedo, personal communication, 1988).

There is almost a century of recorded associations between simple motor tics and OCD. Osler, in his 1894 monograph *On Chorea and Choreiform Affections,* described a girl with "Tic of muscles of the face and neck; fixed ideas; arithromania":

A.B., aged 13, was seen September 6, 1890. She is an only daughter in a family with marked neuropathic taint. The father died insane; the mother is a high-strung, nervous woman. The child is well grown, and well nourished, though rather stout for her age. She is very bright and intelligent, and perhaps has not had as much control as was good for her. For a year or more she has had occasional twitchings of the muscles of the face and neck, noticeable in the quick sudden elevations of the eyebrows, or in movements of the platysma muscles. They have not been severe, and for days it may not have been at all noticeable.

A short time after the onset of the twitchings, it was noticed that she began gradually to have all sorts of queer notions and practices, many of which persisted for some weeks or months, and were then changed for others not less anomalous. Some of her vagaries are as follows, nearly all being modifications of the fixed idea known as arithromania: Before getting into bed at night she lifts each foot and taps nine times on the edge of the bed. After brushing her teeth she has to count to one hundred. For a year at least she has always entered the house by the back door, protesting that she never can enter by the front door again. Lest her mother should prevent her getting in by the back door, she for months carried the key herself. On reaching the door she knocks three times on the edge of the window near by, and three times on the door before unlocking it. She will not under any circumstances button her shoes. For a long time she would not pronounce the name of anyone, but would spell it, and if she wished for anything at the table she would spell the word, but not pronounce it. In drinking water she will take a mouthful, then put the tumbler down, turn it once or twice and repeat this act every time she drinks. She would not brush her hair except at the extreme tips, and it is only under the strictest compulsion that she will allow the hair on the top of the head to be combed. Before putting on clean under-clothes she has to count so many numbers that there is a great difficulty in getting her to make the change, except under the strongest threats from her mother. (p. 82)

Postencephalitic Parkinson's Disease: A Dissociation of Will and Action

The best classic description of neurologically based OCD comes from Constantin von Economo, whose monograph of 1920 (translated to English in

1931) contains elegant clinical descriptions of postencephalitic disorders. In 1916 to 1917, an outbreak in Europe of viral encephalitis lethargica, as it was called, was followed, as previous smaller epidemics had been, by a somnolentlike state accompanied by parkinsonian features. In his study of hundreds of these patients, von Economo provided a comprehensive phenomenology, course, and neuropathology of the disorder. He reported that this infectious, neurotoxic lesion involved the basal ganglia and was associated with a sense of compulsion reminiscent of OCD in addition to motor changes. In discussing the psychological changes in these patients, von Economo argued against a role for the cerebral cortex in the generation of these uncontrollable movements and, instead, focused on subcortical centers, presumably including the basal ganglia:

These patients do not say "I have a twitch in my hand," but rather as a rule "I have got to move my hand that way." The frequent subjectivization of these processes, experienced as compulsory by the patients is, I believe, one of their characteristic attributes. From this subjectivization we may deduce that in cases where the condition manifests itself, centres, probably in the diencephalon-mesencephalon, are affected whose motor function contributes intimately to the constitution of the "sensation of personality" and even to a greater extent than some parts of the cerebral cortex because, for instance, in Jacksonian fits affecting an arm as a result of a lesion of the anterior central convolution of the cerebrum itself, the patient says, "I have a twitch in my arm," that is, the movement does not become subjectivated, though it has its origin in the cerebral cortex. (p. 121)

Von Economo also noted a whole range of peculiar tics associated with these compulsions including blepharospasms, mimetic tics of clucking or hissing, torticollis, and tics of the upper and lower extremities, as well as fits of yelling and yawning. Von Economo concluded that "motor disturbances of encephalitics were reminiscent of compulsive movements and compulsive actions, with frequently ensuing utterances of speech and trends of thought of a compulsive character" (p. 120).

The problem of volitional disabilities continues to plague modern medicine as well as philosophy and reaches far beyond the particular disorders of obsessions and compulsions (Dunnet 1984). There are several disorders in which a dissociation of will and action are observed, as it was in von Economo's patients. But obsessive-compulsive patients are still, in a sense, "free" in that they "will *not* to will." This higher-order free will is a prominent and, in fact, defining feature of OCD: compulsive hand washers know that there are powerful reasons not to wash their hands (e.g., humiliation and waste of time), but simply do not act in accordance with those incentives and, at a simpler level, feel forced to carry out the rituals. Similarly, von Economo's (1931) postencephalitic patients describe "having to" act but not "wanting to":

In spite of intact intelligence and the wish to execute a movement, in spite of the undisturbed possession of the imaginative faculty and the consequent existence of intention (e.g., to change an uncomfortable position) . . . [the] patient is unable to supply the impulse for the act of moving his otherwise sound limbs. (p. 162)

Although the possible linkage between postencephalitic and basal ganglia disease is intriguing, the lesions are by no means exclusively located in the basal ganglia; there tends to be a kaleidoscopic array of focal lesions and several brain regions. Indeed, von Economo stressed the involvement of the cerebral aqueduct, tegmentum, and gray matter ventral to the caudal third ventricle. Nevertheless, the basal ganglia are very much affected in the disease, which has a profound effect on the relation between volition and behavior.

Sydenham's Chorea

Sydenham's chorea, a disorder of children and adolescents, is characterized by sudden, aimless, irregular movements of the extremities frequently associated with emotional instability and muscle weakness. In children, the disorder occurs following rheumatic heart disease, as part of the complex of rheumatic fever. It is associated with high antibody titers to specific streptococcal antigens. These are usually high only for about 2 months following the infection, however, and the test is of limited value in chronic cases. Interestingly, the disorder, like OCD, is extremely rare in black populations. Postmortem studies in Sydenham's chorea have reported that perivascular cellular infiltration and neural degeneration is most pronounced in the striatum (Greenfield and Wolfsohn 1922). Further, Husby et al. (1976) reported that 50 percent of patients with postrheumatic chorea contain specific antibodies to caudate and putamen nucleus neurons, suggesting that the mechanism by which Sydenham's chorea is produced involves the immune system. Thus this disorder is of particular interest since it occurs exclusively in young people, may involve an autoimmunity toward basal ganglia, and has been linked with OCD.

Grimshaw (1964) reported an excess of Sydenham's chorea in the historic patients with OCD compared with a nonobsessional control group. Conversely, Freeman et al. (1965) described an increase in "neuroses," including

OCD, in a group of 40 pediatric cases with Sydenham's chorea. In an ongoing survey of obsessive symptoms of 18 children with Sydenham's chorea, 3 of 18 cases examined to date show a clinical level of symptoms of OCD. Statistically, in the general adolescent population, a sample of 400 would be needed to yield two patients with OCD. This increase in automatic, compulsive, and stereotyped behaviors and thoughts occurred selectively in the patients with Sydenham's chorea and was not prominent in the comparison group of other patients from the same clinics who had rheumatic fever without Sydenham's chorea (Swedo et al. 1987).

Other Presumed Basal Ganglia Disorders and OCD

Several cases have been reported in which discrete lesions of the basal ganglia produced psychological changes that resemble obsessional illness. Laplane et al. (1984) reported a case of a 41-year-old man who suffered a rare but malignant neurotoxic reaction to a wasp sting. His initial drastic neurological disorder, coma followed by choreic movements and gait impairments, diminished over the next several months. But over the following 12 years, he had a rather apathetic, indifferent appearance and, in general, lacked motivation for life. The striking aspect of this case was that

two years after encephalopathy, he began to show stereotyped activities. The most frequent consisted in mental counting, for example up to twelve or a multiple of twelve, but sometimes it was a more complex calculation. Such mental activities sometimes were accompanied by gestures, such as finger pacing of the counts. To switch on and off a light for one hour or more was another of his most common compulsions. When asked about this behavior he answered that he had to count . . . that he could not stop . . . that it was stronger than him. . . . Once he was found on his knees pushing a stone with his hands: he gave the explanation that he must push the stone. (p. 377)

The computed tomography (CT) scan of this patient showed bilateral low-density lesions in the internal part of the lentiform nucleus (i.e., the globus pallidus). The case is of further interest in that after a variety of other drugs has been tried, clomipramine (250/mg/day) greatly improved, although did not cure, his behavior. This is one of the few demonstrations of clomipramine-linked improvement in obsessive-compulsive behavior following a known basal ganglia lesion.

Over the past decade, we and others have evaluated children with choreiform and athetoid movements that presented as OCD. Denckla (1989) summarized her neurological examinations of more than 50 children with OCD. Mild choreiform movements were prominent in this group, although other abnormal patterns were also found. These movements were less prominent in follow-up studies and, thus, seem an early characteristic of the disorder. Similarly, in our series of acute cases of childhood OCD, jerking peripheral movements are particularly prominent and resemble those seen in Sydenham's chorea.

This disturbance is fleeting, however, and disappears over the initial months of the disorder. One rather severe case will illustrate the several we have seen:

A.B. had always been an "uptight" child, who worried at the start of each new school year, and for whom Hebrew school, with its preparation for the Bar Mitzvah, had been full of anxieties. His parents had consulted a psychologist because he was so worried over the ceremony, but reassurance and an easier studying schedule had seemed to solve this. But shortly after his 13th birthday, A. had told his parents of a new problem: He couldn't get "numbers" out of his head, and would say the number 4 and do things, touching, walking, jumping, counting, in 4s over and over again. Psychotherapy and a series of antianxiety and antidepressant medications were tried. At age 14, odd movements, a writhing of his body and arms, began, together with periods of muteness. He complained that he still could not stop numbers and words from going over and over, and that they were worse. The movements were unusual in pattern, puzzling the several neurologists who saw him. He would grimace, pursing his lips while making soft smacking sounds; his head would be to one side resting on his shoulder, and his body would writhe and jerk toward that same side. In between these bursts of writhing activity, he would sit mute, appearing to make a strained effort to respond when spoken to, but not producing any sound. During rare hours free from these symptoms, he complained about "the numbers." There appeared to be intellectual deterioration, but EEG, LP, CT scans were normal.

A diagnosis of atypical Tourette's syndrome was considered. There was slow but steady improvement on clomipramine, together with moderate doses of haloperidol. At 3-year follow-up, he is quite improved, and now attends regular school.

Brain-Imaging Studies

More direct data about a role of basal ganglia in OCD is provided by the study of Luxenberg et al. (1988), in which volumetric CT scan analyses were compared in 10 male patients with OCD (mean age, 20 years) and 10 matched normal controls. The only significant difference between the groups was a decreased volume of the caudate nuclei bilaterally in the patients with OCD ($p = .0002$); the lenticular nuclei and thalami did not differ from controls.

Baxter et al. (1987), using positron emission tomography (PET), found increased metabolic rates bilaterally in the caudate nuclei and the lateral orbito-frontal cortex in 14 obsessive-compulsive patients compared to 14 depressed patients and 14 normal controls. Interestingly, successful treatment with clomipramine did not lessen, and even increased, these differences. These important observations clearly need to be replicated and extended. For example, better quantification of the caudate volume and of associated limbic cortical regions could be achieved with magnetic resonance imaging (MRI) brain scans. Future work should include scans of familial patients with OCD as well as an examination of both state and trait markers and medical history (e.g., birth insults) in relation to these anatomical and metabolic measures.

Psychosurgery

Obsessive-compulsive disorder is one of the few psychiatric disorders for which psychosurgery may be indicated (Kettle and Marks 1986). We have reviewed 29 published reports of psychosurgical treatment in which OCD was one of the main disorders being treated. No studies were ideal; they varied widely in terms of their criteria for diagnosis, rating of illness, follow-up data, and reported improvement. The best documented studies are those following anterior capsulotomy, or cingulectomy, currently the preferred operation.

In capsulotomy, bilateral basal lesions in the anterior limb of the internal capsule are made. The lesions are thought to interrupt frontal cingulate projections, but the target zone for the lesion lies within the striatum, adjacent to the caudate nuclei. In cingulectomy, lesions are made in the anterior portion of the cingulate gyrus, interrupting tracks between cingulate gyrus and frontal lobes and several additional efferent projections of the anterior cingulate cortex. Further, Hassler (1981) reported that stereotaxic lesions in the mediodorsal and anterior nuclei of the thalamus, and their projection systems to the cortex, may diminish both Tourettic and obsessive-compulsive behaviors. It is noteworthy that these are the thalamic nuclei providing the main inputs to the cingulate and frontal cortex.

Although the psychosurgical results are far from conclusive, taken together with other evidence, these data are consistent with a model of OCD involving dysfunction of basal ganglia and frontal lobe–basal ganglia interactions.

Neuropharmacology

In the last decade, clomipramine, a drug with relatively selective action on the serotonergic system, appears to have selective benefit in ameliorating obsessive-compulsive symptoms. This striking clinical phenomenon has led to a "serotonergic hypothesis" of OCD (Flament et al. 1987; Insel et al. 1985). The 2- to 4-week delay before the drug is effective, the efficacy of other serotonergic agents, and the short-term worsening of symptoms following MCPP, a serotonergic agonist (Zohar et al. 1988), suggest that down-regulation of the serotonin system mediates the pharmacological efficacy of clomipramine in OCD.

Serotonin is not the aminergic neurotransmitter/neuromodulator most often thought of in relation to the basal ganglia, especially since the nigrostriatal dopamine system has been so intensively investigated. But recent studies have indicated higher concentration of serotonin receptors (5-HT-2) and serotonin itself in the basal ganglia than has previously been recognized (Pazos and Palacios 1985; Pazos et al. 1985; Steinbusch 1981; Stuart et al. 1986). In rats, concentration of serotonin was particularly high in the nucleus accumbens and ventral striatum, but was present throughout the striatum, including the caudate and putamen.

HYPOTHESIS: BASAL GANGLIA DYSFUNCTION AS A CAUSE OF OCD

There has been a prodigious accumulation of new information about the basal ganglia and its interactions with the cerebral cortex and other subcortical structures, most notably the thalamus (Alexander et al. 1986). The interconnection among these structures can be viewed as forming "loops"; that is, "closed" polysynaptic circuits in which the cortex sends efferents to the basal ganglia, which, while not projecting back to the cortex directly, does so through the dorsal thalamus (Figure 15.1). An earlier concept of basal ganglia function restricted to motor control has proven too limited, and the initial proposals of one "motor loop" and another "complex loop" have also been found too simple. Nevertheless, the concept of a parallel array of "loops," including the striatum, pallidum, thalamus, and cerebral cortex, has found some general support in current anatomical thinking. It seems likely that some of the parallel loops may function primarily in a motor function, whereas others mediate numerous, complex perceptual and cognitive functions.

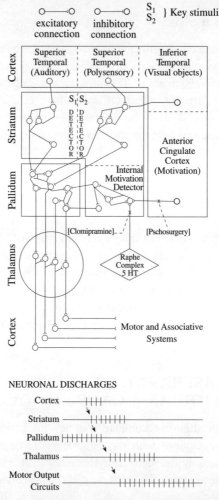

Figure 15.1. *(Top)* A neural model of obsessive-compulsive disorder. Circuits involved in transfer to the striatum of processed sensory information or information about an internal state are shown to emanate from the cerebral cortex. Two of a large number of stimulus detectors are illustrated in the striatum (the S_1 detector and the S_2 detector). The two detection circuits converge with an internal motivation detector onto one pallidal output cell group. This particular pallidal output is thought to project to the mediodorsal and ventroanterior thalamus, which in turn project to the orbito-frontal cortex. *(Bottom)* Timing of the discharges in structures sketched in the top part of the figure. Each vertical line indicates the time of an action potential discharging from the neutral cell group in the structure indicated to the left. The arrows indicate proposed causal relations between the earliest changes in discharge rate of two structures.

Basal Ganglia Anatomy

Before describing our model, it will be valuable to review some basic aspects of basal ganglia anatomy. In addition to the largest and most commonly cited striatal structures, the caudate and putamen, the striatum also includes the nucleus accumbens and parts of the olfactory tubercle. Similarly, in addition to the globus pallidus, the substantia nigra pars reticulata (SNr), parts of the olfactory tubercle, and aspects of the substantia innominata are also pallidal structures (Heimer and Wilson 1975; Heimer et al. 1987; Zahm et al. 1987).

The major input to basal ganglia is a glutamatergic, excitatory projection from the cerebral cortex to the striatum. Additional inputs to the striatum include the well-known dopaminergic input from the midbrain and a serotonergic input from the raphe complex in the brain stem. Within the basal ganglia, inhibitory, GABAergic neurons project from the striatum to the globus pallidus. The major output of the basal ganglia is a GABAergic, inhibitory projection from the globus pallidus to the thalamus, which in turn sends an excitatory input to the cortex. Thus a major pathway to, through, and out of the basal ganglia consists of a "four-neuron loop": (a) from cortex to striatum (excitatory), (b) from striatum to globus pallidus (inhibitory), (c) from globus pallidus to thalamus (inhibitory), and (d) from thalamus to cortex (excitatory). Of course, this simple scheme omits a number of important structures and pathways (including the thalamostriatal projection, the subthalamic nucleus and its connections, and many others). Further, one should not think of this circuit as consisting of four neurons, but rather as four groups of neurons following the basic pattern of the circuit.

The Model

Two ideas about basal ganglia function are central to our hypothesis. One is that the basal ganglia may be a repository of innate motor programs (Greenberg et al. 1979; MacLean 1978; Murphy et al. 1981). The other is that the basal ganglia function, in part, is a gating mechanism for sensory input (Caligiuri and Abbs 1987; Schneider 1984).

Figure 15.1 illustrates our hypothesis concerning the pathways and processes underlying the basal ganglia–OCD relationship. It is based on a simple model of an innate releasing mechanism in the basal ganglia: a detection mechanism for recognizing specific aspects of stimuli (key or sign stimuli) and a releasing mechanism for the species-typical behavioral response (sometimes known as a fixed-action pattern). Usually, detection of the key stimulus causes release (i.e., execution) of the appropriate behavior. But two sorts of behavior can occur in the absence of a key stimulus. Vacuum behaviors (Ingle and Crews 1985), for example, are often actions that would appropriately be directed toward a specific object but when the object is not present. A bird may snap at insects absent and go through the motions of preparing the nonexistent bugs for its meal (Lorenz 1981). Similarly, displacement behaviors are released when there are "conflicts between two strongly activated antagonistic drives" or "when the normal outlet for a certain motivation is blocked." Displacement activity is of particular relevance here since, as Lorenz has summarized:

A vast majority of motor patterns appearing as displacement activities are common "everyday" activities . . . the so-called comfort activities of birds and mammals, such as scratching, preening, shaking, furnish the most common examples of displacement activities; when embarrassed, even humans tend to scratch behind the ear—and in other places. (p. 251)

Note that the term *displacement activity,* as used by ethologists, entirely differs from the term as used in dynamic psychiatry. Lorenz pointed out that the original German term would be translated as "sparking-over activities."

The crux of the model presented in Figure 15.1 involves the convergence of two sets of inputs onto the striatum, particularly the ventromedial aspect of the caudate nucleus and the nucleus accumbens: one from the anterior cingulate cortex and the orbito-frontal cortex and the other from cortical "association" areas thought to be involved in the recognition of objects and sounds (the superior and inferior temporal areas). We postulate that the striatum consists of cell groups acting as stimulus detectors. Some of these detectors can be thought of as innate pattern-recognition circuits; others may be completely or partially learned. We postulate further that in the same general part of the striatum is another type of cell assembly, which we term an "internal motivation detector." These striatal assemblies converge, in our model, to inhibit a pallidal cell assembly, postulated to be tonically discharging. Since the pallidal assembly, in turn, inhibits thalamic neurons, it can be seen that striatal inhibition of the pallidal circuits results in a disinhibition, or release, of the thalamic cell group (labeled "thalamus" in the bottom of Figure 15.1). In addition, it is postulated that the striatal serotonin system potentiates, by excitatory modulation, inputs to the striatum, including those from anterior cingulate cortex to the "internal motivation detector." This circuit corresponds to the "orbito-frontal loop" of Alexander et al. (1986) and includes the orbito-frontal cortex, the caudate nucleus (striatum), the globus pallidus and the SNr (pallidum), and the ventroanterior and mediodorsal thalamic nuclei.

The way in which we envision these circuits to perform is as follows: The sensory apparatus would relay the appropriate sensory information to the cortex and then to the striatum. If the stimulus matches a stored representation in the striatum, then its cells would begin discharging, thus inhibiting the pallidal cells projecting to the thalamus. A simple example might involve the recognition of dirtiness. If sensory input to the striatum indicates that the hands are dirty, an innately programmed striatal cell group would recognize this input as dirtiness. That cell group would then discharge vigorously and stop the tonic discharging of the appropriate pallidal cell. Removal of the inhibitory inputs to the thalamus would release the thalamocortical circuits that lead to the normal behavioral response to dirty hands, hand washing.

The converging circuit, shown in Figure 15.1, originates from the anterior cingulate cortex and relays to the same pallidal cell group through a different set of striatal neurons. We envision that the circuit would provide a signal whenever the animal was to perform an act because of an exclusively internal motivation. There is some experimental evidence that the cingulate cortex could be important in this circuit, at least for learned movements. Brooks (1986) found that no electrical waves are recorded from the cingulate cortex when a monkey correctly performs a visually triggered limb movement. However, during the same behavior, emitted in the absence of the appropriate visual trigger stimulus, large cingulate cortex potentials are observed. Thus the cingulate cortex seems to be involved in generating behavior in the absence of an appropriate sensory signal, at least in this instance. If signals from cingulate cortex to striatum converge on the same pallidal cell group discussed above (the one responsible for producing the species-typical behavior), then activation of the cingulate cortex would serve to release the behavior without an appropriate sensory stimulus. In our example, hand washing is now triggered via this "internal motivation detector" in the absence of any sensory input signaling dirtiness. If, in OCD, hyperactivity in the cingulate cortex or in the striatum causes activation of this circuit in the absence of any motivation to perform the act, the behavior would be executed compulsively. A similar set of arguments could be made for the cognitive functions of the basal ganglia in relation to obsessional thoughts. Further, if the output of another circuit (not illustrated) were blocked or dysfunctional, build-up of basal ganglia activity with its extensive intrinsic collateral interactions might cause the "sparking over" to a displacement activity of the sort described by Lorenz (1981).

The Model and the Phenomenology of OCD

Several aspects of the OCD data are accounted for by this model, and it makes some testable predictions. First, the effects of psychosurgery are explained since destruction of the anterior cingulate cortex, its thalamic input, its efferent pathways to the caudate nucleus, or the caudate itself would eliminate the excitatory drive to the "internal motivation detector." Lesions of the mediodorsal or ventroanterior thalamus would eliminate the output of this cortico-striato-pallidal loop. Since the striatal cell groups involved in this circuit are viewed as releasing a vacuum behavior or displacement activity, destruction of this pathway should help prevent such release. The model also suggests that hyperexcitability of the anterior cingulate cortex or its striatal target cells may lie at the basis of OCD, and that OCD might be profitably considered a vacuum behavior or displacement activity in the sense that the latter term is used by ethologists. Thus, according to the model, a hyperactive striatal circuit (or of input to it) might periodically produce an output causing a movement pattern, such as grooming or obsessive thought.

The model also incorporates the neuropharmacology of OCD. Clomipramine could be viewed as blocking the potentiation by serotonin of striatal neurons by driving down the number of serotonin receptors. It is important to note that serotonin and its 5-HT-2 receptors are especially high in the caudate nucleus and nucleus accumbens (Pazos et al. 1985). One prediction made by the model is that local injection of serotonin and/or glutamate agonists into the ventromedial caudate nucleus or nucleus accumbens should promote vacuum behavior or other stereotypic motor acts. This idea is consistent with the finding of Zohar et al. (1988) that MCPP, a serotonin agonist, worsens OCD. Another prediction of the model is that glutamate and/or serotonin antagonists might inhibit the production of vacuum or stereotypic behavior, especially if locally injected in the appropriate region of the striatum.

Other observations outlined earlier are also consistent with the model. According to Alexander et al. (1986), only the so-called orbito-frontal loop receives converging inputs from the anterior cingulate cortex and from visual, auditory, and polysensory cortical fields. The specific involvement of this particular "loop" in OCD is indicated by the CT data showing shrinkage of caudate nuclei (but not the putamen) and by the PET data showing metabolic abnormalities in the orbito-frontal cortex and caudate nuclei. Further predictions of the model include the possibility that the thalamic relays of this "loop," the magnocellular division of the ventroanterior nucleus and the magnocellular mediodorsal nucleus, play an important role in OCD.

A question naturally arises as to the pathways by which this loop partici-
pates in producing the motor activity. Surprisingly little is known about the
connectivity of the orbito-frontal cortex, but recent anatomical evidence from
nonhuman primates suggests that it could relay information to the primary
motor cortex through the ventral aspects of the premotor cortex (Barbas and
Pandya 1987; Matelli et al. 1986).

DISCUSSION

Several obvious difficulties are encountered by our hypothesis and model.
Clinically, a great deal of information appears to be inconsistent with our
"basal ganglia hypothesis" of OCD. Other neurological disorders of the
basal ganglia, such as Huntington's disease and idiopathic parkinsonism, are
associated with depression and psychotic symptoms, but not with OCD. In
postencephalitic parkinsonian patients, as noted above, lesions outside the
basal ganglia may be related to the obsessions. Moreover, a variety of brain
insults such as head trauma, diabetes, and birth injury appear to be associated
with OCD (Kettle and Marks 1986). It is possible that when these generalized
disorders are associated with OCD, there is also basal ganglia damage, but
we know of no evidence of such damage. However, differential sensitivity of
the basal ganglia to anoxia, and to some neurotoxins, is well established
(Laplane et al. 1984). Newer imaging techniques and/or autopsy data may
eventually resolve these issues in favor of the "basal ganglia hypothesis," but
for now they must be recognized as serious objections.

  The present hypothesis also fails to account for three additional features of
OCD: its time course, behavioral specificity (for one or two thoughts or
actions at a time), and the efficacy of behavior therapy. As for time course,
we can only speculate that degenerative changes in the basal ganglia or
related part of the "orbito-frontal loop" might parallel the time course of the
disease. But why such degeneration would lead to relatively long periods of
symptom stability remains unaddressed by our model. Similarly, we have
little to offer concerning the behavioral specificity of OCD beyond the
invocation of highly localized brain abnormalities and the possibility that
circuits producing one species-typical behavior, such as grooming, might
overlap and share many of the same elements with that for another behavior,
even cognitive functions like checking for contaminants. Regarding behavior
modification, effectiveness of therapies based on behaviorist theory might
appear to contradict our hypothesis, but the relationship between the cause of
a disease and its treatment is not straightforward. A good example of this

principle is seen in dyslexia. Although it is now thought that dyslexia is caused by disruption of species-specific learning (see e.g., Vallutino 1987), and that the disorder is not caused by malfunctional reinforcement history, this does not mean that special education is not an effective treatment. *Mutatis mutandum,* the same might be said of OCD.

In addition to being consistent with the phenomenology of OCD, the present hypothesis views the basal ganglia and OCD in a high, cognitive context, viewing it as did the French, as "folie du doute," the doubting disease. If one for the moment ignores the content of the obsessions and rituals (e.g., contamination, sex, violence), the other striking aspect of the disorder is the defect in knowing. Patients who are "checkers" or "washers" appear to be in a Berkleyan nightmare—tied to their immediate sensory systems, needing continuous reaffirmation that their hands are clean, the door is locked, and so on. The ruminators, on the other hand, are trying to "think their way out" using pure reason as the road to true knowledge. Ultimately, however, checkers and ruminators both are paralyzed skeptics who doubt their own sense and their own reasoning. The hypothesis presented here suggests a biological system underlying an "epistemological sense," in this case involving the rejection or acceptance of sensory input, ideas, explanations, and thoughts.

REFERENCES

Alexander, G., DeLong, M., Strick, P.: Parallel organization of functionally segregated circuits linking basal ganglia and cortex. Annu Rev Neurosci 9: 357–381, 1986

Barbas, H., Pandya, D.: Architecture and frontal cortical connections of the premotor cortex (area 6) in the rhesus monkey. J Comp Neurol 256: 211–228, 1987

Baxter, L., Phelps, M., Mazziotti, J., et al: Local cerebral glucose metabolic rates of obsessive compulsive disorder compared to unipolar depression and normal controls. Arch Gen Psychiatry 44: 211–218, 1987

Brooks, V.: Does the limbic system assist motor learning? A limbic comparator hypothesis. Brain Behav Evol 29: 29–53, 1986

Caligiuri, M. P., Abbs, J. H.: Response properties of the perioral reflex in Parkinson's disease. Exp Neurol 98: 563–572, 1987

de la Tourette, G.: Etude sur une affection nerveuse caraterisee par de l'incoordination motrice accompagnee d'echolalie et de coprolie. Arch Neurol 9: 19–42, 1885

Denckla, M. B.: Neurological Examination, in Obsessive-Compulsive Disorder in Children and Adolescents. Edited by J. L. Rapoport. Washington, DC, American Psychiatric Press, 1989.

Dunnett, D.: Elbow Room: The Varieties of Free Will Worth Wanting. Cambridge, MA, MIT Press, 1984

Flament, M., Rapoport, J. L., Murphy, D., et al: *Biochemical changes during clomipramine treatment of childhood obsessive compulsive disorder.* Arch Gen Psychiatry *44: 219–225, 1987*

Freeman, J., Ann, A., Collard, J., et al: *The emotional correlates of Sydenham's chorea.* Pediatrics *35: 42–49, 1965*

Greenberg, N., MacLean, P. D., Ferguson, J. L.: *Role of the paleostriatum in species-typical display behavior of the lizard.* Brain Res *172: 229–241, 1979.*

Greenfield, G., Wolfsohn, M. J.: *The pathology of Sydenham's chorea.* Lancet *2: 603–607, 1922*

Grimshaw, L.: *Obsessional disorder and neurological illness.* J. Neurol Neurosurg Psychiatry *27: 229–231, 1964*

Hassler, R.: *The role of the thalamus and striatum in the causation of tics and compulsive vocalization. Presented at First International Tourette Syndrome Symposium, New York, 1981*

Heimer, L., Wilson, R.: *The subcortical projections of allocortex: similarities in the neural associations of the hippocampus, the piriform cortex and the neocortex, in* Golgi Centennial Symposium Proceedings. *Edited by M. Santini. New York, Raven Press, 1975*

Heimer, L., Zaborszky, L., Zahm, D., et al: *The ventral striatopallidothalamic projection: I: the striatopallidal link originating in the striatal parts of the olfactory tubercle.* J Comp Neurol *255: 571–591, 1987*

Husby, G., van de Rijn, I., Zabriskie, J., et al: *Antibodies reacting with cytoplasm of subthalamic and caudate nuclei neurons in chorea and rheumatic fever.* J Exp Med *144: 1094–1110, 1976*

Ingle, D., Crews, D: *Vertebrate neurothology: definition and paradigms.* Annu Rev Neurosci *8: 457–495, 1985*

Insel, T., Mueller, E., Alterman, I: *Obsessive compulsive disorder and serotonin: is there a connection?* Biol Psychiatry *20: 1174–1188, 1985*

Karno, M., Golding, J., Sorensun, S., et al: *The epidemiology of obsessive compulsive disorder in five U.S. communities.* Arch Gen Psychiatry 45: 1094–1099, 1988

Kettle, P., Marks, I.: *Neurological factors in obsessive compulsive disorder.* Br J Psychiatry *149: 315–319, 1986*

Laplane, D., Baulac, M., Widlocher, D., et al: *Pure psychic akinesia with bilateral lesions of basal ganglia.* J Neurol Neurosurg Psychiatry *47: 377–385, 1984*

Lorenz, K. Z.: The Foundations of Ethology. *New York, Springer-Verlag, 1981*

Luxenberg, J. S., Flament, M., Swedo, S., et al: *Neuroanatomic abnormalities in obsessive-compulsive disorder detected in quantitative x-ray computed tomography.* Am J Psychiatry 145: 1089–1093, 1988

MacLean, P. D.: *Effects of lesions of globus pallidus on species-typical display behavior of squirrel monkeys.* Brain Res *149: 175–196, 1978*

Matelli, M., Camarda, R., Glickstein, M., et al: *Afferent and efferent projections of the interior area 6 in the macaques monkey.* J Comp Neurol *251: 281–298, 1986*

Murphy, M. R., MacLean, P. D., Hamilton, S. C: *Species-typical behavior of hamsters deprived from birth of the neocortex.* Science *213: 459–461, 1981*

Osler, W.: On Chorea and Choreiform Affections. *Philadelphia, Blakiston & Sons, 1894*

Pauls, D., Towbin, K., Leckman, J., et al: Gilles de la Tourette syndrome and obsessive-compulsive disorder: evidence supporting a genetic relationship. Arch Gen Psychiatry 43: 1180–1182, 1986

Pazos, A., Cortes, R., Palacios, J.: Quantitative autoradiographic mapping of serotonin in rat brain: II: serotonin II receptors. Brain Res 356: 231–249, 1985

Pazos, A., Palacios, J.: Quantitative autoradiographic mapping of serotonin receptors in rat brain: I: serotonin I receptors. Brain Res 346: 205–230, 1985

Schneider, J. S.: Basal ganglia role in behavior: importance of sensory gating and its relevance to psychiatry. Biol Psychiatry 19: 1693–1709, 1984

Steinbusch, H.: Distribution of serotonin-immunoreactivity in the central nervous system of the rat. Neuroscience 6: 557–618, 1981

Stuart, A., Slater, J. M., Unwin, H. L., Crossman, A. R.: A semiquantitative atlas of 5-hydroxytryptamine-1 receptors in the primate brain. Neuroscience 18: 619–639, 1986

Swedo, S., Rapoport, J., Cheslow, D., et al: Increased incidence of obsessive compulsive features in patients with Sydenham's Chorea. Poster presentation at 34th Annual Meeting of the American Academy of Child Psychiatry, Washington, DC, October 1987

Vallutino, F.: Dyslexia. Sci Am 256: 34–41, 1987

von Economo, C.: Encephalitis Lethargica: its sequellae and treatment. London, Oxford University Press, 1931 [Translated from von Economo: Die enceptalitis lethargica Deuticke, Vienna 1917–1918. L'encephalik lethargica, Policlinica Rome, 1920]

Zahm, D. S., Zaborszky, L., Alheid, G. F., et al: The ventral striatopallidothalamic projection: II: the ventral pallidothalamic link. J Comp Neurol 255: 592–605, 1987

Zohar, J., Mueller, E., Insel, T., et al: Serotonin receptor sensitivity in obsessive compulsive disorder: comparison of patients and healthy controls. Arch Gen Psychiatry 44: 211–218, 1988

16. Obsessive-Compulsive Disorder: Psychobiological Approaches to Diagnosis, Treatment, and Pathophysiology

Joseph Zohar and Thomas R. Insel

INTRODUCTION

Obsessive-compulsive disorder (OCD) is a syndrome characterized by recurrent, intrusive thoughts (obsessions), usually accompanied by repetitive, seemingly purposeful behaviors (compulsions), such as ritualistic washing or checking. OCD patients generally recognize their symptoms as senseless and ego-dystonic, and in most cases, struggle against performing their compulsive rituals. As these rituals often appear to be laden with symbolic meaning, OCD traditionally has been assumed to result from an unconscious psychosexual conflict (Salzman and Thaler 1981). Unfortunately, the symptoms are often refractory to psychodynamic treatments (Nemiah 1984), and thus several new approaches to the syndrome have evolved.

There are several reasons to pursue a psychobiologic approach to OCD. A similar syndrome has been associated with certain neurological illnesses (Schilder 1938; Cummings and Frankel 1985), and several reports have noted neurophysiological or neuropsychological abnormalities in OCD patients (Flor-Henry et al. 1979; Insel et al. 1983a; Behar et al. 1984; Shagass et al. 1984). The recent reports of specific improvement in OCD symptoms following psychopharmacological treatment might also suggest a psychobiological abnormality.

In this article, we explore three psychobiological aspects of OCD. First, we review recent studies of the relationship between OCD and affective illness using biological markers. Then we examine whether or not the antidepressant clomipramine (CMI) is specifically antiobsessional and whether or not antiobsessional effects can be demonstrated with other tricyclic antide-

Reprinted by permission of Elsevier Science, Inc., from *Biological Psychiatry* 22 (1987): 667–87.

pressants. Finally, based on results with CMI, we investigate the effects of an acute challenge with a novel serotonin receptor agonist in both OCD patients and healthy volunteers to test the hypothesis that the serotonergic system is involved in the mediation of obsession and compulsions.

OCD: A FORM OF AFFECTIVE ILLNESS?

Although OCD is currently classified as an anxiety disorder (APA Task Force 1980), there is a tradition dating back to the 19th century of grouping this syndrome with melancholy (Maudsley 1895). Over the past 20 years, phenomenological studies have stressed not only the prominence of obsessions in depression (Gittleson 1966; Vaughan 1976), but also that depression is the most common complication of primary OCD (Goodwin et al. 1969). Recently, the Epidemiologic Catchment Area Survey, consistent with earlier results (Lewis 1936; Goodwin et al. 1969), described a significant overlap between OCD and major depressive disorder (Boyd et al. 1984).

One approach to further investigating the link between OCD and affective illness is to examine OCD patients for putative biological markers that have been reported in depression. Table 16.1 reviews our previously reported

Table 16.1. Biological Markers in OCD Patients

Test	n	Result (mean ± SD indicated)		Comment
Dexamethasone Suppression Test	28 OCD	25% nonsuppression ($\geqslant 5$ μg/ml following 1 mg dexamethasone)		Inpatients (n = 10) with AM and PM sampling show 60% nonsuppression
Sleep EEG	14 OCD	REM latency	48.4 ± 8.8 min	REM latency ↓ in
		REM density	1.7 ± 0.1	nondepressed OCD
	14 MDD	REM latency	47.3 ± 5.1 min	patients,
		REM density	2.2 ± 0.2	REM density ↑ in
	14 Controls[a]	REM latency	80.8 ± 5.5	MDD only
		REM density	1.7 ± 0.1	
Platelet ³H-imipramine binding (fmol/mg protein)	12 OCD	B_{max} 584.1 ± 138.5		Differences not significant
	12 Controls[a]	B_{max} 653.4 ± 159.3		
Platelet serotonin uptake (nm/10⁶ platelets/min)	12 OCD	V_{max} 94.1 ± 27.3		Differences not significant
	12 Controls[a]	V_{max} 89.1 ± 32.6		
CSF 5-HIAA (pmol/ml)	8 OCD	98.9 ± 43.1		OCD show ↑ CSF 5-HIAA; no difference in HVA, MHPG
	23 Controls[a]	56.9 ± 24.1		

[a]Healthy volunteers.

results in 39 patients (21 men, 18 women; mean age 31.5 ± 11.6 years, age range 18–57 years) meeting DSM-III criteria for OCD. Patients with OCD resemble depressives in that they manifest an increased incidence of nonsuppression on the Dexamethasone Suppression Test (DST) (Insel et al. 1982b, 1984). Confirmatory studies by Asberg et al. (1982) and Cottraux et al. (1984) have demonstrated this resistance to dexamethasone in OCD patients without secondary depression (although also see Lieberman et al. 1985). Similarly, electrophysiological sleep studies have shown a decreased rapid eye movement (REM) latency that is nearly identical to an age-matched depressed group and significantly less than age-matched controls (Insel et al. 1982a). This finding also was evident in nondepressed OCD patients, including many with normal DSTs. In contrast to the patients with primary depression, REM density was normal in the obsessionals, suggesting some distinctions between the disorders. Platelet ^{3}H-imipramine binding and serotonin uptake, noted to be reduced in several previous studies of depressed patients (Asarch et al. 1980; Paul et al. 1981b; Raisman et al. 1981), were not significantly decreased in our patients with OCD (Insel et al. 1985), although results from a new, larger study in OCD patients suggest that platelet ^{3}H-imipramine binding may in fact be reduced (Weizman et al. 1986).

With each of these findings reported separately, one wonders about the diagnostic accuracy of the sample (perhaps the OCD patients were really depressed) or the diagnostic specificity of the test (none of these "markers" are entirely specific for depression). However, taken together, with the new report on ^{3}H-imipramine binding, the overall picture could be interpreted as a psychobiological link between OCD and affective illness, even in those obsessionals who do not manifest depressive symptoms. Similar studies in other anxiety disorders have generally not found abnormal results (Curtis et al. 1982, Sheehan et al. 1983).

However, the nature of a link between OCD and affective illness is not clear. Neither the DST nor the sleep EEG abnormalities predict response to antidepressants in OCD (Insel et al. 1984). Although it is tempting to speculate that the disorders share a common pathophysiology, the etiological significance of these "markers" remains highly speculative. One explanation for the apparent psychobiological link between the two disorders is that patients with chronic OCD develop episodic depressions and that rather than displaying the affect common in major depressive disorder, these episodes are manifested as exacerbations of obsessions and rituals. Many patients with OCD are ill for years before they seek treatment; some apply for help when they become overtly depressed, some when their OC symptoms are more severe. In both cases, the acute episode superimposed on a chronic disorder may be a form of affective illness.

Recent reports of the successful treatment of OCD with antidepressants could be interpreted as additional evidence that OCD is a variant of affective illness. In the following section, we examine this possibility by asking whether or not all antidepressants are effective for patients with OCD.

OCD AND ANTIDEPRESSANTS: ARE ALL TRICYCLICS ANTIOBSESSIONAL?

The outlook with pharmacological treatments for OCD, until recently, was summed up by Salzman and Thaler (1981) in their review of the pre-1978 literature: "with regard to drugs . . . there is neither convincing nor suggestive evidence that more can be accomplished than the relief of some anxiety—at a cost that often outweighs the potential benefits" (p 295).

In recent years, the therapeutic potential of drugs for OCD has become more promising. Although Reynghe de Voxrie, as early as 1968, reported that clomipramine (CMI) reduced obsessional symptoms, the first double-blind psychopharmacological studies of OCD were not published until 1980 (see Table 16.2). These controlled studies, which collectively have administered CMI to 106 patients, have yielded fairly consistent results. In four studies (Marks et al. 1980; Montgomery 1980; Thoren et al. 1980a, 1980b; Flament et al. 1985a, 1985b) CMI was more effective than placebo in reducing OCD symptomatology.

In several parallel studies, CMI has been compared to nortriptyline (Thoren et al. 1980a, 1980b), amitriptyline (Ananth et al. 1981), and imipramine (Volavka et al. 1985). In a small sample, CMI was slightly better than nortriptyline, although this difference did not reach statistical significance (Thoren et al. 1980a, 1980b). Ananth et al. (1981) reported that CMI, but not amitriptyline, produced significant amelioration of obsessions, depression, and anxiety. Volavka et al. (1985) reported CMI to be slightly more antiobsessional than imipramine at 12 weeks, but probably not at 6 weeks, of treatment, although differences in the baseline scores and in the symptom clusters between the two drug groups complicate the interpretation of these results. CMI was found to be clearly superior to the MAO inhibitor clorgyline in a crossover study (Insel et al. 1983a).

Taken together, these studies suggest that CMI is more potent than placebo and that several excellent antidepressants, including clorgyline, nortriptyline, and amitriptyline, fail to reduce OCD symptoms. Preliminary results from a study of imipramine treatment of OCD found no significant differences

Table 16.2. Double-Blind Studies of CMI in OCD

Study	n	Design	Improvement in obsessed subjects
Thoren et al. 1980a	35(I)	Parallel CMI vs NOR vs PLAC	CMI > PLAC (5 weeks) NOR not > PLAC
Marks et al. 1980	40 (I then O)	Parallel CMI vs PLAC 4 weeks, then behavior Rx	CMI > PLAC (4-week self-rating only) CMI + behavior RX > PLAC + behavior RX (depressed subgroup only)
Montgomery 1980	14	Crossover CMI vs PLAC	CMI > PLAC (4 weeks)
Ananth et al. 1981	20 (I+O)	Parallel CMI vs AMI	CMI not AMI improved from baseline (4 weeks)
Insel et al. 1983a	13 (I+O)	Crossover CMI vs CLG, PLAC control	CMI > CLG (4+6 weeks), PLAC ineffective
Volavka et al. 1985	19 O then 16 O	CMI vs IMI parallel	CMI ≥ IMI (6 weeks) CMI > IMI (12 weeks)
Flament et al. 1985a	19 (I+O)	Crossover CMI vs PLAC	CMI > PLAC (5+5 weeks), childhood OCD

n, Number of patients; I, inpatients; O, outpatients; CMI, clomipramine; NOR, nortriptyline; PLAC, placebo; AMI, amitriptyline; CLG, clorgyline; IMI, imipramine.

between this antidepressant and placebo (Foa et al. 1985). This apparent specificity of CMI for reducing OCD symptoms appears to be strikingly different from the roughly equivalent results with tricyclic drugs in the treatment of depression. However, none of the studies of OCD patients so far has shown that CMI is clearly more effective than another tricyclic.

We chose to directly compare CMI and desipramine (DMI) in a crossover study of patients with OCD. The crossover design, although statistically troublesome, confers the advantage of using each subject as his own control. In a disorder with significant heterogeneity, such as OCD, the crossover design avoids the assumption that one group of subjects is equivalent to another. DMI was chosen as the comparison drug because it predominantly inhibits norepinephrine synaptic uptake, in contrast to CMI, which has potent effects on serotonin uptake (vide infra).

Methods

Subjects.

Twenty-six patients (14 men, 13 women) were referred by private local psychiatrists to the National Institute of Mental Health (NIMH) OCD outpatient program to participate in this study and were screened by at least two clinicians. Inclusion criteria were DSM-III criteria for OCD (as evaluated by two independent clinicians), including (1) obsessions (recurrent, persistent ideas, thoughts, images, or impulses that are ego dystonic), or (2) compulsions (repetitive and seemingly purposeful behaviors that are performed according to certain rules or in a stereotyped fashion), and (3) that either criterion 1 or 2 is a significant source of distress and is not secondary to another psychiatric disorder. Additional inclusion criteria were duration of illness for at least 1 year, age at least 18 years old, and Global–OC rating of at least 6 (1–15 scale).

Of the 26 original referrals, 3 cases were excluded because of other major psychopathology (Tourette's syndrome, alcoholism, borderline character). Two cases who met diagnostic criteria were excluded because the Global–OC rating was less than 6 (mild cases). One severe case was referred for hospitalization. Three referrals declined to stop their medication; two others who met criteria declined to participate in the study protocol.

Patients with mild secondary depression, defined by (1) affective symptoms beginning more than 3 months after onset of obsessional symptoms, (2) main complaint focused on obsessions, and (3) Hamilton Depression Rating Scale (17 items) score of ≤20, were included in this study. One patient was excluded because of a baseline HDRS >20.

The clinical characteristics of the patients that completed the study are summarized in Table 16.3.

Procedure.

Following a thorough psychiatric and medical evaluation, each subject was given unmarked placebo capsules for 2–4 weeks. Subjects were then randomly assigned to either CMI or DMI, beginning at 50 mg/day and increasing at a rate of 50 mg every 2 days until a maximum dose of 300 mg/day. The dosage was lowered below this maximum in increments of 50 mg if side effects were a significant problem. All capsules were identical in appearance, prescribed on a twice per day schedule, and given in a fixed number (6) throughout the entire study. Each week, capsules were prescribed in excess numbers so that remaining capsules could be counted the following week to assure that each patient was taking the full dose. No other psychotropic drugs were given throughout the study, and all patients were medication-free at least 2 weeks prior to beginning placebo. Each active drug was administered for 6 weeks, followed by 4 weeks on placebo, and then crossover to the alternate drug for 6 weeks. Ratings were completed on a weekly basis. The

Table 16.3. Characteristics of Patients with Obsessive-Compulsive Disorder Who Completed the Study

Age/sex	Marital status/ children	Years of education	Major symptoms	Duration current illness (yr)	Age at onset of OCD (yr)	Current impairment	Past treatment	Prior psychiatric diagnosis
22/M	S	13	Slowness Ruminations Washing	7	15	Cannot work, total social isolation	Psychotherapy, DMI, IMI	—
52/F	M/2	12	Washing	1.5	50	Does not function as housewife, some social isolation	IMI, psycho-therapy	—
46/M	M/1	16	Checking	1.5	44	Had to quit job, social isolation	IMI, trazodone alprazolam	—
45/M	Separated	16	Checking Washing	30; exacerbation 6 months	15	Impaired functioning at work, social isolation	Psychotherapy	—
29/F	M	16	Checking	8	11	Affecting her marriage	Psychotherapy, perphenazine, amitriptyline, alprazolam	Bulimia
30/M	M	12	Horrific temp-tations	8	22	Impaired functioning at work	Li, IMI, MAOI, haloperidol carbamazepine	Depression
34/M	S	12	Slowness Checking	2	32	Cannot work, social isolation	Perphenazine, doxepin, IMI	Enuresis, depression
42/F	M/2	16	Washing	1	10	Cannot work, social isolation	Alprazolam, ECT, psychotherapy	Depression
19/M	S	14	Checking	7	12	Affecting school, social isolation	Psychotherapy	Simple phobia
29/M	M	13	Washing Checking	4	25	Affecting work, social isolation	Psychotherapy	Depression
Mean 34.8 SD ± 10.9				4 ± 3.2	23.6 ± 14.2			
Range 19–52				1–30	10–50			

DMI, desipramine; IMI, imipramine; Li, lithium; MAOI, monoamine oxidase inhibitors; ECT, electroconvulsive therapy.

baseline for each drug period was defined as the final week on placebo prior to active drug administration. Patients with more than a 30% decrease in ratings during the initial placebo period where excluded from the analysis of drug effects. Patients who did not meet entry criteria (Global–OC rating ≥6) prior to the second drug trial were dropped from the study.

At the end of each active drug treatment phase, at least 8 hr following the previous dose of drug, a venous blood sample was collected into heparinized polypropylene tubes for plasma drug level measurement. Plasma levels of drug were assayed by mass spectrometry (National Psychopharmacology Laboratory, Knoxville, TN), with a sensitivity of 5 ng/ml.

Throughout the study, the patients continued in psychotherapy with their referring psychiatrist. Although no formal behavioral therapy was carried out either by us or by the referring psychiatrist, patients were encouraged to resist their compulsions and to maintain whatever social and work activities they had been doing prior to the study.

This study was approved by the Clinical Research Review Committee of the NIMH at the Clinical Center of the National Institutes of Health. All patients gave informed consent prior to beginning this study.

Assessment.

The following observer rating scales were administered each week: (1) the NIMH Global Scales—a single point rating over a range of 1 ("no difficulty") to 15 ("most severe") for impairment, obsessive-compulsive, depression, and anxiety (Murphy et al. 1982); (2) the Comprehensive Psychiatric Rating Scale–Obsessive-Compulsive Subscale (CPRS–OC) developed by Thoren and coworkers (1980a, 1980b); and (3) the 17-item Hamilton Depression Rating Scale (Hamilton 1967). As the CPRS–OC includes items for depression, we have modified this scale by scoring only the five items specific for OCD symptoms (i.e., rituals, compulsive thoughts, indecision, worrying over trifles, and lassitude), which we denote CPRS–OC-5, and we have further scored separately the two items, rituals and compulsive thoughts, which we denote as CPRS–OC-2.

All ratings in all patients were performed by the same rater, who was blind to the subject's treatment condition.

Analysis.

The study was designed to answer two questions: (1) Will patients improve on either drug? and (2) Will one drug be more effective? To answer these questions, two basic tests were applied. Clinical ratings were analyzed using a repeated-measures three-way Analysis of Variance for drug, time, and order of presentation on the change score (i.e., change from preceding placebo to the three time points—2, 4, and 6 weeks). In addition, scores between baseline and each of the three time points were compared for each variable using the t-test for paired data. This second test was used to exploit the crossover design by comparing CMI and DMI in each subject. To test for differences in the initial status of the two sequences (CMI–DMI versus DMI–CMI), Student's t-tests were performed on the scores from the end of the first placebo period. Carryover effects were assessed by comparing end of placebo 1 to end of placebo 2 scored by the t-test for paired data in each subject.

Results

Fourteen patients entered the trial. One subject had more than a 30% improvement during the initial placebo period and was excluded from the final data analysis. Three patients were discontinued because of adverse effects of CMI (one with urinary hesitancy; two with fatigue).

Ten patients completed both phases of the crossover. Mean ($\pm$SD) dose of CMI was 235 ± 67 mg/day (range 100–300 mg/day). Mean dose of DMI was 290 ± 32 mg/day (range 200–300 mg/day). For these 10 subjects, there were essentially no differences in the initial clinical status between the two sequences (6 received DMI first, 4 received CMI first). Comparing first and second placebo end-point measurements on all seven rating scales revealed a significant difference only on one scale (CPRS–OC-2) ($t = 2.91, p < 0.05$).

Mean ($\pm$SEM) plasma level of DMI was 189.7 ± 47.1 ng/ml (range 76–397 ng/ml). Mean ($\pm$SEM) plasma level of CMI was 159.2 ± 38.4 ng/ml (range 60–252 ng/ml), and of desmethylclomipramine (DCMI) was 294.6 ± 56.1 ng/ml (range 152–446 ng/ml).

Table 4 shows the means for each rating on DMI and CMI. Significant main effects (i.e., $p \leqslant 0.05$) for drug were evident for CPRS–OC-5 ($F_{1.8} = 8.03, p = 0.022$), CPRS–OC-2 ($F_{1.8} = 5.33, p = 0.05$), and Global–OC($F_{1.8} = 6.9, p = 0.03$). In each case, the CMI effect was greater than the DMI effect, with the paired analysis showing this difference as significant at both weeks 4 and 6. Changes on the Global Impairment rating and HDRS revealed no significant effects or interactions. On the NIMH Global Depression rating there was a significant sequence $\times$ drug interaction ($F_{1.8} = 11.61, p = 0.009$); CMI was more effective than DMI when given first. Finally, changes on the NIMH Global Anxiety rating revealed a significant triple

Table 16.4. Mean $\pm$ SD Behavioral Rating, Clomipramine versus Desipramine

Measure		Baseline	Week 2	Week 4	Week 6	Significance level from repeated measures ANOVA for drug effect[c]
CPRS–OC-5	CMI	8.15 ± 1.76	7.9 ± 1.51	6.70 ± 2.31	6.50 ± 1.70	$F_{1.8} = 8.033$
	DMI	8.15 ± 1.47	8.35 ± 1.90	8.25 ± 1.72	7.85 ± 1.72	$p = 0.022$
Paired t		0.00	0.76	2.48[a]	3.06[b]	
CPRS–OC-2	CMI	4.55 ± 1.30	4.05 ± 0.93	3.60 ± 1.07	3.60 ± 1.15	$F_{1.8} = 5.334$[d]
	DMI	4.70 ± 0.95	4.55 ± 1.14	4.30 ± 0.95	4.25 ± 1.01	$p = 0.0497$
Paired t		0.58	2.02	2.33[a]	3.55[b]	
NIMH Global–OC	CMI	8.2 ± 1.8	7.6 ± 1.3	6.4 ± 1.1	6.4 ± 1.6	$F_{1.8} = 6.998$
	DMI	8.5 ± 1.5	8.4 ± 1.3	8.5 ± 1.4	8.1 ± 1.5	$p = 0.029$
Paired t		0.61	1.50	5.16[b]	2.94[b]	
NIMH Global	CMI	7.0 ± 1.8	6.5 ± 1.4	5.5 ± 1.5	6.0 ± 1.6	NS[e]
Impairment	DMI	7.7 ± 1.3	7.4 ± 1.6	7.5 ± 1.6	7.2 ± 2.0	
NIMH Global	CMI	5.6 ± 2.7	4.9 ± 2.4	3.9 ± 2.1	4.6 ± 2.8	NS
Depression	DMI	5.7 ± 2.2	5.2 ± 2.5	5.6 ± 2.5	4.6 ± 2.0	
NIMH Global	CMI	5.1 ± 1.4	4.7 ± 1.3	4.1 ± 1.1	4.5 ± 1.6	NS
Anxiety	DMI	5.2 ± 1.0	5.4 ± 1.6	5.5 ± 1.1	4.8 ± 1.0	
Hamilton	CMI	13.4 ± 6.4	10.1 ± 4.5	10.7 ± 5.5	11.3 ± 6.2	NS
Depression	DMI	13.8 ± 5.5	14.3 ± 2.5	13.4 ± 3.7	11.6 ± 4.2	
Rating Scale						
(17 items)						
(n = 8)						

[a] Two-tailed, $p < 0.05$.
[b] Two-tailed, $p < 0.01$.
[c] The ANOVA was performed on a change score, i.e., change from preceding placebo to the three time points (2, 4, and 6 weeks) in each drug phase.
[d] The second baseline value for this measure is significantly ($t = 2.91$ $p < 0.02$) lower than the first baseline value.
[e] There is drug $\times$ sequence effect ($F_{1.8} = 11.61$, $p = 0.009$), i.e., whichever drug came first (either CMI or DMI) was effective in reducing global depression.

interaction ($F_{1.8} = 7.41$, $p = 0.026$). It appears that patients who received CMI first demonstrate significantly less anxiety relative to DMI at 4 weeks.

Using the CPRS–OC-5 scale, the mean ($\pm$ SD) improvement during the 6 weeks for CMI was 28.4% $\pm 20.1\%$ (range 0%–75%) compared to 4.2% $\pm 11.4\%$ (range –14%–25%) for DMI. Figure 16.1 demonstrates the range of peak responses to each drug. One patient responded better to DMI (13% improvement) than CMI (0% improvement), one showed equal response (25%) on both drugs, and the remaining 8 showed a superior response to CMI.

Discussion

This study was designed to evaluate the specific question of whether or not CMI may be significantly more effective than DMI in OCD. In a small, carefully selected patient sample, the results demonstrate that in OCD patients

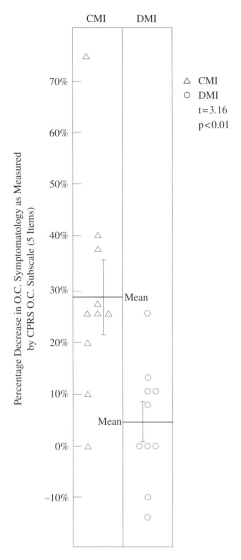

Figure 16.1. Distribution of maximum percent change from pretreatment baseline on clomipramine (CMI) and desipramine (DMI) in obsessive-compulsive (OC) patients (n = 10 for both trials).

with low baseline depression ratings, (1) CMI is significantly more potent than DMI for reducing OC symptoms, and (2) DMI lacks significant antiobsessional effects. After 6 weeks of treatment, the drugs appear to be roughly equivalent for antidepressant effects, but these changes in a mildly depressed cohort are of questionable clinical significance. The CMI–DMI differences in antiobsessional effects are not due to order effects (the drugs were given in a counterbalanced design) and cannot be related to intergroup diagnostic differences, as part of the analysis used each subject as his own control. Plasma levels for DMI and CMI were roughly equivalent and within the therapeutic range for antidepressant effects.

It should be emphasized that the differences in improvement on OC ratings, although clearly significant, were not large. After 6 weeks of CMI treatment, only a 28% improvement in obsessional symptoms was noted. This figure, from the CPRS–OC-5, approximates our earlier results of a 34% improvement (Insel et al. 1983a) and is somewhat less than the 42% improvement reported by Thoren et al. (1980a, 1980b). Both of these latter studies used the full CPRS–OC subscale (including items for depression), which may account for the somewhat greater percentage change. Other studies (Volavka et al. 1985; Zohar and Insel 1986) have reported a relatively long time course for antiobsessional effects with CMI, with reductions significant at 4–6 weeks, but not becoming marked until 12 weeks. Eight of the patients in the current study (including the patient with 0% improvement) entered an open-label extended trial with CMI, leading to improvements of 40%–90% on the CPRS–OC-5. In each case, the symptoms remained to some extent, but were easier to resist and no longer interfered with functioning.

The only previous controlled study of DMI in OCD patients also failed to find significant antiobsessional effects (Insel et al. 1985). In this study, several DMI nonresponders improved significantly during subsequent treatment with CMI, but a direct comparison of the two drugs was not undertaken.

The ineffectiveness of DMI in the current study is also consistent with earlier reports that norriptyline (Thoren et al. 1980a, 1980b), amitriptyline (Ananth et al. 1981), and imipramine (Foa et al. 1985) do not possess significant antiobsessional effects. Taken together, these reports demonstrate that antidepressants are not always antiobsessional, and they highlight the distinctive nature of CMI's consistent (although at times modest) effects in OCD (Table 16.2).

What then sets CMI apart pharmacologically from structurally related antidepressants? CMI differs from imipramine only by the chloride substituent at the number 3 carbon. As with many familiar compounds (such as amphetamine and phenylalanine), this parachloro substitution confers a number of different properties on the tricyclic ring. Compared to other tricyclics, CMI is an extremely potent inhibitor of serotonin reuptake (Table 16.5), is more effective at uncoupling oxidative phosphorylation (Zilberstein and

Table 16.5. Preclinical Comparisons of CMI and DMI

| | In vitro IC 50 (nm) | | | |
| | Synaptosome uptake[a] | | Platelet[b] | In vivo serotonin syndrome– total intensity[c] |
	5HT	NE	^{3}H-IMI Binding	
CMI	18	60	7	37
DCMI	120	2	10	—
IMI	140	28	10	17
DMI	1100	3	120	2

[a] Ross and Renyi 1977.
[b] Paul et al. 1981a.
[c] Wozniak 1984.

Dwyer 1984), and appears to have greater affinity for one of the binding sites on the Ca^{1+} channel (author's unpublished data).

Several lines of evidence point to CMI's effect on serotonin reuptake as most relevant to the drug's antiobsessional effects. Although CMI is metabolized to desmethylclomipramine (DCMI), and DCMI is present at about twice the concentration of CMI in human plasma, the affinity for the ^{3}H-imipramine binding site, believed to be the serotonin transporter, is conserved in the metabolite (Paul et al. 1980). As can be seen in Table 16.5, on this measure of "serotonergic effect," DCMI is an order of magnitude more potent than DMI and is roughly equivalent to CMI. Similarly, comparing tricyclics on their potency for inducing the "serotonin syndrome" in rodents, an in vivo method of assessing direct effects on serotonergic transmission, CMI is considerably more effective than DMI (Table 16.4), as well as imipramine, amitriptyline, and nortriptyline (Wozniak 1984).

Two studies have reported a significant correlation between plasma levels of CMI and clinical improvement in OCD (Stern et al. 1980; Insel et al. 1983a; however, also see Thoren et al. 1980b; Flament et al. 1985a). Thoren et al. (1980b) found a 0.75 correlation between improvement in OCD symptoms during CMI treatment and the decrease in the serotonin metabolite 5-hydroxy-indoleacetic acid (5-HIAA) in cerebrospinal fluid. Flament et al. (1985b) similarly reported a 0.77 correlation between clinical improvement and decreases in platelet serotonin in children with OCD treated with CMI. Several recent studies have reported that nontricyclic selective serotonin uptake blockers, such as zimelidine (Prasad 1984a; Kahn et al. 1984; Fontaine and Chouinard 1985; however also see Insel et al. 1985) and fluoxetine (Fontaine and Chouinard 1985; Turner et al. 1985), are effective antiobsessional agents. Additionally, case reports have described augmentation of CMI's antiobsessional effects with lithium (Rasmussen 1984; Stern and Jenike 1983; Eisenberg and Asnis 1985). In preclinical studies, lithium increases electrophysiological measures of serotonergic functioning in animals during chronic tricyclic treatment (Blier and de Montigny 1985).

All of these studies would be consistent with the hypothesis that the antiobsessional effects of CMI are mediated through the serotonergic system. Whether OCD patients have a psychobiological abnormality that involves serotonergic functioning is an entirely different question that has not been fully addressed. Studies of platelet serotonin uptake have not revealed a difference between OCD patients and controls (Insel et al. 1985; Weizman et al. 1986), although preliminary results in one study (Weizman et al. 1986) suggest a reduction in ^{3}H-imipramine binding in the platelets of OCD patients. As noted in Table 16.1, increases in CSF 5-HIAA have been noted in one small cohort of patients, but this finding still needs to be replicated (Insel et al. 1985). Certainly, there is a temptation to link serotonin with its role in mammalian aggression (Valzelli 1984) and impulse control (Brown et al. 1979) to the phenomenology of OCD, which is replete with guilt and reprehensible aggressive thoughts.

To examine directly the role of serotonin in the mediation of obsessional symptoms, we adopted the "pharmacological challenge strategy," using a novel serotonin receptor ligand, m-chlorophenylpiperazine, which acts at 5HT-1 sites (Sills et al. 1984).

OBSESSIONS AND COMPULSIONS: A ROLE FOR SEROTONIN?

The ideal candidate for studying the serotonergic system in OCD would be a highly selective agent that is safe, well tolerated, and penetrates the blood–brain barrier. None of the traditional serotonergic compounds entirely meet these requirements. Serotonin precursors, such as L-tryptophan and 5-hydroxytryptophan, are not entirely selective (Fernstrom and Wurtman 1974; Saavedra and Axelrod 1974); the serotonin synthesis inhibitor parachlorophenylalanine (PCPA) is associated with nausea and other adverse effects (Engelman et al. 1967); and several "selective" serotonin uptake inhibitors, such as zimelidine or citalopram, have recently been declared unsafe for clinical use. Some direct postsynaptic receptor agonists, such as N, N-dimethyltryptamine, are more specific than the serotonin precursors or uptake inhibitors, but are not useful because of hallucinogenic properties.

Recently, several synthetic nonindole aryl-substituted piperazine derivatives have been demonstrated to have potent effects on central serotonergic function both in vivo and in vitro (Samanin et al. 1979; Fuller et al. 1980). One of these compounds, m-chlorophenylpiperazine (m-CPP), is a metabolite of the antidepressant trazodone (Caccia et al. 1982) and, thus, might be expected to be well tolerated in humans. In vitro studies with m-CPP show potent displacement of ^{3}H-5HT from membrane homogenates (Fuller et al. 1980, 1981; Invernizzi et al. 1981). In vivo administration in preclinical studies of m-CPP has revealed rapid penetration of the CNS (Caccia et al. 1981) and decreased central serotonin synthesis and turnover, which is consistent with a postsynaptic receptor agonist (Rokosz-Pelc et al. 1980; Fuller et al. 1981; Invernizzi et al. 1981; Vetulani et al. 1982). In animal studies, m-CPP produces classic serotonergic behavioral (decreased food consumption and locomotion), neuroendocrine (increased prolactin and ACTH), and physiological (hyperthemia) changes that are reversed by serotonin receptor antagonist administration and responsive to alterations in serotonin receptor sensitivity (Samanin et al. 1979; Maj and Lewandowska 1980); Quattrone et al. 1981; Cohen et al. 1983; Aloi et al. 1984). In the first study of m-CPP administration in humans, the drug was well tolerated, and similar behavioral, endocrine, and physiological effects were observed (Mueller et al. 1985). Using m-CPP as a postsynaptic receptor probe, we investigated whether or not m-CPP would affect the symptoms of OCD patients. In addition, several of the OCD patients were given the serotonin receptor antagonist metergoline in a preliminary comparison with m-CPP administration. As the effects of m-CPP in healthy volunteers has been studied in the same laboratory under identical conditions (Mueller et al. 1985), data from this previous investigation were used for comparison with OCD patients to determine if patients would show an altered sensitivity to this postsynaptic receptor agonist.

Methods

Subjects.

Eight patients (5 men, age 28–46 years, mean 37; 3 women, age 23–64 years, mean 40) who were referred to the National Institute of Mental Health (NIMH) OCD outpatient program were studied. Data from 15 normal volunteers (7 men, age 20–42 years, mean 32; 8 women, age 24–67 years, mean 37) were also included in these studies (Mueller et al. 1985). Inclusive and exclusive criteria for patients were identical to those described in the

CMI–DMI study. None of these patients participated in any of the previous studies that were mentioned. Exclusion criteria for the normal volunteers included any psychiatric disorder, as determined by a formal psychiatric interview, and any medical problems, as determined by a medical evaluation and laboratory tests of renal, hepatic, pancreatic, hematological, and thyroid function.

All the patients and normal volunteers gave voluntary informed written consent to participate in this study, which was approved by the Clinical Research Review Committee of the NIMH.

Procedures.

All studies were limited to a single oral challenge administered under double-blind, placebo-controlled conditions on 3 separate days. Patients were medication-free for at least 3 weeks prior to the study. After an overnight fast, subjects arrived at the clinic between 8:00 AM and 8:30 AM and were kept in bed, with head elevated, throughout the 5-hr study period. Subjects were not allowed to sleep or to eat during this time. For endocrine studies (to be reported elsewhere), an indwelling forearm intravenous catheter was inserted around 9:00 AM. Between 10:00 AM and 10:30 AM, each subject received identical unmarked capsules of placebo, m-CPP, or the serotonin receptor antagonist metergoline. The m-CPP dose was 0.5 mg/kg (mean dose ± SD 36.8 ± 3.7 mg for the volunteers and 34.4±9.8 mg for the OCD patients). The metergoline dose was 4 mg. The challenges were conducted at intervals of at least 48 hr for volunteers and 72 hr for the OCD patients. The m-CPP or placebo capsules were given in random order for both groups. Metergoline, which was given only to the OCD patients, was always given as the last medication because of its long plasma half-life.

Ratings of side effects and mood state were obtained in both volunteers and OCD patients at baseline and at hourly intervals throughout the study using a slightly modified version of the NIMH self-rating scale (Van Kammen and Murphy 1975). In addition, each patient completed, with the aid of an experienced psychiatrist, specific ratings aimed at assessing changes in obsessions and compulsions. The scales that were used included the CPRS–OC-5 and the NIMH global rating scales. The ratings were done prior to and at 90, 180, and 210 min following drug or placebo administration. Patients also completed these ratings at 8:30 PM on the study day and at 9:30 AM and 8:30 PM the following day.

m-CPP was obtained from Aldrich Pharmaceutical Co. (Milwaukee, WI) and metergoline was obtained from Farmitalia (Milan, Italy). The identity and purity of both m-CPP and metergoline were verified by high-performance liquid chromatography by the Pharmaceutical Development Service at the NIH.

Results

Effect of m-CPP and metergoline on obsessive-compulsive symptoms.

After m-CPP administration, obsessive-compulsive symptoms increased significantly more than following placebo administration, as measured by the CPRS–OC-5 ($t = 4.18$, $p < 0.01$) and by the NIMH Global–OC score ($t = 7.18$, $p < 0.001$) (Figure 16.2). The peak response was observed in the first 3 hr following m-CPP administration (except for one patient who responded after 8 hr). This response was measured after 2 days, retrospectively, by the same blind rater using the same scales. The duration of worsening ranged from several hours (2 patients) through a day (4 patients) to 48 hr (2 patients). Five patients spontaneously described emergent obsessions (e.g., concern that touching the investigator might be harmful; inability to leave the clinic because of uncertainty about driving) following m-CPP administration. The effect of metergoline on obsessive-compulsive symptoms was much less pronounced, but generally opposite to m-CPP's effect. Following metergoline administration, scores were significantly decreased on the Global–OC scale ($t = 2.67$, $p < 0.05$), but were not significantly different from placebo on the CPRS–OC-5.

Behavioral effects in OCD patients and healthy volunteers.

A previous report from our laboratory has noted very minimal behavioral effects of m-CPP (Mueller et al. 1985) as measured by the NIMH self-rating score. In contrast to the healthy volunteers, the OCD patients became markedly ($p < 0.01$) more anxious ($t = 3.66$), more depressed ($t = 4.99$), more dysphoric ($t = 4.74$), and showed greater increases in "altered self-reality" ($t = 3.55$). For example, following m-CPP administration mean ($\pm$ SEM) scores on the anxiety, depression, dysphoria, and altered self-reality subscales increased 17.8 ± 5.2, 13.1 ± 3.7, 13.2 ± 3.3, and 7.1 ± 2.3, respectively, in OCD patients compared to 2.9 ± 1.2, 0.0 ± 0.2, 0.4 ± 1.0, and 0.6 ± 0.6, respectively, in the controls. A more detailed analysis of scores on the altered self-reality subscale indicated that m-CPP did not have hallucinogenic properties in either group, but increased reports of being "out of touch" in the OCD

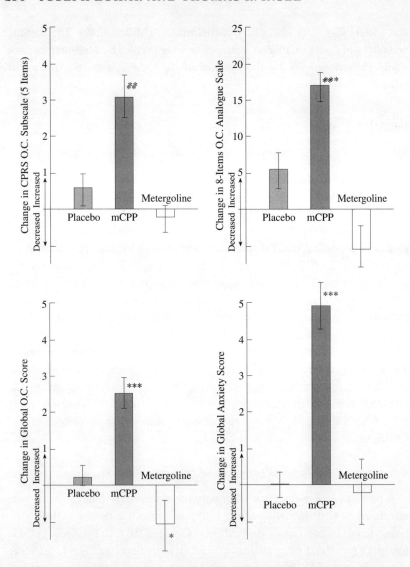

Figure 16.2. Peak changes (±SEM) on behavioral ratings after placebo (n=8), m-CPP (n=8), and metergoline (n=5) administered orally under double-blind conditions to obsessive-compulsive (OC) patients. ***$p \leq 0.001$; *$p < 0.05$ for t-test of paired data comparing change on drug to change on placebo in each individual.

patients. There were no significant changes following placebo administration in either group.

In general, m-CPP was very well tolerated physically by the healthy volunteers and the patients. Physical side effects, if present at all, were mild and included very mild nausea occurring in approximately one-fourth of both the volunteers and the patients. Chilled sensations, however, occurred only in 1 of the 15 volunteers and in half of the patients. Of the eight patients, six described being "slowed down" and seven described feeling "out of focus," effects that were not observed with such frequency in the volunteers. Late onset headache, 10–12 hr after administration of m-CPP, occurred in about one-half of the patients and one-fifth of the volunteers.

Discussion

OCD patients experienced profound behavioral changes following oral administration of m-CPP, whereas healthy volunteers described little, if any, behavioral response to the same challenge. The behavioral effects in the patients specifically included exacerbation of their obsessions (with the emergence of new obsessions in some cases). In addition, increased anxiety, depression, dysphoria, and altered self-reality developed. From these results, it appears that OCD patients are more responsive than healthy volunteers to the behavioral effects of m-CPP and that this selective serotonin receptor agonist significantly increases obsessional symptoms.

Prior to concluding that OCD patients are hyperresponsive to pharmacological challenge with m-CPP, certain methodological problems need to be examined. For instance, sampling intervals for behavioral and temperature measurements were more frequent in the volunteers. This difference would have increased the likelihood of finding greater effects in the volunteers, as peak changes might have been missed in the patients, so it is unlikely that this flaw in the design contributed to the group differences. More important, the concept of supersensitivity implies a leftward shift in the dose–response curve; that is, it assumes that controls given a higher dose would show identical effects as the patients. As only one dose was used for both groups in the present study, such a comparison was not possible. Future studies will need to use a multiple-dose strategy in both patients and controls before concluding that a true difference in sensitivity exists. In addition, the analysis of endocrine effects of the drug may help to refine this difference.

As these results are the first in a patient population, it is not yet known whether m-CPP increases obsessions selectively or whether there is a nonspecific exacerbation of diverse psychopathology following the drug. Certainly, the drug affected several symptoms other than obsessions in the OCD patients and thus, one hypothesis is that the drug is increasing anxiety or dysphoria, with obsessions only increasing as a secondary phenomenon. However, recent reports that the anxiogenic compounds lactate (Gorman et al. 1985), yohimbine (Charney, personal communication, 1985), and caffeine (Zohar and Insel 1986) failed to increase either anxiety or obsessions in OCD patients suggest that these patients are not especially prone to respond to provocative agents that exacerbate other anxiety disorders. Moreover, there is little clinical evidence to support the hypothesis that serotonin agonists induce anxiety (for review, see Gardner 1985). Whether or not a serotonin receptor agonist, such as m-CPP, selectively increases obsessions in these patients cannot be concluded from the current study, but some preliminary evidence linking the serotonin receptor mechanism to obsessions (rather than anxiety) derives from the selective decrease in obsessions observed in a small number of patients given the serotonin receptor antagonist metergoline. Additional studies of m-CPP and metergoline in other patient groups will be necessary to further define the specificity of these effects.

Existing preclinical data are quite strong that m-CPP is a selective postsynaptic agonist at the 5HT-1 receptor. The drug binds only weakly to adrenergic or dopaminergic receptors, does not affect the turnover of central catecholamines (Invernizzi et al. 1981), and lacks activity on behavioral tests sensitive to catecholamine function (Borsini et al. 1980; Maj and Lewandowska 1980). Furthermore, m-CPP's effects are not altered by depletion of presynaptic serotonin by either surgical lesions (Samanin et al. 1979), dihydroxytryptamine (Quattrone et al. 1981), or PCPA administration. Thus, m-CPP is a selective probe for the 5HT-1 receptor. The increase in obsessions following m-CPP administration, combined with the decrease in obsessions with metergoline, a serotonin antagonist, would be consistent with the hypothesis that the 5HT-1 receptor is involved in the acute modulation of OCD symptoms.

What remains unclear is that other agents that *indirectly* increase serotonin postsynaptic receptor activity, such as L-tryptophan or CMI, and hence would be expected to increase OCD symptoms, decrease rather than increase those symptoms (Yaryura-Tobias and Bhagavan 1977; also see Table 16.2). Indeed, chronic treatment with the antidepressant trazodone, which is metabolized in part to m-CPP in humans, has been reported in a single case to decrease obsessions (Prasad 1984b). This apparent paradox may be due to differences in the time course, interaction with the parent compound, or the regional specificity of direct versus indirect agonists. Moreover, it is not yet clear whether these antiobsessional effects are mediated through the same receptor (5HT-1) affected by m-CPP. We are currently investigating the possibility that indirect agonists and reuptake blockers, such as CMI, lead to a subsensitive 5HT-1 receptor by examining the behavioral, physiological, and endocrine effects of m-CPP following chronic administration of CMI.

SUMMARY

In this article, we have presented a series of studies contributing to a psychobiological hypothesis of OCD. At the outset, we asked three questions: (1) Is OCD a form of affective illness? (2) Are all tricyclic antidepressants antiobsessional? and (3) Does serotonin have a role in OCD?

OCD patients resembled those with MDD on certain biological measures (increased incidence of nonsuppression on DST and decreased REM latency on sleep EEG), but not on others (normal REM density, normal platelet serotonin uptake, probably normal ^{3}H-imipramine binding). Unlike depressives, OCD patients may show an elevated level of the serotonin metabolite 5-HIAA in CSF. These results could be interpreted as evidence for some psychobiological overlap between OCD and MDD. The two syndromes share many phenomenological features (e.g., guilt, worry, self-reproach) and frequently coexist. However, the biological marker data are not entirely consistent (four of the six measures are, in fact, different between OCD and MDD patients). Furthermore, the etiological significance of each of these "markers" remains highly speculative. Different approaches, such as comparisons of treatment response, need to be pursued to further investigate the relationship between these two disorders.

In the second section, we asked whether or not all antidepressants are equally effective for OCD, as they are roughly equipotent for patients with MDD. The results of a double-blind crossover comparison of CMI and DMI in 10 carefully selected *nondepressed* OCD patients showed that CMI was more antiobsessional at 4 and 6 weeks. No significant improvement was noted during treatment with DMI, even though plasma levels of the drug were in the range required for antidepressant effects. These results from the first direct crossover comparison of two tricyclics in OCD patients are consistent with earlier reports that CMI appears to be more antiobsessional than a number of structurally related antidepressants. As other selective serotonin uptake blockers, such as zimelidine and fluoxetine, have been reported to be

JOSEPH ZOHAR AND THOMAS R. INSEL

antiobsessional, and CMIs clinical effects have been correlated with decreases in serotonin function in OCD patients, we investigated the role of serotonin in the mediation of obsessional symptoms.

Acutely increasing serotonin function with the 5HT-1 receptor agonist m-CPP markedly increased obsessional symptoms. The serotonin receptor antagonist metergoline was associated with a decrease in obsessions in OCD patients. Not only does acute alteration of the 5HT-1 receptor affect obsessions, but OCD patients appear to be more sensitive than controls to the behavioral and physiological effects of m-CPP.

One hypothesis that would tie these observations together is that OCD patients have supersensitive 5HT-1 receptors, which are unmasked by m-CPP and which become down-regulated by chronic clomipramine administration. This hypothesis can be tested using agonist and antagonist challenges during chronic treatment with clomipramine.

More than 50 years ago, at the end of his classic case history of obsessional neurosis, Freud concluded, "I must confess that I have not yet succeeded in completely penetrating the complicated texture of a severe case of obsessional neurosis. . . . An obsessional neurosis is in itself not an easy thing to understand . . . " (Freud 1909, p. 294). In the current paper, we have done little more than outline approaches for investigating OCD as a psychobiological rather than exclusively a psychodynamic syndrome. Either way, the syndrome is complex. Just as obsessional symptoms are almost certainly not the result of a single developmental trauma, the focus on a single receptor or neurotransmitter is undoubtedly a gross oversimplification of a difficult, intriguing clinical problem. The task ahead is to understand the relationship of a single variable, such as the 5HT-1 receptor, to the multitude of neurobiological *and* psychological variables that contribute to this syndrome.

REFERENCES

Aloi, J. A., Insel, T. R., Mueller, E. A., Murphy, D. L. (1984): Neuroendocrine and behavioral effects of m-chlorophenylipiperazine administration in rhesus monkeysy. Life Sci *34: 1325.*

American Psychiatric Association Task Force (1980): Diagnostic and Statistical Manual of Mental Disorders (DSM-III). *Washington, DC: American Psychiatric Association.*

Ananth, J., Pecknold, J. C., van der Steen, N., et al (1981): Double blind comparative study of clomipramine and amitriptyline in obsessive neurosis. Prog Neuropsychopharmacol Biol Psychiatry *5: 257–264.*

Asarch, K. B., Shih, J. C., Kulescar, A. (1980): Decreased ^{3}H-imipramine binding in depressed males and females. Commun Psychopharmacol 4: 425–429.

Asberg, M., Thoren, P., Bertilsson, L. (1982): Clomipramine treatment of obsessive-compulsive disorder–biochemical and clinical aspects. Psychopharmacol Bull 18: 13–21.

Behar, D., Rapoport, J., Berg, C., et al (1984): Computerized tomography and neuropsychological test measures in adolescents with obsessive-compulsive disorder. Am J Psychiatry 141: 363–368.

Blier, P., de Montigny, C. (1985): Short-term lithium administration enhances serotonergic neurotransmission electrophysiological evidence in the rat CNS. Eur J Pharmacol 113: 69–79.

Borsini, F., Bendotti, C., Velkov, V., Rech, R., Samanin, R. (1980): Immobility test: Effects of 5-hydroxytryptaminergic drugs and role of catecholamines in the activity of some antidepressants. J Pharm Pharmacol 33: 33–37.

Boyd, J. H., Burke, J. D., Gruenberg, E., et al (1984): Exclusion criteria of DSM III. Arch Gen Psychiatry 41: 983–989.

Brown, G. L., Goodwin, F. K., Ballenger, J. C., Goyer, P. F., Major, L. F. (1979): Aggression in humans correlates with cerebrospinal fluid amine metabolites. Psychiatry Res 1: 131–139.

Caccia, S., Ballabio, M., Samanin, R. (1981): m-Chlorophenylpiperazine, a central 5-hydroxytryptamine agonist, is a metabolite of trazodone. J Pharm Pharmacol 33: 477.

Caccia, S., Fong, M. H., Garattini, Zanini, M. G. (1982): Plasma concentrations of trazodone and 1-(3-chlorophenyl)piperazine in man after a single dose of trazodone. J Pharm Pharmacol 34: 605.

Cohen, R. M., Aulakh, C. S., Murphy, D. L. (1983): Long term clorgyline treatment antagonizes the eating and motor function responses to m-chlorophenylpiperazine. Eur J Pharmacol 94: 175.

Cottraux, J. A., Bouvard, M., Claustrat, B., et al (1984): Abnormal Dexamethasone Suppression Test in primary obsessive compulsive patients. A confirmatory report. Psychiatry Res 13: 157–165.

Cummings, J. L., Frankel, M. (1985): Gilles de la Tourette syndrome and the neurological basis of obsessions and compulsions. Biol Psychiatry 20: 117–126.

Curtis, G. C., Cameron, O. G., Nesse, R. M. (1982): The Dexamethasone Suppression Test in panic disorder and agoraphobia. Am J Psychiatry 139: 1043–1046.

Eisenberg, J., Asnis, C. (1985): Lithium as an adjunct treatment in obsessive-compulsive disorder (letter). Am J Psychiatry 142: 663.

Engelman, K., Lovenberg, W., Sjoerdsma, A. (1967): Inhibition of serotonin by parachlorophenylalanine in patients with carcinoid syndrome. N Engl J Med 277: 1103–1108.

Fernstrom, S., Wurtman, R. J. (1974): Nutrition and the brain. Sci Am 230: 84–96.

Flament, M. F., Rapoport, J. L., Berg, C. J., et al (1985a) Clomipramine treatment of childhood obsessive compulsive disorder: A double-blind controlled study. Arch Gen Psychiatry 42: 977–983.

Flament, M. F., Rapoport, J. L., Murphy, D. L., Lake, C. R., Berg, C. J. (1985b): Biochemical changes during clomipramine treatment of childhood obsessive com-

pulsive disorder. Annual Meeting of the American College of Neuropsychopharmacology, p 132 (abstr).

Flor-Henry, P., Yeudall, L. T., Koles, Z. J., Howarth, B. G. (1979): *Neuropsychological and power spectral EEG investigators of the obsessive compulsive syndrome.* Biol Psychiatry *14: 119–130.*

Foa, E. B., Steketee, G., Kozak, M. J., Dugger, D., Simpson, G. M. (1985): *Effects of imipramine on depression and on obsessive-compulsive symptoms. Annual Meeting of the American College of Neuropsychopharmacology, p 38 (abstr).*

Fontaine, R., Chouinard, G. (1985): *Antiobsessive effect of fluoxetine (letter).* Am J Psychiatry *142: 989.*

Freud, S., 1909 (1959): *Notes upon a case of obsessional neurosis. In:* Collected Papers, *vol 3. New York: Basic Books, pp 293–383.*

Fuller, R. W., Mason, N. R., Molloy, B. P. (1980): *Structural relationships in the inhibition of [^{3}H]-serotonin binding to rat brain membranes in vitro by l-phenylpiperazines.* Biochem Pharmacol *29: 833.*

Fuller, R. W., Snoddy, H. D., Mason, N. R., Owen, J. E. (1981): *Disposition and pharmacological effects of m-chlorophenylpiperazine in rats.* Neuropharmacology *20: 155.*

Gardner, C. R. (1985): *Pharmacological studies of the role of serotonin in animal models of anxiety. In Green, A. R. (ed),* Neuropharmacology of Serotonin. *New York: Oxford University Press, pp 281–325.*

Gittleson, N. (1966): *The depressive psychosis in the obsessional neurotic.* Arch Gen Psychiatry *112: 883–887.*

Goodwin, D., Guze, S., Robins, E. (1969): *Follow-up studies in obsessional neurosis.* Arch Gen Psychiatry *20: 182–187.*

Gorman, J. M., Liebowitz, M. R., Fyer, A. J., Dillon, D., Davies, S. O., Stein, J., Klein, D. F. (1985): *Lactate infusions in obsessive-compulsive disorder.* Am J Psychiatry *142: 864–866.*

Hamilton, M. (1967): *Development of a rating scale for primary depressive illness.* Br J Soc Clin Psychol *6: 278–296.*

Insel, T. R., Gillin, J. C., Moore, A., et al (1982a): *Sleep in obsessive-compulsive disorder.* Arch Gen Psychiatry *39: 1372–1377.*

Insel, T. R., Kalin, N. H., Guttmacher, L. B., et al (1982b): *The Dexamethasone Suppression Test in patients with primary obsessive-compulsive disorder.* Psychiatry Res *6: 153–158.*

Insel, T. R., Donnelly, E. F., Lalakea, M. L., Alterman, I. S., Murphy, D. L. (1983a): *Neurological and neuropsychological studies of patients with obsessive-compulsive disorder.* Biol Psychiatry *18: 741–751.*

Insel, T. R., Murphy, D. L., Cohen, R. M., et al (1983b): *Obsessive-compulsive disorder—A double-blind trial of clomipramine and clorgyline.* Arch Gen Psychiatry *40: 605–612.*

Insel, T. R., Mueller, E. A., Gillin, J. C., et al (1984): *Biological markers in obsessive-compulsive and affective disorders.* J Psychiatr Res *18: 407–425.*

Insel, T. R., Mueller, E. A., Alterman, I., Linnoila, M., Murphy, D. L. (1985): *Obsessive-compulsive disorder and serotonin: Is there a connection?* Biol Psychiatry *20: 1174–1188.*

Invernizzi, R., Cotecchia, S., DeBlasi, A., Mennini, T., Pataccini, R., Samanin, R. (1981): Effects of m-chlorophenylpiperazine on receptor binding and brain metabolism of monoamines in rats. Neurochem Int 3: 239.

Kahn, R. S., Westenberg, H. G. M., Jolles, J. (1984): Zimelidine treatment of obsessive-compulsive disorder. Acta Psychiatr Scand 69: 259–261.

Lewis, A. J. (1936): Problems of obsessional illness. Proc R Soc Med 29: 325–336.

Lieberman, J. A., Kane, J. M., Sarantakos, S., Cole, K., Howard, A., Borenstein, M., Novacenko, H., Pluig-Antich, J. (1985): Dexamethasone Suppression Tests in patients with obsessive-compulsive disorder. Am J Psychiatry 142: 747–751.

Maj, J., Lewandowska, A. (1980): Central serotoninmimetic action of phenylpiperazines. Pol J Pharmacol Pharm 32: 495.

Marks, I. M., Stern, R., Mawson, D., et al (1980): Clomipramine and exposure for obsessive compulsive rituals. Br J Psychiatry 136: 1–25.

Maudsley, H. (1895): The Pathology of the Mind. London: Macmillan.

Montgomery, S. A. (1980): Clomipramine in obsessional neurosis: A placebo controlled trial. Pharm Med 1: 189–192.

Mueller, E. A., Murphy, D. L., Sunderland, T. (1985): Neuroendocrine effects of m-chlorophenylpiperazine, a serotonin agonist, in humans. J Clin Endocrinol Metab 61: 1179–1184.

Murphy, D. L., Pickar, D., Alterman, I. S. (1982): Methods for the quantitative assessment of depressive and manic behavior. In Burdock, E. I., Sudilovsky, A., Gershon, S. (eds), The Behavior of Psychiatric Patients. New York: Marcel Dekker, pp 355–391.

Nemiah, J. C. (1984): Forward, In Insel, T. R. (ed), New Findings in Obsessive Compulsive Disorder. Washington, DC: American Psychiatric Press.

Paul, S. M., Rehavi, M., Hulihan, B., Skolnick, P., Goodwin, F. K. (1980): A rapid and sensitive radioreceptor assay for tertiary amine tricyclic antidepressants. Commun Psychopharmacol 4: 487–494.

Paul, S. M., Rehavi, M., Rice, K., Ittah, Y., Skolnick, P. (1981a): Does high affinity [^{3}H]-imipramine binding label serotonin reuptake sites in brain and platelets? Life Sci 28: 2753–2760.

Paul, S. M., Rehavi, M., Skolnick, P., Ballenger, J. C., Goodwin, F. K. (1981b): Depressed patients have decreased binding of ^{3}H-imipramine to the platelet serotonin "transporter." Arch Gen Psychiatry 38: 1315–1319.

Prasad, A. (1984a): A double blind study of imipramine versus zimelidine in treatment of obsessive compulsive neurosis. Pharmacopsychiatry 17: 61–62.

Prasad, A. (1984b): Obsessive compulsive disorder and trazodone (letter). Am J Psychiatry 141: 612–613.

Quattrone, A., Schettini, G., Anunziato, L., DeRenzo, G. (1981): Pharmacological evidence of supersensitivity of central serotonergic receptors involved in control of prolactin secretion. Eur J Pharmacol 76: 9.

Raisman, R., Sechter, D., Briley, M. S., Zarifian, E., Langer, S. Z. (1981): High affinity ^{3}H-imipramine binding in platelets from untreated and treated depressed patients compared to healthy volunteers. Psychopharmacology (Berlin) 75: 368–371.

Rasmussen, S. A. (1984): Lithium and tryptophan augmentation in clomipramine-resistant obsessive-compulsive disorder. Am J Psychiatry 141: 1283–1285.

Reynghe de Voxrie, G. V. (1968): Anafranil (G 34586) in obsessive neurosis. Acta Neurol Belg 68: 787–792.

Rokosz-Pelc, A., Antkiewics-Michaluk, L., Vetulani, J. (1980): 5-Hydroxytryptamine-like properties of m-chlorophenylpiperazine: Comparison with quipazine. J Pharm Pharmacol 32: 220.

Ross, S. B., Renyi, A. L. (1977): Inhibition of the neuronal uptake of 5-hydroxytrypta-mine and noradrenaline in rat brain by (Z) and (E)-3-(4-bromophenyl)-N, N-dimethyl-3-(3-pyridyl)allylamines and their secondary analogues. Neuropharma-cology 16: 57–63.

Saavedra, J., Axelrod, J. (1974): Brain tryptamine and the effect of drugs. Adv Biochem Psychopharmacol 10: 135–139.

Salzman, L., Thaler, F. H. (1981): Obsessive compulsive disorder: A review of the literature. Am J Psychiatry 138: 286–296.

Samanin, R., Mennini, T., Ferraris, A. (1979): m-Chlorophenylpiperazine: A central serotonin agonist causing powerful anorexia in rats. Naunyn Schmiedebergs Arch Pharmacol 308: 159.

Schilder, P. (1938): The organic background of obsessions and compulsions. Am J Psychiatry 94: 1397–1414.

Shagass, C., Roemer, R. A., Straumanis, J. J., et al (1984): Distinctive somatosensory evoked potential features in obsessive-compulsive disorder. Biol Psychiatry 19:1507–1524.

Sheehan, M. B., Clavcomb, J. B., Surman, O. S., Baer, L., Coleman, J., Gelles, L. (1983): Panic attacks and the Dexamethasone Suppression Test. Am J Psychiatry 140: 1062–1064.

Sills, M. A., Wolfe, B. B., Frazer, A. (1984): Determination of selective and nonselec-tive compounds for the 5HT-1A and 5HT-1B receptor subtypes in rat frontal cortex. J Pharmacol Exp Ther 231: 480–487.

Stern, R. S., Marks, I. M., Wright, J., et al. (1980): Clomipramine: Plasma levels, side effects and outcome in obsessive-compulsive neurosis. Postgrad Med J 56: 134–139.

Stern, T. A., Jenike, M. A. (1983): Treatment of obsessive-compulsive disorder with lithium carbonate. Psychosomatics 24: 674–673.

Thoren, P., Asberg, M., Cronholm, B., Jornestedt, L., Traskman, L. (1980a): Clomi-pramine treatment of obsessive-compulsive disorder. I. A controlled clinical trial. Arch Gen Psychiatry 37: 1281–1285.

Thoren, P., Asberg, M., Bertilsson, L., Mellstrom, B., Sjoqvist, F., Traskman, L. (1980b): Clomipramine treatment of obsessive compulsive disorder. II. Biochemi-cal aspects. Arch Gen Psychiatry 37: 1289–1294.

Turner, S. M., Jacob, R. G., Beidel, D. C., Himmelhoch, J. (1985): Fluoxetine treat-ment of obsessive-compulsive disorder. J Clin Psychopharmacol 5: 207–212.

Valzelli, L. (1984): Psychobiology of aggression. Prog Neuro-Psychopharmacol Biol Psychiatry 8: 311–325.

Van Kammen, D. P., Murphy, D. L. (1975): Attenuation of the euphoriant and activat-ing effects of D- and L-amphetamine by lithium carbonate treatment. Psychophar-macologia 44: 215.

Vaughan, M. (1976): The relationship between obsessional personality, obsession in depression and symptoms of depression. Br J Psychiatry 129: 36–39.

Vetulani, J., Sansone, M., Bednarczyk, B., Hano, J. (1982): Different effects of 3-chlorophenylpiperazine on locomotor activity and acquisition of conditioned avoidance response in different strains of mice. Naunyn Schmiedeberg Arch Pharmacol 319: 271.

Volavka, J., Neziroglu, F., Yaryura-Tobias, J. A. (1985): Clomipramine and imipramine in obsessive-compulsive-disorder. Psychiatry Res 14: 83–91.

Weizman, A., Carmi, M., Hermesh, H., Shahar, A., Apter, A., Tyano, S., Rehavi, M. (1986): High-affinity imipramine binding and serotonin uptake in platelets of adolescent and adult obsessive compulsive patients. Am J Psychiatry 143: 335–339.

Wozniak, K. M. (1984): Interaction between inhibitors of monoamine oxidase and amine reuptake in rats. Ph.D. thesis. Department of Pharmacology, Institute of Psychiatry, University of London.

Yaryura-Tobias, J. A., Bhagavan, H. N. (1977): L-Tryptophan in obsessive-compulsive disorders. Am J Psychiatry 234: 1298–1299.

Zilberstein, D., Dwyer, D. M. (1984): Antidepressants cause lethal disruption of membrane function in the human protozoan parasite Leishmania. Science 226: 977–979.

Zohar, J., Insel, T. R. (1986): Drug treatment of obsessive-compulsive disorder. Psychiatr Med.

17. Pharmacologic Treatment of Obsessive Compulsive Disorders

Michael A. Jenike

UNLIKE the situation with affective disorders, obsessive compulsive disorder (OCD) patients tend to respond to medication with only a 30% to 60% symptom reduction, and patients tend to remain chronically symptomatic to some degree despite the best of pharmacologic interventions.[143] Nonetheless, patients usually experience this degree of improvement as quite significant. It is of utmost importance to give OCD patients who have improved with drug treatments a trial of behavior therapy to maximize their potential for recovery.

The number of controlled trials is growing rapidly as OCD clinics are seeing large numbers of patients. The typical randomized prospective placebo-controlled trial, which proved so useful in depression research, had, until recently, been almost impossible because of the small numbers of OCD patients available to any one researcher. As the pharmaceutical industry realizes the potential market for effective antiobsessional agents, they are investing millions of dollars in research into new compounds.

CYCLIC ANTIDEPRESSANTS

The mainstay of pharmacologic treatment for OCD is the antidepressant drugs, especially those with prominent serotonergic reuptake blocking properties. Besides offering effective treatment for depressed OCD patients, these agents are also useful interventions for OCD patients who are not clinically depressed. Because a link between depression and OCD is frequently noted,[42,57,67,83,87,139] it is not surprising that antidepressants have been used extensively in this disorder. Case reports have suggested their usefulness in the treatment of patients with OCD; these drugs include: imipramine,[6,40,56,136] amitriptyline,[56,126] doxepin,[5,13] desipramine,[47] zimelidine,[37,86] fluoxetine,[37] trazodone,[14,89,94,113,114] and citalopram.[144] All of these reports, however, in-

Reprinted by permission of W. B. Saunders Co. from *Psychiatric Clinics of North America* 15 (1992): 895–919.

volved a small number of cases without any controls. Responses were unpredictable and not related clearly to depression; there was, however, dramatic improvement in some cases. There are now a number of carefully controlled trials that demonstrate that some antidepressants are very effective agents, whereas others are quite ineffective in the treatment of patients with OCD. For example, in a placebo-controlled trial involving 37 patients, Foa and colleagues[32,33] showed quite convincingly that imipramine was able to reduce depressive symptoms in OCD patients but that it did not specifically affect OCD symptoms in either depressed or nondepressed OCD patients. Some of the cyclic antidepressants that have been reported to be helpful for OCD are reviewed.

Clomipramine

Early anecdotal studies indicated that clomipramine might have specific antiobsessional properties apart from its antidepressant qualities (see Jenike[69] book chapter on drugs). A number of carefully controlled studies have confirmed preliminary results that clomipramine is indeed superior to placebo in the treatment of OCD.[4,28,45,59,78,132–134] Lopez-Ibor[93] gave clomipramine intravenously to 16 OCD patients and reported improvement over 2 to 5 days in 13 of the patients. Others reported similar findings. Following these successes, other researchers attempted uncontrolled trials with oral clomipramine. These trials had mixed results. Some researchers reported little improvement whereas others reported a good response. Ananth et al[3] compared the efficacy of clomipramine with that of amitriptyline in 20 patients with severe OCD and reported that clomipramine, but not amitriptyline, produced statistically significant improvement in obsessive symptoms, depression, and anxiety. These researchers theorized that the lack of significant effect of amitriptyline on anxiety and depression may have been due to its inability to improve the primary obsessive symptoms and that clomipramine has specific antiobsessional properties superior to those of amitriptyline. Stroebel et al[129] studied the effects of oral clomipramine (maximum dose 300 mg/day) on obsessive symptoms in an open trial of 50 patients with various diagnoses and found that the overall success rate (reduction in obsessive symptoms) was 60%. Of 15 patients with a primary diagnosis of OCD, 12 (80%) improved, whereas only 7 (41%) of 17 schizophrenic patients showed improvement in obsessional symptoms. These findings indicated that clomipramine may have a beneficial effect on obsessive compulsive symptomatology, regardless of the presence of other psychopathology. Unfortunately, the diagnostic criteria were not outlined in this report and it has been documented that severe obsessive compulsive patients frequently are mislabeled as schizophrenic.[22]

Thoren et al[133,134] compared treatment with 150 mg of clomipramine (a fairly low dose) with treatment with 150 mg of nortriptyline and with placebo. Twenty-four patients were distributed among the three groups. Even with this relatively small sample size, a significant change was noted on an obsessive compulsive subscale derived from the Comprehensive Psychiatric Rating Scale.[9] On this scale, 42% (10 of 24) of the clomipramine group showed improvement, 21% (5 of 24) of the nortriptyline group showed improvement, and the placebo group showed no change. The clomipramine–placebo difference was statistically significant. After a 5-week double-blind trial, 22 of the patients were given an open trial of clomipramine and behavior therapy during which 11 (50%) of the patients improved, including three patients who failed to respond to nortriptyline. Interestingly, two of the patients who improved decided to stop taking the drug, preferring their symptoms to the demands of an asymptomatic state.

More recently, carefully controlled double-blind studies using clomipramine have been published[4,28,45,59,78,104,132] which concur that clomipramine is more effective than placebo in reducing obsessional symptoms. Clomipramine helped patients who only had obsessive thoughts as well as those with rituals.

The strongest evidence for the efficacy of clomipramine in OCD comes from a large multicenter trial of clomipramine, funded by CIBA-GEIGY Pharmaceutical Company (Summit, NJ), that was recently completed in the United States.[28,132] Clomipramine's side effects were primarily of an anticholinergic nature. Sexual difficulties (i.e., total or partial anorgasmia, ejaculatory problems) were common[103] and there was a small incidence of seizures at higher doses.[28] There is unpublished anecdotal evidence that the antiserotonergic and antihistaminic agent, cyproheptidine, may be of assistance with sexual side effects and it is now well documented that seizures are very unlikely if the total daily dosage of clomipramine is kept at 250 mg/day or below. Most patients tolerate clomipramine well. Usually to demonstrate a full effect, treatment should extend to at least 10 to 12 weeks and employ dosages as high as 250 mg/day.

Fluoxetine

Fluoxetine came on the United States market in 1987 and a number of open trials suggest that it has antiobsessional effects. Turner and colleagues[137]gave fluoxetine to 10 OCD patients and found that it reduced depressive symptoms but also had an effect (not statistically significant) on self-report measures of obsessions and ritualistic behavior. Fontaine et al[35] performed a 9-week open trial of fluoxetine in nine OCD patients and reported a statistically significant improvement in obsessional symptoms. This group later reported a larger open trial during which 43 of 50 (86%) patients responded to fluoxetine that was sometimes increased to as high as 100 mg/day.

We presently have over 250 well-characterized OCD patients taking fluoxetine in an open trial and early findings appear favorable. In our initial report, 61 outpatients fulfilling DSM-III-R and Research Diagnostic Criteria for OCD (34 men and 27 women, mean age 36.5 ± 10.7 years) completed a 12-week trial.[81] All subjects had duration of OCD over 1 year. As tolerated, fluoxetine was administered as follows: Week 1 (20 mg in morning); Weeks 2 to 4 (20 mg in morning and 20 mg in afternoon); Week 5 (40 mg in morning and 20 mg in afternoon); and Weeks 6 to 12 (40 mg in morning and 40 mg in afternoon). At 4-week intervals, patients were carefully questioned about side effects. Of 72 patients entering the study, 11 dropped out (one weight loss, and five for noncompliance). For the remaining 61 patients, the mean maximum dose of fluoxetine was 75.1 ± 11.3 mg/day. Fifty patients reached the maximum dose of 80 mg/mgday. Fluoxetine produced a significant overall reduction in both OCD symptoms and depression. Fluoxetine's antidepressant effects are well documented[20] and these preliminary data suggest that fluoxetine acts with equal efficacy on OCD symptoms for both depressed and nondepressed patients.

Fluoxetine may be an effective treatment for OCD and a multicenter controlled trial to further investigate the efficacy of this drug and its optimal dosage was completed recently (results not published). Until more definitive data are available, clinicians may wish to give OCD patients a trial of fluoxetine.

Fluvoxamine

Fluvoxamine has been shown to be an effective antidepressant when compared in double-blind trials with clomipramine[26] and imipramine.[48,49,62] A unicyclic agent, fluvoxamine also possesses selective and potent effects on serotonin reuptake inhibition and appears to be helpful in the treatment of severe OCD[44,82,109,115] In one open trial,[115] 6 of 10 inpatients experienced clinically significant improvement, and in a controlled trial,[44] 9 of 21 OCD patients were much improved with fluvoxamine as compared with no responders with placebo. However, because about half of the patients in this report had concurrent major depression, this trial of fluvoxamine did not allow an adequate assessment of its antiobsessional properties separate from its antidepressant effects.[44]

In a more recent study of the efficacy of fluvoxamine in patients with OCD, no other treatments were allowed, depressed patients were excluded, and the double-blind portion of the study was continued for a full 10 weeks in all patients.[82] All subjects were outpatients who met DSM-III-R criteria for OCD, had suffered from OCD symptoms for at least 1 year, and were not depressed by clinical interview. Thirty-eight of 40 patients completed the study. The mean maximum dose during the study was 294 mg/day with 17 of the 18 patients who received fluvoxamine reaching the maximum dose of 300 mg; one could only tolerate 200 mg daily. Side effects were mild and consisted mainly of insomnia, nausea, fatigue, and headache. Overall, fluvoxamine had no serious side effects, and there were no clinically significant alterations on physical examination, laboratory findings, electrocardiograms (ECGs), blood pressure, or pulse in any of the patients during the course of the study. Fluvoxamine was an effective antiobsessional agent when compared with placebo.

Sertraline

Sertraline has recently come on the United States market and there is evidence from a large double-blind, placebo-controlled trial that it is an effective antiobsessional agent.[23,79] There is some very preliminary evidence that it may not be quite as potent as clomipramine and fluoxetine,[82] but clearly some patients have a good response to sertraline after having failed these agents.

MONOAMINE OXIDASE INHIBITORS

There are no large controlled studies using monoamine oxidase inhibitors (MAOIs) in OCD patients but a double-blind, placebo-controlled trial is presently underway in our research unit. As early as 1959, there was a report of iproniazid producing marked improvement in patients who had obsessive compulsive symptoms;[84] diagnostic criteria and symptoms, however, were not described in this paper. Annesley[7] described a 49-year-old man with anxiety, phobias, and disabling obsessions and compulsive rituals, whose symptoms gradually remitted over a 6-week period after starting phenelzine sulfate. At 6-month follow-up, it was noted that the patient's improvement was maintained on a dose of 30 mg twice daily. Prior treatment failures included behavior therapy, electroconvulsive therapy (ECT), insulin therapy, phenothiazines, tricyclic antidepressants, benzodiazepines, and a neurosurgical procedure (bilateral rostral leukotomy).

The case of Jain et al[63] involved a 26-year-old man with anxiety, phobias, and disabling obsessive ruminations who responded to a MAOI with a complete loss of symptoms over a 2-week period and was still symptom-free at 4-month follow-up. In another case report, a 48-year-old man with severe obsessive ruminative thoughts responded well to a combination of thought-stopping plus tranlycypromine.[130] Rihmer et al[119] reported a 50-year-old man with agoraphobia and severe anxiety associated with obsessive ruminations who responded to the MAOI nialamide. Jenike and colleagues[64,65,83] reported six more cases in which MAOI produced dramatic improvement and four cases in which there was no effect. In contrast to the patients in whom there was no improvement, all of the cases reported in which MAOIs were effective had associated panic attacks or severe anxiety. Affective disease in patients or their families did not appear to be a good predictor of responsiveness to MAOI.

Based on these data, a trial of MAOI is indicated in OCD patients who have not responded to cyclic antidepressants, especially when phobic anxiety or panic attacks are part of the clinical presentation. *A full 5 weeks must intervene between stopping clomipramine, fluoxetine, fluvoxamine, or buspirone prior to starting an MAOI because deaths have been reported when these drugs have been used in closer proximity.*

LITHIUM CARBONATE

A link between manic-depressive illness and OCD has been suggested[17,128] (J. Lipinski, personal communication, 1984). Cycling obsessive compulsive symptoms have been described, but there are very few reports on the successful use of lithium carbonate in OCD. One double-blind crossover trial of six OCD patients carried out in Denmark reported lithium was as no more effective than placebo in symptom resolution.[39] On the other hand, there are a few case reports of OCD patients who improved with lithium carbonate.[38,128,138]

Obsessive compulsive behaviors are sometimes found in patients suffering from bipolar affective disorder.[12,17] Although behavior therapy techniques of in vivo exposure and response prevention are highly effective in treating these behaviors, until recently there were no reports of their use in patients with bipolar disorder and concomitant OCD. A report of two patients who met criteria for both disorders and who were treated with a combination of therapist-aided and self-administered exposure and response prevention, demonstrated that behavior therapy was effective only after the major affective disorder was controlled effectively with lithium and neuroleptics.[12]

ANTICONVULSANTS

Anticonvulsants have been studied little as treatments for OCD, but a few case reports suggest only occasional efficacy.[80,85,88] Similarities between OCD patients and those with temporal lobe epilepsy (TLE) have been noted,[66] and involuntary forced thinking is well documented in TLE.[21,51]

In two studies, patients with electroencephalographic (EEG) abnormalities suggestive of epileptic foci were described.[29,80] Four "obsessional psychopaths" did respond to diphenylhydantoin according to one report[106] in which diagnostic criteria were very unclear. In another study, only one of four subjects with temporal lobe EEG findings reported any improvement with carbamazepine.[80] A more recent study found that OCD symptoms did not respond to carbamazepine;[85] these patients were not selected on the basis of abnormal EEGs, however.

Attempting to identify a subgroup of OCD patients who would respond to carbamazepine, Khanna[88] investigated the efficacy of carbamazepine in subjects who showed some indication of temporal lobe dysfunction on EEG. In this study, seven patients were selected from about 50 OCD patients on the basis of EEG abnormalities that were considered to be indicative of a frontotemporal ictal discharge; abnormalities included spikes and sharp waves, periodic discharges, polymorphic delta, or hypsarrhythmia in the frontotemporal leads. Carbamazepine therapy of 200 mg/day was started and gradually increased to between 600 mg/day and 1000 mg/day to maintain a therapeutic blood level for approximately a 12-week study period. Of the seven patients, two reported a reduction of greater than 50% in their clinical symptoms; there were, however, no significant group differences on any of the outcome measures at the end of the 12-week trial. Both patients who were partial responders to carbamazepine had a history of coexistent clinical epilepsy. Khanna hypothesized that the OCD symptoms were probably part of a complex partial seizure disorder in these carbamazepine-responsive patients.

Reference has been made to the ineffectiveness of another anticonvulsant, sodium valproate, in two cases of OCD.[100,101] A case report demonstrated good antiobsessional effects from the benzodiazepine anticonvulsant clonazepam in one patient.[18]

The bulk of the evidence supports the idea that there may well be a small subpopulation of OCD patients in whom anticonvulsant medication may be useful. In patients who suffer concomitant or past seizure disorders, the likelihood of a positive response to carbamazepine may be high. In refractory patients without a seizure disorder, there is some anecdotal evidence to suggest that carbamazepine may be a helpful adjunct to cyclic antidepressants such as fluoxetine or clomipramine, although definite recommendations must await further data.

NEUROLEPTICS

There are only a few case reports of success with neuroleptics.[2,56,120] Most of these patients were atypical and some resembled the clinical picture of schizophrenia rather than classic OCD. It may be that the schizophrenic features were partly, or even substantially, responsible for the favorable outcomes. Under stress, the severe obsessional patient may appear psychotic, an observation that has prompted clinicians to attempt amelioration (often inappropriately) with neuroleptic drugs.[22] Commonly, patients receive neuroleptics for many years even though there is no evidence that they have been of any help.

In view of the absence of data on the efficacy of these agents and the frequency of toxic side effects, the use of neuroleptics can only be recommended for the more acutely disturbed obsessional patient. When these agents are tried, target symptoms should be identified and patients should be evaluated at regular intervals of not more than 1 month and the neuroleptic should be discontinued if there is no definite improvement.

ANXIOLYTICS

There are few anecdotal reports of success with anxiolytic agents[16,18,19,56,131,135] and a couple of controlled trials[105,140] in which both diagnostic and outcome criteria were unclear. Once again, there are no well-conducted studies that addressed the use of anxiolytics in patients with a clear-cut diagnosis of OCD. Most clinicians feel that these agents are of little use in the treatment of obsessions or compulsions but do help with the anxiety that many OCD patients suffer. If antidepressant/antiobsessional agents improve OCD symptoms, anxiety usually decreases without the use of anxiolytics.

Buspirone, an atypical anxiolytic with partial (5-HT$_{1A}$) serotonergic properties, was ineffective in a small (n = 10) open trial.[73] Other researchers, however, found that adding buspirone to an ongoing trial of fluoxetine enhanced efficacy.[74,95] Still others have reported that buspirone is an effective agent when used alone as a treatment for primary OCD.[107,143]

In view of the occasional spontaneous remission and often fluctuating course of OCD, it is difficult to make a strong case for the use of anxiolytic drugs on the basis of available data. There may, however, be a role for the novel anxiolytic, buspirone, as a primary treatment or as an augmenting agent (see later section).

TRYPTOPHAN

Because a deficit in the serotonergic system is sometimes hypothesized in patients with OCD, the use of the serotonin precursor, tryptophan, is of interest. Most of the work on tryptophan has been done by one group and results have not been replicated. Yaryura-Tobias and colleagues[145–147] reported a number of patients who improved with tryptophan.

Steiner and Fontaine[127] reported five patients who developed a toxic reaction when fluoxetine and tryptophan were combined. All of the patients became agitated and some of them developed nausea, worsening of OCD symptoms, abdominal cramps, headache, severe insomnia, aggressive behaviors, chills, and diarrhea. In all of these cases, fluoxetine alone was well tolerated and the toxic reactions occurred after tryptophan was added in dosages ranging from 1 to 4 g/day. Similar reactions have occurred when clomipramine has been used in close proximity (i.e., within 1 month) to MAOI; these reactions have been compared to the serotonin syndrome seen in animals that have received 5-HT (serotonin) precursors pretreated with a drug that increases the availability of 5-HT in the brain.[61] These cases suggest the need for close monitoring when combinations of potent serotonin-enhancing agents are used.

Because the administration of tryptophan stimulates the enzyme that causes the breakdown of tryptophan, to be maximally effective, nicotinamide, and probably vitamins B$_6$ and C also should be administered. It is also likely that the administration of other large neutral amino acids should be controlled in the patient's diet and not taken in close proximity to doses of tryptophan.[25,77]

Recently a syndrome characterized by eosinophilia and myalgia has occurred in patients using tryptophan and the safety of this agent has been
questioned.

YOHIMBINE

In an effort to investigate possibly abnormal adrenergic function in the
pathogenesis of OCD, Rasmussen and associates[117] administered the $alpha_2$-
adrenergic receptor antagonist yohimbine to 12 drug-free OCD patients and
12 healthy subjects and found no significant effect on OCD symptoms.

OXYTOCIN

In animals, oxytocin appears to be an amnestic neuropeptide that prevents the
acquisition of conditioned behavior or facilitates its extinction in a way
opposite to vasopressin.[8] Because compulsions are considered by behavior
therapists to be conditioned responses to anxiety-provoking events, the possible beneficial activity of intranasal oxytocin was investigated. Ansseau et al[8]
administered intranasal oxytocin to a 55-year-old OCD patient during a 4-
week period with resultant clear improvement in symptoms. Unfortunately,
this improvement was concurrent with the development of severe memory
disturbances as well as psychotic symptoms and a marked decrease in plasma
sodium and osmolality, which the authors theorized may have masked the
OCD symptomatology. This initial trial was encouraging in terms of efficacy
but side effects will require close monitoring in future investigations.

NALOXONE

Insel and Pickar[60] performed a double-blind, placebo-controlled trial of naloxone hydrochloride in two patients with OCD. They hypothesized that if
obsessional patients with ruminative doubt had a deficit in an opiate-mediated
capacity to register reward, this deficit would be manifested cognitively as a
difficulty in reaching certainty. The opiate system has been suggested as a
mediator of reward systems. The two subjects in this study specifically
described their obsessional symptoms as spontaneous doubts that required
repeated checks until a point of certainty was reached. They administered the
opiate antagonist naloxone intravenously at 0.3 mg/kg, a dose that is generally free from behavioral effects in normal subjects.[110] On a separate day,
saline was administered similarly and both patients and raters were blind to

the experimental condition. The first patient noticed no change after placebo administration, but while on naloxone became acutely absorbed in checking rituals and was unable to reach certainty about the physical relationships of objects in the protocol room. He had considerable difficulty completing the ratings and this acute exacerbation continued for 24 hours. Similarly, the second patient noted no change with placebo, but became abruptly worse after naloxone with feelings that he could not reach a point of mastery with his intruding thoughts. In both cases, blind self- and observer-ratings corroborated spontaneous self-reports.

Sandyk[122] reported improvement of severe OCD symptoms with naloxone in two patients that also had Tourette's syndrome. These conflicting reports implicate endogenous opiates in the pathophysiology of obsessive doubt and resultant checking and may have further implications in terms of future research on opiate agonists as therapeutic agents in OCD.

PSYCHOSTIMULANTS

The psychostimulant d-amphetamine has been reported to provide brief but significant relief to patients with severe obsessions,[57,58] and the mechanism may involve the opiate system because naloxone blocks d-amphetamine increases in activation and self-stimulation.[123] As mentioned earlier, clomipramine has been demonstrated clearly to improve obsessional symptoms in at least some OCD patients; it has also been reported to potentiate the antinociceptive actions of opiates.[124] A placebo-controlled challenge trial of methylphenidate and dextroamphetamine is presently underway (M. A. Jenike, unpublished data).

FENFLURAMINE

Fenfluramine, an anorectic agent with serotonin reuptake blocking as well as releasing properties, has been reported in one case to potentiate the effects of fluvoxamine when given on a daily basis at 40 mg/day.[55] When compared with placebo and administered as a single dose to seven OCD patients, it was not an effective treatment for OCD.[53]

CLONIDINE

Clonidine, an alpha$_2$-adrenergic agonist, has been reported to be an effective treatment for OCD symptoms in the context of Tourette's syndrome.[24] De-

spite reports of improvement in typical OCD patients with intravenous clonidine[54] and one case report of success with this drug when used alone orally,[90]
our results with oral clonidine are not impressive. Side effects with clonidine,
consisting mainly of excessive sedation and unsteadiness, necessitated stopping the drug before a 1-month trial in over 50% of our patients.

TREATMENT-RESISTANT PATIENTS

Up to the last decade, almost all patients with obsessive compulsive disorder
were thought to be refractory to treatment. Modern therapies, however, have
improved dramatically the prognosis for these patients, although many clinicians are not aware of the effective treatments presently available. The first
tasks of the clinician faced with an OCD patient who has not responded to
treatment is to obtain a careful, detailed history and determine if the patient
has, in fact, received adequate treatment trials (Table 17.1); for each medication, dosage and length of trial must be elicited.[71] There is growing evidence
that a full 10-week trial of potentially effective medications, such as clomipramine or fluoxetine, are required before assuming the drug to be ineffective.
Also, the clinician should assess if specific behavioral techniques (i.e., exposure and response prevention) have been attempted.

We now know that if patients receive appropriate treatment, usually consisting of behavior therapy plus psychotropic medication, the majority will
improve substantially, and occasionally completely, within a few months.[68]
In the experience of our clinic, the most common reason for lack of improvement was that ineffective modalities had been attempted. Many patients
primarily received psychodynamic psychotherapy, ECT, or neuroleptics with-

Table 17.1. Some Common Reasons for Treatment Failure*

1. Incorrect diagnosis; e.g., schizophrenia, obsessive compulsive personality disorder, etc
2. Inadequate treatment:
   a. Inappropriate or ineffective medication
   b. Medication trial too short
   c. Medication dosage too low
   d. No behavior therapy trial
3. Poor compliance:
   a. Willful patient prefers sickness to health, cannot tolerate demands when well
   b. Unrecognized cognitive impairment
   c. Other concomitant psychiatric illness; e.g., schizophrenia, major depression, bipolar
      illness, etc
   d. Poor understanding of treatment plan by patient; e.g., only takes medication when
      feeling "stressed"

*For a more complete discussion of these issues see references 71 and 77.

out result. Despite the well-documented efficacy of behavioral therapies, it is still unusual for patients to arrive at our clinic who have been given even a cursory trial of these treatments.

Even with good treatment, however, certain patients continue to be refractory. Predictors of treatment failure in behavior therapy for OCD include noncompliance with treatment, concomitant severe depression,[31] absence of rituals, fixed beliefs in necessity of rituals, presence of concomitant personality disorder,[102] and type of compulsive ritual. Patients with schizotypal and possibly other severe personality disorders (Axis II in DSM-III-R) also do poorly with pharmacotherapy.[11,75,76] Outcome studies and anecdotal evidence indicate that poor compliance with the behavioral treatment program is the most common reason for treatment failure with behavioral therapy for OCD.[96] Behavior therapy is more demanding of the patient than many other forms of psychotherapy, and the patient must comply with behavioral instructions both during treatment sessions and also during "homework" assignments. If the patient is inconsistent in doing this, treatment is unlikely to be successful. Severe depression also has been found to be a negative predictor for improvement with behavior therapy of OCD,[31] possibly due to impaired learning abilities. In patients with major depression, the behavioral processes of physiologic habituation to the feared stimuli do not occur, regardless of the length of exposure.[91] Because most of the antiobsessional drugs are also powerful antidepressants, depression is not a negative predictive factor for drug outcome.

If a patient has severe obsessive thoughts without rituals, behavior therapy is unlikely to succeed. In these cases pharmacotherapy is the treatment of choice. Patients who strongly hold the belief that their compulsive rituals are necessary to forestall future catastrophes (i.e., "overvalued ideas") have a poorer outcome with behavioral treatments.[31] For example, the patient who really believes that someone in his family will die if he does not wash his entire house every day, is unlikely to give up the rituals with behavior therapy alone.

IMPORTANCE OF CORRECT DIAGNOSIS

Another reason for poor treatment outcome is inaccurate diagnosis. If a patient meets criteria for schizophrenia or suffers exclusively from obsessive compulsive *personality* disorder, the standard treatments for OCD are not likely to be of help. Although patients diagnosed with obsessive compulsive personality disorder may have some obsessions and minor compulsions associated with their perfectionism, indecisiveness, or procrastination, these rituals do not interfere with the patient's life to the extent of OCD. However, some patients with OCD also have compulsive personality traits,[118] and roughly 6%[10] meet DSM-III criteria for obsessive compulsive personality disorder. With the change in diagnostic criteria in DSM-III-R, preliminary data indicate that as many as 20% of OCD patients meet criteria for obsessive compulsive personality disorder (L. Baer, M. A. Jenike, and J. Ricciardi, unpublished data).

The differential diagnosis of these two disorders has important implications for treatment. For example, although traditional psychotherapy produces little change in obsessions and compulsions in the context of OCD, it may be of some value in the treatment of patients with obsessive compulsive personality disorder.[70,121] Conversely, although behavior therapy and psychopharmacologic treatments have been found in controlled trials to be very effective for OCD, there is no evidence that these approaches are helpful for patients with obsessive compulsive personality disorder.

AUGMENTING ANTIOBSESSIONAL DRUGS

As in patients with treatment-resistant depressions, augmentation strategies are worth trying; that is, adding another drug to the treatment regimen when the patient has had no or only a partial response to an antidepressant. A list of potential augmenting agents is given in Table 17.2. Even though the overall percentage of patients that respond may be small, occasionally patients improve quite dramatically, which justifies such trials before switching to another drug. Certain limitations are inherent in these open trials, not the least of which is the possibility that some of the enhanced improvement may, in fact, be secondary to the patient being on the primary drug for a longer duration of time.

There is some very preliminary evidence that not all serotonin reuptake blockers are equally effective as antiobsessional agents; one group reported a meta-analytic comparison of four separate studies of various serotonergic agents (i.e., fluvoxamine, sertraline, fluoxetine, and clomipramine) performed by the same investigators[62] (Table 17.3). Among these potent serotonin reuptake inhibitors, it appeared that a greater effect size was associated with *less* serotonergic specificity, and that some ability to affect other neurotransmitter systems may be a necessary but not sufficient requirement for antiobsessional activity.

The success of a number of serotonergic agents in treating patients with

Table 17.2. Potential Augmenting Agents for
Treatment-Resistant OCD Patients

Augmenting agent	Suggested dosage range *
Lithium	300–600 mg/day †
Clonazepam	1–3 mg/day
Tryptophan	2–10 g/day ‡
Trazodone	100–200 mg/day
Buspirone	15–60 mg/day
Alprazolam	0.5–2 mg/day
Methylphenidate	10–30 mg/day
Nifedipine	10 mg tid
Liothyronine sodium	10–25 μg/day
Clonidine	0.1–0.6 mg/day
Fenfluramine	up to 60 mg/day

* Add these to an ongoing trial of antidepressant medication. It
should be noted that most of these dosages have not been
tested with rigorous clinical trials but simply represent some
of the reported doses tried in the current literature.
† Use with caution—there have been some reports of elevated
lithium levels with ongoing fluoxetine treatment.
‡ Because the use of L-tryptophan recently has been implicated
in an increased incidence of eosinophilia—myalgia syndrome,
the author advises against the prescribing and use of this agent
until the issue is resolved.

OCD lends partial support to a role for serotonin in this illness; however,
because a number of patients fail to respond to these drugs, the role of other
neurotransmitter systems in this disorder must be considered. This suggests
that partially effective drugs that primarily affect the serotonergic system
might have their clinical effectiveness enhanced by the addition of other
agents that have either different effects on the serotonergic system or affect
other neurotransmitter systems (e.g., norepinephrine and dopamine). The
brain's serotonergic system is not composed of a single type of receptor;
there are many different receptor subtypes, each with its own agonists and
antagonists. Thus, at least theoretically, it is likely that some patients fail to
improve because only part of their proposed serotonergic abnormality is
being corrected by a particular drug.

Because of the above findings and theoretical considerations, clinicians
have been attempting to improve OCD symptoms in patients who are only
partially responsive to serotonergic agents by adding other drugs as augmenters. Prior to changing any antidepressant medication, it is worth trying to
augment the response by adding each augmenting agent for a 2- to 4-week
period. Based on published case reports and our anecdotal experience (see
Table 17.2), this strategy will occasionally yield positive results.

Table 17.3. Effect Sizes for Four Trials of Serotonergic Antidepressants *

Study	Relative Potency†	Relative 5-HT Selectivity	Effect Size‡
Sertraline	1.00	Most selective	0.80
Fluvoxamine	0.38	Medium selectivity	1.09
Fluoxetine	0.28	Medium selectivity	1.34
Clomipramine	0.17	Least selective	1.53

* Data demonstrate an inverse relationship between serotonergic potency and selectivity and improvement in OCD symptoms.

† Relative potency of ex vivo inhibition of 5-HT uptake into rat brain synaptosomes.

‡ Calculated as (baseline Y-BOCS mean-end study Y-BOCS mean)/standard deviation for four different studies conducted at same center.

Lithium

Improvement in depressives has been demonstrated in tricyclic nonresponders after addition of lithium to ongoing antidepressant treatment.[27] This strategy has been attempted with refractory or partially responsive OCD patients. Rasmussen[116] reported a 22-year-old woman with classic OCD who did not respond to clomipramine alone, but who improved greatly a few days after lithium carbonate was added with a stabilized blood level of 0.9 mEq/L. Feder[30] reported a similar case in which lithium potentiated ongoing treatment with clomipramine. Golden and associates[41] reported two cases in which lithium augmentation improved response to clomipramine in one patient and doxepin in another.

On the other hand, Hermesh et al[50] found that adding lithium to ongoing clomipramine was relatively ineffective in improving OCD symptoms, with only 1 of 10 patients having any response. Whether or not lithium augmentation of other cyclic antidepressants or MAOIs for obsessive compulsive symptoms is helpful remains to be tested; however, Jenike[71,77] reported that only one of seven OCD patients receiving fluoxetine seemed to derive any additional benefit when lithium was added.

McDougle et al[99] completed 2- and 4-week double-blind, placebo-controlled trials of lithium augmentation of ongoing fluvoxamine treatment trials in 20 and 10 OCD patients, respectively, who had failed to respond to fluvoxamine alone. Although 2 weeks of double-blind lithium augmentation produced a small but statistically significant reduction in OCD symptoms, most patients did not have a clinically meaningful response. Furthermore, there was no statistical or clinical improvement in OCD symptoms during the subsequent 4-week double-blind, placebo-controlled trial of lithium augmentation. On the basis of treatment response criteria, only 18% and 0% of the patients responded to lithium augmentation of fluvoxamine during the 2- and

4-week treatment trials, respectively. McDougle et al noted that in light of the previously reported 44% response rate to lithium augmentation in treatment-resistant depressed patients on fluvoxamine, the results of this study suggested that pathophysiologic differences may exist between OCD and depression, and that the routine use of lithium augmentation in the management of patients with OCD who are refractory or only partially responsive to serotonin reuptake inhibitors is not supported by their findings.

Pigott et al[112] came to similar conclusions about the relative ineffectiveness of lithium in another small (n = 8) controlled crossover trial in which either lithium or L-triiodothyronine (T3) was blindly added to an ongoing trial of clomipramine in patients who had all been partial responders to clomipramine alone. Neither lithium carbonate or T3 added anything to the clinical effect.

Buspirone

One group reported that buspirone, an atypical anxiolytic with partial (5-HT_{1A}) serotonergic agonist properties, was an effective agent when used alone as a treatment for primary OCD.[107] Others found it ineffective when used alone in a small (n = 10) open trial.[73]

Adding buspirone to an ongoing trial of fluoxetine has been reported to diminish OCD symptoms.[1,74,95] Alessi and Bos[1] reported a single case of an 11-year-old girl whose OCD symptoms improved when 30 mg/day of buspirone were added to ongoing fluoxetine treatment. Markovitz et al[95] gave 11 OCD patients a prospective open-label trial of fluoxetine monotherapy followed by buspirone augmentation (up to 30 mg/day) and reported that the combination therapy was statistically superior to fluoxetine monotherapy.

Jenike et al[74] studied 20 outpatients with OCD who had been ill for over 1 year. Ten patients, 5 men and 5 women, were studied prospectively and received fluoxetine alone for 12 weeks (Phase 1) then buspirone plus fluoxetine for another 8 weeks (Phase 2). Ten other consecutively treated outpatients, 7 men and 3 women, who received only fluoxetine for 20 weeks were selected as a post-hoc comparison group. All patients were treated with open fluoxetine for 20 weeks and remained on a constant dose throughout the last 8 weeks of the study. Buspirone was openly administered initially at 15 mg/day in divided doses and increased by 15 mg/day each week to a maximum of 60 mg/day if tolerated. At weeks 1, 12, 16, and 20, the Yale-Brown Obsessive-Compulsive Scale (Y-BOCS)[44] and Beck Depression Inventory (BDI)[15] were administered. Changes in mood and OCD symptoms were assessed by independent *t*-test between buspirone and control groups. The mean maximum dose of buspirone was 54 mg/day with seven patients tolerating the full 60 mg/day dose. The mean maximum dose of fluoxetine was 78 mg/day for the fluoxetine-buspirone group and 76 mg/day for the fluoxetine only group. The two groups did not differ on baseline Y-BOCS score nor Y-BOCS change score over the first 12 weeks of the study. Thus the two groups had similar levels of OCD symptom severity on entering the study, and improved comparable amounts during Phase 1. During Phase 2 of the study, the buspirone augmentation group showed significantly greater change scores at week 20, but not at week 16. However, change scores on the BDI did not differ significantly at either week 16 or week 20. In this study, addition of buspirone to fluoxetine led to greater improvement than continuing on fluoxetine alone. This gradual augmenting effect, which reached statistical significance after 8 weeks, was independent of changes in depression because the two groups did not differ in improvement on this measure. Even though the significant changes in the Y-BOCS were relatively small, patients generally felt that they were clinically improved, and that the quality of their lives had improved when buspirone was added to fluoxetine for 8 weeks. The results of this pilot study must be considered preliminary because of the small sample size, the lack of a double-blind design, and the retrospective nature of the control group.

Pigott et al[111] recently studied 14 OCD patients who had received at least 3 months of treatment with clomipramine. Each patient was initially given placebo for 2 weeks and then treated with buspirone in a 10-week, double-blind study. Prior to the addition of buspirone, these patients had shown a partial but incomplete reduction (average = 28%) in OCD symptoms during clomipramine treatment alone. Although adjuvant buspirone treatment was well tolerated in most subjects, mean OCD and depressive symptoms, as evaluated by standardized rating scales (i.e., Y-BOCS, NIMH-OC), did not significantly change from baseline scores achieved on clomipramine treatment alone. The mean dose of buspirone was 57 ± 7 mg/day. When the response of individual patients was examined, 4 (29%) of the 14 patients did have an additional 25% reduction on OCD symptoms after adjuvant buspirone treatment. Interestingly, 3 (21%) of 14 patients got more than 25% worse when buspirone was added. Pigott et al concluded that adjunctive buspirone therapy is not generally associated with significant further clinical improvement in OCD or depressive symptoms as compared with clomipramine monotherapy, but that there may be a subgroup of patients who do benefit from adjuvant buspirone therapy. They did not speculate on or identify any factors in the drug-responsive patients that differentiated them from the nonresponders.

This study suffers from the obvious weakness that buspirone and placebo were not compared head to head, and there was not even variation in the time that placebo was given (i.e., always the first 2 weeks) over the course of the study.

Tryptophan

Rasmussen[116] reported an OCD patient who had a partial response to clomipramine which was dramatically boosted when 6 g/day of L-tryptophan was added. This patient relapsed when tryptophan was stopped and improved again when it was restarted. Whether tryptophan would boost the antiobsessional effects of other tricyclic antidepressants or MAOIs remains to be determined. Walinder and associates,[141] however, have demonstrated that L-tryptophan potentiates tricyclic antidepressant effects in endogenously depressed patients.

Clonidine

Clonidine, an $alpha_2$-adrenergic agonist, has been reported to be an effective treatment for OCD symptoms in the context of Tourette's syndrome.[24] Despite reports of improvement in typical OCD patients with intravenous clonidine[53] and two case reports of success with this drug when used alone,[90,92] our results with oral clonidine are not impressive. We found that only 3 of 17 patients had a minimal and not clinically significant improvement when clonidine was added to fluoxetine (Table 17.4). Side effects with clonidine,

Table 17.4. MGH Open Trials of Fluoxetine Plus Augmenting Agents *

Drug	Daily dosage range (mg)	No. of patients	% Pts over 20% improvement†	% Stopped for side effects
Clonidine	0.1–0.6	17	19	56
Trazodone	100–200	13	31	31
Lithium	300–600	7	14	29
Clonazepam	1.0–3.0	7	14	0

MGH = Massachusetts General Hospital.
* All trials were roughly 1 month in duration.
† As assessed by Yale-Brown Obsessive-Compulsive Scale.[43]
From Jenike MA: Management of patients with treatment-resistant obsessive-compulsive disorder. *In* Pato MT, Zohar J (eds): Obsessive-Compulsive Disorders. Washington, DC, APA Press, 191, pp 135–156; with permission.

consisting mainly of excessive sedation and unsteadiness, necessitated stopping the drug before a 1-month trial in over 50% of the patients.

Fenfluramine

Fenfluramine, an anorectic agent with serotonin reuptake blocking as well as releasing properties, has been reported in one case to potentiate the effects of fluvoxamine when given on a daily basis at 40 mg/day.[55] Hollander et al[52] gave an open trial of fenfluramine in doses of 20 to 60 mg/day to OCD patients who had only a partial response to fluoxetine, fluvoxamine, or clomipramine or were unable to tolerate therapeutic doses of these agents. Fenfluramine augmentation was well tolerated and resulted in a further decrease in obsessions and compulsions in six of the seven patients.

Antidepressants

Trazodone has been used as an augmenting agent and in one open report[71,77] (see Table 17.4), it improved Y-BOCS scores by greater than 20% in 4 of 13 patients when it was added to ongoing fluoxetine. Almost one third of the patients who were augmented with trazodone, however, had to discontinue the medication because of excessive daily sedation, even though the drug was given at bedtime.

Simeon et al[126] reported adding fluoxetine (20 to 40 mg) to ongoing trials of clomipramine (25 to 50 mg) in six adolescents (4 female, 2 male) with OCD (mean age = 14.8 years, range 13.1 to 16.6 years). Each of the six patients had either not improved or had developed intolerable side effects on clomipramine alone. Before fluoxetine was given, the mean daily dosage of clomipramine was only 92 mg (range 50 to 175 mg) and the duration of treatment ranged from 3 to 32 weeks (mean = 17.5 weeks). In four patients, clomipramine dosage was reduced when fluoxetine was added because patients complained of adverse effects. Two anxious patients also received alprazolam. One patient improved moderately and five improved markedly with combination treatment. The authors concluded that the combination of low doses of clomipramine plus fluoxetine resulted in greater clinical improvement with fewer adverse effects than a trial of clomipramine alone.

Anxiolytic Agents

Anxiolytic agents are often used as adjuncts to other medications and may be helpful in facilitating behavior therapy in patients who are unable to tolerate the anxiety produced by exposure and response prevention techniques. Sometimes these medications can actually interfere with behavior therapy (see article on behavior therapy in this issue). We added clonazepam (0.5 mg two to three times daily) to ongoing fluoxetine in seven patients and only one improved more than 20% after the addition (see Table 17.4).

Neuroleptics

Although neuroleptic agents when used alone are generally not useful for patients with OCD, a recent report by Goodman et al[46] of an open case series of 13 OCD patients in which 8 were much improved after pimozide was added to ongoing fluvoxamine is of interest. McDougle et al[98] presented data on the addition of neuroleptic (haloperidol or pimozide) to ongoing fluvoxamine treatment in 17 OCD patients (includes the same 13 patients as Goodman et al above). Nine of the patients improved to a clinically significant degree. Some of the patients also were taking lithium in combination with fluoxetine during this augmentation trial and its contribution to overall improvement is not clear, but none of the patients had significant improvement prior to neuroleptic augmentation. Because of the dangers of irreversible neurologic sequellae associated with neuroleptic treatments, specific target symptoms should be identified and if there is no improvement within a few months, the neuroleptic should be discontinued. There is some evidence that patients with tic-spectrum disorders or schizotypal features are most likely to respond to neuroleptic augmentation.[98]

MGH Anecdotal Experience with Augmentation

A partial list of potential augmenting agents is given in Table 17.2 and some of our preliminary clinical experience with augmenting agents is presented in Table 17.4. In each of the patients presented in Table 17.4, fluoxetine had been continued alone for a minimum of 10 weeks before the augmenting agent was added. In addition to the seven patients presented in Table 17.4 who were augmented with clonazepam, another nine patients received clonazepam and fluoxetine almost simultaneously; of these, seven (78%) improved at least 20% during the next 10 weeks. A single OCD patient has been reported who had a dramatic response to clonazepam alone, adding further evidence that this agent might have specific antiobessional effects.[18] In our patients, clonazepam was sometimes added early in the course of a fluoxetine trial to counter drug-induced anxiety and restlessness. In two other patients,

Table 17.5. Flow Sheet of Some Treatment Options*

1. Clomipramine trial to 250 mg daily
2. Augment clomipramine
3. Fluoxetine trial to 80 mg daily
4. Augment fluoxetine
5. Stop fluoxetine or clomipramine for 5 weeks
6. MAOI trial
7. Augment MAOI for one month†
8. Trials of experimental agents when available
9. Other medication trials (e.g., trazodone, imipramine, etc)
10. If severe personality disorder presents, consider half-way house placement or day treatment program
11. If patient is severely disabled, despite adequate treatment trials, consider psychosurgical procedure
12. If poor compliance is a persistent problem, or patient prefers symptoms to being rid of them, or if patient also has obsessive compulsive *personality* disorder, consider concomitant psychodynamic psychotherapy

* As soon as patient has at least a partial response to medication; if patient has rituals, begin behavior therapy of exposure and response prevention.
† Do not augment MAOI with buspirone as severe and potentially fatal reactions have been reported.
Modified from Jenike MA: Management of patients with treatment-resistant obsessive-compulsive disorder. *In* Pato MT, Zohar J (eds): Obsessive-Compulsive Disorders. Washington, DC, APA Press, 1991, pp 135–156; with permission.

fluoxetine was augmented with alprazolam (0.5 and 2.0 mg/day) without improvement.

More than 90% of OCD patients have a good outcome (i.e., moderately better to completely cured) with aggressive and appropriate therapy.[77] Some patients, however, fail to improve even with the best of treatments, and future research endeavors will be focused on this still treatment-refractory group of patients. It is hoped that as researchers target these patients, answers will be forthcoming. The use of augmenting strategies in the context of treatment-refractory OCD patients obviously requires more study. Table 17.1 outlines some of the factors to consider when a patient fails to respond to antiobessional medication and Table 17.5 presents a flow sheet of some treatment options and outlines when augmenter drugs may be used. Table 17.6 summarizes the published data on the use of augmenters to treat OCD patients.

It is important to keep in mind that the most likely effective augmenting tactic is to add concomitant behavior therapy consisting of exposure and response prevention; this does not, however, preclude the addition of a second medication to an ongoing trial of antiobessional medication.

Even though the overall percentage of patients that responded is small, occasionally patients have shown quite dramatic improvement which justifies such trials before switching to another drug. Certain limitations are inherent

Table 17.6. Nonneuroleptic augmentation trials in OCD patients

Augmenting agent	Primary drug	Number of subjects	Uncontrolled trials		Reference
			Clinical response	Type of trial	
fenfluramine (dosage = 40 mg)	fluvoxamine	1	improved, discontinued secondary to impotence	open	Hollander and Liebo-witz, 1988[55]
fenfluramine, (dosage = 20–60 mg)	either clomipramine, fluoxetine, or fluvoxamine	7	6 of 7 improved	open	Hollander et al, 1990[52]
lithium	doxepin	1	"striking" improvement	open	Golden et al, 1988[41]
lithium	clomipramine	1	"clinically meaningful" improvement	open	Golden et al, 1988[41]
lithium	clomipramine	10	only 1 improved some improvement	open	Hermesh et al, 1990[50]
lithium	clomipramine	1	improved	open	Feder, 1988[30]
lithium	clomipramine	1	improved	open	Rasmussen, 1984[16]
lithium	fluoxetine	7	1 improved > 20%	open	Jenike, 1991[72]
clonidine	clomipramine	1	much improved	open	Lipsedge & Prothero, 1987[92]
clonidine	fluoxetine	17	3 improved > 20%	open	Jenike, 1991[72]
clonazepam	fluoxetine	7	1 improved > 20%	open	Jenike, 1991[72]
tryptophan (6 g/day)	clomipramine	1	improved. Relapsed when stopped, better when restarted	open	Rasmussen, 1984[116]
buspirone (dosage = 30 mg)	fluoxetine	1 child	improved	open	Alessi and Bos, 1991[1]
buspirone (dosage = 30 mg)	fluoxetine	11	9 improved at least 25%	open	Markovitz et al, 1990[95]
buspirone (dosage = to 60 mg)	fluoxetine	10 F alone / 10 F + B	F + B did significantly better than F alone ($P < .05$). Of minimal clinical significance	open	Jenike et al, 1991[74]

		N	Results	Trial design	Reference
trazodone	fluoxetine	13	4 improved >20% marked improvement (n = 5) moderate improvement (n = 1)	open	Jenike, 1991[72]
fluoxetine (dosage = 20–40 mg)	clomipramine (dosage = 25–50 mg)	6 adolescents		open	Simeon et al, 1990[125]
CONTROLLED TRIALS					
lithium	fluvoxamine	30	very little improvement	2- or 4-week double-blind placebo-controlled trial	McDougle et al, 1991[99]
lithium	clomipramine	9	none	double-blind crossover with T3	Pigott et al, 1991[112]
L-triiodothyronine (T3)	clomipramine	9	none	double-blind crossover with Li	Pigott et al, 1991[112]
buspirone (approx. 60 mg)	clomipramine	14	4 of 14 (29%) improved at least an additional 25% on buspirone; 3 of 14 (21%) got more than 25% worse	2-week placebo, followed by 10 weeks buspirone	Pigott et al, 1992[111]

in these open trials, not the least of which is the possibility that some of the enhanced improvement may, in fact, be secondary to the patient being on the primary drug for a longer duration of time.

HOW LONG TO TREAT?

Response to any of the antidepressants may take 10 to 12 weeks and patients should be advised that medication trials cannot be evaluated if aborted for lack of efficacy until at least 10 weeks have passed at therapeutic levels. Occasionally patients respond earlier. If two serotonergic antidepressant trials fail or if the patient suffers concomitant panic attacks or severe anxiety, an MAOI trial, *after a 5-week waiting period,* is a reasonable next step. Tranylcypromine, to 60 mg daily, or phenelzine, to 90 mg daily, are the MAOIs most commonly used. Prior to changing any antidepressant medication, as noted previously, it is probably worth trying to augment the response by adding other agents for a 2- to 4-week period. Based on case reports with clomipramine and fluoxetine, this strategy will occasionally yield positive results.

Patients who respond to pharmacotherapy are often reluctant to discontinue medication for fear that their symptoms will return. Our enthusiasm to withdraw patients from medication is tempered by the realization that there are no adequate guidelines about when to stop and which patients are likely to be able to maintain their improvement without medication.

In one study,[36] of 35 OCD patients who discontinued fluoxetine after a good response, only eight (23%) relapsed in the first year of follow-up without medication. However, in the only double-blind, placebo-controlled study to date, Pato and colleagues[108] reported that 16 of 18 (89%) patients had substantial recurrence of obsessive compulsive symptoms by the end of a 7-week placebo period. In addition, 11 had a significant increase in depressive symptoms. Treatment duration before discontinuation of clomipramine was not related to the frequency or severity of obsessive compulsive or depressive symptom reappearance.

It is unclear why these two groups had such drastically different relapse rates. In the Pato et al study, none of the patients had concomitant behavior therapy and clomipramine was tapered very rapidly (over 1 week); there was no mention of concomitant treatments by the other group. Behavior therapy that accompanies pharmacotherapy may not only increase the extent of symptom reduction but may also enhance the persistence of improvement after treatment discontinues. It seems unlikely that patients on clomipramine would be more likely to relapse than those taking fluoxetine, but this is one possible explanation for the differences.

Based on clinical wisdom, many clinicians will attempt to keep significantly symptomatic patients on medication for a full year despite symptom reduction, often at a reduced dosage than was required for acute treatment. Patients should be tapered very gradually, perhaps by as little as 20 mg of fluoxetine or 50 mg of clomipramine every 2 months. While patients are doing well, it is important for them to undergo intensive behavior therapy. These recommendations are based on anecdotal evidence; definitive answers concerning the role of behavior therapy and rate of medication tapering in preventing relapse await further controlled studies.

REFERENCES

1. *Alessi, N., Bos., T.: Buspirone augmentation of fluoxetine in a depressed child with obsessive-compulsive disorder.* Am J Psychiatry *148: 1605–1606, 1991*
2. *Altschuler M.: Massive doses of trifluoperazine in the treatment of compulsive rituals.* Am J Psychiatry *119: 367, 1962*
3. *Ananth J., Pecknold J. C., van den Steen N., et al: Double-blind study of clomipramine and amitriptyline in obsessive neurosis.* Prog Neuropsychopharmacol *5: 257–262, 1981*
4. *Ananth J., Solyom L., Bryntwick S., et al: Clomipramine therapy for obsessive-compulsive neurosis.* Am J Psychiatry *136: 700–720, 1979*
5. *Ananth J., Solyom L., Solyom C., et al: Doxepin in the treatment of obsessive-compulsive neurosis.* Psychosomatics *16: 185–187, 1975*
6. *Angst J., Theobald W.: Tofranil.* Berne, Switzerland, Verlag Stampfl, 1980, pp 11–32
7. *Annesley P. T.: Nardil response in a chronic obsessive compulsive.* Br J Psychiatry *115: 748, 1969*
8. *Ansseau M., Legros J. J., Mormont C., et al: Intranasal oxytocin in obsessive-compulsive disorder.* Psychoneuroendocrinology *12: 231–236, 1987*
9. *Asberg M., Montgomery S. A., Perris C., et al: A comprehensive psychopathological rating scale.* Acta Psychiatr Scand Suppl *271: 5–27, 1978*
10. *Baer L., Jenike M. A., Ricciardi J., et al: Standardized assessment of personality disorders in obsessive-compulsive disorder.* Arch Gen Psychiatry *47: 826–832, 1990*
11. *Baer L., Jenike M. A., Black D. W., et al: Effect of axis II diagnoses on treatment outcome with clomipramine in 54 patients with obsessive-compulsive disorder.* Arch Gen Psychiatry *49: 862–866, 1992*
12. *Baer L., Minichiello W. E., Jenike M. A.: Behavioral treatment of obsessive-compulsive disorder with concomitant bipolar affective disorder.* Am J Psychiatry *142: 358–360, 1985*

13. *Bauer G., Nowak H.: Doxepine: ein neues Antidepressivum Wirkungs-Verleich mit Amitriptyline.* Arzneimittelforschung *19: 1642–1646, 1969*

14. *Baxter L. R.: Two cases of obsessive-compulsive disorder with depression responsive to trazodone.* J Nerv Ment Dis *173: 432–433, 1985*

15. *Beck A. T., Ward C. H., Mendelson M.: An inventory for measuring depression.* Arch Gen Psychiatry *41: 561–571, 1961*

16. *Bethume H. C.: A new compound in the treatment of severe anxiety states: Report on the use of diazepam.* N Engl J Med *63: 513–156, 1964*

17. *Black A.: The natural history of obsessional neurosis. In Beech HR (ed):* Obsessional States. *London, Methuen & Co, 1974*

18. *Bodkin A., White K.: Clonazepam in the treatment of obsessive-compulsive disorder.* J Clin Psychiatry *50: 265–266, 1989*

19. *Breitner C.: Drug therapy in obsessional states and other psychiatric problems.* Dis Nerv Syst *21(suppl): 31–35, 1960*

20. *Bremner J. D.: Fluoxetine in depressed patients: A comparison with imipramine.* J Clin Psychiatry *45: 414–419, 1984*

21. *Brickner R. M., Rosen A. A., Munro R.: Physiological aspects of the obsessive state.* Psychosom Med *2: 369–383, 1940*

22. *Carey R. J., Baer L., Jenike M. A., et al: MMPI correlates of obsessive-compulsive disorder.* J Clin Psychiatry *47: 371–372, 1986*

23. *Chouinard G., Goodman W., Greist J., et al: Results of a double-blind placebo controlled trial using a new serotonin uptake inhibitor, sertraline, in obsessive-compulsive disorder.* Psychopharmacol Bull *26: 279–284, 1991*

24. *Cohen D. J., Detlor J., Young J. G., et al: Clonidine ameliorates Gilles de la Tourette syndrome.* Arch Gen Psychiatry *37: 1350–1357, 1980*

25. *Cole J. O., Hartmann E., Brigham P.: L-Tryptophan: Clinical studies.* McLean Hospital Journal *5: 37–71, 1980*

26. *Coleman B. S., Block B. A.: Fluvoxamine maleate, a serotonergic antidepressant: A comparison with chlorimipramine.* Prog Neuropsychopharmacol Biol Psychiatry *6: 475–478, 1982*

27. DeMontigny C., Grunberg F., Mayer A., et al: *Lithium induces rapid relief of depression in tricyclic antidepressant drug non-responders.* Br J Psychiatry *138: 252–256, 1981*

28. *DeVeaugh-Geiss J., Landau P., Katz R.: Treatment of obsessive-compulsive disorder with clomipramine.* Psychiatric Annals *19: 97–101, 1989*

29. *Epstein A. W., Bailine S. H.: Sleep and dream studies in obsessional neurosis with particular reference to epileptic states.* Biol Psychiatry *3: 149–158, 1971*

30. *Feder R.: Lithium augmentation of clomipramine.* J Clin Psychiatry *49: 458, 1988*

31. *Foa E. B.: Failure in treating obsessive-compulsives.* Behav Res Ther *17: 169–176, 1979*

32. *Foa E. B., Steketee G., Kozak M. J., et al: Effects of imipramine on depression and obsessive-compulsive symptoms.* Psychiatry Res *21: 123–136, 1987*

33. *Foa E. B., Steketee G., Kozak M. J., et al: Imipramine and placebo in the treatment of obsessive-compulsives: Their effect on depression and on obsessional symptoms.* Psychopharmacol Bull *23: 8–11, 1987*

34. *Fontaine R., Chouinard G.: Antiobsessive effect of fluoxetine.* Am J Psychiatry *142: 989, 1985*

35. *Fontaine R., Chouinard G.: An open clinical trail of fluoxetine in the treatment of obsessive-compulsive disorder.* J Clin Psychopharmacol *6: 98–101, 1986*

36. *Fontaine R., Chouinard G.: Fluoxetine in the long-term maintenance treatment of obsessive-compulsive disorder.* Psychiatric Annals *19: 88–91, 1989*

37. *Fontaine R., Chouinard G., Iny L.: An open clinical trial of zimelidine in the treatment of obsessive-compulsive disorder.* Curr Ther Res *37: 326–332, 1985*

38. *Forssman H., Walinder J.: Lithium treatment of atypical indication.* Acta Psychiatr Scand Suppl *207: 34–40, 1969*

39. *Geisler A., Schou M.: Lithium ved tvangsneuroser.* Nord Psychiatr Tidsskr *23: 493–495, 1970*

40. *Geissman P., Kammerer T.: L'imipramine dans la neurose obsessionelle: Etude de 39 cas.* Encephale *53: 369–382, 1964*

41. *Golden R. N., Morris J. E., Sack D. A.: Combined lithium-tricyclic treatment of obsessive-compulsive disorder.* Biol Psychiatry *23: 181–185, 1988*

42. *Goodwin D. W., Guze S. B., Robins E.: Follow-up studies in obsessional neurosis.* Arch Gen Psychiatry *20: 182–187, 1969*

43. *Goodman W. K., Price L. H., Rasmussen S. A., et al: Efficacy of fluvoxamine in obsessive-compulsive disorder: A double-blind comparison with placebo.* Arch Gen Psychiatry *46: 36–44, 1989*

44. *Goodman W. K., Price L. H., Rasmussen S. A., et al: The Yale-Brown Obsessive Compulsive Scale (Y-BOCS): Part I. Development, use, and reliability. Part II. Validity.* Arch Gen Psychiatry *46: 1006–1018, 1989*

45. *Greist J. H., Jefferson J. W., Rosenfeld R., et al: Clomipramine and obsessive-compulsive disorder: A placebo-controlled double-blind study in 32 patients.* J Clin Psychiatry *51: 292–297, 1990*

46. *Goodman W. K., Price L. P., Anderson G. M., et al: Drug response and obsessive-compulsive disorder subtypes.* APA Symposium, May 8, 1989, American Psychiatric Association Meetings, San Francisco, CA

47. *Gross M., Slater E., Roth M. (eds):* Clinical Psychiatry. *Bailliere Tindall and Casel, 1969*

48. *Guelfi J. D., Dreyfus J. F., Pichot P.: A double-blind controlled clinical trial comparing fluvoxamine with imipramine.* Br J Clin Pharmacol *15: 411S–417S, 1983*

49. *Guy W., Wilson S. H., Ban T. A., et al: A double-blind clinical trial of fluvoxamine and imipramine in patients with primary depression.* Drug Dev Res *4: 143–153, 1984*

50. *Hermesh H., Aizenberg D., Munitz H.: Trazodone treatment in clomipramine-resistant obsessive-compulsive disorder.* Clin Neuropharmacology *13: 322–328, 1990*

51. *Hill A., Mitchell W.: Epileptic amnesia.* Folia Psychiatr Neurol Jpn *56: 718, 1953*

52. *Hollander E., DeCaria C. M., Schneider F. R., et al: Fenfluramine augmentation of serotonin reuptake blockade antiobsessional treatment.* J Clin Psychiatry *51: 119–123, 1990*

53. *Hollander E., Fay M., Cohen B., et al: Serotonergic and noradrenergic sensitivity*

in obsessive-compulsive disorder: Behavioral findings. Am J Psychiatry *145: 1015–1017, 1988*

54. Hollander E., Fay M., Liebowitz M. R.: *Clonidine and clomipramine in obsessive-compulsive disorder.* Am J Psychiatry *145: 388–389, 1988*

55. Hollander E., Liebowitz M. R.: *Augmentation of antiobsessional treatment with fenfluramine.* Am J Psychiatry *145: 1314–1315, 1988*

56. Hussain M. Z., Ahad A.: *Treatment of obsessive-compulsive neurosis.* Can Med Assoc J *103: 648–650, 1970*

57. Insel T. R. (ed): New Findings in Obsessive-Compulsive Disorder. *Washington, DC, APA Press, 1984*

58. Insel T. R., Hamilton J., Guttmacher L., et al: *d-Amphetamine in obsessive compulsive disorder.* Psychopharmacology *80: 231–235, 1983*

59. Insel T. R., Murphy D. L., Cohen R. M., et al: *Obsessive-compulsive disorder. A double-blind trial of clomipramine and clorgyline.* Arch Gen Psychiatry *40: 605–612, 1983*

60. Insel T. R., Pickar D.: *Naloxone administration in obsessive-compulsive disorder: Report of two cases.* Am J Psychiatry *140: 1219–1220, 1983*

61. Insel T. R., Roy B. F., Cohen R. M., et al: *Possible development of the serotonin syndrome in man.* Am J Psychiatry *139: 954–955, 1982*

62. Itil T. M., Shrivastava R. K., Mukherjee S., et al: *A double-blind placebo-controlled study of fluvoxamine and imipramine in out-patients with primary depression.* Br J Clin Pharmacol *15: 433S–438S, 1983*

63. Jain V. K., Swinson R. P., Thomas J. E.: *Phenelzine in obsessional neurosis.* Br J Psychiatry *117: 237–238, 1970*

64. Jenike M. A.: *Rapid response of severe obsessive-compulsive disorder to tranylcypromine.* Am J Psychiatry *138: 1249–1250, 1981*

65. Jenike M. A.: *Use of monoamine oxidase inhibitors in obsessive-compulsive disorder.* Br J Psychiatry *140: 159, 1982*

66. Jenike M. A.: *Obsessive-compulsive disorder: A question of a neurologic lesion.* Compr Psychiatry *25: 298–304, 1984*

67. Jenike M. A.: *Somatic Treatments. In Jenike M. A., Baer L., Minichiello W. E. (eds):* Obsessive Compulsive Disorders: Theory and Management. *Littleton, MA, PSG Publishing Co., 1986*

68. Jenike M. A.: *Obsessive-compulsive and related disorders: A hidden epidemic.* N Engl J Med *321: 539–541, 1989*

69. Jenike M. A.: *Drug treatment of obsessive-compulsive disorders In Jenike M. A., Baer L., Minichiello W. E. (eds):* Obsessive Compulsive Disorders: Theory and Management, *ed 2. Chicago, Mosby Yearbook Medical Publishing, 1990, pp 249–282*

70. Jenike M. A.: *Psychotherapy of the patient with obsessive-compulsive personality disorder. In Jenike M. A., Baer L., Minichiello W. E. (eds):* Obsessive Compulsive Disorders: Theory and Management, *ed 2. Chicago, Mosby Year Book, 1990*

71. Jenike M. A.: *Approaches to the patient with treatment-refractory obsessive-compulsive disorder.* J Clin Psychiatry *51(suppl 2): 15–21, 1990*

72. Jenike M. A.: *Management of patients with treatment-resistant obsessive-compulsive disorder. In Pato M. T., Zohar J (eds):* Obsessive-Compulsive Disorders. *Washington, DC, APA Press, 1991, pp 135–156*

73. *Jenike M. A., Baer L.: Buspirone in obsessive-compulsive disorder: An open trial.* Am J Psychiatry *145: 1285–1286, 1988*

74. *Jenike M. A., Baer L., Buttolph L.: Buspirone augmentation of fluoxetine in patients with obsessive-compulsive disorder.* J Clin Psychiatry *1: 13–14, 1991*

75. *Jenike M. A., Baer L., Minichiello W. E., et al: Concomitant obsessive-compulsive disorder and schizotypal personality disorder.* Am J Psychiatry *143: 530–533, 1986*

76. *Jenike M. A., Baer L., Minichiello W. E., et al: Concomitant obsessive-compulsive disorder and schizotypal personality disorder: A poor prognostic indicator.* Arch Gen Psychiatry *43: 296, 1986*

77. *Jenike M. A., Baer L., Minichiello W. E.:* Obsessive-Compulsive Disorders: Theory and Management, *ed 2. Chicago, Mosby Year Book, 1990*

78. *Jenike M. A., Baer L., Summergrad P., et al: Obsessive-compulsive disorder: A double-blind, placebo-controlled trial of clomipramine in 27 patients.* Am J Psychiatry *146: 1328–1330, 1989*

79. *Jenike M. A., Baer L., Summergrad P., et al: Sertraline in obsessive-compulsive disorder: A double-blind comparison with placebo.* Am J Psychiatry *147: 923–928, 1990*

80. *Jenike M. A., Brotman A. W.: The EEG in obsessive compulsive disorder.* J Clin Psychiatry *45: 122–124, 1984*

81. *Jenike M. A., Buttolph L., Baer L., et al: Fluoxetine in obsessive-compulsive disorder: A positive open trial.* Am J Psychiatry *146: 909–911, 1989*

82. *Jenike M. A., Hyman S. E., Baer L., et al: A controlled trial of fluvoxamine for obsessive-compulsive disorder: Implications for a serotonergic theory.* Am J Psychiatry *147: 1209–1215, 1990*

83. *Jenike M. A., Surman O. S., Cassem N. H., et al: Monoamine oxidase inhibitors in obsessive-compulsive disorder.* J Clin Psychiatry *44: 131–132, 1983*

84. *Joel S. W.: Twenty month study of iproniazid therapy.* Dis Nerv Syst *20: 1–4, 1959*

85. *Joffe R. T., Swinson R. P.: Carbamazepine in obsessive-compulsive disorder.* Biol Psychiatry *22: 1169–1171, 1987*

86. *Kahn, R. S., Westenberg H. G. M., Jolles J.: Zimelidine treatment of obsessive-compulsive disorder.* Acta Psychiatr Scand *69: 259–261, 1984*

87. *Kendell R. E., Discipio W. J.: Obsessional symptoms and obsessional personality traits in patients with depressive illness.* Psychol Med *1: 65–72, 1970*

88. *Khanna S: Carbamazepine in obsessive-compulsive disorder.* Clin Neuropharmacol *11: 478–481, 1988*

89. *Kim S. W.: Trazodone in the treatment of obsessive-compulsive disorder: A case report.* J Clin Psychopharmacol *7: 278–279, 1987*

90. *Knesevich J. W.: Successful treatment of obsessive-compulsive disorder.* J Clin Psychopharmacol *7: 278–279, 1982*

91. *Lader M., Wing L.: Physiological measures in agitated and retarded depressed patients.* J Psychiatr Res *7: 89–100, 1969*

92. *Lipsedge M. S., Prothero W.: Clonidine and clomipramine in obsessive-compulsive disorder [Letter].* Am J Psychiatry *144: 965–966, 1987*

93. *Lopez-Ibor J. J.: Intravenous infusions of monochlorimipramine. Technique and results. In* Proceedings of the Sixth International Congress of the CINP, *Taragona,*

334   MICHAEL A. JENIKE

Spain, April 1968. Exerpta Medica Foundation Int Congress Series No. 180. Amsterdam, pp 519–521, 1969
94. Lydiard R. B.: Obsessive-compulsive disorder successfully treated with trazodone. Psychosomatics 27: 858–859, 1986
95. Markovitz P. J., Stagno S. J., Calabrese J. R.: Buspirone augmentation of fluoxetine on obsessive-compulsive disorder. Am J Psychiatry 147: 798–800, 1990
96. Marks I. M.: Review of behavioral psychotherapy. I: Obsessive-compulsive disorders. Am J Psychiatry 138: 584–592, 1981
97. Marks I. M., Stern R. S., Mawson D., et al: Clomipramine and exposure for obsessive-compulsive rituals. Br J Psychiatry 136: 1–25, 1980
98. McDougle C. J., Goodman W. K., Price L. H., et al: Neuroleptic addition in fluvoxamine-refractory obsessive-compulsive disorder: An open case series. Am J Psychiatry 147: 552–554, 1990
99. McDougle C. J., Price L. H., Goodman W. K., et al: A controlled trial of lithium augmentation in fluvoxamine-refractory obsessive-compulsive disorder: Lack of efficacy. J Clin Psychopharmacol 11: 175–184, 1991
100. McElroy S. L., Keck P. E., Pope H. G.: Sodium valproate: Its use in primary psychiatric disorders. J Clin Psychopharmacol 7: 16–24, 1987
101. McElroy S. L., Pope H. G. (eds): Use of anticonvulsants in psychiatry: Recent advances. Clifton, NJ, Oxford Health Care, 1988
102. Minichiello W. E., Baer L., Jenike M. A.: Schizotypal personality disorder: A poor prognostic indicator for behavior therapy in the treatment of obsessive-compulsive disorder. J Anxiety Dis 1: 273–276, 1987
103. Monteiro W. O., Noshirvani H. F., Marks I. M., et al: Anorgasmia from clomipramine in obsessive-compulsive disorder: A controlled trial. Br J Psychiatry 151: 107–112, 1987
104. Montgomery S. A.: Clomipramine in obsessional neurosis: A placebo controlled trial. Pharmacol Med 1: 189–192, 1980
105. Orvin G. H.: Treatment of the phobic obsessive-compulsive patient with oxazepam, an improved benzodiazepine compound. Psychosomatics 8: 278–280, 1967
106. Pacella B. L., Polantin P., Nagler S. H.: Clinical and EEG studies in obsessive compulsive states. Am J Psychiatry 100: 830–838, 1944
107. Pato M. T., Pigott T. A., Hill J. L., et al: Clomipramine versus buspirone in OCD: A controlled trial. New Research Symposium. May 8, 1989. American Psychiatric Association Meeting, San Francisco, CA
108. Pato M. T., Zohar-Kadouch R., Zohar J., et al: Return of symptoms after discontinuation of clomipramine in patients with obsessive-compulsive disorder. Am J Psychiatry 145: 1521–1525, 1988
109. Perse T. L., Greist J. H., Jefferson J. W., et al: Fluvoxamine treatment of obsessive-compulsive disorder. Am J Psychiatry 144: 1543–1548, 1987
110. Pickar D., Cohen M. R., Naber D., et al: Clinical studies of the endogenous opioid system. Biol Psychiatry 17: 1243–1276, 1982
111. Pigott T. A., L'Heureux F., Hill J. L., et al.: A double-blind study of adjuvant buspirone hydrochloride in clomipramine-treated patients with obsessive-compulsive disorder. J Clin Psychopharmacol 12: 11–18, 1992
112. Pigott T. A., Pato M. T., L'Heureux F., et al: A controlled comparison of adjuvant

lithium carbonate or thyroid hormone in clomipramine-treated patients with obsessive-compulsive disorder. J Clin Psychopharmacol *11: 242–248, 1991*

113. *Prasad A. J.: Obsessive-compulsive disorder and trazodone.* Am J Psychiatry *141: 612–613, 1984*

114. *Prasad A.: Efficacy of trazodone as an antiobsessional agent.* Pharmacol Biochem Behav *22: 347–348, 1985*

115. *Price L. H., Goodman W. K., Charney D. S., et al: Treatment of severe obsessive-compulsive disorder with fluvoxamine.* Am J Psychiatry *144: 1059–1061, 1987*

116. *Rasmussen S. A.: Lithium and tryptophan augmentation in clomipramine-resistant obsessive-compulsive disorder.* Am J Psychiatry *141: 1283–1285, 1984*

117. *Rasmussen S. A., Goodman W. K., Woods S. W., et al: Effects of yohimbine in obsessive-compulsive disorder.* Psychopharmacology *93: 308–313, 1987*

118. *Rasmussen S. A., Tsuang M. T.: Epidemiology and clinical features of obsessive-compulsive disorder. In Jenike M. A., Baer L., Minichiello W. E. (eds):* Obsessive Compulsive Disorders: Theory and Management. *Littleton, MA, PSG Publishing, 1986, pp 23–44*

119. *Rihmer Z., Szantok, Arato M., et al: Response of phobic disorders with obsessive symptoms to MAO inhibitors.* Am J Psychiatry *139: 1374, 1982*

120. *Rivers-Buckeley N., Hollender M. H.: Successful treatment of obsessive-compulsive disorder with loxapine.* Am J Psychiatry *139: 1345–1346, 1982*

121. *Salzman L.: Obsessional Personality. New York, Science House, 1969*

122. *Sandyk R.: Naloxone abolishes obsessive-compulsive behavior in Tourette's syndrome.* Int J Neurosci *35: 93–94, 1987*

123. *Segal D. S., Brown R. G., Arnsten A., et al: Characteristics of beta endorphin-induced behavioral activation and immobilization. In Usdin E., Bunney Jr W. E., Kline N. S. (eds):* Endorphins in Mental Health Research. *New York, Oxford University Press, 1979*

124. *Sewell R. D. E., Lee R. L.: Opiate receptors, endorphins, and drug therapy.* Postgrad Med *56 (suppl 1): 2530, 1980*

125. *Simeon J. G., Thatte S., Wiggins D.: Treatment of adolescent obsessive-compulsive disorder with a clomipramine-fluoxetine combination.* Psychopharm Bull *26: 285–290, 1990*

126. *Snyder, S: Amitriptyline therapy of obsessive-compulsive neurosis.* J Clin Psychiatry *41: 286–289, 1980*

127. *Steiner W., Fontaine R: Toxic reaction following the combined administration of fluoxetine and L-tryptophan: Five case reports.* Biol Psychiatry *21: 1067–1071, 1986*

128. *Stern T. A., Jenike M. A.: Treatment of obsessive-compulsive disorder with lithium carbonate.* Psychosomatics *24: 671–673, 1983*

129. *Stroebel C. F., Szarek B. L., Glueck B. C.: Use of clomipramine in treatment of obsessive-compulsive symptomatology.* J Clin Psychopharmacol *4: 98–100, 1984*

130. *Swinson R. P.: Response to tranylcypromine and thought stopping in obsessional disorder.* Br J Psychiatry *144: 425–427, 1984*

131. *Tesar G. E., Jenike M. A.: Alprazolam as treatment for a case of obsessive-compulsive disorder.* Am J Psychiatry *141: 689–690, 1984*

132. *The Clomipramine Collaborative Study Group. Efficacy of clomipramine in*

OCD: Results of a multicenter double-blind trial. Arch Gen Psychiatry *48: 730–738, 1991*

133. Thoren P., Asberg M., Cronholm B., et al: *Clomipramine treatment of obsessive-compulsive disorder. I. A controlled clinical trial.* Arch Gen Psychiatry 37: 1281–1285, 1980

134. Thoren P., Asberg M., Cronholm B., et al: *Clomipramine treatment of obsessive-compulsive disorder. II. Biochemical aspects.* Arch Gen Psychiatry *37: 1286–1294, 1980*

135. Tollefson G: *Alprazolam in the treatment of obsessive symptoms.* J Clin Psychopharmacol *5: 39–42, 1985*

136. Turner S. M., Hersen M., Bellack A. S., et al: *Behavioral and pharmacological treatment of obsessive-compulsive disorders.* J Nerv Ment Dis *168: 651–657, 1980*

137. Turner S. M., Jacob R. G., Beidel D. C., et al: *Fluoxetine treatment of obsessive compulsive disorder.* J Clin Psychopharmacol *5: 207–212, 1985*

138. Van Putten T., Sander D. G.: *Lithium in treatment failures.* J Nerv Ment Dis *161: 255–264, 1975*

139. Vangaard T.: *Atypical endogenous depression.* Acta Psychiatr Scand Suppl *267: 5–56, 1976*

140. Venkoba Rao A.: *A controlled trial with Valium in obsessive-compulsive states.* J Indian Med Assoc *42: 564–567, 1964*

141. Walinder J., Skott A., Carlsson A., et al: *Potentiation of the antidepressant action of clomipramine by tryptophan.* Arch Gen Psychiatry *33: 1384–1389, 1976*

142. Watts V. S., Neill J. R.: *Buspirone in obsessive-compulsive disorder.* Am J Psychiatry *145: 1606, 1988*

143. White K., Cole J.: *Pharmacotherapy.* In Bellack A. S., Hersen M. (eds): Handbook of Comparative Treatments. New York, John Wiley & Sons, 1990, pp 266–284

144. White K., Keck P. E., Lipinski J.: *Serotonin-uptake inhibitors in obsessive-compulsive disorder: A case report.* Compr Psychiatry *27: 211–214, 1986*

145. Yaryura-Tobias J. A.: *Tryptophan may be adjuvant to obsessive-compulsive therapy.* Clin Psychiatr News, September 1981, p 16

146. Yaryura-Tobias J. A., Bhagavan H. N.: *L-Tryptophan in obsessive-compulsive disorders.* Am J Psychiatry *134: 1298–1299, 1977*

147. Yaryura-Tobias J. A., Neziroglu M. S., Bhagavan H.: *Obsessive-compulsive disorders: A serotonergic hypothesis.* In Saletu B., Berner P., Hollister L. (eds): Neuropsychopharmacology: Proceedings of the 11th Congress of the CINP, Oxford, England, Pergamon Press, 1979 pp 117–125

18. Caudate Glucose Metabolic Rate Changes with Both Drug and Behavior Therapy for Obsessive-Compulsive Disorder

Lewis R. Baxter, Jr., Jeffrey M. Schwartz, Kenneth S. Bergman, Martin P. Szuba, Barry H. Guze, John C. Mazziotta, Adina Alazraki, Carl E. Selin, Huan-Kwang Ferng, Paul Munford, and Michael E. Phelps

OBSESSIVE-COMPULSIVE DISORDER [1] (OCD) is characterized by recurrent, unwanted thoughts (obsessions) and conscious, ritualized acts (compulsions) usually attributed to attempts to deal with anxiety generated by the obsessions. There is now ample evidence that both medications that are strong serotonin re-uptake inhibitors [2] and specific behavioral therapies that employ the principles of exposure and response-prevention [3] are highly effective in reducing the symptoms of OCD, although the latter may be more effective for compulsions than for obsessions. Based on a wide variety of evidence, many investigators have postulated a role for the basal ganglia, along with limbic, thalamic, and cortical brain regions, in the mediation of OCD symptoms.[4–11] We postulated previously that the head of the caudate nucleus plays a central role in OCD symptom mediation and that successful treatment of OCD by either medication or behavior therapy would be accompanied by a change in caudate nucleus function that might be detected with positron emission tomography (PET) and the 18-F-fluorodeoxyglucose (fludeoxyglucose F 18 [FDG]) method.[5,8] Cerebral glucose metabolism is a sensitive indicator of brain function.[12]

We decided, therefore, to study OCD patients with FDG-PET before and after either drug or behavior therapy. We chose fluoxetine hydrochloride as our treatment drug,[13–15] knowing a similar study was in progress using clomipramine hydrochloride.[16]

Reprinted by permission of the American Medical Association from *Archives of General Psychiatry* 49 (1992): 681–89.

PATIENTS, SUBJECTS, AND METHODS

This study was conducted in accordance with guidelines established by the UCLA Human Subjects' Protection Committee.

Patients

There were initially 10 patients with OCD in each of the two treatment groups, but a computer failure led to the loss of data for the initial scan of one subject in each group. The nine subjects remaining in each treatment group are included in the analyses reported herein.

All patients were clinical outpatients and/or inpatients in the UCLA Neuropsychiatric Hospital Mood and Anxiety Disorders Treatment Program who were asked to undergo PET scanning before and after the clinical treatment they elected (after a careful discussion of all available treatment options), which was either fluoxetine hydrochloride or behavior therapy without drugs. All had a current primary diagnosis of *DSM-III-R* OCD which had been present for at least 1 year. Diagnoses for each patient were made based on both a nonstructured psychiatric interview and the Schedule for Affective Disorders and Schizophrenia–Lifetime version (SADS-L).[17] All patients were drug free for at least 2 weeks before their initial PET scan.

Table 18.1. Characteristics of OCD Patients by Treatment Group*

	Populations	
	Drug treatment	Behavior treatment
No.	9	9
No. drug free	9	9
Age, y	31.2 ± 12.9	34.7 ± 6.0
Sex, M/F	3/6	4/5
No. R-handed	8	8
Y-BOCS		
Total	24.9 ± 3.6	23.9 ± 5.5
Obsessive (items 1–5)	12.7 ± 2.3	12.0 ± 3.8
Compulsive (items 6–10)	12.2 ± 1.6	11.9 ± 2.9
HAM-D	10.4 ± 5.4	7.8 ± 5.7
HAM-A	26.6 ± 9.7	22.8 ± 7.4
GAS	57.8 ± 9.7	59.1 ± 8.6

*OCD indicates obsessive-compulsive disorder; Y-BOCS, Yale-Brown Obsessive-Compulsive Scale; HAM-D, Hamilton Depression Rating Scale; HAM-A, Hamilton Anxiety Rating Scale; and GAS, Global Assessment Scale. Values are numbers or means ± SDs.

In the drug treatment group, there were concomitant diagnosis of cyclothymic disorder, panic disorder, Tourette's disorder (mild), and social phobia in one subject each. In the behavior therapy group, there were concomitant diagnoses of cyclothymic disorder, panic disorder, and acrophobia in one subject each. Many patients in each group had had major depression in the past, but all were euthymic now, as determined by both clinical assessment and the SADS-L. All patients denied substance abuse; we did not do urine drug screens. Patient demographics and rating scale scores are given in Table 18.1.

Normal Control Subjects

Subsequent to analyses of patient PET data, a small group of normal control subjects were collected for comparison. These were two men and two women with a mean ($\pm$SD) age of 29 ± 8 years who were judged to be healthy by history and recent physical examination. None had any personal or family history of an *DSM-III* Axis I disorder. All were drug free by history for at least 1 month before initial PET scanning. They were rescanned 10 ± 2 weeks after initial scanning.

Symptom Severity Ratings

Subject behaviors were rated with the Yale-Brown Obsessive-Compulsive Scale[18,19] (Y-BOCS), the 17-item Hamilton Depression Rating Scale[20] (HAM-D), the Hamilton Anxiety Rating Scale[21] (HAM-A), and the Global Assessment Scale[17] (GAS) at the time of each PET scan. Responders to treatment were defined a priori as those who were rated as either "much improved" or "very much improved" on item 18 of the Y-BOCS (which is taken from the Clinical Global Impression Scale) at the time of the second PET scan. Nonresponders were those who scored "no change" or "minimally improved" on the same item.

Treatments

Drug treatment.

Patients in this group were treated with oral fluoxetine hydrochloride, started at 20 mg/d and titrated within 2 weeks to 60 to 80 mg/d, as tolerated, before the second PET scan was obtained. This is our standard clinical treatment for OCD with this drug. All patients enrolled in drug treatment were able to attain this dosage range with minimal side effects and stay on it for the duration of the study. No other drugs were used, and patients were not in behavior therapy or formal psychotherapy. If they asked about how they should respond to obsessions and compulsive urges, these patients were advised to see if they could refrain from these behaviors, as comfort permitted, if they wished. All did receive supportive advice from their treaters (L.R.B., M.P.S., and J.M.S.), with whom they met once or twice a week.

Behavior therapy.

These patients elected to have behavior therapy consisting of exposure and response-prevention, which was individualized for the patient. Exposure and response-prevention exercises were facilitated by cognitive techniques.[22] Patients met once or twice a week with their therapist (J.M.S., K.S.B., or L.R.B.) for approximately 1 hour to review assignments for exposure and response-prevention, which they did as homework and self-monitored with diaries and/or graphs. Homework was reviewed and evaluated with therapists at the next meeting. Some had occasional therapist-aided exposure and response-prevention sessions. Six also attended a cognitive-behavioral therapy group for patients with OCD run by one of us (J.M.S.). None took any psychoactive medications during the study. All received supportive advice from their individual treaters.

All patients had 10 ± 2 weeks of the therapy they elected before undergoing a second PET scan. Those treated with behavior therapy abstained from medications from the first through the second scan, while those having drug treatment were all on fluoxetine at the time the second scan, with the last dose given the day before scanning.

PET Methods

All subjects were injected with FDG while in the supine position in a room with no conversation, low ambient light, and environmental noise (mostly from the scanner gantry), as previously described.[23] The subjects' ears and eyes were open, and they were instructed to look at the diffusely lit white ceiling above the tomograph. Each subject received 185 to 370 mBq (5 to 10 mCi) of FDG, prepared as previously described.[24] "Arterialized" venous blood was obtained by having the subject's hand in a hand warmer. Blood sampling and determinations of plasma glucose and FDG concentrations have been described in detail previously.[25,26]

Scanning was performed with a PET tomograph (831 Neuro ECAT III, Seimens-CTI, Knoxville, Tenn). Fifteen transverse sections of the brain, spaced 6.75 mm apart, were acquired simultaneously at an angle parallel to the canthomeatal plane. Each subject's head was held in a special head holder[27] during scanning to allow accurate positioning using the low-power laser marker of the tomograph.

Before injection of the tracer, a 2-minute transmission scan with radiation from a germanium Ge 68 (^{68}Ge) ring source was performed to obtain similar planes for intersubject comparisons and to allow accurate repositioning for follow-up scans done after treatment. Next, data for measured attenuation correction were obtained by means of a 20-minute transmission scan using the ring source. Emission scanning commenced 60 minutes after injection of FDG. Total imaging time was 40 minutes, and each image was reconstructed from 2 million to 3 million counts. 18-F-Fluorodeoxyglucose was injected between 10:00 and 15:00. Images were reconstructed by filtered back-projection using of a Shepp filter with a cutoff of 0.6 of the Nyqvist frequency (0.95 cycles/cm). The in-plane resolution used in these studies was 6×6 mm, and the axial resolution was 6.75 mm.[28]

Images were displayed on a video display (SuperMac Technology, Sunnyvale, Calif) in a 256×256 pixel display, with a black-on-white format. Neuroanatomic regions of interest (ROIs) were identified in all tomographic planes in which they occurred, and the glucose metabolic rates were determined as described previously (rate constants used for gray-matter metabolic rate determinations were $k_1 = 0.102$, $k_2 = 0.13$, $k_3 = 0.062$, $k_4 = 0.0068$,[26] and the lumped constant was 0.52[29,30]).[25,26,31] To accomplish this, each scan was compared with template sets obtained from normal anatomic and PET studies with the same tomograph. The size and site of the ROI were then copied from these templates in a standardized fashion appropriate to the individual brain at hand, as previously described.[32] For patients, this was done by one of us (A.A.), who was blind to subject identity, diagnosis, scan sequence, and the hypothesis being tested. Patient scans were scattered among 85 from a variety of studies being processed at the same time. Supratentorial hemispheric values were obtained in a similar fashion and included ventricles. The scans of control subjects analyzed subsequently had their ROIs defined by a technician who was also blind to scan sequence and the hypothesis being tested. For each subject, an average local glucose metabolic rate value (LCMRG1c) was determined for each structure by weighing that structure's planar metabolic value by its cross-sectional area using the following formula:

$$LCMRGlc = \sum_{i=1}^{N} (MR)_i A_i / \sum_{i=1}^{N} A_i$$

where N indicates the number of planes that include the structure, A_i indicates the cross-sectional area of the structure in plane i, and MR_i indicates the metabolic rate of the structure in plane i. The LCMRG1c is expressed in milligrams of glucose used per 100 g of brain tissue per minute. LCMRG1c for each ROI was "normalized" by dividing the LCMRG1c of that region by that of the ipsilateral cerebral hemisphere (ROI/hem), which yielded a dimensionless ratio. Using this metabolic ratio, rather than absolute values, reduces the variance in the resultant data set and gives a measure of activity relative to that in the rest of the hemisphere.

Statistical Analyses

All results are presented as the mean $\pm$ SD. We had made a clear a priori prediction that metabolic rates in the caudate nuclei, normalized to the ipsilateral hemisphere (Cd/hem), would differ significantly before and after treatment for responders to both drug and behavior therapy. In addition, the degree of change in responders would show significantly more change in Cd/hem than in nonresponders or controls, in whom change would not occur after a similar time interval. This was our primary hypothesis.

Statistical comparisons for parametric measures (eg, ROI/hem values) were made with the paired t test for data from the same individual at the two times of scanning. Student's t test was used for comparisons between groups. However, because of low subject numbers and concerns about normal distributions, we also performed the nonparametric Wilcoxon test on critical results that were significant by Student's t test, and the Wilcoxon Signed-Rank test for similar intrasubject evaluations. The report by Benkelfat et al[16] and doubts about our previous report[5] concerning direction of caudate metabolic nucleus change after an unconventional drug treatment of depressed OCD patients (see below) led us to use two-tailed statistical tests to identify a difference, regardless of direction, in Cd/hem values before and after successful treatment.

We also examined the orbital gyrus/hem, putamen/hem, anterior cingulate gyrus/hem, and thalamus/hem, given the findings and theories of others,[6,7,16,33,34] as secondary hypotheses. No corrections were made for multiple tests. Other brain ROIs (anterolateral prefrontal cortex, sensory-motor region, parietal cortex, lateral temporal lobes, hippocampus–parahippocampal gyrus complex, amygdaloid nuclei complex, and cerebellar hemispheres), available for analysis as part of the ROI protocol for scans from the various studies undergoing processing at the time, were examined in an a posteriori survey, with no corrections made for multiple tests.

For comparisons among more than two groups, the nonparametric Kruskal-Wallis analysis of variance was used, since normal distributions and equal variances did not obtain. Post hoc Wilcoxon tests were used to distinguish between relevant pairings of OCD treatment responders and normal controls.

The nonparametric Kendall's τ, with a correction for tied values, was used for rank-order correlations between percentage change in the nonparametric behavioral rating scale scores and percentage change in normalized regional metabolic rates. (The Kendall τ is valid with $n \geq 8$.[35]) The τ was also used for parametric data (metabolic rates), because normal distributions, as determined by visual inspection of frequency histograms, did not obtain for many brain regions.

RESULTS

Drug-treated patients underwent their second PET scanning after 10.5 ± 1.3 weeks of treatment; patients undergoing behavior therapy did so after 10.8 ± 1.1 weeks. Normal control subjects were rescanned after 9.8 ± 1.3 weeks.

Seven of the drug-treated patients and six of the behavior therapy patients were judged to be responders by the preestablished criterion; the rest were nonresponders. Rating scale scores before and after treatment for these groups are presented in Table 18.2. Although not the determinant of response here, there was no overlap between responders and nonresponders in percentage change in the total Y-BOCS score before and after treatment: responders decreased scores by 30% or more and nonresponders by less than 30%, comparable with the differences between responders and nonresponders on the Y-BOCS in other studies.[36]

Table 18.3 presents pretreatment and posttreatment ROI/hem values obtained in those patients judged treatment responders for the brain regions postulated on a primary and secondary a priori basis. Whole-hemisphere LCMRG1c values did not change significantly from before to after treatment in either group of responders (percent change in drug treatment group: left hemisphere, $9.2\% \pm 63.8\%$ [$t = .32$, $df = 6$, $P =$ not significant]; right hemi-

Table 18.2. OCD Patient Treatment Response *

| | Treatment response by group† | | | | | |
| | Drug treatment | | | Behavior treatment | | |
	Pretreatment score	Posttreatment score	P	Pretreatment score	Posttreatment score	P
	Responders					
Y-BOCS						
Total	25.8 ± 3.7	13.0 ± 2.9	.02	22.3 ± 4.1	13.5 ± 4.0	.04
Obsessive (items 1–5)	13.3 ± 2.2	6.6 ± 1.5	.02	11.3 ± 3.6	7.0 ± 2.3	.22
Compulsive (items 6–10)	12.5 ± 1.7	6.4 ± 1.7	.02	11.0 ± 2.4	6.5 ± 2.7	.04
HAM-D	10.3 ± 3.2	5.6 ± 2.2	.04	5.5 ± 3.3	5.2 ± 3.1	NS
HAM-A	24.2 ± 4.2	20.1 ± 4.3	NS	20.2 ± 4.3	18.3 ± 4.4	NS
GAS	57.5 ± 7.7	68.2 ± 6.9	NS	60.0 ± 9.6	71.8 ± 4.8	NS
	Nonresponders					
Y-BOCS						
Total	24.0 ± 2.0	19.5 ± 0.5	NS	27.0 ± 5.7	22.0 ± 4.9	NS
Obsessive (items 1–5)	12.0 ± 2.0	8.5 ± 0.5	NS	13.3 ± 3.1	11.3 ± 2.6	NS
Compulsive (items 6–10)	12.0 ± 0.0	11.0 ± 1.0	NS	13.7 ± 2.6	10.7 ± 2.6	NS
HAM-D	10.0 ± 9.0	5.5 ± 2.2	NS	12.3 ± 5.8	5.3 ± 4.1	NS
HAM-A	32.5 ± 16.5	19.5 ± 3.5	NS	28.0 ± 8.2	21.7 ± 4.6	NS
GAS	56.0 ± 13.0	59.0 ± 11.0	NS	57.3 ± 3.3	58.7 ± 6.3	NS

* OCD indicates obsessive-compulsive disorder.
† In the drug treatment group, seven of nine subjects were responders and two of nine were nonresponders; in the behavior treatment group, six of nine subjects were responders and three of nine were nonresponders. Values are means ± SDs. See Table 1 for expansion of abbreviations. NS indicates not significant.

sphere, $12.1\% \pm 69.45$ [$t = .39$, $df = 6$, $P =$ not significant]; percent change in behavior therapy group: left hemisphere, $11.6\% \pm 16.9\%$ [$t = 1.54$, $df = 5$, $P =$ not significant]; right hemisphere: $14.1\% \pm 18.3\%$ [$t = 1.73$, $df = 5$, $P =$ not significant]).

Although right anterior cingulate gyrus/hem and left thalamus/hem showed significant changes with successful drug treatment, only the head of the right caudate nucleus showed a significant change with both successful drug and behavior therapies—values decreased. While responders changed right caudate nucleus ratios $-5.2\% \pm 2.3\%$ for drug treatment and $-8.0\% \pm 4.8\%$ for behavior therapy, nonresponders changed only $0.3\% \pm 1.0\%$ ($P =$ not significant) and $2.6\% \pm 3.2\%$ ($P =$ not significant), respectively. Normal controls changed only $0.4\% \pm 2.0\%$ ($P =$ not significant). Individual subject values for percentage change in right Cd/hem are represented in Fig. 18.1. The Kruskal-Wallis analysis of variance, applied to right Cd/hem among all groups, was significant (Kruskal-Wallis test statistic, 14.17; $P = .007$). Differences between responders and nonresponders were significant for both drug treat-

Table 18.3. Responders to Treatment,* Pretreatment and Posttreatment Normalized Glucose Metabolic Rate† Values for Brain Regions of Interest‡

Site	Drug treatment ($df=6$)				Behavior treatment ($df=5$)			
	Pretreatment	Posttreatment	t	P	Pretreatment	Posttreatment	t	P
R head of caudate nucleus	1.23 ± 0.08	1.17 ± 0.10	5.81	.001§	1.28 ± 0.12	1.18 ± 0.15	4.12	.009‖
L head of caudate nucleus	1.10 ± 0.09	1.08 ± 0.09	1.07	.33	1.14 ± 0.13	1.10 ± 0.13	1.41	.20
R putamen	1.38 ± 0.08	1.38 ± 0.10	0.06	.96	1.44 ± 0.12	1.42 ± 0.16	0.56	.60
L putamen	1.33 ± 0.09	1.37 ± 0.10	1.21	.27	1.46 ± 0.15	1.40 ± 0.14	2.24	.08
R anterior cingulate gyrus	1.20 ± 0.05	1.14 ± 0.06	2.89	.03	1.18 ± 0.07	1.18 ± 0.05	0.01	.99
L anterior cingulate gyrus	1.26 ± 0.04	1.28 ± 0.07	0.84	.43	1.25 ± 0.08	1.24 ± 0.08	0.75	.49
R orbital gyri	1.17 ± 0.09	1.17 ± 0.11	0.12	.91	1.15 ± 0.04	1.12 ± 0.08	0.93	.40
L orbital gyri	1.18 ± 0.07	1.23 ± 0.10	0.12	.30	1.17 ± 0.07	1.16 ± 0.09	0.31	.77
R thalamus	1.17 ± 0.11	1.10 ± 0.09	1.71	.14	1.15 ± 0.14	1.12 ± 0.13	1.07	.33
L thalamus	1.23 ± 0.09	1.16 ± 0.09	2.75	.03	1.19 ± 0.13	1.20 ± 0.13	0.29	.78

* Fluoxetine hydrochloride-treated responders (n = 7) and behavior therapy-treated responders (n = 6).
† Ratio of glucose metabolic rate in brain region of interest, divided by that in the ipsilateral hemisphere.
‡ Head of caudate nuclei predicted a priori to show significant changes.
§ Wilcoxon $z = 2.27$, $P = .02$.
‖ Wilcoxon $z = 2.04$, $P = .04$.

ment ($t = 2.84$, $df = 7$, $P = .025$; Wilcoxon $z = 1.90$, $P = .06$) and behavior therapy ($t = 3.15$, $df = 7$, $P = .02$; Wilcoxon $z = 2.19$, $P = .03$). Right Cd/hem percentage changes for normal controls were less than those for drug treatment ($z = 2.17$, $df = 9$, $P = .03$) and behavior therapy ($z = 2.24$, $df = 8$, $P = .025$) responders. For illustration, Fig. 18.2 presents FDG-PET scans of representative OCD treatment responders before and after each treatment.

Contrary to our expectations of significant Cd/hem results for both sides of the brain, the left Cd/hem did not show a statistically significant change with either treatment. Therefore, separate analyses of results in relationship to handedness were conducted. Results were unchanged when left and right caudate nucleus values for the one left-handed patient in each treatment group (both responders) were switched, and when they were excluded from the analyses.

There was a significant, positive rank-order correlation between percentage change in total Y-BOCS score before and after treatment and the percentage change in right Cd/hem when considering all nine subjects having drug therapy ($\tau = .48$, $P = .04$) and a trend for those patients undergoing behavior therapy ($\tau = .37$, $P = .09$).

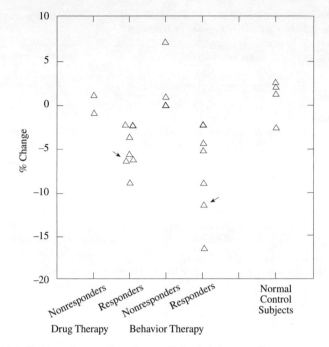

Figure 18.1. Percent change after drug or behavior therapy {[(posttreatment value–pretreatment value)/pretreatment value] $\times$ 100} in glucose metabolic rate in the right head of the caudate nucleus, divided by that of the ipsilateral hemisphere (Cd/hem) for responders and nonresponders to treatment, as well as normal controls scanned twice with a between-scan interval similar to that of the patients. Differences between responders and nonresponders to treatment are significant (P < .05) for both treatment groups, as are differences between treatment responders and normal controls. Arrows indicate data for subjects illustrated in Fig. 18.2.

None of the other brain regions surveyed that are not listed in Table 18.3 showed significant changes in pretreatment to posttreatment results in the treatment responders (all $P > .10$).

Since there were significant changes with both successful drug and behavior treatment only for right Cd/hem, and we have always observed high correlations between normalized left and right head of caudate nucleus values in normal controls (J.C.M. and L.R.B., unpublished data, 1982 to 1992), we wondered what happened to such a correlation in the OCD treatment responders before and after treatment. To have adequate numbers for valid correlation coefficients, we had to combine responders to both treatments.

As shown in Table 18.4, before treatment there was not a significant correlation of left and right Cd/hem in responders. After successful treatment

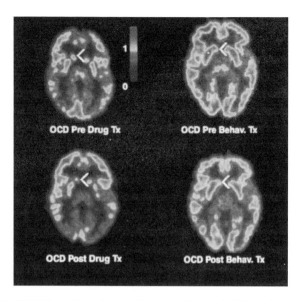

Figure 18.2. 18-F-Fluorodeoxglucose (fludeoxyglucose F 18) positron emission to-mographic scans of representative patients in a horizontal plane at a middle level of the head of the caudate nuclei before and after successful drug treatment or behavior theray (Behav Tx) for obsessive-compulsive disorder (OCD). Scans were processed to reflect the ratio of glucose metabolic rate registered by each pixel element, divided by that of whole brain; color bar reflects this with linear scaling. Arrowheads indicate right head of caudate nucleus. (Display follow radiologic and anatomic convention of displaying the right side on the viewer's left.) These particular examples were chosen for illustration because of exactness of scan repositioning and because they demonstrate various degrees of visible left-right asymmetry of caudaute nucleus change from before to after treatment.

there was a significant positive correlation between left and right Cd/hem. At this point, since we and others have postulated pathology in brain circuits involving the caudate, thalamus, orbital, and cingulate gyrus brain regions in OCD,[5–11] we examined correlations among these regions, too (Table 18.4).

Right orbital cortex/hem was significantly correlated with ipsilateral Cd/hem and thalamus/hem before treatment but not after, and the differences before and after treatment were clearly significant ($P<.0.5$). There was a similar pattern of correlation among these structures on the left side. Also of interest, there was no significant correlation between left cingulate/hem and left Cd/hem before treatment, but a clearly significant change to a significant positive correlation obtained after successful treatment. No other correlations

Table 18.4. Normalized Region of Interest Rank-Order Correlations (Kendall's τ) before and after Treatment for Responders to Either Treatment (n = 13)

	τ Value before treatment	τ Value after treatment
L to R caudate	.28	.77*
L to R orbit	.54†	.59†
L to R thalamus	.67†	.69*
L to R cingulate	.17	.03
L caudate to L orbit	**.49‡**	**.00**
R caudate to R orbit	**.44‡**	**−.03**
L orbit to L thalamus	**.33**	**−.21**
R orbit to R thalamus	**.41‡**	**−.21**
L caudate to L thalamus	.28	.33
R caudate to R thalamus	.21	.46‡
L caudate to L cingulate	−.10	.41‡
R caudate to R cingulate	−.04	−.03
L cingulate to L orbit	.00	.33
R cingulate to R orbit	.12	.03
L cingulate to L thalamus	−.05	.00
R cingulate to R thalamus	−.01	.05

*P < .001 (two-tailed).
†P < .01 (two-tailed).
‡P < .05 (two-tailed).

between ROIs were calculated. Numbers of nonresponders and controls were too small for valid correlation coefficients.

COMMENT

Although subject numbers are small, and our findings clearly in need of replication, we were able to provide evidence that glucose metabolic rates in the right head of the caudate nucleus change when OCD is treated successfully with either fluoxetine or behavior therapy. Normal subjects scanned twice under similar conditions hours to days apart have not shown such changes in other laboratories,[37,38] nor did our small group of normal subjects with a time interval between scans similar to that of our patients with OCD.

We also found evidence for significant correlations of orbital cortex activity with both the caudate nucleus and the thalamus before treatment in treatment responders. These correlations disappeared with successful treatment. Left cingulate glucose metabolism was not significantly correlated with left caudate nucleus activity before treatment but was significantly correlated after treatment.

Although half of our primary a priori hypothesis concerning the caudate nuclei was fulfilled, we did not provide evidence that left Cd/hem changes with effective OCD treatment. We had expected similar findings for both left and right Cd/hem. This seems all the more confusing in that Benkelfat et al[16] observed a statistically significant decrease in the normalized left caudate nucleus of OCD responders vs nonresponders, but did not do so for the right caudate nucleus in a group of patients with OCD undergoing FDG-PET before and after clomipramine hydrochloride treatment. They did, however, find a similar mean percentage decrease in right caudate nucleus glucose metabolic rates in responders $(-7.4\% \pm 18.6\%)$ vs nonresponders $(0.07\% \pm 8.7\%)$, as we did, but the variance in their data for the right caudate nucleus was much greater than that obtained for the left caudate nucleus, and, thus, results were not significant for the right side. Clomipramine has significant direct interactions with the dopamine system[16,39] in addition to its better-known serotonin reuptake blockade properties.[2,40] Both dopamine agonists and antagonists have been shown to have strong effects on caudate nucleus glucose metabolic rates, and Benkelfat et al acknowledged that such effects, unrelated to OCD symptom response, could have confounded their caudate nucleus findings. Fluoxetine itself, however, has indirect effects on the dopamine system, as should all agents affecting serotonin.[41]

Likewise, in our data, despite the fact that some cases that showed a clear response-related change in the right Cd/hem had a visible lack of similar effects on the left (Fig. 18.2), it should be emphasized that we did observe an overall mean decrease in left Cd/hem with both OCD treatments, even though this change was not statistically significant. Also, our correlational analysis implicates the left caudate nucleus almost as strongly as the right.

Our study findings should not be taken as evidence against the findings of Benkelfat et al.[16] Both studies had a high probability of Type II error, and taken together they are complementary in showing a similar change in caudate nucleus glucose metabolism after treatment with two chemically different drugs and after behavior therapy. It is noteworthy, however, that Hollander et al.[42] found increased right compared with left brain neurologic soft signs in their population of patients with OCD, perhaps implying that right brain function is more disordered than left in OCD.

Type II error is also possible in the evaluation of the other brain regions we surveyed. Surrounded by white matter and ventricular space, the head of the caudate nucleus is one of the easiest brain regions to determine visually with high-resolution FDG-PET scanning. The boundaries of most of the other brain regions we examined are not as distinct. Both Benkelfat et al[16] and

Swedo et al[34] report significant changes in normalized orbital cortex after OCD treatment, yet we note that only subregions of orbital cortex showed this change; we did not attempt such subdivisions. We did find significant changes in correlations between orbital gyrus and caudate nucleus and thalamus before and after successful treatment, however. We also note that Swedo et al did not find caudate nucleus changes with OCD treatment. Differences in treatment duration might account for these seeming disparities among the three studies of OCD before and after treatment. We have suggested that orbital brain function changes with OCD treatment would occur some time after caudate nucleus changes.[8] Further, work in our laboratory[43] has demonstrated that as an individual learns to perform a motor task more efficiently, the critical brain structures mediating the behavior show a reduction in both spatial extent and magnitude of activation on PET scanning while performing the task than when the task was new. With time, might the caudate nucleus become "more efficient" in controlling OCD symptoms and its change(s) in critical functions no longer be detectable with present PET methods? Swedo et al restudied their subjects after at least 1 year (mean, 20 months), Benkelfat et al did so after a mean of 16 weeks, and we did so after only 10 weeks. It is interesting that the study of intermediate length found both caudate nucleus and orbital changes, while the shorter and longer ones found only caudate nucleus and orbital changes, respectively. Whether those who respond to OCD treatment show various regional brain changes before, at the time of, or after clinical response could be investigated with FDG-PET.

We also found decreases in right anterior cingulate gyrus/hem and left thalamus/hem with successful drug treatment but not behavior therapy. These findings may be specific to OCD treatment with fluoxetine vs exposure and response-prevention, but could also be related to other factors in those patients who chose drug treatment over behavior therapy. Other studies are needed to resolve this issue.

In our first report of FDG-PET findings in OCD, we reported *increases* in both left and right Cd/hem ratios after treatment with trazodone hydrochloride and tranylcypromine sulfate.[5] However, most of those subjects had major depression as well as OCD. We had previously reported a similar increase in Cd/hem with treatment of unipolar major depression[44] and observed that the change in depression scores in the depressed patients with OCD gave a significant negative correlation with the change in Cd/hem, while the change in the OCD scale used did not.[5] Nevertheless, we associated this increase in Cd/hem with improvement in OCD symptoms, not just depression.[5] We now believe that that conclusion was in error and that both the increases in Cd/

hem and the decreased OCD symptoms observed in that study population were secondary to an improvement in depression, rather than a primary improvement in OCD per se. Obsessive-compulsive disorder often worsens when major depression is superimposed.[45,46] The findings of Benkelfat et al[16] in a group of nondepressed patients with OCD, and our own failure to show significant improvement in a placebo and doxepin hydrochloride controlled treatment study of trazodone hydrochloride in nondepressed patients with OCD (L.R.B., J. M. Thompson, MD, and J. M. Schwartz, MD, unpublished data, 1990) led us to suspect this error. Consequently, we used a two-tailed hypothesis and statistics in the present study.

It should be pointed out, however, that a decrease in Cd/hem does not imply a "decrease" in some critical caudate nucleus "function." There are so many interacting excitatory and inhibitory circuits in the caudate nucleus[47] that all one can say is that there is a change in function; the critical element(s) in the behavioral mediation may be either increasing or decreasing.

Known functions of the caudate nucleus, however, do seem to fit the symptomatology of OCD. Rapoport and colleagues[11] have pointed out the similarities between the behaviors commonly seen in compulsive rituals and innate, species-specific behavioral routines that may be released when the caudate nucleus is dysfunctional. (Also, see Villablanca and Olmstead[48] for a detailed review of relevant behaviors in cats with caudate nucleus lesions.) Another basal ganglia function, "gating," by which certain motor, sensory, and perhaps cognitive impulses are either allowed to proceed through to perception and behavior or are held back ("filtered") and dissipated, seems to speak to the psychodynamic concept of disordered "repression" in OCD.[8] In this regard, it seems appropriate to note that individuals likely to develop Huntington's disease, who have Cd/hem values that are significantly below those of normals, have increased expressions of "anger and hostility" on the Profile of Mood States compared with siblings with normal Cd/hem values who are less likely to develop this neurologic disorder.[49] Obsessive-compulsive disorder symptoms have often been viewed as the result of attempts to overcontrol these same emotions. Further, specifically in regard to the localization of this brain change after behavior therapy for OCD, there is now a wealth of data implicating the caudate nucleus in "procedural" or "process learning," including the ability to acquire new habits and skills necessary for the successful initiation of approach or avoidance behaviors.[50–53]

Although our findings are consistent with the idea that the head of the caudate nucleus is involved in the mediation of OCD's symptomatic expression,[8] and there is an attractive theory as to how caudate nucleus dysfunction may develop in OCD and related disorders,[54] our data do not prove that caudate nucleus dysfunction is the "cause" of OCD. That may be further up the afferent stream. Indeed, brain glucose metabolic rates largely reflect the work of neuronal firing at synaptic nerve terminals, and not the metabolic demands of cell bodies in and processes efferent from a structure.[55] The orbital region of the brain has been demonstrated to be abnormal in OCD with FDG-PET[5,33,56,57] and sends extensive efferent projections to both the head of the caudate nucleus and the thalamus.[7] Our correlational analysis of brain region activity suggests that in symptomatic, treatment-responsive OCD activity in the orbital region is closely coupled with that in the caudate nucleus and thalamus, while with symptom improvement these relationships are broken, perhaps through a change in caudate nucleus function.

Although it seems hazardous to tally pluses and minuses among the multiple excitatory and inhibitory elements in orbital-basal ganglia-thalamic circuits to predict a final outcome, we will now invoke our data to support proposed theories[6,7,9,10] of OCD symptom mediation by elements in these same circuits[6–11] (Fig. 18.3[58]). According to our present view, before effective treatment a deficit in caudate nucleus function leads to inadequate "filtering" (or "repression") of orbital "worry" inputs, and thus allows them to drive the relevant fraction of inhibitory caudate nucleus output to the globus pallidus. This results in decreased pallidal inhibitory output to relevant parts of the thalamus. Consequently, orbital worry inputs may also come to have an undue, rigid influence on thalamic outputs to other brain regions mediating OCD symptoms that are not localized to the orbit. Further, excitatory thalamic input to the orbit makes this a potentially self-reinforcing loop that is difficult to "break." With effective treatment, however, adequate filtering activity in the caudate nucleus damps out this self-driving circuitry, and thereby allows the individual to better limit OCD symptoms once an obsessive worry is "launched" from the orbital region. These orbital-basal ganglia-thalamic circuits may have evolved to allow significant threats involving OCD themes (violence, contamination, etc) to capture and direct attention for needed action—and to rivet behavior to those concerns until the danger is judged passed. In treatment-responsive OCD the threshold for system "capture" may be too low. Caution is warranted about the generalizability of these ideas, however, since we do not have adequate subject numbers to examine drug treatment and behavior therapy separately or to comment on treatment nonresponders. In addition to further human PET work, PET studies and simultaneous electrophysiologic recordings from these same brain regions in

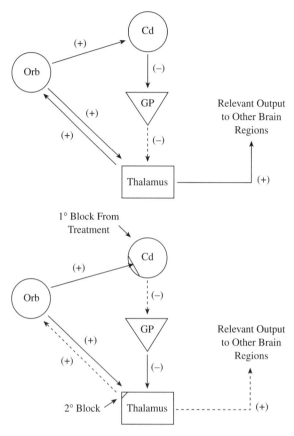

Figure 18.3. Although known connections among brain systems proposed to be involved in obsessive-compulsive disorder (OCD) symptom mediation[6,7,10] *(top)* are complex,[58] a subsystem *(top)* may be the locus of pathologic dysfunction. Pretreatment correlations suggest that "worry" outputs from the orbital (Orb) region of the brain may be driving OCD-relevant circuits in the caudate nucleus (Cd), and thus increase inhibitory output to relevant regions of the globus pallidus (GP). This would reduce inhibition of the thalamus, making it vulnerable to being driven by the orbit as well. The excitatory connections between thalamus and orbit make this a potentially self-sustaining circuit, and thus difficult to break. With effective treatment *(bottom),* increases in filtering functions in the caudate nucleus may reduce its inhibitory output to the globus pallidus, which in turn would increase inhibitory output to the thalamus. This would result in an uncoupling of this fixed "worry circuit" and allow the patient to more easily terminate OCD behaviors. With time, orbital "worry activity" may also decrease. Arrows indicate effect of stimulating one brain region on the rate of neuronal firing in the other; plus signs, excitory output; minus signs, inhibitory output; and broken lines, reduced effect.

animal models of OCD, before and after effective drug treatment,[59] are warranted.

Based on reported effects of cingulotomy in OCD[60] and theory put forward by others,[6] we expected significant cingulate-caudate correlations before but not after effective treatment. Instead, we observed the opposite. This may have been a chance occurrence, although we have some ideas as to how cingulate-mediated "will" and/or "suppression" functions might be operating.[22] Such discourse is beyond space limitations here.

A significant input to the caudate nucleus comes from serotonin neuron bodies in the dorsal raphe.[61] Serotonin is highly implicated in the pathophysiology of OCD.[40] We believe it unlikely, however, that changes in the activity of these serotonin terminals themselves are what is being measured directly when Cd/hem changes with successful treatment of OCD. These terminals are but a tiny fraction of those in the caudate nucleus,[61] and changes in glucose utilization in serotonin terminals alone are thus not likely to be directly responsible for as large a percentage change in Cd/hem as measured in our study. A more specific PET neurotracer than FDG may be needed to detect changes in activity at serotonin synapses. (A comparable situation exists with dopamine terminals in Parkinson's disease where FDG-PET does not show consistent striatal abnormalities but ^{18}F-fluoro-DOPA-PET does.[62]) It seems more likely that the changes in Cd/hem we observed are a reflection of changes in the activity of one or more of the many neurochemically diverse populations of small interneurons in the caudate nucleus.[61] Our correlational analysis suggests the possibility, however, that loss of a key modulating process in the caudate nucleus may allow inputs from the orbital region to drive interneuron activity in the caudate nucleus and that with successful treatment adequate regulatory control is (re)established. Serotonin agonists have generally been observed to decrease brain glucose metabolic rates in animals, but effects in the caudate nucleus are complex, presumably dependent on the classes of serotonin receptors that may be most affected by any given agent, and are not easily interpreted.[63] Critical interneuron function changes with OCD treatment could be effected by serotonin afferents to the caudate nucleus acting on other, larger populations of neurons, but there are many possible candidates for the title of "critical element" in the neurochemical mosaic of the caudate nucleus.

The "serotonin hypothesis" of OCD rests most firmly on evidence that chemically diverse drugs that are strong serotonin re-uptake inhibitors are effective in the treatment of OCD, while similar agents that affect other neurotransmitters are ineffective.[40,64,65] Some may wonder how behavior therapy could produce brain function changes similar to neurochemically specific drugs. Even in lower animals, such as the sea slug, *Aplysia,* however, it is changes at synapses that use serotonin that seem to mediate learned changes in stimulus-response behavior (see Kandel[66] for review). Further, direct applications of serotonin at these synapses can produce the same lasting changes in synaptic function and behavior as seen with behavior modification in *Aplysia.*[66,67] Thus, the possibility of both a serotonin reuptake inhibitor and behavior modification treatments having the same neural effects is not as farfetched as it might seem to some at first glance.

Unipolar major depression[68–70] and the panic/agorophobia disorder complex[71–75] can also be treated with either drugs or behavior therapy, although, as in OCD, certain symptoms may respond better to one intervention than to another. Positron emission tomography has provided significant, replicated findings in mood disorders (see Baxter[76] for review) and anxiety disorders. [5,33,56,57,76–79] Positron emission tomographic studies that compare and contrast the effects of these overtly different treatment interventions may provide a powerful method for investigating the brain mediation of symptoms in these disorders, too.

REFERENCES

1. *Jenike, M. A., Baer, L., Minichiello, W. E., eds.* Obsessive-Compulsive Disorders: Theory and Management, *2nd ed. St. Louis, Mo: Mosby–Year Book; 1990.*
2. *DeVeaugh-Geiss, J. Pharmacologic treatment of obsessive-compulsive disorder. In: Zohar, J., Insel, T., Rasmussen, S., eds.* The Psychobiology of Obsessive-Compulsive Disorder. *New York: NY: Springer Publishing Co Inc; 1991: 187–207.*
3. *Baer, L., Minichiello, W. E. Behavior therapy for obsessive-compulsive disorder. In: Jenike, M. A., Baer, L., Minichiello, W. E., eds.* Obsessive-Compulsive Disorders: Theory and Management. *2nd ed. St. Louis, Mo: Mosby–Year Book; 1990: 203–232.*
4. *Cummings, J. L., Frankel, M. Gilles de la Tourette's syndrome and the neurological basis of obsessions and compulsions.* Biol Psychiatry. *1985; 20: 1117–1126.*
5. *Baxter, L. R., Phelps, M. E., Mazziotta, J. C., Guze, G. H., Schwartz, J. M., Selin, C. E. Local cerebral glucose metabolic rates in obsessive-compulsive disorder: a comparison with rates in unipolar depression and normal controls.* Arch Gen Psychiatry. *1987; 44: 211–218.*
6. *Rapoport, J. L., Wise, S. P. Obsessive-compulsive disorder: is it a basal ganglia dysfunction?* Psychopharmacol Bull. *1988; 24: 380–384.*
7. *Modell, J. G., Mountz, J. M., Curtis, G. C., Greden, J. F. Neurophysiologic dysfunction in basal ganglia/limbic striatal and thalamocortical circuits as a pathogenetic mechanism of obsessive-compulsive disorder.* J Neuropsychiatry. *1989; 1: 27–36.*

8. *Baxter, L. R., Schwartz, J. M., Guze, B. H., Bergman, K., Szuba, M. P. Neuroimaging in obsessive-compulsive disorder: seeking the mediating neuroanatomy. In: Jenike, M. A., Baer, L., Minichiello, W. E., eds.* Obsessive-Compulsive Disorders: Theory and Management. *2nd ed. St. Louis, Mo: Mosby–Year Book; 1990: 167–188.*

9. *Insel, T. R. Obsessive-compulsive disorder: a neuroethological perspective.* Psychopharmacol Bull. *1988; 24: 365–369.*

10. *Insel, T. R., Winslow, J. T. Neurobiology of obsessive-compulsive disorder. In: Jenike, M. A., Baer, L., Minichiello, W. E., eds.* Obsessive-Compulsive Disorders: Theory and Management. *2nd ed. St. Louis, Mo: Mosby–Year Book; 1990: 116–131.*

11. *Rapoport, J. L. Recent advances in obsessive-compulsive disorder.* Neuropsychopharmacology. *1991; 5: 1–10.*

12. *Phelps, M. E., Mazziotta, J. C. Positron emission tomography: human brain function and biochemistry.* Science. *1985; 228: 799–809.*

13. *Pigott, T. A., Pato, M. T., Bernstein, S. E., Grover, G. N., Hill, J. L., Tolliver, T. J., Murphy, D. L. Controlled comparisons of clomipramine and fluoxetine in the treatment of obsessive-compulsive disorder.* Arch Gen Psychiatry. *1990; 47: 926–932.*

14. *Turner, S. M., Jacob, R. G., Beidel, D. C., Himmelhoch, J. Fluoxetine treatment of obsessive-compulsive disorder.* J Clin Psychopharmacol. *1985; 5: 207–212.*

15. *Jenike, M. A., Buttolph, L., Baer, L., Ricciardi, J., Holland, A. Open trial of fluoxetine in obsessive-compulsive disorder.* Am J Psychiatry. *1989; 146: 909–911.*

16. *Benkelfat, C., Nordahl, T. E., Semple, W. E., King, C., Murphy, D. L., Cohen R. M. Local cerebral glucose metabolic rates in obsessive-compulsive disorder: patients treated with clomipramine.* Arch Gen Psychiatry. *1990; 47: 840–848.*

17. *Spitzer, R. L., Endicott, J. Schedule for Affective Disorders and Schizophrenia. New York, NY: New York State Psychiatric Institute; 1978.*

18. *Goodman, W. K., Price, L. H., Rasmussen, S. A., Mazure, C., Fleischmann, R. L., Hill, C. L., Heninger G. R., Charney, D. S. The Yale-Brown Obsessive Compulsive Scale, I: development, use, and reliability.* Arch Gen Psychiatry. *1989;46: 1006–1011.*

19. *Goodman, W. K., Price, L. H., Rasmussen, S. A., Mazure, C., Delgado, P., Heninger, G. R., Charney, D. S. The Yale-Brown Obsessive Compulsive Scale, II: validity.* Arch Gen Psychiatry. *1989; 46: 1012–1016.*

20. *Hamilton, M. Development of a rating scale for primary depressive illness.* Br J Soc Psychol. *1967; 6: 278–296.*

21. *Hamilton, M. Diagnosis and rating of anxiety.* Br J Psychiatry. *1969; 3 (special issue): 76–79.*

22. *Schwartz, J. M., Martin, K., Baxter, L. R. Neuroimaging and cognitive-behavioral self-treatment in obsessive-compulsive disorder: practical and philosophical considerations. In: Hand, I., Goodman, W., eds.* Obsessive-Compulsive Disorder: Recent Research. *New York, NY: Springer-Verlag NY Inc. In press.*

23. *Mazziotta, J. C., Phelps, M. E., Miller, J. Tomographic mapping of human cerebral metabolism: normal unstimulated state.* Neurology. *1981; 31: 503–516.*

24. *Barrio, J. R., MacDonald, N. S., Robinson, G. D., Najafi, A., Cook, J. S., Kuhl,*

D. E. Remote, semiautomated production of F-18-labeled 2-deoxy-2-fluoro-D-glucose. J Nucl Med. *1981; 22: 372–375.*

25. *Phelps, M. E., Huang, S. C., Hoffman, E. J., Selin, C., Sokoloff, L., Kuhl, D. E. Tomographic measurement of local cerebral glucose metabolic rate in humans with (F-18) 2-fluoro-2-deoxyglucose: validation of method.* Ann Neurol. *1979; 6: 371–388.*

26. *Huang, S. C., Phelps, M. E., Hoffman, S. C., Sideris, K., Selin, C. E., Kuhl, D. E. Noninvasive determination of local cerebral metabolic rate of glucose in man.* Am J Physiol. *1980; 238: E69–E82.*

27. *Mazziotta, J. C., Phelps, M. E., Meadors, A. K., Ricci, A., Winter, J., Bentson, J. R. Anatomical localization schemes for use in positron computed tomography using a specially designed headholder.* J Comput Assist Tomogr. *1982; 6: 848–853.*

28. *Cherry, S. R., Dahlbom, J., Hoffman, E. J. 3D PET using a conventional multislice tomograph without septa.* J Comput Assist Tomogr. *1991; 15: 655–668.*

29. *Reivich, M., Alavi, A., Wolf, A. P., Fowler, J., Russell, J., Arnett, C., MacGregor, R. R., Shiue, C. Y., Atkins, H., Anaud, A., Dahn, R., Greenberg, J. H. Glucose metabolic rate kinetic model parameter determination in man: the lumped constants and rate constants for [^{18}F]fluorodeoxyglucose and [^{11}C]deoxyglucose.* J Cereb Blood Flow Metab. *1985; 5: 179–192.*

30. *Brooks, R. A., Hatazawa, J., Di Chiro, G., Larson, S. M., Fishbein, D. S. Human cerebral glucose metabolism determined by positron emission tomography: a revisit.* J Cereb Blood Flow Metab. *1987; 7: 427–432.*

31. *Reivich, M., Kuhl, D., Wolf, A., Greenberg, J. H., Phelps, M. E., Ido, T., Cassella, V., Fowler, J., Hoffman, E. J., Alvani, A., Sokoloff, L. The [^{18}F]fluorodeoxy-glucose method for the measurement of local cerebral glucose utilization in man.* Circ Res. *1979; 44: 127–137.*

32. *Mazziotta, J. C., Phellps, M. E., Plummer, D., Optimization and standardization of anatomical data in neurobehavioral investigations using positron CT.* J Cereb Blood Flow Metab. *1983; 3(suppl): S266–S267.*

33. *Swedo, S. E., Schapiro, M. B., Grady, C. L., Cheslow, D. L., Leonard H. L., Kumar, A., Friedland, R. P., Rapoport, S. I., Rapoport, J. L. Cerebral glucose metabolism in childhood-onset obsessive-compulsive disorder.* Arch Gen Psychiatry. *1989; 46: 518–523.*

34. *Swedo, S. E., Pietrini, P., Leonard, H. L., Schapiro, M. B., Rettew, D. C., Goldberger, E. L., Rapoport, S. I., Rapoport, J. L., Grady, C. L. Cerebral glucose metabolism in childhood-onset obsessive-compulsive disorder: revisualization during pharmacotherapy.* Arch Gen Psychiatry. *1992; 49: 690–694.*

35. *Hayes, W. L. Statistics. New York, NY: Holt Rinehart & Winston; 1963.*

36. The Clomipramine Collaborative Study Group. *Clomipramine in the treatment of patients with obsessive-compulsive disorder.* Arch Gen Psychiatry. *1991; 48: 730–738.*

37. *Bartlett, E. J., Brodie, J. D., Wolf, A. P., Christman, D. R., Laska, E., Meissner, M. Reproducibility of cerebral glucose metabolic measurements in resting human subjects.* J Cereb Blood Flow Metab. *1988; 8: 502–512.*

38. *Bartlett, E. J., Barouche, F., Brodie, J. D., Wolkin, A., Angrist, B., Rotrosen, J.,*

Wolf, A. P. The stability of resting deoxyglucose metabolic values in PET studies of schizophrenia. Psychiatry Res. *1991; 40: 11–20.*

39. *Austin, L. S., Lydiard, R. B., Ballenger, J. C., Cohen, B. M., Laraia, M. T., Zealberg, J. J., Fossey, M. D., Ellinwood, E. H. Dopamine blocking activity of clomipramine in patients with obsessive-compulsive disorder.* Biol Psychiatry. *1991; 30: 225–232.*

40. *Zohar, J., Insel, T. R. Obsessive-compulsive disorder: psychobiological approaches to diagnosis, treatment, and pathophysiology.* Biol Psychiatry. *1987; 22: 667–687.*

41. *Lipinski, J. F., Mallya, G., Zimmerman, P., Pope, H. G. Fluoxetine-induced akathisia: clinical and theoretical implications.* J Clin Psychiatry. *1989; 50: 339–342.*

42. *Hollander, E., Schiffman, E., Cohen, B., Rivera-Stein, M. A., Rosen, W., Gorman, J. M., Fyer, A. J., Papp, L., Liebowitz, M. R. Signs of central nervous system dysfunction in obsessive-compulsive disorder.* Arch Gen Psychiatry. *1990; 47: 27–32.*

43. *Mazziotta, J. C., Grafton, S. T., Woods, R. C. The human motor system studied with PET measurements of cerebral blood flow: topography and motor learning. In: Lassen, N. A., Ingvar, D. H., Raichle, M. E., Frieberg, L., eds.* Brain Work and Mental Activity: Quantitative Studies With Radioactive Tracers: Proceedings of the 31st Alfred Benzon Symposium. *Copenhagen, Denmark: Munksgaard; 1991: 280–293.*

44. *Baxter, L. R., Phelps, M. E., Mazziotta, J. C., Schwartz, J. M., Gerner, R. H., Selin, C. E., Sumida, R. M. Cerebral metabolic rates for glucose in mood disorders: studies with positron emission tomography and ^{18}F-fluorodeoxyglucose.* Arch Gen Psychiatry. *1985; 42: 441–447.*

45. *Mavissakalian, M., Michelson, L. Tricyclic antidepressants in obsessive-compulsive disorder: antiobsessional or antidepressant agents?* J Nerv Ment Dis. *1983; 171: 301–306.*

46. *Fogelson, D. L., Bystritsky, S. Imipramine in the treatment of OCD with and without major depression.* Ann Clin Psychiatry. *1991; 3: 233–237.*

47. *Penney, J. B., Young, A. B. Speculations on the functional anatomy of basal ganglia disorders.* Annu Rev Neurosci. *1983; 6: 73–94.*

48. *Villablanca, J. R., Olmstead, C. E. The striatum: a finer tuner of the brain.* Acta Neurobiol Exp (Warsz). *1982; 42: 227–299.*

49. *Baxter, L. R., Mazziotta, J. C., Pahl, J. J., Grafton, S. T., St George-Hyslop, P., Haines J. L., Gusella, J., Szuba, M. P., Selin, C. E., Guze, B. H., Phelps, M. E. Psychiatric, genetic and PET evaluation of persons at-risk for Huntington's disease.* Arch Gen Psychiatry. *1992; 49: 148–154.*

50. *Phillips, A. G., Carr, G. D. Cognition and the basal ganglia: a possible substrate for procedural knowledge.* Can J Neurol Sci. *1987; 14: 381–385.*

51. *Packard, M. G., Hirsh, R., White, N. M. Differential effects of fornix and caudate nucleus lesions on two radial maze tasks: evidence for multiple memory systems.* J Neurosci. *1989; 9: 1465–1472.*

52. *Mittleman, G., Whishaw, I. Q., Jones, G. H., Koch, M., Robbins, T. W. Cortical,*

hippocampal and striatal mediation of schedule-induced behaviors. Behav Neurosci. *1990; 104: 399–409.*

53. *Packard, M. G., White, N. M. Lesions of the caudate nucleus selectively impair 'reference memory' acquisions in the radial maze.* Behav Neural Biol. *1990; 53: 39–50.*

54. *Swedo, S. E., Rapoport, J. L., Cheslow, D. L., Leonard, H. L., Ayoub, E. M., Hosier, D. M., Wald, E. R. High prevalence of obsessive-compulsive symptoms in patients with Sydenham's chorea.* Am J Psychiatry. *1989; 146: 246–249.*

55. *Mazziotta, J. C., Phelps, M. E. Positron emission tomography studies of the brain. In: Phelps, M. E., Mazziotta, J. C., Schelbert, H. R., eds.* Positron Emissioni Tomography and Autoradiography. *New York, NY: Raven Press; 1986.*

56. *Baxter, L. R., Schwartz, J. M., Mazziotta, J. C., Phelps, M. E., Pahl, J. J., Guze, B. H., Fairbanks, L. Cerebral glucose metabolic rates in nondepressed patients with obsessive-compulsive disorder.* Am J Psychiatry. *1988; 145: 1560–1563.*

57. *Nordhal, T. E., Benkelfat, C., Semple, W. E., Gross, M., King, A. C., Cohen, R. M. Cerebral glucose metabolic rates in obsessive compulsive disorder.* Neuropsychopharmacology. *1989; 2: 23–28.*

58. *Albin, R. L., Young, A. B., Penney, J. B. The functional antaomy of basal ganglia disorders.* Trends Neurosci. *1989; 12: 366–375.*

59. *Rapoport, J. L., Ryland, D. H., Kriete, M. Drug treatment of canine acral lick: an animal model of obsessive-compulsive disorder.* Arch Gen Psychiatry. *1992; 48: 517–521.*

60. *Jenike, M. A., Bear, L., Ballantine, H. T., Martuza, R. L., Tynes, S., Giriunas, I., Buttolph, L., Cassem, N. H. Cingulotomy for refractory obsessive-compulsive disorder: a long-term follow-up of 33 patients.* Arch Gen Psychiatry. *1991; 48: 548–555.*

61. *Greybiel, A. M., Ragsdale, C. W. Biochemical anatomy of the striatum. In: Emson, P. C.* Chemical Neuroanatomy. *New York, NY: Raven Press; 1983: 427–504.*

62. *Leenders, K. L., Salmon, E. P., Tyrrell, P., Perani, D., Brooks, D. J., Sager, H., Jones, T., Marsden, C. D., Frackowiak, R. S. J. The nigrostriatal dopaminergic system assessed in vivo by positron emission tomography in healthy volunteer subjects and patients with Parkinson's disease.* Arch Neurol. *1990; 47: 1290–1298.*

63. *Grome, J. J., Harper, A. M. Local cerebral glucose utilization following indoleamine- and piperazine-containing 5-hydroxytryptamine agonists.* J Neurochem. *1986; 46: 117–124.*

64. *Leonard, H. L., Swedo, S. E., Koby, E. V., Rapoport, J. L., Lengne, M. C., Cheslow, D. L., Hamburger, S. D. Treatment of obsessive-compulsive disorder with clomipramine and desmethylimipramine in children and adolescents: a double-blind crossover comparison.* Arch Gen Psychiatry. *1989; 46: 1088–1092.*

65. *Goodman, W. K., Price, L. H., Delgado, P. L., Palumbo, J., Krystal, J. H., Nagy, L. M., Rasmussen, S. A., Heninger, G. R., Charney, D. S. Specificity of serotonin reuptake inhibitors in the treatment of obsessive-compulsive disorder: comparison of fluvoxamine and desipramine.* Arch Gen Psychiatry. *1990; 47: 577–585.*

66. Kandel, E. R. Genes, nerve cells, and the remembrance of things past. J Neuro-psychiatry. 1989; 1: 103–125.
67. Montarolo, P. G., Goelet, P., Castellucci, V. F., Morgan, J., Kandel, E. R., Schacher, S. A critical period for macromolecular synthesis in long-term heterosynaptic facilitation in Aplysia. Science. 1986; 234: 1249–1254.
68. Elkin, I., Shea, M. T., Watkins, J. T., Imber, S. D., Sotsky, S. M., Collins, J. F., Glass, D. R., Pilkonis, P. A., Leber, W. R., Docherty, J. P., Fiester, S. J., Parloff, M. B. National Institute of Mental Health treatment of depression collaborative research program: general effectiveness of treatments. Arch Gen Psychiatry. 1989; 46: 971–982.
69. Frank, E., Kupfer, D. J., Perel, J. M., Comes, C., Jarrett, D. B., Mallinger, A. G., Thase, M. E., McEachran, A. B., Grochocinsky, V. J. Three-year outcomes for maintanance therapies in recurrent depression. Arch Gen Psychiatry. 1990; 47: 1093–1099.
70. Klerman, G. L. Treatment of recurrent unipolar major depressive disorder: commentary on the Pittsburgh study. Arch Gen Psychiatry. 1990; 47: 1158–1162.
71. Mavissakalian, M., Michelson, L. Agoraphobia: relative and combined effectiveness of therapist-assisted in vivo exposure and imipramine. J Clin Psychiatry. 1986; 47: 117–122.
72. Mavissakalian, M. Imipramine in agoraphobia. Compr Psychiatry. 1986; 27: 401–406.
73. Ballenger, J. C., Burrows, G. D., DuPont, R. L., Jr., Lesser, I. M., Noyes, R. Jr., Pecknold, J. C., Rifkin, A., Swinson, R. P. Alprazolam in panic disorder and agoraphobia: results from a multicenter trial, I: efficacy in short-term treatment. Arch Gen Psychiatry. 1988; 45: 413–422.
74. Marks, I. M., Gray, S., Cohen, D., Hill, R., Mawson, D., Ramm, E., Stern, R. S. Imipramine and brief therapist-aided exposure in agoraphobics having self-exposure homework. Arch Gen Psychiatry. 1983; 40: 153–162.
75. Salkovskis, P. M., Jones, D. R. O., Clark, D. M. Respiratory control in the treatment of panic attacks: replications. Br J Psychiatry. 1986; 148: 526–532.
76. Baxter, L. R. PET studies of cerebral function in major depression and obsessive-compulsive disorder: the emerging prefrontal cortex consensus. Ann Clin Psychiatry. 1991; 3: 103–109.
77. Reiman, E. M., Raichel, M. E., Butler, F. K., Herscovitch, P., Robins, E. A focal brain abnormality in panic disorder, a severe form of anxiety. Nature. 1984; 310: 683–685.
78. Reiman, E. M., Raichle, M. E., Robins, E., Minton, M. A., Fusselman, M. J., Fox, P. T., Price, J. L., Hackman, K. A. Neuroanatomical correlates of a lactate-induced anxiety attack. Arch Gen Psychiatry. 1989; 46: 493–500.
79. Nordahl, T. E., Semple, W. E., Gross, M., Mellman, T. A., Stein, M. B., Goyer, P., King, A. C., Uhde, T. W., Cohen, R. M. Cerebral glucose metabolic differences in patients with panic disorder. Neuropsychopharmacology. 1990; 3: 261–272.

19. Childhood-Onset Obsessive Compulsive Disorder

Susan E. Swedo, Henrietta L. Leonard, and Judith L. Rapoport

B ASED ON psychiatric clinic populations,[6,17,21,33] childhood-onset obsessive compulsive disorder (OCD) was considered to be rare until Flament and colleagues,[12] in a survey of 5596 high school students, demonstrated that the disorder had a lifetime prevalence rate of at least 0.4%. When the sample was weighted to reflect sampling design, this lifetime prevalence rate approached 1.0% ($\pm 0.5\%$), making it clear that childhood-onset OCD is not uncommon. The disparity between clinic-based estimates and population rates may be the result of the secrecy manifested by patients with the disorder. Children and adolescents who are afflicted with OCD recognize the irrationality of their obsessive thoughts and compulsive rituals and make concerted efforts to hide their disorder.[35] Frequently, patients will have been treated for depression or another anxiety disorder for several months before they disclose their OCD symptoms. It is for this reason that clinicians need to be well versed in the various clinical presentations of childhood-onset OCD. This article reviews the phenomenology, treatment, and outcome of the disorder in pediatric patients.

CLINICAL PRESENTATION

Information about the clinical presentation of childhood-onset OCD was obtained from clinical interviews of 70 children and adolescents (47 boys, 23 girls) enrolled in psychopharmacologic treatment studies at the Child Psychiatry Branch of the National Institute of Mental Health (NIMH)[10,26] as well as from 18 OCD subjects in a New Jersey epidemiologic sample.[12] The clinical presentation of the epidemiologic subjects[5,12] was similar to those of the more intensely studied NIMH clinic sample and thus, their data are not

Reprinted by permission of W. B. Saunders Co. from *Psychiatric Clinics of North America* 15 (1992): 767–75.

presented separately here. In addition, the phenomenologic data from the NIMH sample are similar to those recently reported by Riddle et al[32] and Thomsen and Mikkelsen.[38]

The NIMH study subjects were 6 to 18 years old, had had symptoms for at least 1 year, and met DSM-III[1] criteria for the disorder. Exclusionary criteria included a concurrent diagnosis of Tourette's syndrome, schizophrenia, primary major depression, organic mental disorder, or mental retardation, but not tic disorders, secondary depressive symptoms, lifetime diagnosis of depressive disorder, or Axis II disorders, such as learning disabilities.

In general, children with OCD presented with both rituals and obsessions and the content of these obsessive compulsive behaviors changed over time in 95% of subjects (Rettew et al, 1992, unpublished data). "Pure obsessives," or those with only obsessive thoughts, were rare (3 of 70 subjects [4%]), but "pure ritualizers" were not uncommon.[37] Very young children (ages 6 to 8 years) in particular would have elaborate washing or checking rituals without cognitive obsessions. For example, one 7-year-old boy repeatedly washed his hands to the point where they cracked and bled. When prevented from using the sink, he would lick his hands in a stylized manner, but denied any preceding obsessional thought. Rather, he said that it was merely an irresistible urge to wash or lick his hands.

Washing rituals were the most common OCD symptom, affecting over 85% of the children at some point in time. When asked specifically (for example, after observing raw, reddened hands), the children reluctantly would acknowledge their excessive washing, but rarely volunteered the information. The excessive washing could be manifested as either increased frequency (10 to 20 times/hour) of handwashing; or elaborate, ritualized washing patterns that took several minutes or longer to complete. No child reported excessively long or frequent baths, but several teenagers complained of troublesome showering rituals, wherein they were "required" to wash in a set pattern and to do it "perfectly." Parents would report increased laundry requirements (from towels that could only be used one time or more frequent clothes changes), increased hot water bills from excessively long showers, or toilet stoppages from excessive toilet paper use. In about half of the 70 NIMH cases (48% of sample), the excessive washing was accompanied by an obsessional concern with dirt, germs, body excretions (urine, saliva, or stool), or environmental toxins. The obsessional feared objects varied from rabies and AIDS viruses, to spearmint gum, ball-point pen ink, and battery acid. There were no consistent patterns and there did not seem to be a "rational" basis for the symptom choice.

A lifetime history of repeating rituals was present in over one half of the sample (n = 36,51%).[37] Many children would have to repeatedly draw a letter or number until it was "perfect." Their teachers noticed the abrupt onset of erasure holes in their papers, whereas parents observed increasing amounts of time being spent on homework assignments. The repeating rituals could be as simple as going back and forth through a doorway three times or getting up from a chair twice; or as complicated as a young man's 2-hour-long ritual of repeatedly getting in and out of the car, circling a tree in the front yard, checking the mailbox, climbing the porch steps, and entering and re-entering the house. If an obsessive thought accompanied these rituals, it was usually one of harm coming to self or a loved one, and the ritual was necessary to neutralize the thought. The children reported, as adult OCD patients do, that performing the repeating ritual perfectly could "protect" them or their loved ones. Whenever possible, the patients would resist the urge to repeat, but when unable to do so, would disguise their repeating as "forgetting" their books by the chair, turning back to engage someone in conversation in order to re-enter the doorway, and so on. In a few cases, certain numbers would become "lucky" and actions would have to be repeated that number of times; for example, one girl felt that 5 was a good number and repeated her actions five times. If she didn't do it perfectly, she had to do it over five times five times (25 times). The patient reported, with good humor, that "five times is okay, but those double-digits are killers!"

Checking rituals also were common and were reported by 32 children (46% of sample). Again, in general, there was no set ending to the checking rituals; the child would check until it "felt right" or the urge had dissipated. This checking also was characterized by "rational irrationality." For example, despite a complicated checking ritual involving the stove, curling iron, electric iron, toaster, and other appliances, one 14-year-old girl did not check the home's smoke detectors. This is particularly ironic because the patient's obsessional fear was that an appliance would cause a fire and injure her parents.

Obsessional symmetry, ordering, or exactness was experienced by 12 subjects (17%). Young children would require that their stuffed animals be lined up "just so" on the bed, whereas older children might try to make their steps exactly even or arrange the books and papers in their desk or bookbag in a precise order. One young man had trichotillomania (compulsive hair-pulling) and symmetry concerns, which were manifested as pulling out his arm hairs to try to get the same number on each side. Other common obsessions included aggressive or sexual images (3 subjects, 4%) and scrupulosity (9 subjects, 13%). These scrupulous adolescents reported that they were consumed with worry about going to hell if they were not able always to do the right thing and have only good thoughts. As one might imagine, this was particularly painful and distressing because it was impossible to control their thoughts and comply with the requirements of the scrupulosity obsession.

Miscellaneous compulsions included rituals of writing, moving, or speaking (18 subjects, 26%) and ordering and arranging (12 subjects, 17%). Some children repeated "hum" until they had a good thought, or would blink and carry a bad thought away to a safe corner with a staring ritual. These vocal and ocular rituals, as well as the touching rituals experienced by one fifth of the subjects (14 of 70), closely resemble the motor and vocal tics of Tourette's syndrome and can be very difficult to distinguish. In most cases, the children with OCD were able to verbalize an obsessional thought preceding the ritual and considered the ritual a response to that thought, rather than a motor response to a nondefined urge. The distinction between symptoms of Tourette's syndrome and OCD can be unclear, however, and the two disorders may lie on a single continuum, representing different phenotypic presentations of a single genetic abnormality.[30,34]

Associated Disorders

Only one quarter (26%) of the children had OCD as their sole diagnosis.[37] Associated diagnoses seen most frequently were depression (39%), other anxiety disorders (simple phobia [17%], overanxious disorder [16%], and separation anxiety disorder [7%]), developmental disabilities (24%), oppositional disorder (11%), and attention-deficit disorder (10%). Tourette's syndrome was an exclusionary criterion for the NIMH studies; however, at 2- to 7-year follow-up, 6 of 52 (12%) OCD children met criteria for Tourette's syndrome.[27] (Note: Fifty-two is used as the denominator, rather than 54, because in retrospect, two children might arguably have had Tourette's syndrome at the time of presentation.) Five of these boys had had chronic motor tics at baseline and had "developed" additional vocal and motor tics during the interim. All had had an early presentation of their OCD with typical symptoms of washing or checking. In addition, however, all had had other symptoms that were difficult to categorize as a ritual or a tic; e.g., smelling, spitting, touching, tapping, or bouncing. These behaviors again demonstrate the difficulty of distinguishing between the compulsive rituals of OCD and the complex tics of Tourette's syndrome and speak to the apparent close association between the two disorders.

The relationship between childhood-onset OCD and obsessive compulsive personality disorder (OCP) is unclear. Eleven percent of the NIMH sample[37] met criteria for OCP, in keeping with adult studies. It appears that pediatric subjects initially may present with OCD and at follow-up, meet criteria for OCP; whereas others begin with OCP and later, "develop" OCD. Two-year follow-up of the New Jersey epidemiologic sample revealed that several subjects with early-onset OCD (without obsessive compulsive personality) had developed compulsive personality traits.[5] These adolescents reported that they had developed careful, structured routines to prevent performing their compulsive rituals (e.g., carefully placing objects to avoid straightening rituals) or that they had withdrawn socially, either to prevent contamination or to conserve energy for obsessive compulsive behaviors.

TREATMENT

As with adult-onset OCD, childhood-onset OCD has been treated with a variety of modalities, including pharmacotherapy and behavioral, family, and individual therapy. Although insight-oriented psychotherapy generally has not been helpful for patients with OCD and is not currently the primary treatment of the disorder, it provides an important adjunctive role in decreasing patient anxiety, identifying the role the symptoms play in the patient's life, and increasing coping skills. Group therapy can be particularly helpful as patients clinically improve; helping them to "rebuild" their lives and refocusing on peer and socialization issues. Particularly for adolescents, it is an opportunity to acquire socialization skills—neglected because their OCD may have kept them isolated and "too busy" with their symptoms during crucial formative years.

Family therapy is another important adjunct to the treatment of childhood-onset OCD as it can improve compliance with behavior therapy and pharmacotherapy. Lenane[23] has reviewed the role of family therapy for childhood-onset OCD. One of the major goals of family therapy is to decrease the parental involvement in the child's rituals, helping the parents to realize that their interventions, although well-meaning, may worsen the OCD symptomatology.

Although behavior therapy has not been studied systematically in pediatric patients, open trials suggest that it is as effective for children as it is for adults (see Berg et al[5] for a review). Bolton et al,[7] who conducted a retrospective chart review and identified 15 OCD adolescents treated with behavior therapy over a 4-year period, reported the efficacy of response prevention in

11 obsessive adolescents. Nine additional behavioral treatment case studies used response prevention, frequently in addition to other therapeutic modalities, to treat pediatric patients. Response prevention combined with in vivo exposure, thought to be the most effective combination for adults, was used in only two studies (Apter et al,[2] 8 patients; Zikis,[40] 1 patient) and was effective. Thought stopping for obsessive ruminations was used in three cases, also with good results (Campbell,[8] Friedman and Silvers,[13] and Ownby[29]). Controlled studies of behavior therapy for children, particularly in contrast to drug treatment, are needed and warranted.

Some very young children, who lack the necessary cognitive abilities, may not be suitable for behavioral therapy; but, in general, if the child is motivated and able to understand directions, he or she may be a candidate for behavioral therapy. The information gathering phase of treatment is important but challenging because of the child's secrecy. Use of structured symptom checklists (such as the Yale-Brown Obsessive Compulsive Symptom Checklist[14,15] or Leyton Obsessional Inventory—Child Version[3] can be helpful, as can questioning parents about observed rituals prior to meeting with the child. External and internal cues for obsessive thoughts, importance/consequences of the obsessional thoughts, responsive rituals, and avoidance patterns should be determined through a semi-structured interview, and the child should be asked to identify a chief complaint. Subjective Units of Discomfort (SUDs)[16] should be assigned and designated exposure items should be arranged hierarchically. The exposure items are then presented in ascending order beginning midway. A given item is presented repeatedly until it evokes no more than minimal anxiety. In addition to therapist-guided sessions, exposure homework is assigned after establishing rules for response prevention. In some cases, parents might be involved in monitoring homework,[4] but care must be taken to avoid parental overinvolvement, such as actively prohibiting ritualistic responses.

Pharmacotherapy

Serotonin-reuptake inhibitors, such as clomipramine, fluoxetine, and fluvoxamine, which have been used successfully for the treatment of OCD in adults, also have been used effectively for pediatric patients. Of these medications, clomipramine is the only one to have been systematically evaluated in children. Flament and colleagues[10,11] conducted the first double-blind placebo-controlled trial of clomipramine. Nineteen pediatric patients (mean age of 14.5 ± 2.3 years) took part in a crossover-design study and received 5 weeks of placebo and 5 weeks of clomipramine, with dosages targeting 3 mg/kg/day. Fourteen patients completed the trial and clomipramine was demonstrated to be significantly superior to placebo at week 5 of treatment (P = 0.02 on NIMH-OC scale).[19] Frequently, symptom improvement was observed by week 3 and overall, three quarters of the patients had moderate to marked improvement. There were no baseline predictors of drug response; and as with adults, the response of the obsessive compulsive symptoms was independent of the antidepressant effect.

Leonard et al[26] reported the results of a double-blind crossover comparison of clomipramine and desipramine—a more noradrenergic tricyclic antidepressant—in 48 children and adolescents with OCD. Desipramine was chosen because of its similar side-effect profile and equivalent antidepressant and anxiolytic effectiveness, thus, any difference between the drugs might reflect clomipramine's unique serotonergic properties.[18] The mean age of the 31 male and 18 female participants was 13.9 ± 2.8 years (range 7 to 19 yrs), with a mean age of onset of 10.2 ± 5.8 years (range 5 to 16 yrs). After an initial 2-week single-blind placebo phase, the active treatment phase consisted of a double-blind crossover of two consecutive 5-week treatments of clomipramine and desipramine. Both drugs were targeted at 3 mg/kg/day and the average clomipramine dose was 157 ± 53 mg/day, and the dosage of desipramine was similar at 153 ± 55 mg/day. Clomipramine and desipramine were both well tolerated, and the side-effects profiles of the two drugs were quite similar, although the incidence of tremor and other (sweating, flushing, middle insomnia) side effects was slightly greater with clomipramine than desipramine.

Clomipramine was clearly superior to desipramine in ameliorating OCD symptomatology.[26] On some scales, significant differences were demonstrated by week 3; and at week 5, clomipramine was found to be strikingly and significantly better than desipramine on all measures (e.g., $P = 0.00001$ on the NIMH-OC scale). Two thirds of the patients who received desipramine as their second medication relapsed (worsened OCD and depressive symptom ratings) during the active phase of the study and desipramine was found to be no more effective than placebo had been in the previous study.[10]

Fluoxetine, which currently is indicated by the Food and Drug Administration for the treatment of depression in adults, was used for 28 of the NIMH pediatric subjects who could not tolerate a sufficient dose of clomipramine to maintain symptom remission, who wished to try a second medication, or who had failed to respond completely to clomipramine. Fluoxetine was well tolerated by these adolescents and many showed a clinical response when treated with 20 to 80 mg/day (most patients were started at a lower dosage, 5 to 10 mg/day, because of their weight). Riddle et al[31] reported the results of open trials of fluoxetine in dosages of 10 to 40 mg/day for a group of 10 children and adolescents with primary OCD or Tourette's syndrome with obsessive compulsive symptomatology. Here again, the drug appeared to be well tolerated and effective. These two series and recent anecdotal reports suggest that fluoxetine may be safe, effective, and useful for younger patients with OCD, although large controlled trials are necessary.

PROGNOSIS

Historically, childhood-onset OCD has been considered to be chronic and debilitating.[6,17,39] Flament and colleagues[9] conducted the first prospective study of the clinical prognosis of childhood OCD by following 25 of 27 consecutive OCD patients and 23 of 29 matched controls for 2 to 7 years. The majority of the OCD patients had remained ill. Seventeen patients (68%) still met diagnostic criteria for OCD and 12 of these had other psychopathology, usually depressive or anxiety disorders. Of the eight patients who no longer met criteria for OCD, only three were considered to be well. Outcome was unrelated to any baseline measures, such as severity; neurologic abnormalities; or family history of depression, anxiety disorder, or OCD. Further, initial good response to clomipramine therapy did not convey any prognostic benefit. Some nonresponders did well, whereas others who initially had responded well, were troubled again with OCD symptoms at follow-up.

Leonard and colleagues[25] recently have completed a follow-up study of 54 consecutively admitted children and adolescents with OCD, who had participated in drug treatment studies in the Child Psychiatry Branch of the NIMH. The interval between presentation and follow-up assessment was 3.4 ± 1.0 years (range 2 to 7 years). The mean age of the 36 boys and 18 girls in the sample was 17.4 ± 3.0 years at follow-up. The mean age of onset of OCD was 9.9 ± 3.3 years range (2 to 16 years). At follow-up, 38 of the 54 subjects (70%) were on psychoactive medication. The outcome for this group seemed to be improved over that of Flament et al,[9] as less than half (23 of 54, 43%) of the patients still met diagnostic criteria for OCD and 80% were improved from baseline (5 [15%] were "minimally improved," 16 [30%] were "much improved," and 23 [43%] were "very much improved"). Six patients (11%) were totally asymptomatic and of those, three were on medication at the time of re-evaluation. The majority of patients were still on medication at the time of follow-up (38 subjects, 70%) and one third (18 subjects) had had a behavior therapy trial. A number of baseline variables, including presence of tics, measures of family functioning (as assessed by the Family Environment Scale), neuropsychological test results, and severity of OCD, depression, and anxiety symptoms after 5 weeks of clomipramine therapy, were found to be significantly correlated with long-term outcome. When these variables were entered into a multiple regression, only the NIMH global OCD and NIMH global depression ratings at week 5 of treatment with clomipramine, and father's rating of family activities (from the Family Environment Scale) remained significantly associated.

In a related study, Leonard et al[24] conducted a double-blind substitution (with desipramine) during clomipramine maintenance to determine whether long-term medication is required. The mean duration of treatment prior to enrollment in the study was 17.1 ± 8.3 months (range 4 to 32 months). Twenty-six pediatric patients participated in the 8-month trial (note that this was a self-selected population already known to require clomipramine treatment). All patients received clomipramine for the first 3 months, then half continued with clomipramine therapy and half were (blindly) switched to desipramine for 2 months (substituted patients), and all subjects again received clomipramine for the last 3 study months. Six patients dropped out of the study. Eight (89%) of the nine remaining substituted patients and only two (18%) of the 11 subjects in the clomipramine group relapsed during the 2-month comparison period. It appears that long-term clomipramine treatment conveys benefit and is necessary for symptom relief in pediatric OCD. It is noteworthy that even patients receiving clomipramine maintenance had continued obsessive compulsive symptoms, which varied in severity over time. These results and the follow-up data reviewed previously suggest that although pharmacotherapy and behavior therapy have improved the outcome for pediatric patients with OCD, the disorder remains chronic.

SUMMARY

The clinical presentation of OCD in children and adolescents is quite similar to that in adults, with overlapping obsessional content and compulsive ritualistic patterns. In addition, both age groups provide essentially identical descriptions of the anxiety accompanying their compulsions and invoke similar mechanisms to resist acting out the ritualistic behavior. Responses to behavioral treatment and pharmacotherapy are similar across ages, and the disorder appears to be chronic and unremitting in the studied populations whether its onset is in childhood or adulthood. Conversely, the strong familial influence,[22] male predominance, neuro-endocrine abnormalities,[36] presence of tics and other neurologic abnormalities, and possible impact on personality development suggest that pediatric OCD has important differences from its adult counterpart. Further investigations of these unique features of childhood-onset OCD are warranted and may provide etiologic clues to the disorder.

REFERENCES

1. *American Psychiatric Association:* Diagnostic and Statistical Manual of Mental Disorders, *ed 3. Washington, American Psychiatric Association, 1980.*
2. *Apter, A., Bernhout, E., Tyano, S.: Severe obsessive compulsive disorder in adolescence: A report of eight cases.* J Adolesc *7: 349–358, 1984.*
3. *Berg, C. Z., Rapoport, J. L., Flament, M.: The Leyton Obsessional Inventory— Child Version.* J Am Acad Child Adolesc Psychiatry *25: 84–91, 1986.*
4. *Berg, C. Z., Rapoport, J. L., Wolff, R. P.: Behavioral treatment for obsessive-compulsive disorder in childhood. In Rapoport J. L. (ed):* Obsessive-Compulsive Disorder in Children and Adolescents. *Washington, American Psychiatric Association, 1989 pp 169–185.*
5. *Berg, C. Z., Rapoport, J. L., Whitaker, A., et al: Childhood obsessive compulsive disorder: A two-year prospective follow-up of a community sample.* J Am Acad Child Adolesc Psychiatry *28: 528–533, 1989.*
6. *Berman, L.: Obsessive-compulsive neurosis in children.* J Nerv Ment Dis *95: 26–39, 1942.*
7. *Bolton, D., Collins, S., Steinberg, D.: The treatment of obsessive-compulsive disorder in adolescence: A report of fifteen cases.* Br J Psychiatry *142: 456–464, 1983.*
8. *Campbell, L. M.: A variation of thought-stopping in a twelve-year-old boy: A case report.* J Behav Ther Exp Psychiatry *4: 69–70, 1973.*
9. *Flament, M. F., Koby, E., Rapoport, J. L., et al: Childhood obsessive compulsive disorder. A prospective follow-up study.* J Child Psychol Psychiatry *31: 363–380, 1990.*
10. *Flament, M. F., Rapoport, J. L., Berg, C. J., et al: Clomipramine treatment of childhood compulsive disorder.* Arch Gen Psychiatry *42: 977–983, 1985.*
11. *Flament, M. F., Rapoport, J. L., Murphy, D. L., et al: Biochemical changes during clomipramine treatment of childhood obsessive compulsive disorder.* Arch Gen Psychiatry *44: 219–225, 1987.*
12. *Flament, M. F., Whitaker, A., Rapoport, J. L., et al: Obsessive compulsive disorder in adolescence: An epidemiological study.* J Am Acad Child Adoles Psychiatry *27: 764–771, 1988.*
13. *Friedman, C. T. H., Silvers, F. M.: A multimodality approach to inpatient treatment of obsessive compulsive disorder.* Am J Psychother *31: 456–465, 1977.*
14. *Goodman, W. K., Price, L. H., Rasmussen, S. A., et al: The Yale-Brown Obsessive*

Compulsive Scale (Y-BOCS), Part I. Development, use and reliability. Arch Gen Psychiatry *46: 1006–1011, 1989.*

15. *Goodman, W. K., Price, L. H., Rasmussen, S. A., et al: The Yale-Brown Obsessive Compulsive Scale (Y-BOCS), Part II: Validity.* Arch Gen Psychiatry *46: 1012–1016, 1989.*

16. *Grayson, J. B., Foa, E. B., Steketee, G. S.: Obsessive compulsive disorder. In Hersen, M., Bellack, A. S. (ed):* Handbook of Clinical Behavior Therapy with Adults. *New York, Plenum, 1985.*

17. *Hollingsworth, C., Tanguey, P., Grossman, L., et al: Long-term outcome of obsessive compulsive disorder in children.* J Am Acad Child Psychiatry *19: 134–144, 1980.*

18. *Insel, T. R., Mueller, E. Z., Alterman, I., et al: Obsessive compulsive disorder and serotonin: Is there a connection?* Biol Psychiatry *20: 1174–1188, 1985.*

19. *Insel, T. R., Murphy, D. L., Cohen, R. M., et al: Obsessive–compulsive disorder: A double-blind trial of clomipramine and clorgyline.* Arch Gen Psychiatry *40: 605–612, 1983.*

20. *Joffe, R. T., Swinson, R. P., Regan, J. J.: Personality features of obsessive-compulsive disorder.* Am J Psychiatry *145: 1127–1129, 1988.*

21. *Judd, L.: Obsessive compulsive neurosis in children.* Arch Gen Psychiatry *12: 136–143, 1965.*

22. *Lenane, M., Swedo, S., Leonard, H. L., et al: Psychiatric disorders in first degree relatives of children and adolescents with obsessive compulsive disorder.* J Am Acad Child Adolesc Psychiatry *29: 407–412, 1990.*

23. *Lenane, M. C.: Family therapy for children with obsessive-compulsive disorder. In Pato M. T., Zohar, J. (eds):* Current Treatments of Obsessive-Compulsive Disorder. *Washington American Psychiatric Press, 1991, pp 103–113.*

24. *Leonard, H. L., Swedo, S. E., Lenane, M. C., et al: A double-blind desipramine substitution during long-term clomipramine treatment in children and adolescents with obsessive-compulsive disorder.* Arch Gen Psychiatry *48: 922–927, 1991.*

25. *Leonard, H. L., Swedo, S. E., Lenane, M. C., et al: A 2- to 7-year follow-up study of 54 obsessive compulsive children and adolescents.* Arch Gen Psychiatry, *50: 429–439, 1993.*

26. *Leonard, H. L., Swedo, S. E., Rapoport, J. L., et al: Treatment of childhood obsessive compulsive disorder with clomipramine and desipramine: A double-blind crossover comparison.* Arch Gen Psychiatry *46: 1088–1092, 1989.*

27. *Leonard, H. L., Swedo, S. E., Rapoport, J. L., et al: The diagnosis of Tourette's syndrome at two to seven year follow-up of 54 obsessive-compulsive children.* Am J Psychiatry, *in press.*

28. *Moos, R. H., Moos, B. S.:* Family Environment Scale Manual. *Palo Alto, CA, Consulting Psychologists Press, 1986.*

29. *Ownby, R. L.: A cognitive behavioral intervention for compulsive handwashing for a thirteen-year-old boy.* Psychology in the Schools *20: 219–222, 1983.*

30. *Pauls, D. L., Towbin, K. E., Leckman, J. F., et al: Gilles de la Tourette's syndrome and obsessive-compulsive disorder: Evidence supporting a genetic relationship.* Arch Gen Psychiatry *43: 1180–1182, 1986.*

31. *Riddle, M. A., Hardin, M. T., King, R., et al: Fluoxetine treatment of children*

and adolescents with Tourette's and obsessive compulsive disorders: Preliminary clinical experience. J Am Acad Child Adoles Psychiatry 29: 45–48, 1990.

32. Riddle, M. A., Scahill, L., King, R., et al: Obsessive compulsive disorder in children and adolescents: Phenomenology and family history. J Am Acad Child Adolesc Psychiatry 29: 766–772, 1990.

33. Rutter, M., Tizard, J., Whitmore, K.: Education, Health and Behavior. London, Longmans, 1970.

34. Swedo, S. E.: Rituals and releasers: An ethological model of obsessive-compulsive disorder. In Rapoport, J. L. (ed): Obsessive-Compulsive Disorder in Children and Adolescents. Washington, American Psychiatric Association, 1989.

35. Swedo, S. E., Rapoport, J. L.: Phenomenology and differential diagnosis of obsessive-compulsive disorder in children and adolescents. In Rapoport, J. L. (ed): Obsessive-Compulsive Disorder in Children and Adolescents. Washington, American Psychiatric Association, 1989.

36. Swedo, S. E., Leonard, H. L., Kruesi, M. J. P., et al: Cerebrospinal fluid neurochemistry in children and adolescents with obsessive-compulsive disorder. Arch Gen Psychiatry 49: 29–36, 1992.

37. Swedo, S. E., Rapoport, J. L., Leonard, H., et al: Obsessive-compulsive disorder in children and adolescents: Clinical phenomenology of 70 consecutive cases. Arch Gen Psychiatry 46: 335–341, 1989.

38. Thomsen, P. H., Mikkelsen, H. U.: Children and adolescents with obsessive-compulsive disorder. The demographic and diagnostic characteristics of 61 Danish patients. Acta Psychiatr Scand 83: 262–266, 1991.

39. Warren, W.: A study of adolescent psychiatric in-patients and the outcome six or more years later. J Child Psychol Psychiatry 6: 141–160, 1965.

40. Zikis, P.: Treatment of an 11-year-old obsessive compulsive ritualizer and Tiquer girl with in vivo exposure and response prevention. Behavior Psychotherapy 11: 75–81, 1983.

20. The Spectrum of Obsessive-Compulsive–Related Disorders

Dan J. Stein and Eric Hollander

Recent advances in our understanding of obsessive-compulsive disorder (OCD) have led to increased attention to a number of apparently related disorders. The notion of a spectrum of obsessive-compulsive–related disorders (OCRDs) has gained some popularity (Jenike 1990). In this chapter we review several ways of thinking about the OCD spectrum of disorders. We discuss two traditional clinically based approaches to the OCRDs: that of the early descriptive psychiatrists and that of the classical psychoanalysts. We also note the existence of some less clinically based work on the spectrum of ruminative thoughts. We then consider the relationship between OCD and anxiety, and between OCD and depression. Finally, we consider the evidence of a spectrum between OCD and tic, somatoform, grooming, eating, and impulse disorders. We begin, however, with some comments on the general nature of spectrums of psychopathology and on the value of exploring such spectrums.

SPECTRUMS OF PSYCHOPATHOLOGY

The traditional way of classifying psychiatric disorders entails a categorical approach. Categories are convenient abstractions of clinically important information. They enable the clinician to readily classify different patients, and they may suggest a standard clinical approach.

Categorical classifications may also use hierarchies and groupings to establish relationships between different entities. The various disorders that have been discussed in this book, for example, are classified in DSM-III (American Psychiatric Association 1980) and DSM-III-R (American Psychiatric Association 1987) as quite separate entities that fall in different groupings. Thus, OCD is classified as an anxiety disorder, Tourette's syndrome (TS) as a tic

Reprinted by permission of the American Psychiatric Press from *Obsessive-Compulsive Related Disorders,* edited by Eric Hollander, Washington, D.C., 1993, 241–62.

disorder, anorexia nervosa as an eating disorder, body dysmorphic disorder (BDD) and hypochondriasis as somatoform, or perhaps delusional, disorders, trichotillomania as an impulse disorder, and compulsive sexuality as a sexual dysfunction disorder. Because hierarchical considerations apply, the diagnosis of OCD is not given if, for example, the obsessions occur in relation to food and an eating disorder is present. This diagnostic approach provides the clinician with a series of categories that are useful insofar as they allow classification of patients and suggest appropriate clinical approaches. It is also useful, for example, in pointing out that obsessive-compulsive symptoms occur in the context of anorexia nervosa.

On the other hand, there are reasons for employing a dimensional approach in classifying psychopathology. First, the phenomena of the world are only rarely classifiable into categories that are homogeneous, mutually exclusive, and jointly exhaustive. Psychiatric phenomena often fall on a continuum (Kendell 1975). Thus a dimensional approach allows the classification of patients who fall at the border of classical entities or who are otherwise atypical. Similarly, if a patient has the signs and symptoms of two categorical entities, these can be seen as related rather than as merely comorbid. A dimensional perspective may be useful, for example, in working with a patient who appears to fall on the border of OCD and BDD; who simultaneously has TS, trichotillomania, and OCD; or who presents with anorexia nervosa and then goes on to develop OCD.

The DSM manuals note in the introductory section that there are no sharp and natural boundaries that separate mental disorders from normality and from one another. The DSM-III and DSM-III-R emphasize polythetic diagnostic criteria, encourage the use of multiple diagnoses, and include a multiaxial system—all features that make them more flexible than their predecessors, which were more categorical in spirit (Frances 1982). Nevertheless, as can be seen from the classification of OCD and its related disorders, the DSM manuals ultimately retain a focus on *categories* of obsessive-compulsive symptoms. In the remainder of this chapter we will discuss a number of *dimensions* of obsessive and compulsive symptoms.

A second reason for employing a dimensional rather than a categorical approach to psychopathology concerns the different emphasis that each gives to theoretical relationships between disorders. In a categorical system, hierarchies and groupings may be used to suggest relationships between different entities. In a dimensional system, these kinds of relationships may be more overtly specified as particular dimensions are employed to draw attention to particular relationships between different entities. Thus a classification in which rituals and tics fall along a continuous dimension specifies a relationship between OCD and TS. Such a classification may more readily suggest that rituals and tics have a similar etiology, or that they respond to similar treatment.

The introductory section to the DSM manuals argues that these classification systems are atheoretical with respect to the question of etiology. The use of hierarchies and groupings in the manuals does, however, embody some theory about the relationships between disorders. Thus the classification of OCD as an anxiety disorder suggests a relationship between OCD and anxiety. Conversely, the classification of BDD in an entirely different section implies that OCD and BDD are not related. On the other hand, the exclusion criteria in OCD concerning anorexia nervosa point to a relationship between these two disorders. Nevertheless, it may be argued that more detail deserves to be paid to specifying the relationships between different OCRDs. In the remainder of this chapter we will consider possible relationships between the OCRDs at some length.

The categorical and dimensional approaches to psychopathology are not necessarily exclusive. In this book we have already taken a categorical approach to the OCRDs, and we now explore the dimensions along which these disorders fall. It is useful perhaps to list the criteria for considering two categories as dimensionally related. We suggest that diagnostic categories are initially considered along a spectrum if there is considerable symptom overlap. Associated features such as age at onset, clinical course, comorbidity, level of impairment, and prevalence provide further evidence of a spectrum. Similar etiology, as demonstrated by familial linkage, biological markers, or therapeutic (pharmacological) dissection, perhaps provides the most convincing justification for a spectrum.

OBSESSIVE-COMPULSIVE DISORDER AND DELUSIONS

Early descriptions portray obsessive-compulsive symptoms as related to psychotic states. Westphal contended that obsessions represent a disorder of thinking, and Bleuler regarded obsessive-compulsiveness as a prodrome or variant of schizophrenia (Insel and Akiskal 1986). Both OCD and schizophrenia have early onset, a chronic and debilitating course, and intrusive thoughts and bizarre behavior. OCD patients have been noted to have perceptual distortions (Yaryura-Tobias and Neziroglu 1984). Early authors had limited means with which to investigate organic factors. The etiologic basis for the phenomenological spectrum between OCD and psychosis was, however, considered by these authors to be organic in nature.

Obsessive-compulsive disorder and schizophrenia appear, however, to be readily distinguishable. Although the delusions of schizophrenia can resemble particular obsessional concerns, there is usually less insight into the former. The rituals of schizophrenic patients do not appear to be purposeful and are often in response to what the patient perceives as an external force. Other core positive and negative symptoms of schizophrenia are not present in OCD. Moreover, it has been found that OCD patients only rarely become schizophrenic (Goodwin et al. 1969) and that schizophrenic patients only rarely have OCD (Fenton and McGlashan 1985; Rosen 1957). No family study has suggested a genetic relationship between OCD and schizophrenia, and findings from imaging studies and medication responsivity data do not suggest similarities between the two disorders. However, Kindler et al. (1993) emphasized the need for further research on schizophrenic patients with obsessive-compulsive symptoms. They pointed out that the prevalence of such symptoms in schizophrenia may be higher than previously thought, that dopamine appears to play a role in both schizophrenia and OCD, and that schizophrenic patients with OCD may respond to serotonin reupake blockers.

Furthermore, there are a considerable number of reports that describe a transition from obsessions to delusions (Insel and Akiskal 1986). The similarity between delusional disorder and OCD has perhaps been underplayed. The two are traditionally distinguished as follows: in OCD, symptoms are recognized as senseless or excessive, while in the delusional disorder, symptoms are, by definition, delusional in intensity. Also, OCD is thought to begin in childhood, adolescence, or early adulthood, while delusional disorder begins in late adulthood. Nevertheless, the obsessional concerns and consequent behaviors of patients with delusional disorder may mimic those of the OCD patient. Conversely, in many cases of OCD, obsessions are ego-syntonic and compulsions are not thought unreasonable (Insel and Akiskal 1986; Stern and Cobb 1978). In both OCD and delusional disorder the obsession or delusion is fairly restricted, and there is no evidence of thought disorder or other positive and negative symptoms.

In addition, the content of such obsessions may be similar in OCD and delusional disorder. Thus a concern with contamination may be present in both. Jealousy may be present in both erotomania and OCD, and somatic concerns may be present in both somatic delusion disorder and OCD. The severe dysfunction and perhaps poorer prognosis of OCD patients with ego-syntonic symptoms may parallel that seen in psychotic patients. Again, there may be some overlap in treatment response of OCD and delusional disorder (Jenike 1990; McDougle et al. 1990).

OBSESSIVE-COMPULSIVE DISORDER AND OBSESSIVE-COMPULSIVE PERSONALITY DISORDER

Freud and subsequent psychoanalysts substituted for the early connection between obsessive-compulsive symptoms and psychosis an emphasis on the concepts of neurosis and character. In his classic volume, Salzman (1968), a contemporary analyst, describes the phenomenology of obsessive-compulsivity as existing on a spectrum between a character problem and a neurotic problem in which symptoms manifest. Both clinical presentations are explicable on the basis of a particular set of underlying dynamic mechanisms, but in the case of the character problem these mechanisms are more functional and more ego-syntonic. In addition, Salzman describes a set of OCD-related disorders, namely phobias and alcoholism. The basis on which he considers these to be related disorders is again the existence of similar underlying psychodynamics. Such disorders as TS, trichotillomania, BDD, hypochondriasis, and anorexia nervosa are not referenced in the book.

Contemporary thinking does not support the notion of OCD as on a spectrum with obsessive-compulsive personality disorder (OCPD). Modern nosology emphasizes the traditional phenomenological distinction between OCD and OCPD patients: the former have ego-dystonic obsessions and compulsions, whereas the latter have ego-syntonic character traits without obsessions and compulsions. However, obsessions and compulsions are sometimes ego-syntonic, and OCPD patients often experience discomfort and disability. Furthermore, some overlap in symptoms may be present—for example, both OCD and OCPD patients may be hoarders, or have extreme moral scrupulosity. Nevertheless, the phenomenological distinction between OCD and OCPD appears statistically reproducible (Pollack 1979). More closely related to the phenomenology of OCD is subclinical OCD—that is, obsessions and compulsions that are only minimally resisted and that do not cause significant distress or dysfunction and therefore do not meet the criteria for OCD (Rachman and Da Silva 1978).

The idea that a particular etiologic mechanism accounts for both OCD and OCPD has also not received much support. Several studies have indicated that OCPD neither precedes nor is always associated with OCD (Baer et al. 1990; Black 1974; Joffe et al. 1988; Pollack 1987). Conversely, patients with

OCPD may not develop other psychiatric disorders, or they may develop psychiatric disorders other than OCD. Neuropsychological studies of patients with OCD (Rosen et al. 1988) and of patients with OCPD (Reed 1977) have not clearly pointed to a continuum between the disorders, although more work needs to be done. Early family studies suggesting increased obsessional traits in relatives of OCD patients, and more recent controlled studies pointing to an increase in OCD in relatives, have been reviewed by Rasmussen and Eisen (1990). These authors argue, however, that further diagnostic clarity between OCD and OCPD is necessary in such work. Finally, although there is a lack of controlled studies, it appears that patients with OCD respond to behavior treatment, while the psychotherapy of choice for OCPD patients is insight oriented.

The relationship between OCD and OCPD nevertheless remains of interest. Swedo et al. (1989b) have suggested that OCPD may develop in some OCD patients as an adaptation to the illness. There are anecdotal reports of OCPD patients experiencing subjective alleviation and improved functioning on serotonergic agents. Understanding the etiologic mechanisms of OCPD may therefore contribute to our knowledge of OCD.

OBSESSIVE-COMPULSIVE DISORDER AND RUMINATION

While obsessive-compulsive phenomena have been approached by psychiatrists from a clinical perspective, psychologists have tackled similar phenomena from a somewhat different viewpoint. Martin and Tesser (1989), for example, have explored rumination using a cognitive-psychology framework. They define rumination as conscious thinking directed toward a given object for an extended period of time. The concept therefore refers to a broad range of cognitive phenomena, including problem solving and anticipation as well as a number of different thoughts seen in the clinic, such as negative thoughts in depressed patients and intrusive thoughts in OCD.

Martin and Tessler (1989) emphasize that ruminations involve both automatic and controlled processes. For example, following a negative event such as the death of a close relative, a person may attempt to analyze the implications of this loss for his or her life and try to form new strategies and plans. At the same time the person may find that he or she is subject to images of the relative, images that appear unpredictably and that have an intrusive, disturbing quality. The authors argue that rumination involves attempts to find ways of reaching important unattained goals or attempts to find ways of reconciling oneself to not reaching those goals.

It is unlikely that this explanation of rumination provides a comprehensive account of the genesis of OCD and related disorders. Stressors appear to play only a minor role in OCD, and a characteristic feature of the symptoms of OCD is their senselessness, or the lack of relation between goals and symptoms. Advances in cognitive psychology may, however, have clinical relevance. Cognitive theories that employ cybernetic constructs, for example, may be useful in explaining the characteristic senselessness of ruminations in OCD. Thus it has been suggested that in OCD there is a persistence of high error signals or mismatch, resulting in subjective incompleteness and doubt as well as repetitive behaviors to reduce such signals (Pitman 1987a). Furthermore, cognitive theories of clinical phenomena may be useful in suggesting different methods for cognitive-behavioral therapy, and, as Josephson and Brondolo (1993) argue, such therapy can be efficacious in the treatment of OCD and OCRDs.

OBSESSIVE-COMPULSIVE DISORDER AND ANXIETY AND DEPRESSION

Although the DSM classification system claims to be atheoretical, we have argued that it does embody certain theoretical assumptions. For example, in terms of the differentiation that we have drawn between OCD as on a spectrum with psychotic or personality problems, the DSM rejects this and places OCD on a spectrum with the anxiety disorders. Furthermore, the diagnostic criteria for OCD emphasize that obsessions are senseless and elicit resistance, thus differentiating them from the delusionality of psychosis and the ego-syntonicity of personality disorder. Finally, the diagnostic criteria suggest that compulsions occur in order to decrease anxiety.

These operational definitions warrant further consideration. While the DSM manuals note that overvalued ideas may occur, some studies suggest that up to 35% of patients with OCD do not regard their obsessions as senseless (Stern and Cobb 1978) and that a proportion of patients are absolutely convinced of them (Insel and Akiskal 1986). Resistance to obsessions varies a great deal (Insel and Akiskal 1986; Stern and Cobb 1978). Compulsions may take place divorced from obsessional ideas and may be experienced as involuntary and purposeless. On the other hand, others have been concerned that the worries of generalized anxiety disorder may be classified as obsessions (Mackenzie et al. 1990), or that subclinical OCD may be ignored by the DSM. The DSM-IV Task Force is presently conducting field trials with the goal of reformulating the diagnostic criteria for OCD.

The classification of OCD as an anxiety disorder also bears further consideration. Again, there are a number of arguments for and against this position. It is clear that many patients with OCD do suffer from anxiety. It may also be argued that there is some phenomenological overlap between the various anxiety disorders. Thus there appears to be some similarity between the experience of phobia and consequent avoidance, and that of obsessionality and subsequent compulsivity. Compulsive cleaning behavior, for example, can be construed as the consequence of a dirt-disease-contamination phobia (Rachman 1976). The pattern of fear and avoidance in panic disorder has also been compared with OCD, and it has been noted that agoraphobic individuals often have obsessional concerns and compulsive behaviors related to traveling (Turner et al. 1979). On the other hand, phobias and phobic avoidance generally require the presence of the feared object or situation to trigger symptomatology, whereas this is not the case in OCD. Obsessional doubts may become *more,* not less, certain with reassurance, and it has been noted that the performance of rituals may increase anxiety. Finally, when there is an increase in external stress, some OCD patients may have a decrease in symptoms (Insel 1982).

A number of studies indicate that patients with OCD are more likely to have symptoms of other anxiety disorders, as are relatives of patients with OCD (Rasmussen and Eisen 1990). Furthermore, there appears to be some overlap in neurobiological markers and therapeutic response. Thus *m*-chlorophenylpiperazine (m-CPP), a partial serotonin agonist, causes an exacerbation of OCD symptomatology (Hollander et al. 1988a; Zohar et al. 1987) in a subgroup of OCD patients and can trigger panic-like attacks (Kahn et al. 1988) in panic-prone individuals. Fluoxetine, a serotonin reuptake blocker, appears useful in the treatment of both panic disorder (Gorman et al. 1987) and OCD (Liebowitz et al. 1989). On the other hand, a variety of panicogens, including lactate (Gorman et al. 1985) and yohimbine (Rasmussen et al. 1987), do not exacerbate OCD. Furthermore, fluoxetine is effective at much lower doses and the response time is quicker in panic disorder than in OCD. Clomipramine appears to have a differential benefit over other antidepressants in the case of OCD (Leonard et al. 1988; Zohar and Insel 1987), whereas this difference is not apparent when these agents are used to treat other anxiety disorders.

Although the DSM manuals do not indicate that OCD is a mood disorder, the relationship between OCD and depression has also received some consideration. OCD was considered a variant of depression by Maudsley, and psychoanalysts have long argued that most depressive patients have obsessional personalities. Certainly, OCD is often accompanied by depression (Rasmussen and Eisen 1990). Depression, on the other hand is accompanied by ruminations that may have an obsessive nature, as well as by obsessive-compulsive symptoms (Kendell and Discipio 1970; Peselow et al. 1990; Vaughan 1976). Nevertheless, the ruminations of depression occur against the background of depressed mood and, within that context, differ from the senseless intrusion of OCD obsessions. A number of biological markers suggest similarities between OCD and depression (Insel 1983). Serotonin has long been thought to play an important role in depression (Meltzer 1990), and OCD has been found to respond to a variety of antidepressants. Nevertheless, serotonin has been more closely linked to OCD than to depression, and the specificity of the response of OCD to serotonergic medication differs from the general response to antidepressants seen in mood disorders. Again, in the case of fluoxetine, antiobsessional doses are higher and take longer to work than antidepressant doses. Furthermore, the efficacy of antidepressant medication in OCD is not dependent on the presence of coexistent depression (DeVeaugh-Geiss et al. 1988). In short, it seems that some of the links between OCD and anxiety also pertain to OCD and depression.

In summary, we would conclude that although there is some evidence for retaining the concept of OCD as an anxiety disorder, further consideration and validation are required. Alternative ways of conceptualizing (and therefore perhaps of classifying) the OCD spectrum also require exploration. In the following sections we consider the overlap between OCD and TS, trichotillomania, BDD, hypochondriasis, and eating disorders.

OBSESSIVE-COMPULSIVE DISORDER AND TOURETTE'S SYNDROME

In this section we will discuss some of the neurological and organic disorders that appear to be on a spectrum with OCD. Advances in the neurobiology of both OCD and these various disorders allow us to consider in greater depth the neurochemical and neuroanatomical substrate of the spectrum of obsessive-compulsivity.

One of the most intriguing relationships of OCD is that with Tourette's syndrome. Gilles de la Tourette's (1885) initial description of the syndrome included a patient with tics, vocalizations, and perhaps obsessions. Recent studies have confirmed this association between recurrent motor and phonic tics of TS and obsessive-compulsive symptomatology (Hollander et al. 1989b; Leckman 1993). The occurrence of tics in patients with OCD has also been noted (Pitman et al. 1987; Rasmussen and Tsuang 1986). Indeed, Pitman et al. (1987) found that tics were more useful in distinguishing relatives of patients with OCD from relatives of control subjects than were obsessions or compulsions.

To some extent, the ego-dystonic experience of obsessions as intrusive and senseless differentiates OCD from TS, in which tics are not necessarily perceived as intrusive and may be accompanied by a welcome release of tension. Furthermore, while compulsions are defined as purposeful and intentional and are designed to prevent discomfort or some dreaded event, tics are often purposeless and involuntary and are not generally connected with dread or prevention of some future event. Nevertheless, obsessions may become ego-syntonic, and compulsions may be felt as involuntary and need not be associated with future harm, particularly in patients with the need for perfection or symmetry. Conversely, just as obsessions may be resisted by the patient, so tics may be suppressed for a brief period of time. Also, just as compulsions often result in a reduction of anxiety, so tics result in reduced tension. The distinction between complex tics and compulsions may therefore be difficult to make.

The term "impulsions" was employed by Bender and Schilder (1940) to describe a childhood phenomenon in which there was preoccupation with a specific subject (e.g., motor cars), leading to the performance of specific actions (e.g., painting cars). Impulsions differed from obsessions and compulsions in that patients were not bothered by them. Shapiro et al. (1988) have used the term "impulsions" to describe the obsessive-compulsive–like symptoms frequently found in TS (e.g., repeated touching). Touching and symmetry behavior is more common in TS than in OCD (Pitman et al. 1987). Often there is only mild resistance to such activities, and the activities may not interfere with functioning. We would agree that while the lack of distress and dysfunction often means that these symptoms do not meet the criteria for OCD, they are a common subtype of compulsion, and like compulsions they are followed by a reduction in anxiety. We would therefore consider these activities obsessive-compulsive behaviors characteristic of subclinical OCD.

It should be noted, however, that a number of symptoms commonly seen in TS, such as echo phenomena, coprolalia, self-destructive behavior, and childhood attention-deficit disorder, are seen much less frequently in OCD (Pitman et al. 1987).

Family studies indicate a high rate of OCD and/or tics in relatives of TS patients (Comings and Comings 1987; Pauls et al. 1984, 1986) and a high rate of TS and/or tics in relatives of OCD patients (Pauls 1989; Pitman et al. 1987). These authors argue that at least a subgroup of OCD patients may represent a different manifestation of the same underlying factors that are responsible for TS and chronic multiple tic disorder.

A relationship has also been established between OCD or obsessive-compulsiveness and other movement disorders including Sydenham's chorea (Rapoport 1989), von Economo's encephalitis (Jenike 1984; Schilder 1938), Huntington's disease (Dewhurst et al. 1969), and Parkinson's disease (Menza et al. 1990). Obsessive-compulsive symptoms have been noted in various organic illnesses such as Lesch-Nyhan syndrome (Yaryura-Tobias and Neziroglu 1984) and Prader-Willi syndrome. Obsessive-compulsive symptoms have occurred in a variety of other neurological disorders, including head injury (McKeon et al. 1984), birth trauma (Capstick and Seldrup 1977), seizure disorder (Bear and Fedio 1977; Kettl and Marks 1986), brain tumors (Cambier et al. 1988), diabetes insipidus (Barton 1965), and others (Grimshaw 1964). More specifically, OCD symptoms have occurred after damage to the basal ganglia (Laplane et al. 1989) and with frontal cortical lesions (Ward 1988).

An immediate question is the underlying neurochemical and neuroanatomical basis for a link between such disorders as OCD and TS. A good deal of research is now available on neurobiological similarities and differences when OCD and TS are compared. We can begin with the neurochemical.

On the basis of cerebrospinal fluid (CSF) measurements of dopamine metabolites, exacerbation of symptoms with dopamine agonists, and treatment response to dopamine blockers in TS, and on CSF 5-hydroxyindoleacetic acid (5-HIAA), pharmacological challenges with serotonin agonists and antagonists, and therapeutic response to serotonergic medication in OCD, TS has been thought of as a disorder of dopamine function, and OCD as a disorder of serotonin function (Hollander et al. 1989b; Leckman 1993). Nevertheless, there are a number of preclinical and clinical findings which suggest that the picture is more complex than this. On the one hand there is substantial interlinkage between serotonin and dopamine tracts (Gabay 1981). Dopaminergic agents lead to a variety of stereotypies that mimic obsessive-compulsive symptoms, and dopamine is implicated in hoarding behavior (Goodman et al. 1990). OCD does not always respond to serotonergic medication, and it turns out that if medications are highly serotonin selective, they may not lead to as good a response (Jenike et al. 1990). McDougle et al.

(1990) have shown the value of dopamine blockers in the treatment of some OCD patients. Conversely, in some TS patients, CSF 5-HIAA is decreased (Butler et al. 1979; Cohen et al. 1979), and postmortem studies show decreased tryptophan and serotonin in various brain regions, including the basal ganglia (Anderson et al. 1989). Studies of serotonergic probes have not yet been undertaken in TS. Clomipramine has been useful in some TS patients (Ciprian 1980; Yaryura-Tobias and Neziroglu 1977), and fluoxetine has been shown to improve obsessions and compulsions in these patients (Riddle et al. 1990). While the neurochemistry of these disorders clearly requires further investigation to clarify the exact nature of the dysfunctions and the precise contribution of the various neurotransmitter systems (including the noradrenergic system), it is apparent that there are not only differences in the underlying neurochemistry of OCD and TS, but also important similarities.

This account may also have applicability to the relationship between OCD and other neurological and organic disorders. Thus in Parkinson's disease, a disorder in which patients are noted to be stoic, industrious, and inflexible, there is not only dopaminergic dysfunction but also serotonin involvement (Mayeux et al. 1984). In Lesch-Nyhan syndrome, which is characterized by compulsive self-mutilation, 5-hydroxytryptophan has been found useful (Mizuno and Yugari 1975; Mizuno et al. 1970), and Yaryura-Tobias and Neziroglu (1984) report that clomipramine is also useful. Although the obsessive-compulsiveness in such disorders may be more dissimilar from OCD than even the obsessive-compulsive symtomatology seen in TS, the investigation of such disorders may turn out to enhance our understanding of the neurobiology of OCD and related disorders.

Attention has also been paid to possible neuroanatomical similarities between OCD and TS that would fit with the phenomenological and neurochemical similarities. Increasing mention is made of the importance of basal ganglia and orbitofrontal cortex neurocircuitry in these disorders (Modell et al. 1989; Leckman 1993). The association between OCD and site-specific neurological disorders supports the involvement of such pathways. Furthermore, abnormal movements and soft-sign examinations are present in OCD and TS (Hollander et al. 1989b). Neuropsychological testing and electrophysiological studies in OCD and TS indicate heterogeneity within the disorders, but suggest some similar abnormalities in the two disorders (Hollander et al. 1989b). More specific evidence lies in neuropathological studies of the striatum in TS (Chase et al. 1986). Brain imaging in OCD (Baxter 1990) and TS (Chase et al. 1984) also suggests involvement of the basal ganglia and orbitofrontal cortex. Finally, psychosurgical ablation of corresponding neurocircuitry has had therapeutic efficacy in OCD (Modell et al. 1990).

Involvement of these pathways may again be of importance in understanding the association between OCD and other organic and neurological disorders.

In summary, advances in modern neurobiology suggest that OCD is related to various organic and neurological disorders on the basis of overlapping pathogenic mechanisms. Such research contributes in turn to the way in which we think of the phenomenology of the OCD spectrum. Thus it becomes increasingly likely that we will focus on tics and other neurological signs and symptoms in OCD patients and their relatives.

OBSESSIVE-COMPULSIVE DISORDER AND THE BODY: GROOMING, SOMATOFORM, AND EATING DISORDERS

The finding that obsessive-compulsiveness in a variety of different disorders may have underlying pathogenic similarities leads to a review of obsessions and compulsions that are not traditionally included under the category of OCD but appear to be phenomenologically related. In this section we will focus on ruminations and rituals that concern the body. Under this rubric we will look at trichotillomania, BDD, hypochondriasis, depersonalization disorder, and anorexia nervosa. Other obsessive-compulsive habits revolving around the body include certain forms of scratching, nail biting, oral habits, head banging, and self-mutilation (Hollander et al. 1988b; Koblenzer 1987; Primeau and Fontaine 1987).

Trichotillomania

In describing the difference between the compulsions of OCD and trichotillomania, Skodol (1989) notes that although hair pulling is associated with relief, this action may not be purposeful or closely connected with preventing or producing some future event. Patients with trichotillomania appear to have only this one symptom, rather than the multiple obsessions and compulsions often found in OCD patients (Jenike 1990). While both OCD and trichotillomania have an early onset, the sex ratio in the two disorders differs markedly, with many more females than males suffering from the latter disorder (Swedo et al. 1989a). Anecdotal findings suggest that such patients have impulsive rather than compulsive personality disorders.

Nevertheless, as Swedo (1993) notes, there is some evidence that OCD and trichotillomania have similar underpinnings. Hair pulling is often described as ego-dystonic and is resisted. Swedo reported a preliminary family study indicating a higher-than-normal incidence of both OCD and trichotillomania in first-degree relatives of patients with trichotillomania. Brain imaging in patients with trichotillomania (Swedo et al. 1990) indicates differences from OCD patients but shows that treatment efficacy is negatively correlated with anterior cingulate and orbital frontal metabolism, a finding that corresponds with data from OCD studies. Finally, Swedo et al. (1989a) report that clomipramine is more efficacious than desipramine in treating trichotillomania. Preliminary work by Winchel et al. (1989) suggests that fluoxetine is also helpful in treating trichotillomania, although our own observations (unpublished) are that fluoxetine is often not helpful. A neuroethological model suggests that OCD and trichotillomania may involve disturbances in grooming behaviors.

Somatoform Disorders: Body Dysmorphic Disorder and Hypochondriasis

Body dysmorphic disorder is characterized by preoccupation with some imagined defect in appearance in a normal-appearing person. In hypochondriasis there is preoccupation with the fear, or the belief, of having a serious disease, in the absence of a physical evaluation of abnormality. As these are somatoform disorders, it is implied that these preoccupations are not intrusive and senseless. By definition they are not of delusional intensity. Nevertheless, in BDD, hypochondriasis, and OCD, the fixity of and resistance to the pathological thought vary greatly and may change in the individual patient over time. It is therefore possible to see a phenomenological similarity between BDD, hypochondriasis, and OCD, and to postulate that the continuum between OCD and delusional disorder is seen also in BDD and hypochondriasis. As Hollander and Phillips (1993) and Fallon et al. (1993) point out, both BDD patients and hypochondriacal patients may have other obsessions and compulsions, and OCD patients may have concerns about body defects or disease. Obsessive-compulsive traits may be more common in BDD (Andreasen and Bardach 1977; Thomas 1984). A number of validators, such as course, prevalence, age at onset, comorbidity, level of impairment, and sex ratio, appear to be similar in BDD and OCD (Hollander et al. 1992b). At times there may be a family history of OCD in patients with BDD (Hollander et al. 1989c). Body dysmorphic symptoms of delusional intensity have been reported to be exacerbated with marijuana (Hollander et al. 1989c), and this also has been reported secondary to cyproheptadine administration (Craven and Rodin 1987), suggesting possible serotonergic involvement.

There are reports of these disorders responding to antidepressants (Jenike et al. 1990), and our group has found fluoxetine to be helpful in treatment of both disorders (Hollander 1991; Hollander et al. 1989c; Fallon et al. 1993). When hypochondriasis is of delusional intensity, a dopaminergic agent may be helpful (Munro and Chmara 1982).

Depersonalization Disorder

In depersonalization disorder there are concerns about the reality of one's sense of self. As this is a dissociative disorder, it is again implied that these concerns are not intrusive and senseless. Nevertheless, as Hollander and Phillips (1993) point out, such symptoms may well be experienced as ego-dystonic. Premorbid obsessional traits have been reported in depersonalized patients (Roth 1959; Torch 1978). Conversely, doubt has long been thought central to OCD, and Janet emphasized the role of depersonalization in OCD (Pitman 1987b). More recently, Hollander and colleagues (1990b) have noted depersonalization symptoms in OCD and panic disorder patients. Depersonalization occurs with migraine (Comfort 1982) and is exacerbated by marijuana (Szymanski 1981), suggesting the involvement of serotonin. Hollander et al. (1989a, 1990b) have suggested that depersonalization disorder responds to fluoxetine.

Anorexia Nervosa

Patients with eating disorders are classically distinguished from OCD patients in that the former have obsessions and compulsions relating to the body and to eating. The obsessions and compulsions of eating disorders are often described as more ego-syntonic than those of OCD, but once more this is a variable finding. A number of early authors conceived of anorexia as a subtype of OCD (Dubois 1949–1950; Palmer and Jones 1939). Indeed, as Kaye et al. (1993) note, a high proportion of eating disorder patients have other obsessions and compulsions. Conversely, some patients with OCD have concerns with the body and with eating.

Family studies indicate a high incidence of obsessive character traits in family members of anorexic patients (Crisp et al. 1974; Hecht et al. 1983; Kalucy et al. 1977), but work on familial incidence of OCD remains to be done. Some preliminary neurobiological research has attempted to explore the relationship between anorexia nervosa and OCD. Kaye et al. (1993) report that high levels of CSF 5-HIAA are found in a subgroup of eating disorder patients, and a subgroup of OCD patients may also have increased levels of CSF 5-HIAA (Goodman et al. 1989; Insel et al. 1985; Thorén et al. 1980). Studies of behavioral and serotonergic responsivity to serotonergic agonists reveal similar patterns in patients with OCD and eating disorders (Brewerton et al. 1989; Buttinger et al. 1990; Jimerson et al. 1989; McBride et al. 1990). There are reports of the use of clomipramine (Crisp et al. 1987) and fluoxetine (Kaye et al. 1990) in the treatment of eating disorders. Nevertheless, it is not clear that the response to these medications is as specific as that seen in OCD.

COMPULSIVITY AND IMPULSIVITY

At first glance, OCD and impulsive symptoms such as kleptomania, fire setting, self-mutilation, explosive aggression, compulsive gambling and shopping, and some patterns of sexuality and drug abuse, seem inversely related. Obsessions are experienced as intrusive, senseless, and repetitive, whereas impulsive thoughts may be ego-syntonic and unpremeditated. Compulsions are related to the avoidance of discomfort or future harm, whereas impulsive acts can be pleasurable and can result in harm. Moreover, psychodynamic theory teaches us to think of obsessive-compulsivity as a neurotic regression to anal-sadistic concerns, whereas impulsivity is conceived of as a more pathological consequence of ego and superego deficits. Nevertheless, both obsessive-compulsive and impulsive symptoms fall on a spectrum from ego-syntonic to ego-dystonic, and both types of symptoms may involve repetitive patterns. Both symptom groups may elicit resistance and result in anxiety reduction. Furthermore, many patients with OCD have aggressive thoughts, focusing on impulsive acts toward self or others. There appears to be a subgroup of OCD patients with a history of poor impulse control (Gardner and Gardner 1975; Hoehn-Saric and Barksdale 1983), or with primitive defenses (Insel 1982). In some of the OCRDs such as TS or pathological gambling, self- and other-directed impulsivity is even more apparent (Pitman et al. 1987; Yaryura-Tobias and Neziroglu 1984; DeCaria and Hollander 1993). Conversely, Kernberg (1985) has noted the presence of obsessive-compulsive symptoms in impulsive borderline patients.

Cloninger (1987) has proposed that harm avoidance comprises a personality dimension that can be reliably measured. We elected to administer his Tridimensional Personality Questionnaire (TPQ) to patients who appeared to fall on the compulsive-impulsive spectrum. Fifty patients who met DSM-III criteria for OCD, TS, trichotillomania, anorexia nervosa or bulimia, or bor-

Table 20.1. Tridimensional Personality Questionnaire (TPQ) Scores in Compulsive and Impulsive Patients

	Obsessive-compulsive	Tourette's syndrome	Hair pulling	Eating disorder	Borderline personality
Reward dependence	14.9	19.3	19.3	20.8	20.4
Novelty seeking	13.1	17.5	16.7	15.7	16.9
Harm avoidance	26.1	18.7	19.8	19.6	21.5

derline personality disorder (BPD) ($n = 10$ for each group) completed the questionnaire. Results were tabulated and compared (see Table 20.1).

Harm-avoidance scores in OCD patients (mean = 26.1) were higher than in patients with OCRDs and impulsive personality disorders. Nevertheless, harm-avoidance scores in all patient subgroups were higher than published scores of harm avoidance in control subjects (mean = 8.3; Cloninger 1987). Thus, although patients with OCD have the highest harm-avoidance scores, patients with OCD and OCRDs are more similar to one another than to control subjects on this dimension. Reward-dependence scores were lower in OCD subjects (mean = 14.9), and higher in patients with OCRDs, than in control subjects (mean = 17.4). Novelty-seeking scores in OCD patients (mean = 13.1) were similar to those of control subjects (mean = 12.9), but these scores were higher in patients with OCRDs. Relatively low reward-dependence and novelty-seeking scores in OCD patients are not inconsistent with clinical experience (i.e., OCD patients may be detached or rigid). In sum, it appears that the compulsive-impulsive spectrum cannot simply be divided into poles of high and low harm avoidance. Rather, there may be abnormal harm avoidance in the different patient groups that fall on this spectrum.

Cloninger (1987) has argued that harm avoidance reflects serotonergic function, with high harm avoidance correlating with a hyperserotonergic state. While a subgroup of OCD patients have high CSF levels of 5-HIAA, this is not true for all patients. Administration of the serotonin agonist m-CPP to OCD patients reveals both serotonin receptor hypersensitivity (associated with behavioral exacerbation) and subsensitivity (associated with endocrine blunting) (Hollander et al. 1992a; Zohar et al. 1987). On the basis of central and peripheral measures of serotonergic function, as well as serotonergic challenge studies, serotonin has also been implicated in a wide variety of impulsive behaviors, with low serotonin function correlating with high impulsivity (Brown and Goodwin 1986; Coccaro et al. 1989; Kavoussi and Coccaro 1993). In a pilot study of m-CPP in patients with impulsive personality disorders, we found that behavioral and neuroendocrine responses differed from those of OCD patients. Thus, while there is some support for Cloninger's hypothesis, the biochemistry of compulsivity and impulsivity appears to be complex.

The role of serotonergic medications in the treatment of the OCRDs has also been mentioned in many chapters. Fenfluramine treatment, for example, may be helpful in decreasing suicidal ideation (Meyendorff et al. 1986) and OCD symptoms (Hollander et al. 1990a). Serotonin reuptake blockers may be useful in the treatment of both OCD and impulsivity, and there are case reports of the response of kleptomania, self-mutilation, and sexual compulsivity to these medications (Hollander et al. 1988b; Levy 1990).

Several possibilities exist. Increased serotonergic function in OCD may correlate inversely with impulsivity. This is supported by the idea that compulsive patients differ from impulsive patients in their focus on harm avoidance. This might account for anecdotal reports of decreased obsessive-compulsivity but increased impulsive aggression during fluoxetine treatment of OCD. On the other hand, low serotonin function in OCD may lead to increased impulsivity. This would explain the subgroup of impulsive aggression in OCD and related disorders. Leckman et al. (1990) reported low levels of CSF 5-HIAA in two patients with aggressive obsessions. A third alternative is that a variety of receptor changes occur in OCD and that in some patients the receptor profile overlaps with that seen in impulsive patients.

The neurobiological basis for the link between OCD and impulsivity may also be investigated from a neuroanatomical viewpoint. Laplane et al. (1989) reported a number of patients with bilateral basal ganglia lesions who manifest obsessive-compulsive symptoms as well as frontal-lobe syndrome, classically reported as characterized by impulse dyscontrol. Modell et al. (1990) have argued that orbitofrontal cortex and basal ganglia neurocircuitry may also be central in alcoholism, a disorder that is typically conceived of as impulsive.

CONCLUSIONS

We have characterized several spectrums of OCD. OCD has been discussed in relation to delusions and obsessive-compulsive personality, anxiety and depression, disorders of grooming and the body, and impulsivity. We have indicated not only that there is some degree of phenomenological overlap between OCD and these disorders, but also that there is evidence of an overlap in pathogenic mechanisms. Several nosologic, clinical, and research implications are apparent.

Our review indicates that the current classification of OCD perhaps over-emphasizes the link between OCD and anxiety and downplays the relationships between OCD and its related disorders. Operational criteria for obsessions and compulsions may also neglect the delusional and subclinical dimensions of OCD symptoms. Further consideration ought to be given to making the links between the various OCRDs more explicit in DSM-IV. Hopefully, the current DSM-IV field trials will help in the revision of the diagnostic criteria for OCD.

A careful history of tics, physical illness, body concerns, and impulsivity in patients and family should be taken in OCD and its related disorders. In treating OCRDs, consideration should be given to medications that have proven useful in treating OCD.

Further research on the relationships of OCD to its related disorders is required. These relationships may be investigated using phenomenological studies, family data, neurochemical and neuroanatomical studies, and pharmacotherapeutic dissection. Pharmacological challenges and brain imaging studies appear to be particularly promising methodologies for understanding the neurobiology of the OCD spectrum. Ultimately, family studies using the methods of molecular genetics may lead to even more detailed knowledge. Exploration of the spectrums of OCD will in turn contribute to our understanding of OCD and will lead to new ways of characterizing this important and complex disorder.

REFERENCES

American Psychiatric Association: Diagnostic and Statistical Manual of Mental Disorders, *3rd Edition. Washington, DC, American Psychiatric Association, 1980*

American Psychiatric Association: Diagnostic and Statistical Manual of Mental Disorders, *3rd Edition, Revised. Washington, DC, American Psychiatric Association, 1987*

Anderson, G. M., Leckman, J. F., Riddle, M. A., et al: Recent neurochemical research on Tourette's syndrome. Paper presented at the Regional Congress on Biological Aspects of Nonpsychotic Disorder, World Federation of Societies of Biological Psychiatry, Jerusalem, 1989

Andreasen, N. C., Bardach, J.: Dysmorphophobia: symptom or disease? Am J Psychiatry *134: 673–676, 1977*

Baer, L., Jenike, M. A., Ricciardi, J. N., et al: Standardized assessment of personality disorders in obsessive-compulsive disorder. Arch Gen Psychiatry 47: 826–830, 1990

Barton, R.: *Diabetes insipidus and obsessional neurosis: a syndrome.* Lancet 1: 133–135, 1965

Baxter, L. R.: *Brain imaging as a tool in establishing a theory of brain pathology in obsessive compulsive disorder.* J Clin Psychiatry 51 (no 2, suppl): 22–25, 1990

Bear, D. M., Fedio, P.: *Quantitative analysis of interictal behavior in temporal lobe epilepsy.* Arch Neurol 34: 454–467, 1977

Bender, L., Schilder, P.: *Impulsions: a specific disorder of the behavior of children.* Archives of Neurology and Psychiatry 44: 990–1008, 1940

Black, A.: *The natural history of obsessional neurosis,* in Obsessional States. Edited by Beech, H. R. London, Methuen, 1974, pp 1–23

Brewerton, T., Murphy, D., Jimerson, D. C.: *A comparison of neuroendocrine responses to L-TRP and m-CPP in bulimics and controls.* Biol Psychiatry 25 (no 7A, suppl): 19A, 1989

Brown, G. L., Goodwin, F. K.: *Cerebrospinal fluid correlates of suicide attempts and aggression.* Ann N Y Acad Sci 487: 175–188, 1986

Butler, I. J., Koslow, S. H., Seifert W. E. Jr., et al: *Biogenic amine metabolism in Tourette syndrome.* Ann Neurol 6: 37–39, 1979

Buttinger, K., Hollander, E., Walsh, B. T.: *m-CPP challenges in anorexia nervosa. Paper presented at the 143rd annual meeting of the American Psychiatric Association, New York, May 1990*

Cambier, J., Masson, C., Benammou, S., et al: *La graphomanie, activité graphique compulsive manifestation d'un gliome fronto-calleux.* Rev Neurol (Paris) 144: 158–164, 1988

Capstick, N., Seldrup, U.: *Obsessional states: a study in the relationship between abnormalities occurring at birth and subsequent development of obsessional symptoms.* Acta Psychiatr Scand 56: 427–439, 1977

Chase, T. N., Foster, N. L., Fedio, P., et al: *Gilles de la Tourette syndrome: studies with the fluorine-18–labeled fluorodeoxyglucose positron emission tomographic method.* Ann Neurol 15 (suppl): S175, 1984

Chase, T. N., Geoffrey, V., Gillespie, M., et al: *Structural and functional studies of Gilles de la Tourette syndrome.* Rev Neurol (Paris) 142: 851–855, 1986

Ciprian, J.: *Three cases of Gilles de la Tourette's syndrome. Treatment with chlorimipramine: a preliminary report.* Journal of Orthomolecular Psychiatry 9: 116–120, 1980

Cloninger, C. R.: *A systematic method for clinical description and classification of personality variants: a proposal.* Arch Gen Psychiatry 44: 573–588, 1987

Coccaro, E. F., Siever, L. J., Klar, H. M., et al: *Serotonergic studies in patients with affective and personality disorders: correlations with suicidal and impulsive aggressive behavior.* Arch Gen Psychiatry 46: 587–599, 1989

Cohen, D. J., Shaywitz, B. A., Young, J. G., et al: *Central biogenic amine metabolism in children with the syndrome of chronic multiple tics of Gilles de la Tourette: norepinephrine, serotonin, and dopamine.* J Am Acad Child Adolesc Psychiatry 18: 320–341, 1979

Comfort, A.: Out-of-body experiences and migraine (letter). Am J Psychiatry 139: 1379–1380, 1982

Comings, D. E., Comings, B. G.: Hereditary agoraphobia and obsessive-compulsive behaviour in relatives of patients with Gilles de la Tourette's syndrome. Br J Psychiatry 151: 195–199, 1987

Craven, J. L., Rodin, G. M.: Cyproheptadine dependence associated with an atypical somatoform disorder. Can J Psychiatry 32: 143–145, 1987

Crisp, A. H., Harding, B., McGuinness, B.: Anorexia nervosa. Psychoneurotic characteristics of parents: relationship to prognosis, a quantitative study. J Psychosom Res 18: 167–173, 1974

Crisp, A. H., Lacey, J. H., Crutchfield, M.: Clomipramine and 'drive' in people with anorexia nervosa: an in-patient study. Br J Psychiatry 150: 355–358, 1987

DeCaria, C. M., Hollander, E: Pathological gambling, in Obsessive-Compulsive Related Disorders. Edited by Hollander, E. Washington, DC, American Psychiatric Press, 1993

DeVeaugh-Geiss, J., Katz, R., Landau, P., et al: A multicenter trial of Anafranil in obsessive compulsive disorder. Paper presented at the 141st annual meeting of the American Psychiatric Association, Montreal, May 1988

Dewhurst, K., Oliver, J., Trick, K.L.K., et al: Neuro-psychiatric aspects of Huntington's disease. Confinia Neurologica 31: 258–268, 1969

Dubois, F. S.: Compulsion neurosis with cachexia (anorexia nervosa). Am J Psychiatry 106: 107–115, 1949–1950

Fallon, B. A., Rasmussen, S. A., Liebowitz, M. R.: Hypochondriasis, in Obsessive-Compulsive Related Disorders. Edited by Hollander, E. Washington, DC, American Psychiatric Press, 1993

Fenton, W., McGlashan, T.: Obsessional/compulsive symptoms in schizophrenia, in New Research Program and Abstracts, the 138th annual meeting of the American Psychiatric Association, Dallas, TX, May 1985, NR12, p 24

Frances, A.: Categorical and dimensional systems of personality diagnosis: a comparison. Compr Psychiatry 23: 516–527, 1982

Gabay, S.: Serotonergic-dopaminergic interactions: implications for hyperkinetic disorders, in Advances in Experimental Medicine and Biology. Edited by Haber, B., Gabay, S., Issidorides, M. R., et al. New York, Plenum, 1981, pp 285–291

Gardner, A. R., Gardner, A. J.: Self-mutilation, obsessionality and narcissism. Br J Psychiatry 127: 127–132, 1975

Gilles de la Tourette: Étude sur une affection nerveuse caractérisée par de l'incoordination motrice accompagnée d'echolalie et de coprolalie. Arch Neurol 9: 19–42, 158–200, 1885

Goodman, W. K., Price, L. H., Anderson, G. M., et al: Drug response and obsessive compulsive disorder subtypes. Paper presented at the 142nd annual meeting of the American Psychiatric Association, San Francisco, CA, May 1989

Goodman, W. K., McDougle, C. J., Price, L. H., et al: Beyond the serotonin hypothesis: a role for dopamine in some forms of obsessive-compulsive disorder? J Clin Psychiatry 51 (no 8, suppl): 36–43, 1990

Goodwin, D. W., Guze, S. B., Robins, E.: Follow-up studies in obsessional neurosis. Arch Gen Psychiatry 20: 182–187, 1969

Gorman, J., Leibowitz, M., Fyer, A., et al: Lactate infusions in obsessive-compulsive disorder. Am J Psychiatry 142: 864–866, 1985

Gorman, J. M., Liebowitz, M. R., Fyer, A. J., et al: An open trial of fluoxetine in the treatment of panic attacks. J Clin Psychopharmacol 7: 329–332, 1987

Grimshaw, L: Obsessional disorder and neurological illness. J Neurol Neurosurg Psychiatry 27: 229, 1964

Hecht, A. M., Fichter, M., Postpischil, P.: Obsessive-compulsive neurosis and anorexia nervosa. International Journal of Eating Disorders 2: 69–77, 1983

Hoehn-Saric, R., Barksdale, V. C.: Impulsiveness in obsessive-compulsive patients. Br J Psychiatry 143: 177–182, 1983

Hollander, E., Fay, M., Cohen, B., et al: Serotonergic and noradrenergic sensitivity in obsessive-compulsive disorder: behavioral findings. Am J Psychiatry 145: 1015–1017, 1988a

Hollander, E., Papp, L., Campeas, R., et al: More on self mutilation and obsessive compulsive disorder (letter). Can J Psychiatry 33: 675, 1988b

Hollander, E., Fairbanks, J., DeCaria, C., et al: Pharmacological dissection of panic and depersonalization (letter). Am J Psychiatry 146: 402, 1989a

Hollander, E., Liebowitz, M. R., DeCaria, C. M.: Conceptual and methodological issues in studies of obsessive-compulsive and Tourette's disorders. Psychiatr Dev 7: 267–296, 1989b

Hollander E., Liebowitz, M. R., Winchel, R., et al: Treatment of body-dysmorphic disorder with serotonin reuptake blockers. Am J Psychiatry 146: 768–770, 1989c

Hollander, E., DeCaria, C. M., Schneier, F. R., et al: Fenfluramine augmentation of serotonin reuptake blockade antiobsessional treatment. J Clin Psychiatry 51: 119–123, 1990a

Hollander, E., Liebowitz, M. R., DeCaria, C., et al: Treatment of depersonalization with serotonin reuptake blockers. J Clin Psychopharmacol 10: 200–203, 1990b

Hollander, E.: Serotonergic drugs and the treatment of disorders related to obsessive-compulsive disorders, in Current Treatments of Obsessive-Compulsive Disorder. Edited by Pato, M. T., Zohar, J. Washington, DC, American Psychiatric Press, 1991, pp 173–191

Hollander, E., DeCaria, C., Nitescu, A., et al: Serotonergic function in obsessive-compulsive disorder: behavioral and neuroendocrine responses to oral m-chloro-phenylpiperazine and fenfluramine in patients and healthy volunteers. Arch Gen Psychiatry 49: 21–28, 1992a

Hollander, E., Neville, D., Frenkel, M., et al: Body dysmorphic disorder: diagnostic issues and related disorders. Psychosomatics 33: 156–165, 1992b

Hollander, E., Phillips, K. A.: Body image and experience disorders in Obsessive-Compulsive Related Disorders. Edited by Hollander, E. Washington, DC, American Psychiatric Press, 1993

Insel, T. R.: Obsessive compulsive disorder—five clinical questions and a suggested approach. Compr Psychiatry 23: 241–251, 1982

Insel, T. R.: Biological markers and obsessive compulsive and affective disorders. J Psychiatr Res 18: 407–423, 1983

Insel, T. R., Akiskal, H. S.: Obsessive-compulsive disorder with psychotic features: a phenomenologic analysis. Am J Psychiatry 143: 1527–1533, 1986

Insel, T. R., Mueller, E. A., Alterman, I., et al: Obsessive-compulsive disorder and serotonin: is there a connection? Biol Psychiatry 20: 1174–1188, 1985

Jenike, M. A.: Obsessive-compulsive disorder: a question of a neurologic lesion. Compr Psychiatry 25: 298–304, 1984

Jenike, M. A.: Illnesses related to obsessive-compulsive disorder, in Obsessive-Compulsive Disorders: Theory and Management, *2nd Edition. Edited by Jenike, M. A., Baer, L. B., Minichiello, W. E. Chicago, IL, Year Book Medical, 1990, pp 39–60*

Jenike, M. A., Hyman, S., Baer, L., et al: A controlled trial of fluvoxamine in obsessive-compulsive disorder: implications for a serotonergic theory. Am J Psychiatry 147: 1209–1215, 1990

Jimerson, D. C., Lesem, M. D., Kaye, W. H., et al: Serotonin and symptom severity in eating disorders. Biol Psychiatry 25 (suppl): 141A, 1989

Joffe, R. T., Swinson, R. P., Regan, J. J.: Personality features of obsessive-compulsive disorder. Am J Psychiatry 145: 1127–1129, 1988

Josephson, S. C., Brondolo, E.: Cognitive-behavioral approaches to obsessive-compulsive-related disorders, in Obsessive-Compulsive Related Disorders. *Edited by Hollander, E. Washington, DC, American Psychiatric Press, 1993*

Kahn, R. S., Wetzler, S., van Praag, H. M., et al: Neuroendocrine evidence for serotonin receptor hypersensitivity in panic disorder. Psychopharmacology (Berlin) 96: 360–364, 1988

Kalucy, R. S., Crisp, A. H., Harding, B.: A study of 56 families with anorexia nervosa. Br. J. Med Psychol 50: 381–395, 1977

Kavoussi, R. J., Coccaro, E. F.: Impulsive personality disorders and disorders of impulse control in Obsessive-Compulsive Related Disorders. *Edited by Hollander, E. Washington, DC, American Psychiatric Press, 1993*

Kaye, W., Wletzin, T., Hsu, G.: An open trial of fluoxetine in adolescent weight-recovered anorexics. Paper presented at the annual meeting of the American College of Neuropsychopharmacology, San Juan, Puerto Rico, 1990

Kaye, W. H., Weltzin, T., Hsu, L.K.G.: Anorexia nervosa, in Obsessive-Compulsive Related Disorders. *Edited by Hollander, E. Washington, DC, American Psychiatric Press, 1993*

Kendell, R. E.: The Role of Diagnosis in Psychiatry, *Oxford, UK, Blackwell, 1975*

Kendell, R. E., Discipio, W. J.: Obsessional symptoms and obsessional personality traits in patients with depressive illness. Psychol Med 1: 65–72, 1970

Kernberg, O.: Borderline Conditions and Pathological Narcissism. *New York, Jason Aronson, 1985*

Kettl, P. A., Marks, I. M.: Neurological factors in obsessive compulsive disorder: two case reports and a review of the literature. Br J Psychiatry 149: 315–319, 1986

Kindler, S., Kaplan, Z., Zohar, J.: Obsessive-compulsive symptoms in schizophrenia, in Obsessive-Compulsive Related Disorders. *Edited by Hollander, E. Washington, DC, American Psychiatric Press, 1993*

Koblenzer, C. S.: Psychocutaneous Disease. *New York, Grune & Stratton, 1987*

Laplane, D., Levasseur, M., Pillon, B., et al: Obsessive-compulsive and other behavioral changes with bilateral basal ganglia lesions. Brain 112: 699–725, 1989

Leckman, J. F., Goodman, W. K., Riddle, M. A., et al: Low CSF 5-HIAA and obsessions of violence: report of two cases. Psychiatry Res 33: 95–99, 1990

Leckman, J. F.: Tourette's Syndrome, in Obsessive-Compulsive Related Disorders. Edited by Hollander, E. Washington, DC, American Psychiatric Press, 1993

Leonard, H., Swedo, S., Rapoport, J. L., et al: Treatment of childhood obsessive compulsive disorder with clomipramine and desmethylimipramine: a double-blind crossover comparison. Psychopharmacol Bull 24: 93–95, 1988

Levy, R.: Is obsessive-compulsive disorder (OCD) the basis for several pathological states? Paper presented at the annual meeting of the American Academy of Clinical Psychiatry, October 1990

Liebowitz, M. R., Hollander, E., Schneier, F., et al: Fluoxetine treatment of obsessive-compulsive disorder: an open clinical trial. J Clin Psychopharmacol 9: 423–427, 1989

Mackenzie, T. B., Christenson, G., Kroll, J.: Obsession or worry (letter)? Am J Psychiatry 147: 1573, 1990

Martin, L. L., Tesser, A.: Toward a motivational and structural theory of ruminative thought, in Unintended Thought. Edited by Uleman, J. S., Bargh, J. A. New York, Guilford, 1989, pp 306–326

Mayeux, R., Stern, Y., Cote, L., et al: Altered serotonin metabolism in depressed patients with Parkinson's disease. Neurology 34: 642–646, 1984

McBride, P. A., Anderson, G. M., Khait, V. D., et al: Serotonergic responsivity in eating disorders. Paper presented at the annual meeting of the American College of Neuropsychopharmacology, San Juan, Puerto Rico, 1990

McDougle, C. J., Goodman, W. K., Price, L. H., et al: Neuroleptic addition in fluvoxamine-refractory obsessive-compulsive disorder. Am J Psychiatry 147: 652–654, 1990

McKeon, J., McGuffin, P., Robinson, P.: Obsessive-compulsive neurosis following head injury: a report of four cases. Br J Psychiatry 144: 190–192, 1984

Meltzer, H. Y.: Role of serotonin in depression. Ann N Y Acad Sci 600: 486–500, 1990

Menza, M. A., Forman, N. E., Goldstein, H. S., et al: Parkinson's disease, personality, and dopamine. Journal of Neuropsychiatry and Clinical Neurosciences 2: 282–287, 1990

Meyendorff, E., Jain, A., Träskman-Bendz, L., et al: The effects of fenfluramine on suicidal behavior. Psychopharmacol Bull 22: 155–159, 1986

Mizuno, T., Yugari, Y.: Prophylactic effect of L-5-hydroxytryptophan on self-mutilation in the Lesch-Nyhan syndrome. Neuropaediatrie 6: 13–23, 1975

Mizuno, T., Segawa, M. Kurumada, T., et al: Clinical and therapeutic aspects of the Lesch-Nyhan syndrome in Japanese children. Neuropaediatrie 2: 38–52, 1970

Modell, J. G., Mountz, J. M., Curtis, G. C., et al: Neurophysiologic dysfunction in basal ganglia/limbic striatal and thalamocortical circuits as a pathogenetic mechanism of obsessive-compulsive disorder. Journal of Neuropsychiatry and Clinical Neurosciences 1: 27–36, 1989

Modell, J. G., Mountz, J. M., Beresford, T. P.: Basal ganglia/limbic striatal and thalamocortical involvement in craving and loss of control in alcoholism. Journal of Neuropsychiatry and Clinical Neurosciences 2: 123–144, 1990

Munro, A., Chmara, J.: Monosymptomatic hypochondriacal psychosis: a diagnostic checklist based on 50 cases of the disorder. Can J Psychiatry 27: 374–376, 1982

Palmer, H. D., Jones, M. S.: Anorexia nervosa as a manifestation of compulsion neurosis: a study of psychogenic factors. Archives of Neurology and Psychiatry 41: 856–860, 1939

Pauls, D. L.: The familial relationship of obsessive compulsive disorder and Tourette's syndrome. Paper presented at the 142nd annual meeting of the American Psychiatric Association, San Francisco, CA, May 1989

Pauls, D. L., Kruger, S. D., Leckman, J. F., et al: The risk of Tourette's syndrome and chronic multiple tics among relatives of Tourette's syndrome patients obtained by direct interview. J Am Aca Child Adolesc Psychiatry 23: 134–137, 1984

Pauls, D. L., Towbin, K. E., Leckman, J. F., et al: Gilles de la Tourette's syndrome and obsessive-compulsive disorder: evidence supporting a genetic relationship. Arch Gen Psychiatry 43: 1180–1182, 1986

Peselow, E. D., DiFiglia, C., Fieve, R. R.: Obsessive-compulsive symptoms in patients with major depression: frequency and response to antidepressant treatment. Paper presented at the annual meeting of the American College of Neurpsychopharmacology, San Juan, Puerto Rico, 1990

Pitman, R. K.: A cybernetic model of obsessive-compulsive psychopathology. Compr Psychiatry 28: 334–343, 1987a

Pitman, R. K.: Pierre Janet on obsessive-compulsive disorder (1903): review and commentary. Arch Gen Psychiatry 44: 226–232, 1987b

Pitman, R. K., Green, R. C., Jenike, M. A., et al: Clinical comparison of Tourette's disorder and obsessive-compulsive disorder. Am J Psychiatry 144: 1166–1171, 1987

Pollack, J. M.: Obsessive-compulsive personality: a review. Psychol Bull 86: 225–241, 1979

Pollack, J. M.: Relationship of obsessive-compulsive personality to obsessive-compulsive disorder: a review of the literature. J Psychol 121: 137–148, 1987

Primeau, F., Fontaine, R.: Obsessive disorder with self-mutilation: a subgroup responsive to pharmacotherapy. Can J Psychiatry 32: 699–701, 1987

Rachman, S.: The modification of obsessions: a new formulation. Behav Res Ther 14: 437–443, 1976

Rachman, S., Da Silva, P.: Abnormal and normal obsessions. Behav Res Ther 16: 233–248, 1978

Rapoport, J. L.: The biology of obsessions and compulsions. Sci Am 3: 83–89, 1989

Rasmussen, S. A., Eisen, J. L.: Epidemiological and clinical features of obsessive-compulsive disorder, in Obsessive-Compulsive Disorders: Theory and Management, 2nd Edition. Edited by Jenike, M. A., Baer, L. B., Minichiello, W. E. Chicago, IL, Year Book Medical, 1990

Rassmussen, S. A., Tsuang, M. T.: Clinical characteristics and family history in DSM-III obsessive-compulsive disorder. Am J Psychiatry 143: 317–322, 1986

Rasmussen, S. A., Goodman, W. K., Woods, S. W., et al: Effects of yohimbine in obsessive-compulsive disorder. Psychopharmacology (Berlin) 93: 308–313, 1987

Reed, G.: Obsessional personality disorder and remembering. Br J Psychiatry 130: 177–183, 1977

Riddle, M. A., Hardin, M. T., King, R., et al: Fluoxetine treatment of children and adolescents with Tourette's and obsessive compulsive disorders: preliminary clinical experience. J Am Acad Child Adolesc Psychiatry 29: 45–48, 1990

Rosen, I.: The clinical significance of obsessions in schizophrenia. Journal of Mental Science 103: 773–785, 1957

Rosen, W., Hollander, E., Stannick, V., et al: Task performance variables in obsessive-compulsive disorder. J Clin Neuropsychol 10: 73, 1988

Roth, M.: The phobic anxiety depersonalization syndrome. Journal of Neuropsychiatry 1: 293–306, 1959

Salzman, L.: Obsessional Personality, New York, Science House, 1968

Schilder, P.: The organic background of obsessions and compulsions. Am J Psychiatry 94: 1397–1416, 1938

Shapiro, A. K., Shapiro, E. S., Young, J. G., et al: Gilles de la Tourette Syndrome, 2nd Edition. New York, Raven, 1988

Skodol, A. E.: Problems in Differential Diagnosis: From DSM-III to DSM-III-R in Clinical Practice. Washington, DC, American Psychiatric Press, 1989

Stern, R. S., Cobb, J. P.: Phenomenology of obsessive-compulsive neurosis. Br J Psychiatry 132: 233–239, 1978

Swedo, S. E.: Trichotillomania, in Obsessive-Compulsive Related Disorders. Edited by Hollander, E. Washington, DC, American Psychiatric Press, 1993

Swedo, S. E., Leonard, H. L., Rapoport, J. L., et al: A double-blind comparison of clomipramine and desipramine in the treatment of trichotillomania (hair pulling). N Engl J Med 321: 497–501, 1989a

Swedo, S. E., Rapoport, J. L., Leonard, H., et al: Obsessive-compulsive disorder in children and adolescents: clinical phenomenology of 70 consecutive cases. Arch Gen Psychiatry 46: 335–341, 1989b

Swedo, S. E., Grady, C., Leonard, H. L.: PET examination of women with trichotillomania. Paper presented at the annual meeting of the American College of Neuropsychopharmacology, San Juan, Puerto Rico, 1990

Szymanski, H. V.: Prolonged depersonalization after marijuana use. Am J Psychiatry 138: 231–233, 1981

Thomas, C. S.: Dysmorphophobia: a question of definition. Br J Psychiatry 144: 513–516, 1984

Thorén, P., Asberg, M., Bertilsson, L., et al: Clomipramine treatment of obsessive-compulsive disorder, II: biochemical aspects. Arch Gen Psychiatry 37: 1289–1294, 1980

Torch, E.: Review of the relationship between obsession and depersonalization. Acta Psychiatr Scand 58: 191–198, 1978

Turner, S. M., Hersen, M., Bellack, A. S., et al: Behavioral treatment of obsessive-compulsive neurosis. Behav Res Ther 17: 95–106, 1979

Vaughan, M.: The relationships between obsessional personality, obsession in depression, and symptoms of depression. Br J Psychiatry 129: 36–39, 1976

Ward, C. D.: Transient feelings of compulsion caused by hemispheric lesions: three cases. J Neurol Neurosurg Psychiatry 51: 266–268, 1988

Winchel, R., Stanley, B., Guido, J.: A pilot study of fluoxetine for trichotillomania. Paper presented at the 28th annual meeting of the American College of Neuropsychopharmacology, Maui, HI, 1989

Yaryura-Tobias, J. A., Neziroglu, F. A.: Gilles de la Tourette syndrome: a new clinico-therapeutic approach. Progress in Neuro-psychopharmacology *1: 335–338, 1977*
Yaryura-Tobias, J. A., Neziroglu, F. A.: Obsessive-Compulsive Disorders: Pathogenesis, Diagnosis, Treatment. *New York, Marcel Dekker, 1984*
Zohar, J., Insel, T. R.: Obsessive-compulsive disorder: psychobiological approaches to diagnosis, treatment, and pathophysiology. Biol Psychiatry *22: 667–687, 1987*
Zohar, J., Mueller, A., Insel, T. R., et al.: Serotonergic responsivity in obsessive-compulsive disorder: comparison of patients and healthy controls. Arch Gen Psychiatry *44: 946–951, 1987*

Epilogue
Dan J. Stein and Michael H. Stone

IN THE INTRODUCTION to this volume, we noted the enormous strides that have been made in understanding the psychology and neurobiology of obsessive-compulsive disorder (OCD) and related disorders over the last century. The reader of the papers in this volume cannot fail to be impressed by the dramatic advances made in the theoretical understanding and clinical management of this disorder. Nevertheless, OCD is a complex and often refractory disorder, and after reading the papers presented here the reader will surely agree with Sigmund Freud's (1926) confession that "as a problem obsessional neurosis has not yet been mastered." In this epilogue, we briefly consider some issues in the OCD field that require further investigation.

The papers on psychodynamic approaches to OCD raise a number of important issues for contemporary researchers and clinicians. First, how can current neurobiology address the role of some of the affects emphasized by psychoanalysts? While it is clear that anger, guilt, and impulsivity may at times be important components of the clinical picture, our understanding of their neurobiology remains rudimentary.

It seems clear that OCD is not a homogenous entity, but the extent to which OCD can usefully be subclassified on the basis of its clinical phenomenology remains unknown. Further work also needs to be done to clarify the relationship of OCD to different personality traits, a project to which neurobiological methodologies may well be able to contribute (Stein et al. 1995).

Second, current work on OCD tends to ignore the possible meaningfulness of symptoms. Certainly, it is possible that many OCD symptoms are in fact meaningless and reflect only the pathological triggering of primitive brain alarm systems. However, it is also possible that in some patients OCD symptoms develop as a meaningful response to specific stressors. One subset of such cases may comprise patients with histories of sexual abuse who have repetitive symptoms as a result of this trauma (Stone, unpublished data).

Third, psychoanalysis raises the issue of the overlap between normal and abnormal obsessive-compulsive symptomatology. Modern work has tended to draw a strict boundary to delineate psychopathology. However, closer investigation of normal obsessive-compulsive phenomena may provide useful insights. Freud's (1907) observation that rituals are an important part of day-to-day life deserves further consideration. Similarly, repetitive thoughts and actions may play an important role in everyday problem solving (Martin and Tesser 1990).

Finally, the phenomenon of subclinical OCD and the relationship between habits and OCD are both under-researched areas. There is some evidence that sub-clinical OCD is more common than might be expected in relatives of OCD patients, and there is some evidence that habits such as severe nail-biting respond selectively to serotonergic reuptake inhibitors. Questions about convergences and divergences in the neuroanatomical and neurochemical mediation of OCD, sub-clinical OCD, and habits are immediately raised by such preliminary data.

Psychological research on OCD also raises a number of issues for the researcher and clinician. First, while neuropsychiatric research has demonstrated that psychotherapeutic intervention impacts on brain activity (Baxter et al. 1992), the incorporation of neurobiological constructs into cognitive-behavioral models remains incomplete. Cognitive science is currently the predominant paradigm in the psychological sciences, so that a integrative cognitivist approach to OCD remains an important challenge for both clinicians and cognitivists (Stein and Hollander 1992). In particular, it is possible that further attention to putative psychobiological disturbances in goal assessment and determination in OCD will not only provide clearer explanations of OCD, but will also contribute to cognitive science (Stein and Hollander 1992).

Similarly, more trials are needed that compare rigorously pharmacotherapeutic, cognitive-behavioral, and combined treatments. Although preliminary evidence suggests that cognitive-behavioral intervention may have more long-lasting effects than pharmacotherapy, further work is necessary to demonstrate this more conclusively. Further research is also necessary to delineate factors that predict response to psychotherapy and to devise strategies for the management of patients who are reluctant to undertake psychotherapy.

The success of the neuropsychiatric approach in both theory and practice has led to its current domination of the OCD field. Nevertheless, much further work remains to be done. With regard to the neuroanatomy of OCD, Steven P. Wise and Judith L. Rapoport (1989) point out that a basal ganglia hypothesis fails to account for certain neuroanatomical data. Indeed, it remains unclear whether basal ganglia lesions or frontal lesions are primary in OCD (Insel 1992). While the hypothesis that prefrontal–basal ganglia circuits mediate OCD is a useful one, additional work to define the precise neuroanatomy of OCD remains necessary.

Similarly, further research on the neurochemistry of OCD is essential. Given the complexity of the serotonin system with its multiple receptors, the current view that this system is "involved" in OCD is obviously incomplete. Furthermore, it is likely that other neurotransmitters and neurochemicals also play a significant role in the mediation of OCD (Goodman et al. 1990). The development of more precise pharmacological challenges and the combination of such challenges with functional brain imaging studies will no doubt lead to further advances in our understanding.

From a clinical perspective, it is clear that while the serotonergic reuptake inhibitors (SRIs) are safe and effective in OCD, there are many patients who do not respond to these medications. We now know that dopaminergic agents also have a role in the treatment of some patients with OCD (McDougle et al. 1994). However, the literature on augmentation of SSRIs in OCD remains largely anecdotal and incomplete. Better understanding of the neurochemistry of OCD will hopefully lead to advances in its pharmacotherapy. More clinical research is needed on patients who are treatment-refractory.

The concept of an OCD spectrum of disorders remains a tentative one that currently has primarily heuristic value. Further research is necessary to determine the precise relationship between OCD and other conditions on this spectrum. The exciting work of Lewis R. Baxter and colleagues (1992) on the neurobiological changes effected by both psychotherapy and pharmacotherapy may provide a useful paradigm for further investigation in this area. Other particularly promising research avenues in understanding both OCD and the OCD spectrum are the hypothesis that these involve auto-immune mechanisms (Swedo et al. 1994) or genetic factors (Pauls et al. 1986) and the investigation of animal analogues (Rapoport et al. 1992; Stein et al. 1992).

Despite the excitement generated by the success of the neuropsychiatry approach, this paradigm may run the risk of ignoring important phenomenological and psychological data on OCD. Just as the psychoanalytic concept of OCD as a neurotic spectrum disorder turned attention away from important aspects of the disorder, viewing OCD too narrowly as a neuropsychiatric disorder may prove disadvantageous both in the clinic and in the research setting. A challenge for the future is the development of research models and clinical practices that integrate successfully the broad range of OCD data collected by the writers of the past century.

ACKNOWLEDGEMENT

Dan J. Stein is supported by a grant from the Medical Research Council of South Africa and the Lundbeck Fellowship Award.

REFERENCES

Baxter, L. R., Schwartz, J. M., Bergman, K. S., et al. 1992. Caudate glucose metabolic rate changes with both drug and behavior therapy for OCD. Arch Gen Psychiatry 49: 681–89.

Freud, S. 1907. Obsessive actions and religious practices. Standard Edition 9: 115–28.

———. 1926. Inhibitions, symptoms, and anxiety. Standard Edition 20: 111–31.

Goodman, W. K., McDougle, C. J., Price, L. H., et al. 1990. Beyond the serotonin hypothesis: a role for dopamine in some forms of obsessive compulsive disorder? J Clin Psychiatry 51: S36–S43.

Insel, T. R. 1992. Toward a neuroanatomy of obsessive-compulsive disorder. Arch Gen Psychiatry 49: 739–44.

Martin, L. L., Tesser, A. 1990. Toward a motivational and structural theory of ruminative thought. In J. S. Uleman, J. A. Bargh, eds, Unintended Thought. New York: Guilford Press.

McDougle, C. J., Goodman, W. K., Leckman, J. F., et al. 1994. Haloperidol addition in fluvoxamine-refractory obsessive-compulsive disorder: A double-blind placebo-controlled study in patients with and without tics. Arch Gen Psychiatry 51: 302–8.

Pauls, D. L., Towbin, K. E., Leckman, J. F., et al. 1986. Gilles de la Tourette's syndrome and obsessive compulsive disorder: evidence supporting a genetic relationship. Arch Gen Psychiatry 43: 1180–82

Rapoport, J. L., Ryland, D. H., Kriete, M. 1992. Drug treatment of canine acral lick: An animal model of obsessive-compulsive disorder. Arch Gen Psychiatry 48: 517–21.

Stein, D. J., Hollander, E. 1992. Cognitive science and obsessive-compulsive disorder. In D. J. Stein, J. E. Young, eds. Cognitive Science and Clinical Disorders. San Diego: Academic Press.

Stein, D. J., Shoulberg, N., Helton, K., Hollander, E. 1992. The neuroethological model of obsessive-compulsive disorder. Comprehensive Psychiatry 33: 274–81.

Stein, D. J., Trestman, R., Coccaro, E., et al. 1995. Serotonergic responsivity in compulsive personality disorder. Biol Psychiatry 37: 645

Swedo, S. E., Leonard, H. L., Kiessling, L. S. 1994. Speculations on antineuronal antibody-mediated neuropsychiatric disorders of childhood. Pediatrics 93: 323–26

Wise, S., Rapoport, J. L. 1989. Obsessive-compulsive disorder: is it basal ganglia dysfunction. In J. L. Rapoport, ed., Obsessive-Compulsive Disorder in Children and Adolescents. Washington, DC: American Psychiatric Press.

Author Index

Subject Index